Introduction to
Mythology

J.G. Farrow
Macomb Community College
Third Edition Revised Printing 2019

Kendall Hunt
publishing company

Kendall Hunt
publishing company

www.kendallhunt.com
Send all inquiries to:
4050 Westmark Drive
Dubuque, IA 52004-1840

Copyright © 2009, 2012, 2016 by J.G. Farrow

ISBN 978-1-5249-9164-7

CONTENTS

Appendix   Last poem of the Troy Cycle

PART 1

Vital Information

CHAPTER 1

What Is Myth?

The word *myth* is often misunderstood, to the point that some people can even be quite offended when it is used in the "wrong" context. If the term is so sensitive, then why study it or even acknowledge the validity of such a subject as mythology in our class-rooms? When we study the subject at college or university level, there is a lot more to it than just the adventures of gods or heroes who, in many cases, are not even believed in any more, at least in a literal sense. At this level of the subject we are far more concerned with the real people who actually did (or in some cases still do) believe in the gods and heroes of the systems we will be studying in the course. We are also concerned with the critics and theorists who have been contributing to the subject over the last two cen-turies. We cannot understand myths fully without having in our minds a complete "tool kit" of theories and interpretations, some of which are new, others which have stood the test of time for a century or more.

If you are buying this book, you are probably a serious student who wants to know more about the subject, not just get a couple more credits (though we all know what a big incentive that can be). Mythology has grown as a subject in the past century, espe-cially in the American higher education system. This is a great contrast from European countries, where students are expected to study the original languages of the **sources** first (especially Latin and Greek), then get to grips with the myths when they read the works of ancient poets such as Homer, Hesiod, Vergil, and Ovid. Even in our system we cannot avoid one basic fact: **the word *source* is the most important word in mythology.**

Don't panic—the sources used in this book are all translated into plain English for you. Care has been taken to keep it simple. Where there are important issues arising from the use of a particular word or name in a written source, there are footnotes to explain those issues. The shorter examples given in chapters 9 to 12 of this book are each followed by discussion questions which are designed to get you, as a beginning student of mythology, used to knowing what kind of details to look for and how to rec-ognize structures. It helps if you know some actual history and geography, too. At no point must we ever forget that our sources were real people, living in a real place and at a real time.

Before we start to read actual myths from actual sources, we must take some time to examine what thinkers across the last couple of centuries have said about myths, especially the important truths they can still find in them. For this reason the bulk of this chapter is taken up with a list of definitions of myth: not just diction-ary-style definitions, but important statements reflecting attitudes toward the sub-ject which have developed as tastes, fashions, and technological innovations have changed. You don't need to memorize these definitions, but you do need to be aware of the possibilities they offer in the interpretation of myths and in the choices we make in accepting or rejecting the claims given for treating a particular story as truly being a myth.

MODERN DEFINITIONS OF MYTH

1. Webster's **Third New International Dictionary**:

   "A story that is usually of unknown origin and at least partially traditional, that ostensibly relates to historical events usually of such character as to serve to explain some practice, belief, institution, or natural phenomenon, and that is especially associated with religious rites and beliefs."

2. Charles M. Gayley, **The Classic Myths in English Literature and Art** (Boston, 1939, p. 2):

   "Myths are born, not made."

3. H.J. Rose, **A Handbook of Classical Mythology** (6th ed., 1958, pp. 12–14):

   "[True myth is...] the result of the working of naive imagination upon the facts of experience."

4. a) Geoffrey S. Kirk, **The Nature of Greek Myths** (Penguin Books, 1974, p. 27):

   "A Traditional tale... a myth is a story, a narrative with dramatic structure and a climax. ...[Myths] have succeeded in becoming traditional... [and in being considered] important enough to be passed from generation to generation."

4. b) G.S. Kirk, **Methodological Reflexions on the Myth of Herakles** (from *Il Mito Greco*, International Conference, Rome 1973, p. 293):

   "All universal theories of myth are automatically wrong."

5. Robert W. Brockway, **Myth from the Ice Age to Mickey Mouse** (SUNY Press, 1993, p. 10):

"The confusions with the word myth rest, in part, with its modern usages, as in 'the American Dream,' and, with philosophers, as Cassirer says. Twentieth century theorists in various relevant disciplines such as the history of religions, literature, anthropology, archeology, and popular culture have coined private definitions so that definitions have proliferated to the point of chaos. Their problem and ours is the isolation of the disciplines from one another where mythic studies are concerned. There is very little dialogue between workers in these various fields. As a result, we are bedeviled by problems in definition and meaning, some of which are contradictory.

Since archaic myths are only known to us in literary form, literary critics are best equipped to deal with them in my view. Classical scholars such as Robert Graves and G.S. Kirk tell us that we do not have a single Greek myth, by which they mean that all so-called Greek myths are authored works of literature. The same is true of other archaic cultures as well, such as Egypt and Mesopotamia. What we call 'myth' is literature unless we refer to the traditional stories of native peoples. Even here, most are known because they have been written and, when written, they have been altered."

6. F. Max Müller, **Comparative Mythology** (London [1856, 1909], 1977, p. 178):

"Mythology, though chiefly concerned with nature, and here again mostly with those manifestations which bear the character of law, order, power and wisdom impressed on them, was applicable to all things. Nothing is excluded from mythological expression; neither morals nor philosophy, neither history nor religion, have escaped the spell of that ancient sibyl."

7. E.B. Tylor, **Anthropology** (London, Macmillan, 1924, p. 387):

"Myth is not to be looked upon as mere error and folly, but as an interesting product of the human mind. It is sham history, the fictitious narrative of events that never happened."

8. Sir James Frazer, **Introduction to Apollodorus: The Library** (translation & notes, Loeb Classics, 1921, p. xxvii):

"By myths I understand mistaken explanations of phenomena, whether of human life or of external nature. Such explanations originate in that instinctive curiosity concerning the causes of things which at a more advanced stage of knowledge seeks satisfaction in philosophy and science, but being founded on ignorance and misapprehension they are always false, for were they true they would cease to be myths. The subjects of myths are as numerous as the objects which present themselves to the mind of man; for everything excites his curiosity, and of everything he desires to learn the cause. Among the larger questions which many peoples have attempted to answer by myths are those which concern the origin of the world and of man, the apparent motions of the heavenly bodies, the regular recurrence of the seasons, the growth and decay of vegetation, the fall of rain, the phenomena of thunder and lightning, of eclipses and earthquakes, the discovery of fire, the invention of the useful arts, the beginnings of society and the mystery of death. In short the range of myths is as wide as the world, being coextensive with the curiosity and the ignorance of man.

[*Frazer then continues by distinguishing myths from legends.*]

...which relate to the fortunes of real people in the past, or which describe events, not necessarily human, that are said to have occurred at real places. Since the term 'legend' is used so loosely by many authors, I prefer to use the term *saga* to describe the kind of legendary narrative which is closest to the history of real people."

[*Note that Harrison, in the next definition, used "legend" in a much more general sense than Frazer did.*]

9. Jane Ellen Harrison, with Margaret Verral, **Mythology and Monuments of Ancient Athens** (London, 1890, p. iii):

"I have tried everywhere to get at, where possible, the cult as the explanation of the legend. My belief is that in many, even in the large majority of cases, **ritual practice misunderstood** explains the elaboration of myth.

Some of the loveliest stories the Greeks have left us will be seen to have taken their rise, not in poetic imagination, but in primitive, often savage, and I think, always practical ritual."

10. Robert Graves, **The Greek Myths** (Penguin Books, 1955, vol. 1, p. 10) in defining "true myth" and distinguishing it from twelve other categories of narrative genre:

"The reduction to narrative shorthand of ritual mime performed in, public festivals, and in many cases recorded pictorially on temple walls, vases, seals, bowls, mirrors, chests, shields, tapestries and the like."

[*Graves's other categories include philosophical allegory, satire or parody, minstrel romance, political propaganda, theatrical melodrama, and realistic fiction.*]

11. Andrew Lang, **Mythology** (London, 1897, pp. 55–56):

"The difficulty that Mythology faces (as 'science') lies in explaining the following points among other seemingly irrational elements contained in myths: the barbaric and absurd stories concerning the beginnings of things, the origin of mankind, of the sun, of the stars, of animals, of death and of the world in general; the vile and ridiculous behaviour of the gods; why divine beings are considered incestuous, adulterous, murderers, thieves, cruel and cannibals; why they take the form of animals; myths of metamorphosis into plants, animals and stars; repulsive stories of the kingdom of the dead: descent of the gods to the regions of the dead and their return from those places."

12. Sigmund Freud, in a preface to Theodore Reik's **Ritual: Psycho-analytic Studies** (New York, 1946):

"[Myths are] [t]he echo of that occurrence* which threw its shadow over the whole development of mankind."

* The "occurrence" here is the death of the archetypal father of the human horde; compare Freud's remark in his **Moses and Monotheism** *(tr. Katharine Jones, Vintage Books, 1955):*

"From Darwin I borrowed the hypothesis that man originally lived in small hordes, each of the hordes stood under the leadership of an older male, who governed by brute force, appropriated all the females, and belabored or killed all the young males, including his own sons. From Atkinson I received the suggestion that this patriarchal system came to an end through the rebellion of the sons, who united against the father, overpowered him, and together consumed his body. Following Robertson Smith's totem theory I suggested that the horde, previously ruled by the father, was followed by a totemistic brother clan. In order to be able to live in peace with one another the victorious brothers renounced the women for whose sake they had killed the father, and agreed to practice exogamy.

The power of the father was broken and the families were regulated by matriarchy. The ambivalence of the sons toward the father remained in force during the whole further development. Instead of the father, a certain animal was declared the totem; it stood for their ancestor and protecting spirit, and no-one was allowed to hurt or kill it. Once a year, however, the whole clan was assembled for a feast at which the otherwise revered totem was torn to pieces and eaten. No one was permitted to abstain from this feast; it was the solemn repetition of the father-murder, in which social order, moral laws, and religion had their beginnings."

13. C. G. Jung, in the preface to **Psyche and Symbol** (1957):

"The primitive mentality does **not invent** myths, it **experiences** them. Myths are original revelations of the pre-conscious psyche, involuntary statements about unconscious psychic happenings, and anything but allegories of physical[1] processes."

14. a) Bronislaw Malinowski, **Myth in Primitive Psychology** (1926, pp. 18–19):

"Myth as it exists... in its living primitive form, is not merely a story told but a reality lived. It is not of the nature of fiction, such as we read today in a novel, but it is a living reality, believed to have once happened in primeval times, and continuing ever since to influence the world and human destinies."

"The limitation of the study of myth to the mere examination of texts has been fatal to a proper understanding of its nature. The forms of myth which come to us from classical antiquity and from the ancient sacred books of the East and other similar sources have come down to us without the context of living faith, without the possibility of obtaining comments from true believers, without the concomitant knowledge of their social organization, their practiced morals, and their popular customs—at least without the full information which the modern field-worker can easily obtain. Moreover, there is no doubt that in their present literary form these tales have suffered a very considerable transformation at the hands of scribes, commentators, learned priests, and theologians. It is necessary to go back to primitive mythology in order to learn the secret of its life in the study of a myth which is still alive—before, mummified in priestly wisdom, it has been enshrined in the indestructible but lifeless repository of dead religions.

Studied alive, myth, as we shall see, is not symbolic, but a direct expression of its subject-matter; it is not an explanation in satisfaction of a scientific interest, but a narrative resurrection of a primeval reality, told in satisfaction of deep religious wants, moral cravings, social submissions, assertions, even practical requirements. Myth fulfills in culture an indispensable function: it expresses, enhances, and codifies belief; it safeguards and enforces morality; it vouches for the efficiency of ritual and contains practical rules for the guidance of man. Myth is thus a vital ingredient of human civilization; it is not an idle tale, but a hard-worked active force; it is not an intellectual explanation or an artistic imagery, but a pragmatic charter of primitive faith and moral wisdom."

---

[1]The phrase "physical processes" refers specifically to Freud's theories, partially outlined above in #12.

14. b) Chief Nalubutua, of the Trobriand Islands, speaking of Bronislaw Malinowski in a 1990 interview with Paul Theroux, published in **National Geographic** (July 1992, pp. 120–121):

"We could not pronounce his name, we called him Tolibogwa. It means, 'Telling old stories.' He did nothing but write down the old stories, which is how he got the name.

Theroux: What did people think of him?

Nalubutua: Not many people were interested in him. He was accepted because he was kind. He was known as the man who liked to ask questions."

[**Note:** *Theroux pointed out that the Chief was over 70 at the time of this interview. Theroux also observes on p. 120 of the same article*]:

"Most islanders claim to be Protestant or Catholic, but Christian theology does not impinge very much on their traditional beliefs. In a village one day I found the pastor of a Christian church revolving a small child over some smoke coming from a coconut shell. 'A burning grasshopper's egg,' he explained: so the child would have strong legs."

15. Joseph Campbell, introduction to **The Flight of the Wild Gander** (Harper, 1990, p. 6):

"The common tendency today to read the word 'myth' as meaning 'untruth' is almost certainly a symptom of the incredibility and consequent inefficacy of our own outdated mythic teachings... but also of the various, more modern, secular 'Utopiates' (let us call them) that are being offered in their place. Living myths are not mistaken notions, and they do not spring from books. They are not to be judged as true or false but as effective or ineffective, maturative or pathogenic... They are not invented but occur, and are recognized by seers, and poets, to be then cultivated and employed as catalysts of spiritual (i.e. psychological) well-being. And so, finally, neither a stale and overdue nor a contrived, plastic mythology will serve; neither priest nor sociologist takes the place of the poet-seer—which, however, is what we all are in our dreams, though when we wake we may again render only prose."

16. Alexander Eliot, in the Introduction to **The Universal Myths** (Meridian Books, 1990, p. 1):

"Myths are never factual, but seldom are they totally 'untrue.' That's because they have to do with what we don't know and yet can't dismiss. The more adventurous reaches of our thinking are not wholly rational; they do partake of faith as well."

17. Walter Burkert, in **Structure and History in Greek Mythology and Ritual** (University of California Press, 1979, Sather Classical Lectures, vol. 47, p. 1):

   "To modern man, the word, 'myth', while retaining a certain fascination even outside Classical circles, has quite an ambivalent appeal: to denounce some opinion or attitude as 'myth' means to reject it as irrational, false and potentially harmful; at the same time, 'myth' has a nostalgic ring, indicative of some meaningful reality hidden or lost in the depths of the past or of the psyche, which might be resuscitated as an antidote to a present that seems both rational and absurd."

18. Jaan Puhvel, in the introduction to **Comparative Mythology** (Johns Hopkins University Press, 1987, p. 2):

   "A myth in its pristine state is by definition specific to a given human environment. How it fares from then on (its 'life,' 'afterlife,' survival, transposition, revival, rediscovery, or whatever) is a matter of historical accident. It follows that the study of any specific past body of myth has to be mainly a historical discipline employing written sources, whereas contemporary myth can be pursued by the methods of field anthropology."

19. Manfred Korfmann (in a 2002 TV interview):
   "A myth needs a place to which you can attach it."

20. C. Kerényi, **The Primordial Child in Primordial Times** (published in **Essays on a Science of Mythology**, by C.G. Jung & C. Kerényi, Bollingen series XXII, Princeton University Press, 1969, 1989, p. 25):

   "Mythology is never the biography of the gods, as often appears to the observer. This is particularly true of 'mythology properly so called': mythology in its purest, most pristine form. It is both more and less. It is always less than a biography, even though it tells of the birth and childhood of the gods, the deeds of their youth, and sometimes of their early death. The remarkable thing about these childish or youthful feats is that they show the god in the full perfection of his power and outward form, and thus really preclude biographical thinking—thinking in periods of life as stages of development. At the same time mythology is more than any biography. For, although it may tell us nothing that relates organically to a particular period of life, it nevertheless comprehends the periods themselves as timeless realities: the figure of the child plays a part in mythology equal to that of the marriageable girl, or Koré, and the mother. In mythology these too, like every other possible form of being, are manifestations of the Divine."

21. Joseph Campbell, **Myths from West to East** (in Eliot's **The Universal Myths**, p. 59):

"The Hindus, like Adolf Bastian, have noticed the difference between *Völker* and *Elementargedanken,* ethnic and elementary ideas. Their terms for the same are *Dési* and *Màrga. Dési* means 'That which is local, provincial' and refers to those forms of myth and ritual that we recognize as culturally shaped, and whose areas of origin can be mapped. *Màrga* on the other hand, means 'path or track, trail of an animal, to be followed' and this is precisely what is meant by C.G. Jung's term, 'the archetypes of the unconscious.'"

22. George Lucas (in a 1999 PBS TV interview with Bill Moyers):

"Mythology is... a context for the unknown."

23. The Ferengi Rules of Acquisition (edited by Steven Behr, Pocket Books, 1995):

"Rule #60: Keep your lies consistent."

SUMMARY: WHAT WE CAN NOW SAY ABOUT MYTH

MYTH	FACT	FICTION
Starts with casual conversations about what people see as **"true"** (subjective truth). These observations are remembered as **motifs** and passed on (not always accurately) taking on the best **structure** as they are repeated and a story develops. Participants are **unaware** of the story-building process.	What we **KNOW** to be true (objectively) based on 1) eyewitness **and** 2) science.	A story made up **consciously** by a **known** author.

"Fact" without science is myth. For example, we still use terms like "sunrise" and "sunset" even though we, as modern people, understand how the earth rotates within the solar system.

Science without eyewitness evidence is theory. An example is the idea, once debated amongst some mathematicians, that the world exists in the form of a Möbius strip!

The simplest definition of **motif** is "idea-unit," in the form of a detail, character, action, or situation. The most important and formative character-motifs are **archetypes**.

Motifs are explained more fully, with some of the most popular examples, below in chapter 4.

As you can see from the above diagram, a myth seems to "grow" by itself in the same way that a living, organic being grows. The growth and transmission process is entirely **unconscious** on the part of those involved. In most of the cases we will be dealing with, these people can fairly be defined as a **culture**. Most of the modern research on this process has been done by anthropologists and by psychologists following C.G. Jung's theory of the Archetypes of the Collective Unconscious. This theory will be explained in terms of the hero (Chapter 6) and trickster (Chapter 7) archetypes.

Students in a creative writing class are often advised to "write what you know best." This is why so much of the best fiction seems credible even when we know it isn't. Myth creates the same effect for the opposite reason: people are discussing and trying unconsciously to explain to themselves the realities they see around them. The most memorable features of these ancient but ongoing conversations are remembered in the form of motifs which in turn grow into story-form.

CHAPTER 2

Ancient Critics of Myth

1. XENOPHANES OF COLOPHON (500–440 B.C.?)

📖 Xenophanes, whose poems do not survive, was the earliest known philosopher to express direct criticism of **ANTHROPOMORPHIC POLYTHEISM**. The fragments below are translated from H. Diels, rev. W. Kranz, *die Fragmente der Vorsokratiker* (Zürich & Berlin, 1934, 1964). For a good collection of the fragments in English, see *Xenophanes of Colophon: Fragments* (Text & Translation with Commentary) by J.H. Lesher (U. of Toronto Press, 1992); as a Philosophy text, I can also recommend Philip Wheelwright, *The Presocratics* (Macmillan, NY 1966), p. 31–39. I have included here my own translations of the fragments which clarify Xenophanes' attitude to myth.

a) Diels 21 B 15 = Clement of Alexandria, **Stromata** V.110

If oxen or lions had hands which enabled them to draw pictures and create images as human beings do, they would portray their gods as having bodies like their own: horses would portray them as horses, and oxen as oxen.

b) Diels 21 B 14 = Clement of Alexandria, **Stromata** V.109

But mortals suppose that gods have been born, that they have voices and bodies and wear clothing like human beings.

c) Diels 21 A 13 = Aristotle, **Rhet.** 1400b

When the people of Elea asked Xenophanes whether or not they should sacrifice to Leucothea[1] and sing her a dirge, he advised them that if they believed that she had become a goddess they should not sing her a dirge, but if they believed her to be human, they should not sacrifice to her.

---

[1]Ino, a daughter of Cadmus, was believed to have been turned into a goddess instead of dying. The full story is outlined in Hyginus, *Fabula* 2. Her divine name was Leucothea, the "White Goddess." We are probably dealing with a legend of a drowned woman and an etiological myth for the foam and spray of the sea. She appears in Homer's *Odyssey*, V. 333–462. For partially rationalized versions of the story, see Hyginus *Fabulae* I–IV(given in chapter 13, below).

d) From Plutarch, **Isis and Osiris**, Ch. 70

[People once] attributed to the gods the fortunes of their crops, not only calling the availability of necessary resources "births of the gods" and the disappearance of such resources "deaths of the gods," but also believing that this
was the case. And so they filled their minds with unlikely, illogical, and confused teachings, even though they had before their eyes the illogicality of such
reasoning.

Xenophanes of Colophon rightly maintained that the Egyptians, if they believe
in gods, should not weep; if they weep, they should not believe in their gods.
Isn't it ridiculous that, even while they are lamenting, they should pray for their
crops to reappear once more and be caused to ripen, just so as to be consumed
and made the subject of lamentation once again?

e) 21 A 28 = Pseudo-Aristotle, **On Melissus, Xenophanes, and Gorgias** 977b

On the issue of divine supremacy in all things, Xenophanes draws the conclusion that God is One. For, if there were two or more gods, each of them would
be supreme; thus ultimately neither would be supreme and best. For the very
meaning of God and of divine power involves supremacy over all else. So far as
he is not superior he is not God.

2. THE LOGOGRAPHERS AND SOPHISTS

The *Logographoi* (word-writers, or writers of story/argument) were the first ancient
Greek authors to use prose as a medium (all previous literary composition had been in
verse). The earliest logographoi were in some cases the predecessors of systematic historians, in other cases professional speech-writers hired by politicians or by people involved
in litigation before the days of an organized legal profession. "Logographers" of the latter
type were often described also as "sophists." *Sophist* means "wisdom specialist." Strictly
speaking, these were people who applied the disciplines of planned, logical argument to
the understanding of philosophy and/or science. After the Peloponnesian War (431–404
B.C.), when Athens was finally defeated by Sparta, the sophists fell into disrepute: the term
acquired all the negative connotations of "wise guy." This becomes clear to anyone who
reads Aristophanes' comedy *The Clouds* and Plato's account of Socrates' defense-speech,
The Apology. To understand that Socrates was not a logographer or a sophist, see below,
#3 and #4.

The earliest sophist of whom we know anything was **Gorgias of Leontini**. Gorgias
moved to Athens around 440 B.C. and set himself up as a teacher of rhetoric, the art and
science of public speaking. Gorgias' own treatment of myths is limited to the use of

situations from myth as speech-material: for example, there is a speech in defense of the Greek hero Palamedes, prosecuted for treachery by Odysseus. This is clearly a kind of educational showpiece. Another example is the *Encomium of Helen*, praising the famous queen of Sparta and excusing her from the charge of provoking the Greek invasion of Troy.

In the early days of the Logographers, sophists, and students of "natural philosophy," there was much questioning of myths, their meaning and their plausibility. Historians were especially interested in whether the events had actually taken place in a way resembling the stories. The method preferred by this early generation of critics was one which I usually call "materialist criticism." The standard approach in applying this method is to isolate the most incredible or least acceptable motif in a given myth and to explain it away with reference to a noteworthy detail in an everyday object. This same approach is still often used by individuals who try to rationalize myths. It has also achieved success in the media with popular shows such as *Mythbusters*. The main difference between these ancient critics and their modern TV counterparts is the modern reliance on physical experiment and the application of scientific enquiry as we would expect for the 21st century. Logographers and sophists simply argued about plausibility in a way we would now consider "armchair" criticism. The following examples illustrate this well.

a) Hecataeus of Miletus

Hecataeus was probably active around 500 B.C.. He was the first recorded prose historian in Greece. None of his works survive in a complete text. The complete testimonies and fragments (usually in quotations, given in the original text only) are found in F. Jacoby, *die Fragmente der Griechischen Historiker*, Vol. I, where Hecataeus is Nr.1.

1F26 = Arrian, *Alexander's Advance (Anabasis) II.16.5–6*

Hecataeus the historian says that Geryon, against whom the Argive Herakles was sent by Eurystheus to drive off Geryon's cattle and bring them back to Mycenae, had nothing to do with the land of the Iberians,[2] nor was Herakles sent to some

---

[2]Iberia = Spain. In each successive generation of Greeks from Hesiod's time to the Roman period, the location of Geryon's land of supernaturally large cattle was moved progressively westward "as colonization increased public awareness of the western Mediterranean and its geography". A semi-dramatized version of the story was sung by the poet Stesichorus, about a century before Hecataeus' time. Only fragments of Stesichorus' poems now survive. The *Geryoneis* apparently told the story of Herakles borrowing the cup of Helios to sail into the western sea to attack Geryon and steal his cattle. Evidently the story in its oldest form must have been a solar myth as well as containing elements of a traditional cattle-rustling adventure.

kind of island called Erytheia outside the Mediterranean Sea. [Hecataeus says that] Geryon was king of Epirus, the mainland area in the region of Ambracia[3] and the territory of the Amphilochians, and that Herakles drove the cattle from this area.

Indeed, this was no mean task to be assigned to him. I personally know that this mainland area is even now rich in pasture and produces excellent cattle.

b) Herodorus of Heraclea (c.450–380 B.C.)

Herodorus wrote at least two major works, *The Story of Hercules* and *The Argonauts*. In addition to preserving the myths with a lot of details from non-Greek sources he included his own personal explanations of the stories; I have concentrated here on examples of the latter. His works only survive in fragments, collected by F. Jacoby, in *Die Fragmente der Griechischen Historiker*, where Herodorus is #31.

i) 31 F 13 = Clement of Alexandria, Stromata I.73.2

Herodorus says that Hercules became a seer and a natural philosopher, receiving from Atlas the pillars (movements) of the universe, so that the story grew as a pun that he had received knowledge of heavenly matters by learning.

ii) 31 F 28 = Scholion on Lycophron, Alexandra 522

Herodorus says that in reality Poseidon and Apollo did not build the city.[4] but Laomedon squandered on the building of walls money that had been set aside for sacrifices to these gods.

iii) 31F30 = Scholion on Apollonius Rhodius, Argonautica II.1248

Herodorus has this different interpretation of Prometheus' chains: he says Prometheus was a king of the Scythians, and, being unable to provide the necessities of survival for his subjects, because the river Aetos was flooding the plains, he was chained up by the Scythians. Hercules presented himself and channeled the river into the sea. For this

---

[3]Northwestern Greece, towards the present Albanian border.

[4]This is from the story of Old Troy, before the more famous war involving the Wooden Horse story. The old king, Laomedon, tricked Poseidon and Apollo into building the walls of the city for him.

reason the story arose that Hercules had killed the Eagle [Gk. *Aetos*] and had freed Prometheus from his bonds.

c) Palaephatus

Palaephatus was a contemporary of Plato (see #4 below) or of Aristotle. He collected over 60 myths, attaching rational explanations to each one. The surviving manuscripts which bear Palaephatus' name probably contain only a summary of his original arguments rather than his complete works. His technique was probably becoming old-fashioned by the time he was writing, between 370 and 320 B.C.. The following extracts are translated from the only "modern" printed text of Palaephatus, Vol. III of the series *Mythographi Graeci* (ed. N. Festa, 1903, pub. Teubner, Stuttgart). A modern translation is now available, *Palaephatus on Unbelievable Tales*, with an introduction & commentary by Jacob Stern (Chicago, Bolchazy-Carducci 1996).

i) IX. On Lynceus

It is said of Lynceus that he could even see things that were under the ground. This is false. The truth is as follows: Lynceus was the first man to begin the mining and smelting of bronze, silver, and other metallic ores. In mining for ores he took a lamp under the ground with him so that he could see.

ii) XVII. On Aeolus

It is said that Aeolus was a man who had power over the winds, and that he gave the winds to Odysseus in a leather bag. As for this, it could never have happened, and I think that is obvious to everyone. More likely, Aeolus was an astrologer who told Odysseus the times and bearings of certain winds. They also say he had a bronze[5] wall built around his castle, which is false. He had armed guards stationed around his city.

iii) XXX. On Phrixus and Helle

As for Phrixus, they say a ram prophesied to him that his father was going to kill him and his sister Helle. Taking his sister he rode on the ram across the sea until they reached the Black Sea, spending three or four days in the whole journey. It is hard to believe that a ram could swim faster than a ship, especially carrying two children

---

[5]For another interpretation of the "bronze wall" with accompanying photograph, see Tim Severin, *The Ulysses Voyage* (NY 1987).

on its back, presumably carrying also a supply of food and water for them all (there is no record that they starved).

Then (allegedly) Phrixus killed the very ram that could speak and had saved them. People say that he skinned it and gave its fleece to Aeëtes as a bride-price for his daughter (Aeëtes was king of the country at the time). Fleeces must have been very rare in those days for a king to accept one as a dowry for his daughter! Did he really consider his daughter so worthless? Some people, to avoid seeming ridiculous at this point, claim that the fleece was golden. If that had been so, it would have been improbable for the king to take it from a foreigner.

People also say that this fleece was the reason why Jason set out in the Argo with the best of the Greeks. But Phrixus would not have been so ungrateful as to kill the very animal that had helped him, nor would the Argo have sailed after a fleece, even if it was made from emeralds.[6]

The truth is like this: Athamas the son of Aeolous and grandson of Hellen, was king of Phthia. He had a steward in charge of his treasury and government, the very trustworthy and reliable Krios.[7] When Phrixus' mother died, Athamas designated Phrixus his successor as the elder child. At a later time Krios discovered [a plot against Phrixus' life[8]]. He said nothing to Athamas, but spoke to Phrixus and warned him to leave the country. Krios personally equipped a ship and loaded it with all of Athamas' valuables, both goods and money. Amongst these was a life-size golden statue which a lady called Kôs[9] (daughter of Helios and mother of Merops) once had made of herself, at her own expense (there was a lot of gold involved, and there's a big story about that too). Krios stowed these items on board the ship with Phrixus and Helle, then sailed off. During the course of the voyage Helle became ill[10] and died: the Hellespont is named in her memory.

The rest reached the river Phasis and settled there. Phrixus married a daughter of Aeëtes the king of Colchis, giving as a dowry the golden statue of Kôs. Later, when

---

[6]Pindar (*Pythian* IV.160) seems to have known another rationalization, this time a political one, in which the primary object of the quest was to find the mortal remains of Phrixus (presumably as a hero whose bones were considered talismanic) and return them to Greece.

[7]*Krios* means *fleece* and is translated by some modern scholars as *Mr. Ram*.

[8]There are gaps in the Greek text here. See Stern's notes (1996, pp. 60–61). To fill the gaps, see Hyginus, *Fabulae* I–IV, where Athamas has two other wives, Themisto and Ino. Both of them, in different versions of the story, perform the role of "Wicked Stepmother."

[9]*Kôs* is another word for *fleece*. The character Merops may have been mentioned in the missing part of the story (see previous note).

[10]Another rationalization: the traditional etiological myth for the Hellespont is that Helle fell from the Golden Ram's back as it was traveling over that stretch of water.

Athamas died, Jason sailed off in the Argo to get the "Golden Kôs," not the skin of a ram (*krios*). This is the true story.

iv) XXXIV. Pandora

The story of Pandora is unlikely: that she was moulded from earth and passed on her shape to others. It doesn't seem likely to me. But Pandora was a very rich Greek woman, and when she saw fit she would put on make-up made from clay.[11] She was the first to discover the cosmetic use of facial colouring mixed with a lot of clay (which a lot of women do these days, but none of them get a special name for doing so). This is what really happened, but the story became impossibly twisted.

3. SOCRATES (470–399 B.C.)

📖 Socrates, who was sentenced to death in Athens in 399 B.C. for blaspheming against the gods and corrupting the minds of young people, never wrote any books or poems. All his teaching was done in dialogue form (see example in #3, below). His method was to try to get participants in a conversation to make their own definitions of important terms and to apply those definitions to the practical values of their own lives. Naturally, this involved some questioning of traditional religion, especially since the religious views of ancient Athenians were based on the myths of the gods.

Socrates' main objection to the traditional characterizations of the gods in myths was that humans should look up to their gods. The gods of Greek myth, he argued, were often portrayed as very poor role-models, not as fit beings for humans to imitate.

4. PLATO (C. 429–347 B.C.)

📖 Plato was a student of Socrates (#3) and is still for us the main source of Socrates' teachings. Plato's dialogues always have Socrates as the main character, acting as the chairman of a discussion-group. It is therefore often difficult to separate Plato's own ideas from those of his teacher. One of Plato's largest and best-known works is the *Republic*, a lengthy discussion of the qualities needed to furnish the constitution and government of the ideal state. The moral values of the traditional myths (especially as they were, and still are, represented in the poetry of Homer and Hesiod) were regarded

---

[11]In ancient Greece women wore face-packs in the daytime, made from white lead applied on a clay base. The object was to make them look as pale as possible, but it must also have been dangerous.

as being especially open to question. The following extract from Book II of the *Republic* illustrates this: the aspect of civic life under discussion is the education of the young.

Socrates: What, then, must this "education" be? I suppose we shall begin with the mind, before we deal with the training of the body?

Adeimantus: Of course.

Socrates: Under that category will come stories. There are two kinds: some are true, others fictitious. Both are relevant, but we must begin our education with the fictitious kind.

Adeimantus: I don't understand.

Socrates: Don't you understand that we shall begin by telling children stories, that the general details of the stories are fictitious, but that they contain some truth? Such storytelling begins at an earlier age than physical training, so that's why we must start with the mind.

Adeimantus: You are right.

Socrates: The beginning, as you know, is the most important part, especially when dealing with anything young and tender. That is when the character is molded and is easily impressionable.

Adeimantus: That's true.

Socrates: Then shall we simply allow our children to listen to any stories that anyone happens to make up, and so receive into their minds the very opposite kind of ideas from those which we think they ought to have when they grow up?

Adeimantus: Certainly not.

Socrates: Then, it seems, our first job will be to supervise the making of fables and legends, rejecting all which are unsatisfactory. We shall encourage mothers and nurses to tell their children only the stories which we have approved, and to pay more attention to molding the children's souls with these stories than they pay now to rubbing their limbs, trying to make them strong and shapely. Most of the stories now in use must be discarded.

Adeimantus: What sort of stories do you mean?

Socrates: Let us take the great ones as examples of all the rest.

Adeimantus: Which ones do you mean by "the great ones"?

Soc.: The stories in Homer and Hesiod and the poets generally, whenever they have composed fictitious tales and told them to people.

Adeimantus: Which kind do you mean, and what kind of faults do you find in them?

Socrates:The worst of all faults, especially if the story is nasty and immoral as well as false; if it misrepresents the nature of gods and heroes, like the work of an artist who draws something which is entirely unlike the object he first set out to draw.

Adeimantus:That's a fault all right, but give me an example in a story.

Socrates:A prize example of unacceptable fiction about the highest affairs is that foul story which Hesiod tells, about the deeds of Uranus and the revenge of Cronus.Then there are the adventures of Cronus, and his son's treatment of him in turn. Even if such stories were true, I would hardly have thought they were to be thoughtlessly told to young people. If the stories can't be suppressed altogether, then they should only be revealed in a mystery, to which access should be restricted as far as possible by requiring an expensive sacrifice, not just a piglet.[12]

Adeimantus: It's true; such stories are unacceptable.

Socrates:Yes, and not to be repeated in our republic, Adeimantus.We shall not tell a child that, whatever vile crime he commits or whatever he does to punish his father's misdeeds, he won't be doing anything unusual but just what the first and greatest of the gods have done before him.

From the above extract we can see not only Socrates' objection to the gods as role-models, but the argument being taken a stage further to suit the overall scheme of Plato's ideal state, namely that a form of censorship should be instituted. It is difficult to believe that Socrates himself would have gone so far as to advocate such censorship; probably this is an instance of Plato's use of Socrates as a dialogue-character to propagate his own views of what should happen in an ideal state.

5. The Stoics

About 300 B.C. **Zeno of Citium**, who had moved to Athens, began to teach in the **Stoa Poikile** (Painted Gateway), a well-known public building in Athens.After Zeno's death the teachings which he had begun were carried on by his successors. Stoicism as a collection of doctrines became popular amongst the Romans from the second century B.C. to the death of Marcus Aurelius at the end of the second century A.D..

Among Zeno's teachings were:

a) the importance of **Logos** (reason, system), identified with a unified divine will (**Nous**);

---

[12]A piglet was the required sacrifice, a sort of admission charge, for candidates who were to be initiated into the Eleusinian Mysteries. See *Homeric Hymn to Demeter*, 470-489(given in chapter 14, below).

b) **Pronoia** (literally meaning *forethought*, but having now the sense of divine providence), which can be seen reflected in human reason.

While it is not strictly accurate to see the Stoics as monotheistic in their beliefs, it is certainly fair to see their later influence in the development of Christianity, especially in the use of **Logos** as The Word of God, in St. John's Gospel, I.1–19.

In explaining the Greek (and, later, Roman) gods, the Stoics saw the traditional polytheistic system as a reflection of the forces of nature, which we experience around us with our sensory perceptions, existing in eternal balance under a central control defined variously as the Will of Zeus or as Logos.

Likewise, other divine forces could be interpreted as abstract concepts perceived by our intellect. Thus, anthropomorphic polytheism was not to be considered a reason for embarrassment, but could be understood by the tool of **allegory**, the examination of hidden or inner meanings in myths and in the characteristics of gods and goddesses.

6. EPICURUS (BORN IN SAMOS, 341 B.C.; DIED ATHENS 270)

Epicurus took his basic ideas from the **Atomists**, especially from Democritus, who had taught in Athens over a century earlier. The writings of Epicurus are almost entirely lost, but there is a poetic outline of the Epicurean system, including an account of the creation (or rather evolution) of the Universe, in the Roman poet **Lucretius**' great epic, *On the Nature of the Universe*, composed in Latin around 70 B.C..

Epicurus' teachings may be summarized thus:

a) All matter is made up of particles (atoms);

b) The world as we know it came into shape as a result of a natural process, a combination of pure chance or coincidence and of simple rules, e.g., that the heaviest atoms sank to the bottom of the universe; the roughest atoms stuck to one another; the lightest and most slippery atoms floated on top.

c) There was no divine plan, or any creator god to put such a plan into action.

d) When we die, it is like a lamp or a machine running out of fuel. Thus, there is no eternal afterlife.

e) If there is no afterlife, all the more reason to respect and make full provision for what we can enjoy on earth. The Epicurean ideal was **Ataraxia**, or *untrouble*.

f) If gods exist, they are made of more refined atoms than the mediocre, short-term stuff of which we are made; thus, they live in an entirely different world or set of dimensions. This being the case, there is no reason why anyone as intelligent as this superior life-form would ever want to interfere in the affairs of humanity: they don't want their **Ataraxia** to be disturbed!

Epicurean teaching on myth may now be seen to stem from the above: heroes, when they lived, were made of better stuff than most people; monsters, on the other hand, were simply evolutionary freaks. The confusion of gods with the characteristics of heroes (hence such demigods as Herakles and Perseus) is mainly a result of poetic fancy.

7. EUHEMERUS OF MESSENE

Euhemerus claimed to have worked as a diplomat for King Cassander, who ruled Northern Greece from 318 to 298 B.C.. Cassander rose to power shortly after the death of Alexander the Great. Euhemerus wrote a book entitled *The Sacred History*, probably after Cassander's death. We know from extract (a) below that Euhemerus spent the last part of his life in Alexandria, the great coastal city in Egypt which became a Greek-speaking metropolis with a library and educational centre under the Ptolemaic dynasty (320 B.C.–31 B.C.). It is obvious from the same source, as well as from extract (b), that Euhemerus' ideas were ridiculed by his contemporary Greek counterparts who still supported the traditional views of the gods. In fact, Euhemerus was not taken seriously as a thinker until Christian times, see extract (c) below.

Euhemerus claimed to have visited an island called Panchaea in the Indian Ocean, where he saw and transcribed a memorial biography of the hero Zeus, written in ancient times by Zeus' son Hermes. Euhemerus framed his theory about the gods in the form of a fictional story surrounding a collection of rationalized myths: the outer story purports to describe his own travels in Egypt, then down the Red Sea and into the Indian Ocean. The inner story is the "biographical" information on the gods.

The fragments of Euhemerus are found (some in Greek, others in the Latin translation made by Ennius in the second century B.C.) in the first volume of F. Jacoby, *die Fragmente der Griechischen Historiker*, where Euhemerus is #63. Complete versions of both the Greek text of the *Sacred History* and Ennius' Latin translation are now lost. The Greek text was used extensively by Diodorus of Sicily in his *Universal History* (between 60 and 30 B.C.) which was in turn used for a Christian world history by Eusebius (300–350 A.D.). The Latin version was similarly used by another Christian writer, Lactantius, a contemporary of Eusebius. Altogether Jacoby lists just over thirty fragments in his collection, but the complete fragments have never so far been published in a collected English translation. I am currently in the process of re-editing and translating the complete fragments and other evidence of Euhemerus' work and influence.

a) Callimachus, **Iambic Poem** I. 9–11

> Come, gather at the shrine outside the walls,
> Where the old man who invented past-time Panchaean Zeus
> Babbles and scribbles his wrongful volumes.

b) Plutarch, **Isis and Osiris** 23 (Jacoby, T4e)

> This [the questioning of anthropomorphism in religion] is little short of ousting and dissolving the honour and faith with which everyone is endowed as soon as he is born, opening the great doors to the atheistic crowd and reducing divine matters to a human level, giving the limelight and platform to the deceits of Euhemerus of Messene, who personally compiled forgeries of an incredible and untenable mythology, spreading every kind of godlessness around the civilized world, by reducing all the believed-in gods alike into the names of generals, admirals, and kings, as if they had indeed lived in ancient times, having them commemorated in gold inscriptions at Panchaea, which no-one had ever encountered, whether a foreigner or a Greek, except Euhemerus alone, so it seems. He says he sailed to the lands of the Panchoans and the Triphyllians, which never existed anywhere on earth and do not now exist.

c) Eusebius, **Preparation for the Gospel** II.2, 59B (Jac. F2)

> Euhemerus, being a friend of king Cassander, was compelled by him to fulfill certain imperial functions and to undertake great journeys abroad. He says he travelled south as far as the Ocean. Having embarked from Arabia the Blessed he travelled through the ocean for several days and reached some islands in the sea, one of which happened to be called Panchaea. The island is sacred to the gods, and there are many things marvelous for their antiquity and their workmanship. There is also on the island, located on a very high hill, a temple of Zeus Triphyllius, founded by him when he was king of all the civilized world and was amongst humanity. In this temple there is a plaque of gold on which are written in the Panchaean alphabet the deeds of Uranus, Cronus, and Zeus. Euhemerus says that Uranus was first to rule, that he was a distinguished and beneficent man, that he was knowledgeable in the movements of the stars, and that he was the first to honour the heavenly gods with sacrifices, for which reason he was called "Heaven" (Ouranos). There were born to him by his wife Hestia two sons, Titan and Cronus, and two daughters, Rhea and Demeter.

Cronus became king after Uranus; he married Rhea and fathered Zeus, Hera, and Poseidon.

Note:

Since the appearance of Euhemerus' work, probably around 280 B.C., students of myth have begun to use the term *Euhemerism*. To euhemerize a myth is to interpret the myth on the understanding that all the so-called gods and goddesses are really people who once lived, but are now dead; we still respect their memory because of their contributions (especially inventions and discoveries) to humanity. Such a human benefactor is normally defined as a **Culture Hero**.

📖 In the interpretation of myths, it is a good practical rule of thumb to treat allegory and Euhemerism as opposites. **Allegory** concentrates on symbolic representations, while Euhemerism concentrates on treatment of myths as exaggerated history.

8. ASTROLOGICAL INTERPRETATIONS

📖 There is some controversy as to whether this type of approach can strictly be termed "elimination of the supernatural," since it usually substitutes the concept of birth-signs and other astrological phenomena for the influence of gods. The following extract is taken from an essay, *On Astrology*, by the satirical author Lucian of Samosata, who lived in Syria in the late second century A.D.. The following example, on Bellerophon, is plainly a mixture of allegory and a demythologization similar to the approaches of the logographers and sophists (compare the Hercules and Atlas story in part 2, above).

13. This is what I think about the Bellerophon story: I certainly do not believe that he acquired a flying creature in the form of a horse, but I think he pursued wisdom and had high thoughts, keeping his mind focused on the stars in the sky: he did not reach the sky on a horse, but in his intellect.

14. Let the same be said of Phrixus the son of Athamas.[13] The story goes that he was carried through the air on a golden ram. Likewise goes the story of Daedalus the Athenian.[14] The story may be strange, but I don't think it is foreign to astrology: rather, he practiced it himself and taught it to his son.

---

[13]See above (2.c.iii) for Palaephatus' rationalization of this story.

[14]Daedalus was the legendary designer of the Labyrinth, which ancient Athenians believed had once contained the monstrous Minotaur. See paragraph 16, below on Pasiphae, believed to have been the monster's mother.

15. But Icarus, because he was prone to immaturity and poor judgment, did not aim for what was attainable. He climbed to the very peak in his mind and fell from the truth and strayed away from every kind of reason. So he fell into a sea of unfathomable intricacies and this is why the Greeks made up a story about him, calling a bay in their sea "Icarian" after his name.

16. Presumably Pasiphae[15] too, when she heard from Daedalus about the bull who appears amongst the stars [i.e., *Taurus*] and about the subject of astrology itself, fell in love with the subject. This is why people think Daedalus arranged her union with the bull.

---

[15]See Hyginus, *Fabulae* XXXIX & XL in chapter 13 below

CHAPTER 3

The Development of Modern Mythology

Student guide by J.G. Farrow

The following 12 scholars have been selected because of their memorable contributions to the study of mythology over the past 200 years. In class we refer to these scholars collectively as "the modern critics."

1. JACOB GRIMM (1785–1863)

Early years: studied law, but his academic career was partially interrupted by Napoleon's invasion. During his student days, Grimm took an interest in languages and was intrigued by recent discoveries in the history of the Indo-European language family. His most significant research was in the ways in which phonic shifts occur when one language splits into dialects, then those dialects in turn evolve into languages in their own right. It was already common knowledge that French, modern Italian, Spanish, Portuguese, and Romanian had all begun as different provincial dialects of Latin, becoming known as the "Romance" languages. Likewise Old English, Dutch, and Norse are all Germanic languages. Questions arose as to how each of these European groups are inter-related. Those questions became even more intriguing when, in the mid- to late-1700s, Europeans became aware of the relationship between Sanskrit and the modern languages of India, compounded by similarities between these Indic languages and the major European groups, but quite independent of Mid-Eastern languages. Grimm also began to examine the role of traditional stories in the growth of language.

- **1812:** *Kinder- und Hausmärchen* (better known in English as *Grimm's Fairy Tales*), 1st edition, edited in collaboration with his brother Wilhelm. Jacob insisted on maintaining as much as possible of the authentic flavour of primary sources[1].

---

[1]For detailed discussions and arguments, see "Little Red Riding Hood: A Casebook" by Alan Dundes (U. of Wisconsin Press, 1989) and an article by Donald Haase, "Yours, Mine, or Ours? Perrault, the Brothers Grimm, and the Ownership of Fairy Tales" in "The Classic Fairy Tales, ed. Maria Tatar, Norton N.Y. 1999.

The brothers conveyed a strong impression to their readers that their versions of these tales were the results of research amongst rural story-tellers in Germany. Modern researchers have often questioned the accuracy of this claim.

- **1819:** *Kinder- und Hausmärchen*, 2nd edition, somewhat larger and with expanded footnotes. In Grimm's lifetime there were seven editions published in German alone; brother Wilhelm exercised increasing control over the publication of this work. Elements of sex and violence in the content of the stories were considerably toned down in later editions.

- **1835:** *Deutsche Mythologie*, later translated into English under the title *Teutonic Mythology* (reprinted by Dover, 1966). Even though he did not try to produce a "theory" of myth, as such, Grimm was one of the first scholars to realize and apply the fact that **myth is a function of language.** The link between myth and language is developed in chapter 8 of this book.

2. F. Max Müller (1823–1900)

Born in Germany, but moved to Oxford in the 1840s as a postgraduate student to study Indo-European languages and culture based on evidence from religion and art including sources gathered from India. Lived in Oxford for the rest of his life.

- **1861–71:** *Lectures on the Science of Language* delivered and published
- **1872:** *Lectures on the Science of Religion*
- **1867–87:** Miscellaneous works published as *Chips from a German Workshop*
- **1895–1900:** *Sacred Books of the East* (major series of which Müller was general editor)
- **1909:** *Comparative Mythology* published separately (originally written as an essay in *Chips*) reprinted 1977, Arno Press, NY. More recently, Müller's most important works on mythology have been reprinted by Kessinger reprints (kessinger.net)

Müller's basic view of myth is that myths came into being as a way of explaining the apparent behavior of nature before the days of science (see definition 6 in Chapter 1). He is especially famous for his "solar myth" theory as a way of classifying and interpreting many myths including the vast majority of hero-stories. According to this theory, a large number (possibly the majority) of myths are etiological for the way the sun appears to behave, either on a day-night or a seasonal basis. If the casual reader does not see the etiology at first glance, Müller's explanation rested in his well-known joke, "Myth is a disease of language."

3. HEINRICH SCHLIEMANN (1822–1890)

Left school in his early teens and rose to wealth as a merchant, so he had very little formal education. He wanted to prove that the myths of the Trojan War were based on real events which could be located in history. He was not satisfied with myths merely as nature-symbols or explanations. After becoming rich enough to finance his own excavations and having taught himself Homeric Greek, he studied archaeology (a brand-new science at the time) in Paris in the late 1860s.

1871–80: Schliemann excavated the site of **Hisarlik**, northwest Turkey, believing from evidence in Homer and Strabo that this was the site of the ancient city of Troy. He found that the site contained evidence of settlements at nine different levels. After Schliemann's death his successor on the excavation, Wm. **Dörpfeld**, decided that **Troy Level VI**, marked by extremely strong walls, had been badly damaged by an earthquake; **Level VIIa**, which immediately followed it, was marked by inferior construction and had been destroyed by fire. The approximate time of these settlements corresponded to the end of the Greek Bronze Age, when the wars were believed to have taken place. Clearly the archaeological solution to the Trojan War was not so simple, even though Schliemann died believing that he had proved the war's reality. Modern archaeologists are still trying to analyze much of the rubble thrown up during Schliemann's excavations, since modern science can add much to any inferences Schliemann may have been able to draw in his own day.

4. ANDREW LANG (1844–1912)

Spent most of his life in Scotland. Lang was famous as an editor and collector of folk-tales. He also contributed an enormous number of articles and reviews to magazines.

1870–early 1890s: Lang devoted much energy to ridiculing some of the wilder excesses of the "Solar" theorists (see #2), but from 1890 onwards his reviews and articles showed increasingly strong attacks on the "Ritualists" (#5 & 6 below), especially Frazer. Lang believed in a devolution or degeneration of religion in the early stages which had led to Polytheism, with present-day monotheism preserved (throughout and in spite of a long series of external and internal distractions) by the Judeo-Christian system.

Lang believed that myths had grown as a response to material, social, and economic systems in which the whole of mankind had lived: they were not necessarily etiological for the apparent behavior of nature, as Müller had preferred to believe, or just for rituals (see below). For more on Lang's definition of myth, see definition 11, Chapter 1.

5. WILLIAM ROBERTSON SMITH (1846–1894)

Was Professor of Hebrew in the Free Church College, Aberdeen, until he was accused of heresy for some articles in the *Encyclopedia Britannica* on ancient religion. He was one of the first Biblical scholars to acknowledge the effect of evolution on religion as a distinctly human phenomenon and to advocate a specific course for this evolutionary pattern. He believed that myths had begun to develop at a very early date, occupying the same functional place which **dogma** occupies in modern religions. His ides on the evolution of religion, including the role of totemism, were very controversial

He was one of the first proponents of **ritual theory**, the view that rituals had been originally devised as attempts to control nature by **sympathetic magic**. The practice of the rituals had become habitual to the point that, even when their original form and purpose had been long forgotten, etiological myths had grown up around them to explain otherwise illogical actions. As Robertson Smith's ideas became widely recognized, other authors and teachers used the idea that myths were not always a mere substitute for science (as Müller had believed), but that the myths were etiological for ritualized behavior which otherwise defied explanation. Scholars who used his methods were therefore known collectively, after their own time, as **the Cambridge Ritualists**. One of the most prominent Cambridge Ritualists, **Jane Ellen Harrison**, gave a very accurate and concise definition of the ritualist position: definition 9 in Chapter 1.

6. SIR JAMES G. FRAZER (1854–1935)

Spent most of his life pursuing research at Trinity College, Cambridge. Based his theories of myth on the principle (starting from theories of **Ch. Darwin**, **E.B. Tylor**, and **Wm. Robertson Smith**) that religion, as an anthropological phenomenon, had undergone basic evolution from primitive animism, via polytheism, to modern monotheistic systems. For Frazer's own definition of myth, see definition 8, Chapter 1.

1890–91: *The Golden Bough*, 1st edition, published. This major work provoked much controversy at the turn of the century. In a very long and rambling discussion, with worldwide examples, Frazer demonstrates that certain themes constantly recur in combination with each other as religious symbols in myths and folktales. Frazer's chief themes are **tree-worship** (especially of evergreens) and **Sacral Kingship**. Frazer examines kingship as not simply leadership (whether political manipulation or military strategy) but more importantly as a perceived line of direct communication between people, land, and the forces of nature. In early communities, Frazer claimed, magical ceremonies (sympathetic magic, to make crops grow and cause other benefits to visit the tribe) had been performed by a priest or king: the Latin word for priest, *pontifex*, for example, means *bridge-builder*. A king's function was to represent his people to the gods and the gods to his people. Thus there was a lot of similarity between priest and king. Frazer contrasts king-as-priest with sacrificial victim, comparing both with the recurrent **dying god** theme of worldwide seasonal myths.

7. SIGMUND FREUD (1856–1939)

Freud's basic position on myths was that they, like dreams, act as a safety-valve for the human mind. Freud, following the early evolutionists, assumed that human behavior had once (in our early tribal development) formed a series of behavioral patterns in order to ensure survival. Such behavior is now programmed unconsciously into our genetic make-up even though it is undesirable in modern social conditions. We thus work out our unacceptable behavior in dreaming and in perpetuating myths. For more, see definition 12, Chapter 1.

8. CARL GUSTAV JUNG (1875–1961)

Born in Switzerland, Jung perceived myths as reflections of **Archetypes** (originals from which moulds are made) **of the Collective Unconscious**. See definitions 13, 19, Chapter 1.

Jung's own language sometimes conveys to the modern reader a sense of the prophetic pronouncement, as if he really believed that his archetypes had an independent and objective existence of their own. Students must realize that such language is meant to be read as figurative or symbolic. The "collective unconscious" is actually manifest in such everyday concepts as peer-pressure and has been, quite consciously and deliberately, exploited and modernized by the advertising and entertainments industries during the last fifty years (especially in the US).

9. BRONISLAW MALINOWSKI (1884–1942)

Was born and studied at Krakow, Poland. He was intrigued by the concept of a "mythopoeic society" (a phrase already in use since the days of Müller and Tylor) and decided to go to the Trobriand Islands to study life in such a society. He wished to demonstrate that myths are not just stories, but an essential part of daily life for those who believe in them. See definition 14, Chapter 1.

In his essays, *Magic, Science and Religion* (1925, 1954) Malinowski discussed the role of myth and of sympathetic magic within a larger context of social organization.

10. VLADIMIR PROPP (1895–1970)

Propp's most important contribution to research in mythology is his *Morfologia Skazki* (1928), published in English in 1958 as *Morphology of the Folktale*. Propp's research consisted of taking typical examples of the *Skazka* form (traditional Russian folktales in which something supernatural often happens) and analyzing them. Most of the samples used by Propp were different kinds of "Myth of the Quest."

Propp formulated a system by which each story follows a regular pattern of episodes. Each motif in the story performs its own particular function and has its own particular value, determined principally by the stage of the story in which we find the motif. For Propp's view of the functions of the *Dramatis personae* (cast of characters) see below, Chapter 5.

11. CLAUDE LÉVI-STRAUSS (B. BELGIUM, 1908, DIED PARIS 2009)

Educated in France, Lévi-Strauss spent much of his professional life in Brazil and made many specialized studies of native American myths. Like Propp, Lévi-Strauss has often been classified as a **Structuralist**, but the two scholars differ strongly in the ways in which they examine myths and folktales to find an inherent structure.

Unlike Propp, Lévi-Strauss disregards the narrative order of a story because it tends (especially in European and other literary treatments of stories) to be excessively regulated by rules of sequential logic and other forms of artificial packaging.

In Lévi-Strauss' approach, it is necessary to understand a myth by looking for patterns such as polarization of motifs: to put it simply, look for groupings of "likes" and "opposites" (such as male/female, raw/cooked, hot/cold, dark/light, etc.) and list them. Ideally, if we can find two such pairings in a story, we may be able to assemble the pairlists in graph form and, from the graph, derive a reading which tells us something about the social organization or attitudes of the people who produced the myth.

Lévi-Strauss admitted that his approach does not work very well with Classical Greek myths (see "The Structural Study of Myth" in *Structural Anthropology*, 1963, pp. 206–231). He tried applying the system to the myths of Thebes, achieving two pairgroups (nature plus vs. nature minus; over-attachment towards relatives vs. violence towards relatives) but was unable to form a graph. Presumably he decided that the present form of the myths had suffered from too much elaboration by poets and tragedians.

12. WALTER BURKERT (B. 1931, D. 2015, SWITZERLAND)

Demonstrated that Lévi-Strauss' approach to structural analysis can be applied to Classical Greek myths if a scholar has a strong enough background in linguistic, social, and religious history to assemble all the required background information. Burkert has been especially helpful in applying knowledge of archaeological research to applications of literary and structural, as well as ritual understanding of our sources. For more on his *Structure and History in Greek Mythology and Ritual*, see definition #17, Chapter 1.

Examples of Motifs

For purposes of this course we will define *motif* as an **idea-unit**, a single unit when we are counting or listing the ideas which make up a story. They should be seen as the building-bricks of stories. When you proceed to more advanced studies in the subject, the definition becomes more complex. The ultimate reference guide to myths and folktales as they are classified by motifs is the "Motif Index," first compiled by the Finnish scholar Antti Aarne and continued first by the American Stith Thompson and more recently by Hans- Jörg Uther. In this important reference work motifs are classified on a larger scale by the story-types in which they occur. For more on this Index, see Chapter 5.

Here are a few examples of motifs which commonly occur in myths and in folktales, together with the meanings they most often carry.

1. "CHALLENGE AT THE DOOR" MOTIF

How often have you heard a joke which starts, "Knock, knock"?

Any form of knocking or calling out at a door or barrier is an instance of this motif. It is especially used in myths in the same way (but obviously on a bigger scale) as a conjunction is used in a sentence: it links component episodes. Consider the way in which the challenge is traditionally used in Little Red Riding Hood: the first knocking is done by the wolf (who does not admit who he is) and is answered by the "real" Grandmother. In the second instance the "real" Red Riding Hood knocks at the door, answered by the "fake" Grandmother. The narrator has repeated the motif almost word-for-word, but has inverted the role of the characters. The relationship between character-roles and the sequencing of motifs was very effectively explored by the Russian folklorist Vladimir Propp (see chapter 3 #10 above & chapter 5 on structure, below).

2. BIRDS

The single most common function of the bird as a motif is to be a messenger. It doesn't always matter (depending on the culture) what kind of bird it is. We still continue to use the phrase, "A little bird told me," especially when confronting children with an uncomfortable truth.

Birds can have other functions depending on the species, color, or habits:

a) **Black birds** can sometimes represent **shamanism** (see below) or in some cultures they can indicate an omen of death.

b) **White birds** most frequently represent a person's soul or spirit (see **Aschenpüttel** and **Swing on the Pictured Rocks**, chapters 10 & 12 below). In another Ojibwa myth, **Sun-Catcher** (given chapter 11 below), the adjective *gitchee* (big) is used twice for emphasis before the bird's name (snow bird) so the whiteness together with this probably symbolizes the strength and power of the Northern Michigan winter.

c) **Carrion-eating birds** most commonly represent the **Psychopomp** (see chapter 7 below). Examples of this are the Egyptian god Thoth (represented as an ibis) and Oðin's ravens, allegorically portrayed as Valkyries escorting the souls of dead warriors to Valhalla.

3. TREES

Occasionally one meets the motif of a tree which has the attributes of a person. J.R.R. Tolkien exploited this motif most effectively with the Ents, a fictitious species in the *Lord of the Rings* trilogy. In ancient Greek rural belief the **Dryads** were specifically oak-tree goddesses, while the **Meliai** (*Meliae* in Latin spelling) were ash-tree goddesses. The idea of the ash-tree as a precursor of the human being is explicit in Norse myth (Snorri's *Gylfaginning* Chapter 28, below, section 9), while it seems to be implied by Hesiod (in chapter 18, below) if there is any particular purpose in his reference to the Meliai (see the translation of the *Theogony*, below, with relevant footnote).

Other functions of trees depend on the species. Here are some examples.

a) **Fruit-bearing trees:** (e.g., apple, pear, nut) represent the act of **giving**. In ancient Greek religion the olive was the gift of Athene, the grape that of Dionysus. In Grimm's **Aschenpüttel** part of the role we might have expected to be given to the Fairy Godmother is assigned instead to a hazel-nut tree which the girl plants by her mother's grave.

b) Hardwood trees symbolize strength and endurance. In Northern Europe this is typified by the oak and ash trees. In Greece the olive is especially significant for the hardness of its wood, a theme prominent throughout Homer's *Odyssey*. Thus we can see that the olive plant, which fits both the "giving" and the "strength" categories, was regarded by ancient Greeks as a particularly holy tree.

c) Evergreen trees symbolize life, especially during the winter when everything else around them seems dead or sleeping. All those familiar with the words of the traditional German carol "O Tannenbaum" will understand that the song probably originated as a hymn to the tree for this quality. Several types of evergreen common in Northern Europe produce, even during decomposition, a substance called tannic acid. It is a natural preservative and is responsible for the still-fresh condition of corpses found in peat-bogs in Denmark and the British Isles. For some good examples, try an Internet search on the **Tollund Man**, the body of a man executed or sacrificed by hanging in Denmark some 2,000 years ago.

For some vivid examples of tree-motifs used sometimes in an attractive context, sometimes gruesome, read the script of Euripides' play *The Bacchae*. A slightly abridged translation is given as chapter 22, below.

4. MOTIFS ASSOCIATED WITH SHAMANISM

The shaman is believed by his people to have powers of "crossing over," whether it is to the world of spirits, gods, or the animal kingdom. Thus people expect him to have abilities which sometimes include seeing into the future or communicating with the dead. We therefore find this type of character depicted by marginality, i.e., he/she lives on borderlines, whether between human and animal, male and female, god and human, or living and dead. This habit of defying what people see as the normal parameters of nature helps classify the shaman as a **trickster** to whom such polarizations do not apply.

Motifs of physical transformation associated with shamanism:

a) Dressing in animal skins or masks is a motif still sometimes used in the entertainment industry as a stereotypical indicator of a "witch doctor." When the boy in **Sun-Catcher** dresses in the skins of the Snow Bird he is obviously entering a stage of shamanic initiation. When Menelaus goes to consult Proteus who is introduced by Homer in a way which clearly shows him to be a shaman, Menelaus himself must put on a seal-skin as a disguise (*Odyssey* IV, 395-480). A recent pair of films recycling ideas from the Grimm Brothers "Snow White" introduced the name Ravenna, developing the evil queen as an obvious and stereotypical shamaness.

b) **Trans-gender characteristics**, depicted as ambiguous or as actual changes in gender, are also common. A glance at the biography of the ancient Greek seer **Teiresias**, especially as given by Apollodorus, shows how much this character was associated with changes of sex. See chapter 7, below.

c) **Sensations of flight** may be associated with **birds** (see above) or with aspects of **mental or spiritual transformation** (see below). The association between birds and the shaman was certainly known to the ancient Greeks: Herodotus (IV.15–16) included in chapter 25 below, mentions a tradition passed on by people in Metapontum (a Greek colony in Southern Italy, near which the followers of Pythagoras maintained a kind of college in Herodotus' time). According to this tradition the famous shaman Aristeas of Marmora, or Proconessus (a Greek colony on the inlet to the Black Sea), had appeared in Metapontum 240 years after his previous disappearance in Marmora and explained to the people there that he traveled with Apollo, taking on the form of a raven to do so. The link between shamanism and the mental sensation of flight lies also at the origin of the ancient European motif of the witch who flies on a broomstick.

Motifs of mental/spiritual transformation associated with shamanism:

a) **Ritual fasting** is seen by believers as a cleansing process to prepare the body for a visit by a god. The non-believer sees it as hallucination caused by dramatic fluctuations in blood sugar and other chemical levels within the body.

b) **Ritual dancing** is seen as the performance of an ecstatic rite to a god, leading to the possession of the dancer's spirit. When the dancer collapses and "receives spiritual visions" the non-believer sees hallucinations caused again by internal chemical fluctuations.

c) **Intoxicating liquids** are similarly seen in primitive religions as inducing spiritual visitation. A reading of Euripides' *Bacchae* (Chapter 22, below) will show many examples of this.

d) **Inhaling certain smokes and gases** was also seen by the ancients as inviting a visit from a god. There has been much argument in recent years as to whether the trances of the **Pytho** (the title of Apollo's main prophetess in the Oracle at Delphi) were caused by geological gases issuing from a fault under the oracle building or from the smoldering of certain leaves on a metal plate (the "Holy Tripod") over a fire.

e) **Eating hallucinogenic fungi** can be extremely dangerous and ancient people attached supernatural causes to its results. In the seventeenth century there was a notorious incident in Salem, Massachusetts, attributed at the time to witchcraft. In recent years there has been a growing perception that the incident was likely caused by the accidental eating of bread and other cereal crop products by local people when the harvest had been tainted with ergotine, a chemical produced by a fungus which sometimes grows in cereals. Since ergotine is a naturally occurring form of LSD, it is hardly surprising that the victims believed themselves to be visited by demons.

CHAPTER

Myth and Structure

There are several ways to approach the question: "Do myths follow a set of structural rules—for example, like the rules of grammar?"

The main approaches are:

1. **Linear sequence:** Taking the view that every story has a beginning, a middle, and an end, with certain motifs belonging in their respective places. Some of the most popular sequences are outlined below.

2. **Binary polarization:** An approach pioneered by the Belgian anthropologist Claude Lévi-Strauss (chapter 3 #11) and extended into the area of classical myths since the 1970s, especially following the publications of Walter Burkert on Greek religion and its impact on the contents of myth.

3. **Classification by theme:** A useful way of cross-referring to myths internationally (pioneered by the Finnish scholar Antti Aarne, continued by the American scholar Stith Thompson and more recently updated by Hans-Jörg Uther (see http://www.folklorefellows.fi/?page_id=103), resulting in a major reference work usually known as the "Motif Index." For example stories of the *Little Red Riding Hood* type, grouped as *The Glutton*, are Type 333. *Cinderella* is Type 510A, while *Snow White* is Type 709.

Linear sequence was considered a standard approach until the mid-20th century. The best argument in its favor is still the analogy with jokes: we have all met a person who, in telling a joke, introduces a motif that he should have saved until the end, or "punch line." A motif presented out of sequence can ruin the entire telling of the joke. Before continuing to the other approaches, we must consider some important and still popular linear sequences.

POPULAR LINEAR SEQUENCES

1. The Two-Step Trickster Story

Let us call the two main characters A and B.

- Step 1: A tricks, or tries to trick, B.
- Step 2: B turns the tables by foiling A and/or by tricking him back.

We will all recognize this as the basic format of cartoon films and other Saturday-morning media entertainment.

2. The Three-Step "Significant Exception" Sequence

- Step 1:Attempt 1 has result A (Wolf eats the Pig in the straw house).
- Step 2:Attempt 2 also has result A (Wolf eats the Pig in the twig house).
- Step 3:Attempt 3 has a new result, B, thus breaking the pattern set by the repetition in the first two attempts (Wolf fails to eat the Pig in the brick house).

This sequence can be multiplied to a high degree of complexity. Goldilocks, for example, goes through three layers of testing (chairs, porridge, beds) while in the home of the three bears (one of each for father, mother, child). Some Norse myths take this three-pattern to an even higher degree of complexity, such as the *Song of Rig* (*Rigsthula*), in which the solar god Heimdallr visits three homes in ascending order of wealth, spending three days and nights in each home as the third person in the bed and the offspring of each family is listed with growing complications of numerical repetition.

3. The Five-Step Myth of the Quest

Before listing the steps, we must consider an important issue, which resembles the rules of grammar: **every quest must have a subject and an object.** The subject is the one "looking," while the object is what this person is looking for. This "object" may or may not necessarily be a physical object. More often it is a problem that needs to be solved. So, if Jason and the Argonauts are the subject, we assume that the object is going to be the Golden Fleece.

- Step 1:We meet the characters and form sympathies (decide who is a "good guy" or a "bad guy").
- Step 2:We meet the quest-object or the problem.

   Note: Before continuing, observe that steps 1 and 2 may overlap. There is no problem in meeting new characters later in the story, as long as we meet enough at the beginning to make sense of the story. Some sources set up the object first and then introduce us to the subject(s) as a new set of characters. Hyginus does this in the first 20 of his *Fabulae* (chapter 13 below), introducing the man Phrixus and setting up the Golden Fleece in Colchis before even mentioning Jason or the other Argonauts.[1]

---

[1]Early versions of the Grail-quest often follow the same pattern: Joseph of Arimathea leaves the Holy Land with the Cup of the Last Supper (in later sources also with a cutting from the Crown of Thorns) and travels across the Roman Empire, settling in the far Northwest on the island of Great Britain and building the first Christian Church there in what later became the town of Glastonbury. The narrator can then jump forward over 400 years to the time of King Arthur and his knights.

- Step 3: The "wandering" stage: The subject does not know where to look for the object, so he can easily be sidetracked on apparent tangents. As in a good computer game, these sidetracks can, in the hands of a good story-teller, produce material that becomes useful later.
- Step 4: The confrontation: The subject confronts the object, the problem, the romance-interest, or the villain (or any combination of these).
- Step 5: Conclusion.

We will easily recognize from the above that this formula is not just used in traditional stories but is the basic blueprint for over 90 percent of Hollywood films.

SPECIALIZED FORMS OF LINEAR SEQUENCE

There are many more linear sequences than those mentioned in this chapter; they are simply three of the most popular. Other forms include the following:

- **Creation myths:** Usually follow a pattern dictated by local living conditions. One of the most popular types of creation myth is the one we call "Sacred Marriage of Earth and Sky," outlined in its own section below in chapter 17.
- **Katabasis myths:** A person goes to the underworld (sometimes, but not always, on a quest) and returns. The katabasis is explained more fully below in chapter 14.

ADVANCED THEORIES OF LINEAR SEQUENCE

The most notable of these, advanced in the 1920s, is that of Russian folklorist **Vladimir Propp**. Propp's approach is to equate the linear progression of a story with the functions of its main characters, treating these characters like the cast of a play. The theory will be outlined in the next section. One of the most interesting and appealing features of this theory is that we can use Propp's 31 character-functions as pin-points on the map of a story, using them as a vertical axis to stack up on each one an entire menu of possible motifs. With modern computers this makes it possible to design a kind of "story-writing software." It is indeed unfortunate that Propp died before the modern personal computer was invented.

THE FUNCTIONS OF THE *DRAMATIS PERSONAE*

Summarized from *Morphology of the Folktale* by Vladimir Propp
(1928, 2nd Edition of English translation, 1968)

The following is a sequential list of functions for the *Dramatis Personae* ("Characters of the Play"), as Propp found the most popular structural pattern recurring in his research on **Skazki** (Russian for "Folk Tales"). Propp's research was based exclusively on Russian samples, but his findings can be applied to any broad group of folk tales or myths that are based on heroic adventures and quests.

The list is a series of stages, called **functions** by Propp. In each "function" particular characters perform their roles (that's why we call them "functions") in a typical story. Other motifs (such as objects, situations, etc.) fall into place around the characters in an order dictated by the "grammar" of the story. Each motif has its own most likely place (or choice of places) in sequence, determined by its function (the job it does) and value (its particular kind of importance) in the story.

- **Roman figures** represent Propp's numbering (2nd English language edition, University of Texas Press 1968, 1988).

- **The story begins with its initial situation** (labeled α by Propp: not a **function** as such, but still an important stage in the story) in which the main family or character is introduced.

   I. One member of a family absents himself from home (labeled β by Propp).

   II. An **interdiction** ("Don't do this," "Don't go there," etc.) is addressed to the hero.

   III. The interdiction is violated.

   *This is a very popular point for the introduction of the villain/monster/ wicked stepmother/uncle, etc.

   IV. Reconnaissance: Usually the villain asks a question, for example, location of children/jewels, or sometimes the hero asks the villain a question, thus enabling a trick or trap to be set.

   V. The villain receives information about his intended victim (usually in answer to #IV).

   VI. The villain attempts to trick his victim, to take something from him, or to cast a spell on him.

   VII. The hero submits to deception and thus unwittingly helps his enemy.

VIII. The villain causes damage or injury to a member of a family.

> *Propp believed that this was an especially crucial stage in the story and that the first seven functions were all building up toward it. It is also important, Propp believed, that our attention is drawn at this stage to a character's **lack** of something. This lack or need may be caused by the villain's trick or it may already have existed at the beginning of the story.

IX. The misfortune or lack is made known; the hero is approached with a request or command and is sent or allowed to go.

X. The hero counteracts (this is a minor function, limited to stories about a "seeker hero," in Propp's terms).

XI. The hero leaves home; if he has already done so in function **I**, then **XI** is for a longer time.

> *At this stage a new character often appears, termed by Propp the "donor" or "provider."

XII. The hero is tested, interrogated, or attacked. This usually prepares the way for his receiving a helper or magical agent. Propp called this the **first function of the Donor**.

XIII. The hero reacts to the future donor's actions.

XIV. The hero acquires the use of a magical agent.

XV. The hero is taken to the location of an object of search. This object is often in a "different" world, reality, or country. The hero's transportation can be magical (flying, special boat, etc.) or natural but dramatic (following a thread, footprints, bloodstains, etc.).

XVI. The hero struggles with the villain (direct combat).

XVII. The hero is marked or branded.

XVIII. The villain is defeated (hero's victory).

XIX. **Liquidation** of the original misfortune or lack (already sensed in functions **I** through **IX**).

XX. The hero returns.

XXI. The hero is pursued. Often the pursuer tries to trick, trap, or kill the hero.

XXII. The hero is rescued from pursuit. There is usually a helper (compare functions **XII** and **XV**) or a change of appearance involved; alternatively, the hero hides in/as a tree.

XXIII. The hero, unrecognized, arrives home or in another country.

XXIV. The false hero presents unfounded claims. If the hero arrives home in the previous function (**XXIII**), then the false claims may be presented by his brothers. If the hero is a warrior, then another officer poses as killer of a monster, etc.

XXV. The hero is challenged to perform a difficult task or undergo an ordeal.

XXVI. The task (**XXV**) is resolved.

XXVII. The hero is recognized.

XXVIII. The false hero is exposed.

XXIX. The hero is given a new appearance (usually with a magical helper's assistance; see **XV, XXII**), new clothing, or a new palace.

XXX. The false hero is punished.

XXXI. The hero is married and/or ascends the throne.

CHAPTER 6

Introduction to the Hero

There are two basic approaches to the study of heroes in myths. In the first, or "old" approach, we examine the hero in terms of what the sources say about him and how he was viewed in historical antiquity by his believers. We call this factor **historicity**. Some modern scholars consider this approach to be antiquated or "irrelevant," but it can tell us a very great deal, not only about the history and development of religious belief but also about unchanging factors in human psychology, such as the ever-popular recurrence of hero shrines visited by large numbers of pilgrims. Since the middle ages shrines of saints have fulfilled a very similar function. More recently visitors have thronged the burial-places or former homes of deceased rock stars and respected royalty.

The second approach, widely accepted and pursued in the middle and late twentieth century, has been to point out that every individual and every culture has a Hero in some sense of the term. The Hero is an **archetype**: no single version is "the only true and original." If we need to find "the original," then we must look into our own minds rather than into the facts of history.

Too often students have been encouraged to consider these two approaches a matter of polarized choice: they have been urged to choose either the objective study of how real people in the past worshipped their long-dead mythic heroes, or to treat myths as a shopping-mall where you can go looking for an archetype to adopt in forming your own outlook on life. The student who wishes to be most fully prepared for the 21st century should not see the approaches as an either/or choice, but as two halves or aspects of the same tool which, once they understand both parts better, they can use more fully.

1. HISTORICALLY-BASED STUDY OF THE HERO

A. Hero Cults: research on the overlapping areas of anthropology and ritual in the explanation of myths began with the Cambridge Ritualists (Sir James Frazer, Jane Harrison, A.B. Cook, L.R. Farnell, and others) and has continued to the present time with the recent works of Walter Burkert (*Greek Religion* 1977, 1985; *Structure and History in Greek Mythology and Ritual* 1979; *Ancient Mystery Cults* 1986–87). See chapter 3 critics 5, 6 and 12 above.

1. L.R. Farnell (*Greek Hero-Cults and Ideas of Immortality*), H.J. Rose (various works), W.K.C. Guthrie (*Greek Religion*) all assert that the hero is definitely in origin a man who may later have risen to status of a god—this seems to be essentially a variation of **Euhemerism**, the standard explanation that gods in bygone religions were men who distinguished themselves (became culture-heroes) and were venerated as gods after their death. See Chapter 2 (Ancient Critics) #7.

2. Guthrie makes the following observations regarding hero-cults:

a) The hero was a man, not a god—some heroes were historical, and others were not.

b) Hero-worship rests on the belief that the dead have power in and from the grave—there would have been no cult without such a belief.[1]

c) The hero is still imagined as dwelling in his tomb—this explains the magnificence of the tombs like the massive *tholoi* at Mycenae—hence the great treasures stored in tombs.

d) The tomb, whether it contains the body or the ashes (there was a change in practice from burial to cremation) of the hero, is his dwelling-place, and around the tomb his influence is felt—hence cult observed at the tomb with offerings of blood and wine.[2]

e) Hero-cults were established either in expectation of benefits to come or to avert the effects of the dead man's wrath—due to belief that the dead have power for good or evil.

f) Farnell's view that Homeric poems had powerful influence for the spread of hero-cults in post-Homeric times is accepted as valid by Guthrie.

B. Lord Raglan (in *The Hero*) in essence denies all historicity (historical existence) to most true heroes (i.e., heroes in the true and Classical sense of the term). Raglan was, in essence, a ritualist in his view of myths and how they develop. He was very much influenced by the Cambridge Ritualists, especially Jane Ellen Harrison, A.B. Cook, and Sir James Frazer.

The following synopsis of Lord Raglan's *The Hero*[3] takes the form of a biographical sketch:

---

[1] The endurance of this belief, together with some insight into its workings, can be seen in the *Heroikos* of Flavius Philostratus, probably written in the early 3rd century AD. See J.K. Berenson Maclean and E.B Aitken, *Flavius Philostratus: Heroikos* (Atlanta, 2001).

[2] This type of ritual is outlined by Homer as already being familiar to Odysseus and his audience: *Odyssey* XI, 23-50.

[3] Lord Raglan's *The Hero* was first published in the U.K. in 1936. Since 1990 it has been reprinted several times in the Princeton/Bollingen *Mythos* series.

1. The hero's mother is a royal virgin;
2. his father is a king, and
3. often a near relative of the mother, but
4. the circumstances of his conception are unusual, and
5. he is also reputed to be the son of a god, (i.e., he has supra-personal parents as well as personal).
6. At birth an attempt is made, usually by his father or maternal grandfather (or uncle) to kill him, or
7. he is spirited away and
8. reared by foster-parents in a far country.
9. We are told almost nothing of his childhood, but
10. on reaching manhood he returns or goes to his future kingdom.
11. After a victory over the king and/or a giant, dragon, or wild beast,
12. he marries a princess, often the daughter of his predecessor,
13. and becomes king.
14. For a time he reigns uneventfully, and
15. prescribes laws (or bestows a blessing or gift upon the community) but
16. later he loses favor with the gods and/or his subjects and
17. is driven from the throne and city, after which
18. he meets with a mysterious death,
19. often at the top of a hill.
20. His children, if any, do not succeed him.
21. His body is buried, but nevertheless
22. he has one or more holy sepulchres.

(Lord Raglan, *The Hero* – modified)

2. PSYCHOANALYSIS AND THE HERO AS AN ARCHETYPE OF THE COLLECTIVE UNCONSCIOUS

The first thinker to use the expression **archetype** in this context was the psychologist Sigmund Freud. Many of Freud's students and followers developed the use of the term, especially **C.G. Jung**, who linked it to what he called the **collective unconscious**, i.e., the terms and images humans use when they communicate with each other within a frame of mutually understood cultural allusions. Such allusions are so strong that they seem real to those who use them uncritically.[4]

Jung's list of "archetypes of the collective unconscious" includes the following:

1. The Trickster (see chapter 7, below);
2. The Great Mother;
3. The Hero;
4. The Divine Child; and
5. The **Maiden Goddess (Kore)**. This theme is developed below in chapter 14 with the Homeric Hymn to Demeter.

After Jung's ideas had been published and discussed internationally, a number of his followers extended his findings or tried applying them to specific areas of myth. Joseph Campbell is the best-known recent example of the followers of Jung in this respect. For comparison, examples will also be given from writings by scholars of cult and ritual on hero-cults amongst the Greeks (see part C, below).

A. Joseph Campbell:

"The hero is the man of self-achieved submission," of submission to the experience of "a continuous 'recurrence of birth' (**Palingenesia**) to nullify the unremitting recurrences of death."[5]

The first step in the process, detachment or withdrawal, consists of a retreat from the external to the internal world, macro- to microcosm, a retreat to the everlasting realm within; but, says he,

"This realm, as we know from psychoanalysis, is precisely the infantile unconscious. It is the realm that we enter in sleep. We carry it within ourselves forever. All the ogres and secret helpers of our nursery are there, all the magic of childhood. And more important, all the life-potentialities that we never managed to bring to adult realization, those other portions of ourselves, are there.... If only a portion of that lost totality could be dredged up into the light of day, we should experience a marvelous expansion of our powers, a vivid renewal of life...."

"Moreover, if we could dredge up something forgotten not only by ourselves but by our whole generation or our entire civilization, we should become indeed the boon-bringer, the culture hero of the day—a personage of not only local but world historical moment. In a word: the first work of the hero is to retreat from the world

---

[4]The references here to Jung's ideas are derived from a general reading of his works. For principal sources, see *The Archetypes and the Collective Unconscious*, 1959, vol. 9 of his collected works (Princeton).

[5]*The Hero with a Thousand Faces,* 1st edition 1949, p.25. 3rd edition 2008.

scene of secondary effects to those causal zones of the psyche where the difficulties really reside, and there to clarify the difficulties, eradicate them in his own case (i.e., give battle to the nursery demons of his local culture) and break through to the undistorted, direct experience and assimilation of what C.G. Jung has called '**the archetypal images....**'.

"The archetypes to be discovered and assimilated are precisely those that have inspired, throughout the annals of human culture, the basic images of ritual, mythology, and vision. These 'Eternal Ones of the Dream' are not to be confused with the personally modified symbolic figures that appear in nightmare and madness to the still tormented individual. Dream is the personalized myth, myth the depersonalized dream; both myth and dream are symbolic in the same general way of the dynamics of the psyche. But in the dream the forms are quirked by the peculiar troubles of the dreamer, whereas in myth the problems and solutions shown are directly valid for all mankind."

"The hero, therefore, is the man or woman who has been able to battle past his personal and local historical limitations to the generally valid, normally human forms. Such a one's visions, ideas, and inspirations come pristine from the primary springs of human life and thought. Hence they are eloquent, not of the present, disintegrating society and psyche, but of the unquenched source through which society is reborn. The hero has died as a modern man; but as eternal man—*perfected, unspecific, universal man—he has been reborn. His second solemn task and deed therefore ... is to return then to us, transfigured, and teach the lesson he has learned of life renewed.*"

(Campbell *The Hero*, pp. 16–20)

More on Campbell is given below in a short section entitled **The Monomyth**. A critical present-day reader who studies Campbell's works will observe one consistent feature of his publications. They are aimed at moderately well-educated adults who may already have some idea as to what archetypes are, and who wish to do two basic things:

a) acquaint themselves with myths of different times and places, probably going beyond the usual fodder of the most popular Classical myths read to children in the home or at elementary school; and/or

b) investigate archetypes which they may then apply to their own lives and how they perceive themselves in their own internal struggles on their own "epic" journeys through life.

Taken in the wide context we considered at the beginning of this chapter, Campbell's works are very useful in letting us see what the myths can mean to us. At worst, however, the application of what we can only call psychological subjectivism can narrow down our understanding of myths by limiting us to internalization at the expense of trying to understand geographical and/or historical context.

B. Otto Rank

A pupil of Freud who later broke with him, wrote his *The Myth of the Birth of the Hero* in his definitely Freudian stage. In his introductory chapter he gives some credence to the dispersionist theory of mythology (the belief in *an original community* from which sprang all the tales which then were spread as a result of migration or borrowing through oral tradition or literary influence), and he lends some support to the then-popular theory of nature myths which saw in the birth myths of heroes a personification of the processes of nature, although in later writings he paid scant attention to this "naturalistic" approach to mythology.

Rank emphasizes the importance of seeking

"the reason for the general unanimity of these myths in the very general traits of the human psyche" and he asserts that "the manifestation of the intimate relationship between dream and myth... entirely justifies the interpretation of myth as a dream of the masses of the people." (pp. 4–9, passim)

Rank suggests that

"the hero should always be interpreted **merely as a collective ego**, which is equipped with all the excellences."

He further notes that the ego of the child behaves like the hero of the myth in that

"the myth throughout reveals an endeavor to get rid of the parents, and that the same wish arises in the fantasies of the individual child at the time when he is trying to establish his personal independence." (pp. 71–72)

Hero myth, like romantic fantasy, begins with noble parents in conformity with the overvaluation of the parents in early childhood. The hostility of the father, and the resulting exposure, accentuate the motive which has caused the ego to indulge in the entire fiction. The fictitious romance, in the fantasy of a family romance, is the excuse for a child's hostility toward his father which in this fiction is projected against the father. The exposure in the myth, therefore, is equivalent to the repudiation or non-recognition in the romantic fantasy. The child simply gets rid of the father in the neurotic romance, while in the myth the father endeavors to lose the child. Rescue and revenge are the natural terminations, as demanded by the essence of the fantasy. The utilization of the same material in the dreams of healthy persons and neurotics indicates that the exposure in the water signifies no more and no less than the **symbolic expression of birth**. The children come out of the water. The basket, box, or receptacle simply means the container, the womb; so that the exposure directly signifies the process of birth, although it is represented by its opposite. (Rank defends this representation of opposites by appealing to dream patterns.) The tendency to represent the parents as the first and most powerful opponents of the hero is related to the family romance which derives from a feeling of being neglected, i.e., the assumed hostility of the parents. In the myth, this hostility goes so far as to refuse to allow the child to be born; moreover, the myth plainly reveals the desire to enforce his materialization, even against his parents' will. The vital peril is the birth process itself, which is concealed in the representation of birth through exposure. The overcoming of all these obstacles also expresses the idea that the future hero has actually overcome the greatest difficulties by virtue of his birth, for he has victoriously thwarted all attempts to prevent it.

The refusal to let the child be born, which belongs especially to the father (or grandfather), is frequently concealed by the contrast motif, the wish for a child (as in Oedipus, Perseus, and others), while the hostile attitude toward the future successor on the throne and in the kingdom is projected to the outside—it is attributed to an oracular verdict.

From another point of view Rank sees the family romance as the confirmation of the parents as the real parents: the exposure myth, translated with the assistance of symbolism, likewise contains nothing but the assurance: "This is my mother, who has borne me at the command of my father." But this assurance can only be expressed as the repudiation of such parentage.

The exposure of the child with the mother (Perseus, Telephus, and others) enables the hero to acquire a more intimate connection with the mother, who is nearer to him on account of the erotic relation.

The person of the grandfather in the Perseus myth illustrates the father-daughter erotic complex: the father refuses to give his daughter to any suitors because he really wishes to possess her himself. When his command to protect his daughter's virginity is disobeyed, he pursues the daughter and her offspring with insatiable hatred. The hero, when getting vengeance, kills his grandfather, killing in him the man who is trying to rob him of the love of his mother, i.e., the father. The birth from a virgin represents the repudiation of the father, and the lowly father's secondary elevation to the rank of a god represents merely the most exalted childish idea of the magnitude, power, and perfection of the father.

Rank also sees in the hero myths (i.e., myths of the birth of a hero) the equivalence in many essential features to the delusional ideas of certain psychotic individuals who suffer from delusions of persecution and grandeur—the so-called paranoiacs.

C. Robert W. Brockway

In *Myth from the Ice Age to Mickey Mouse*, pp. 71–2, Brockway has an interesting perception of the hero and other archetypes as their roles and functions have changed throughout the evolution of Western attitudes, reflected in our preferences for the kinds of narratives and images we pass on to our children. Note that his use of the term *Comedic Mode* has nothing to do with the concept of being funny. It simply refers to a structural build-up to a happy conclusion.

"In the archetypal myth, the hero defeats the dragon, rescues the maiden, and inherits the kingdom. In the Christian version of the myth, Christ confronts Satan, ransoms humanity, and founds the Kingdom of God. This, the comedic mode, supplanted the tragic mode of Greek drama in which the hero falls because of his own error and, by so doing, brings ruin on his society as well as himself. As a literary mode, comedy is not funny but fulfilling. The hero is challenged but wins. In tragedy, which is not just any sad story, the hero achieves much but errs because of a flaw. He falls and in his fall brings down a society. The comedic mode has been superseded in our time by the ironic mode in which the anti-hero is a victim. He is a bungler and we look down on him with pity and contempt. From the demonic perspective, in comedy the dragon loses; in tragedy he is severely challenged but ultimately wins; and in irony he is not even challenged. All three are variants of the archetypal Myth of the Hero and Dragon, but the ironic mode is a very recent development. We do not encounter irony in traditional Western literature or art. Today, we encounter little else. In itself, the predominance of the ironic version of the Hero and Dragon myth is a moral commentary on our age since it is the dragon who is really the hero. Only the dragon acts with courage and determination, but of course, he is bound to lose as well since there are no winners or losers."

We must, in the above passage, be aware of Brockway's ambivalent use of the word *hero*. In the Classical sense, the word simply denotes a man who has experienced the dangers, rewards, and sufferings of life beyond the normal span of human expectation or endurance, usually to become immortalized in one sense or another. In the nineteenth and early twentieth centuries, molded by conventions of presentation in novels, melodramatic plays, and early films, the hero was simply the central character with whom the reader/ audience was intended to identify in a positive way.

The Monomyth

Joseph Campbell in *The Hero with a Thousand Faces* makes use of James Joyce's term *monomyth* for the pattern that seems to be evident in the hero stories. The scheme he works out has profound psychological implications, but considered even superficially it gives formal meaning to the hero adventure. The following simplified summary of Campbell's ideas shows his debt to the psychoanalytical teachings of C.G. Jung. The standard path of the mythological adventure of the hero is a magnification of the formula represented in the rites of passage: separation, initiation, return, which might be named the nuclear unit of the monomyth.

1. The hero ventures forth from the world of common-day into a region of supernatural wonder. Fabulous forces are there encountered and a decisive victory is won. The hero comes back from the mysterious adventure with the power to bestow boons on his fellow men (i.e., he gives laws, restores order).

2. Everywhere, no matter what the sphere of interest, the really creative acts are represented as those deriving from some sort of dying to the world; and what happens in the interval of the hero's nonentity, so that he comes back as one **reborn**, made great and filled with **creative power**, mankind is also unanimous in declaring. We shall have only to follow, therefore, a multitude of heroic figures through the classic stages of the universal adventure in order to see again what has already been revealed. This will help us to understand not only the meaning of those images for contemporary life, but also the singleness of the human spirit in its aspirations, powers, vicissitudes, and wisdom.

The mythological hero, setting forth from his common-day hut or castle, **(1)** is lured, carried away, or else voluntarily proceeds, **(2)** to the threshold of adventure. The hero receives definite signs of his vocation, he has a "call." Often he refuses the call and needs some sort of coercion to get him started. He receives divine aid of some sort. In Greek myths Athene is generally the prime divine aid to the hero. He sometimes has aids such as a sword, helmet, or magic charm. At the threshold of adventure, **(3)** he encounters a shadow presence that guards the passage. The hero may defeat or conciliate this power and go alive into the kingdom of the dark (battle with a human opponent or with a monster; offering; charm), or be slain by the opponent and descend in death (dismemberment, crucifixion). In the epic poems and literary versions of the myths, the approach to the threshold is announced by a storm which symbolizes the cosmic importance of the adventure. **(4)** Beyond the threshold, the hero journeys through a world of unfamiliar yet strangely intimate forces, some of which severely threaten him (tests), some of which give magical aid (helpers). When he arrives at the nadir, **(5)** of the mythological round, he undergoes a supreme ordeal and gains his reward. The supreme ordeal is frequently a death experience of some sort, such as visiting Hades, the abode of the dead. Regressive action such as the sexual union with the goddess-mother of the world leads the hero into the bliss of infancy from which he emerges as one reborn. This is known in comparative religion as the sacred marriage. Sometimes the supreme ordeal consists in bride theft or treasure theft. This stage also marks in some cases the reconciliation with the father-creator. Intrinsically it is an expansion of the consciousness and therewith of being. The expanding of consciousness is symbolized by bringing instinctual powers under rational control and an increase of spiritual knowledge and power. The hero becomes free from the downward pull of the unconscious, and is illuminated by special knowledge and power to complete his task on earth. The final work is that of return, **(6)**. If the powers have blessed the hero, he now sets forth under their protection: if not, he flees and is pursued (transformation flight, obstacle flight).

At the return threshold, **(7)** the transcendental powers must remain behind: the hero re-emerges from the kingdom of strange and unfamiliar forces, **(8)** (return, resurrection). The boon that he brings restores the world, so we are back where we started **(1)**.

(*The Hero with a Thousand Faces,* page 245 ff. modified)

Sources for Greek Hero-myths

A guide for student research projects J.G. Farrow

1. THE ARGONAUTS

An extremely old story, already in circulation by the Homeric period and familiar to the audiences of Homer (e.g., Od. XI.254-9, XII.69-72) and Hesiod (Theog. 956-962). None of the early epics on this theme survive, so for material before around 500 B.C. we must depend on Black-figure and Red-figure vases.

The earliest literary source is Pindar, *Pythian* IV (in Chapter 24 of this textbook). Note that narrative was not the primary purpose of this poem. When reading Pindar, pay special attention to the homeward itinerary which he sketches in the final verses of the poem.

The most detailed sources for the myth may be found in the following ancient texts:

> **Euripides:** *Medea* (tragedy, 431 B.C.) takes place after the Argonauts return to Greece. Link to the *Medea*: http://www.gutenberg.org/files/35451/35451-h/35451-h.htm
>
> **Apollonius of Rhodes:** *Argonautica* (Voyage of Argo): epic poem in four books, first composed between 290 and 260 B.C.. Book IV possibly revised after 218, if Apollonius lived so long! This is the fullest complete story of the expedition, therefore the single most important source. Note structure of the four books. Link to a translation of Apollonius: http://www.theoi.com/Text/ApolloniusRhodius1.html
>
> **Valerius Flaccus:** *Argonautica* (Voyage of Argo): incomplete epic poem in eight books (author died suddenly, c.94 A.D., and had probably intended twelve books). Much material modeled on Apollonius, but amplified for Roman interest (e.g., the Argonauts stop at Troy on the outward journey). Link to a translation of Valerius: http://www.theoi.com/Text/ValeriusFlaccus1.html
>
> See also episodes in **Apollodorus**, *The Library of Mythology*, I.ix; Hyginus *Fabulae* I-III (on the background of Phrixus, Helle, and the Golden Ram); XII-XXVII. The Hyginus material is in chapter 13, below. Ovid also covers the Argonauts in *Metamorphoses* VII: http://www.theoi.com/Text/OvidMetamorphoses7.html

2. PERSEUS

The early epic material is lost, apart from some extremely brief references in Hesiod, *Theog.* 274-286. There are many scenes from the story in Black-figure and Red-figure art. There are somewhat fuller references to the story in Pindar, *Nemean* X and *Pythian* X.

For the best outlines, see Ovid, *Metamorphoses* IV.629–V.250; Diodorus of Sicily IV; Apollodorus II.iv; Hyginus: *Poetica Astronomica* II.10–12, *Fabulae* LXIII–LXIV. Hyginus is in chapter 13, below; Apollodorus is part 2 of chapter 23.

3. HERAKLES

All the earliest epic material is lost apart from scattered references in Hesiod, *Theog.* and Homer, *Odyssey* XI. Again, there are many visual treatments surviving on vases.

Apart from the hero's madness (theme of Euripides' *Herakles in a Rage*), Herakles' death is the most commonly represented theme in drama: see Sophocles, *Women of Trachis* and references in *Philoctetes*; Euripides, *Children of Herakles*. The story of the hero's conception was treated as a situation comedy by the Roman playwright Plautus in his *Amphitruo*. Euripides' *Alcestis* was used for some motifs in the recent Disney film and in some of the *Legendary Journeys* TV material. The Alcestis story is summarized by Hyginus, *Fab.* XLIX, LI. For links to the play *Alcestis,* see:

http://www.gutenberg.org/cache/epub/10523/pg10523-images.html

or

http://classics.mit.edu/Euripides/alcestis.html

For Plautus, see: http://www.gutenberg.org/files/16564/16564-h/16564-h.htm

There are summaries of Herakles' labors in Apollodorus (occupying most of Book II), in Diodorus of Sicily Book IV and in Hyginus, *Fabulae* XXIX–XXXVI. See chapters 13 & 23 below.

4. THEBAN CYCLE

Early epic treatments and native Theban versions of the stories are all lost. Individual episodes are represented now by traditions of varying antiquity and quality. For dramatic treatments, see also **Development of Greek Drama** section in this textbook. Remember that all the surviving plays were written by Athenians, and therefore are usually unsympathetic to Thebans as a group.

a) Europa:

Apollodorus, III.i; Ovid, *Metamorphoses* (end of Bk.II – beginning of III) Hyginus, *Fabula* CLXXVIII.

b) Cadmus in Greece:

Ovid, *Met.* III; Nonnos, *Dionysiaca* V (Chapter 20 below); Apollodorus III. iii–v: Hyginus, *Fabulae* I–VI.

c) Actaeon:

   📖 Check Black-figure and Red-figure vases for versions earlier than Euripides!

   Euripides, *Bacchae* (Scene 2 in Chapter 22 version); Ovid, *Met.* III.138–252

   Nonnos, *Dionysiaca* V (Chapter 20 below); Apollodorus III.iv.4 (w/Frazer's notes!)

   Hyginus, *Fabula* CLXXX–CLXXXI.

d) Semele, Dionysus:

   Euripides, *Bacchae* (whole play: most of it translated in Chapter 22 below); Ovid, *Met.* III.

e) Oedipus Cycle:

   Sophocles, *King Oedipus* (*Oedipus Rex*); *Oedipus at Colonus*;

   Euripides: *Phoenician Women* 1–62; Apollodorus, III.v.6–9; Hyginus *Fabula* LXVII.

f) The Sons of Oedipus:

   Aeschylus: *Seven against Thebes*; Sophocles: *Antigone*;

   Euripides: *Phoenician Women*; Apollodorus III. vi–vii;

   Hyginus LXVIII–LXXII.

   Links for Sophocles (all 7 extant plays):
   http://www.gutenberg.org/files/14484/14484-h/14484-h.htm

IMPORTANT FOR ALL PROJECTS

Apollodorus and **Hyginus** are both mythological collections from the ancient world, compiled probably in the second century A.D.. This means that they are the Roman Empire's equivalent of mythology textbooks.

Apollodorus is in a Greek text of which approximately the last quarter is missing from surviving manuscripts. The English translation with the most informative footnotes is still that of Sir James Frazer (Loeb series). There is also a new paperback translation by Robin Hard (*Apollodorus:The Library of Greek Mythology*, Oxford Univ. Press, World's Classics Series, 1997).

Hyginus is a Latin text from about the 2nd century A.D. (English trans. of selected parts in this textbook), but many of the stories were taken from the plots of Greek tragedies. Papyrus fragments of similar works in Greek have been found.

Diodorus of Sicily's *Universal History* was composed probably between the 40s and 20s B.C.. Diodorus takes some of his accounts of hero-myths from euhemerizing authors such as Dionysius Skytobrachion (Dionysius the Leather-Armed), a prolific author and collector who had flourished in the previous century.

Mythology Essay Projects

How to answer the questions and submit your work:

1. Each question on the sheet is carefully phrased to offer you an opportunity to show what you have understood in this course, both from lectures and from assigned reading. Many of them also offer opportunities for research. Some of them are based on just a limited range of reading (e.g., the *Odyssey*) but expect imaginative, clear and well-reasoned essay writing. In order to offer all of these opportunities in such a wide range of choice, it is especially important that you **read the question and copy out all of its pertinent words as the title of your essay**. I really must see, **before** I even begin to read the actual essay, precisely which question you are answering and whether you understand its component parts (e.g., the difference between the words *and* and *or*). So please don't try to give your essay an imaginative title! If you are an imaginative writer you will probably find a question which gives your imagination plenty of scope **inside** the essay. When a question involves internal choices it is especially important for your title to be clear and to reflect the question exactly.

   Example: If we take Question #1, on the comparison of Creation Myths, your title should read: "Compare the account of creation given by [*your choice*] with [*your other choice*]. Draw attention to parallels and contrasts, both in content and in intention."

2. **All** these questions require that you understand and actually **use** technical terms **correctly** when they have been explained and used in class. Points are deducted for misuse of, and failure to use appropriately, terms adequately covered in class and/or in the texts.

3. All questions deal, directly or indirectly, with the **sources** of particular myths. Make sure you pay due attention to a myth's sources and to the difference between a **primary** and a **secondary** source. If you don't know what the main (fullest) source is, or what the primary source of a myth is, don't be afraid to ask!

4. It is **very important that your work should be handed in at the right time, in the right place, and in the right way**. Essays submitted in any unorthodox way are apt to be misplaced. Even if they aren't misplaced, they are **certain** to be put in a miscellaneous/low-priority pile. My classes are large and

many of the essays are well-written and substantial, so I spend a lot of time reading them and assigning a grade which reflects the quality of your research and discussion. Work submitted late may not reach me in time for full consideration. There is a penalty of 5 points deducted per class-period by which an essay is late. A further 5 points may be deducted if you fail to hand your work to me **personally**. Any attempt to submit your essay in such unorthodox ways as putting it in my mail-box, stuffing it under my office door, or dumping it on my secretary are considered "hit-and-run," which is risky for you (I might need to ask you a question about the absence of an appropriate title, or some other detail which might cost you even more points) as well as professionally insulting to me.

CHAPTER 7

Tricksters, Psychopomps, and Shamans

Student guide by J.G. Farrow

The Trickster is an important mythical archetype in every required sense of the term. **Tricksters are not simply characters who play tricks.** The most important requirement for a mythical Trickster is to be an outcast or outsider: an individual **who does not conform to normal category-divisions** of species (human vs. animal), gender (male vs. female), or some other division normally observed in myths, such as god vs. mortal. The same qualities which make a person a mythical trickster can also indicate shamanism (see below).

In our study of the trickster archetype we need to observe a distinction between **primary tricksters**, characters whose sole or primary purpose in myth is to be a trickster, from **secondary tricksters**, meaning characters whose primary purpose is something else (such as psychopomps, deities linked to the workings of Sympathetic Magic, or destroying deities) but who need trickster qualities in order to fulfill their main functions. This is an entirely experimental mode of classification.

In the case of Prometheus, the primary ancient Greek trickster, we are dealing with an individual who has all the qualifications to be a god (his parents are Titans) but who fails in his attempts to join the power-clique. His adventures thus cast him as the agent of **Hubris** between mortals and gods. In this respect he is often compared with the Norse trickster Loki.

In English folklore the trickster of the rural midlands was Puck, or Robin Goodfellow (see Shakespeare, *A Midsummer Night's Dream*). He was a kind of cross between an anthropomorphic elf-type being and a local nature spirit. His Northern counterpart (Northeast Midlands and Yorkshire) was Robin Hood, probably a name used by more than one real-life bandit in the Middle Ages as a badge of anonymity.

The equivalent in Lancashire and the West Midlands was Ned Ludd (possibly a corruption of the Romano-British estuary-god Nodens, who was known to the ancient Irish as Nuadu and to the Welsh as Llydd). During the Industrial Revolution anti-machinery groups sabotaged factories during the night and called themselves "Luddites."

ANIMAL TRICKSTERS

Most areas of the world have a traditional trickster-character preserved in native folklore. In the Plains of North America it is usually the coyote, the four-legged mammal who shows curiosity towards humans and their campfires. Compare the Navaho myth "Coyote Brings Fire" with Hesiod's Prometheus story (*Theog.* 507–616 in chapter 18, below).

In the Southwestern states many native tribes have stories of **Iktome**, the Spider Trickster. Spiders are arachnids, not really insects. Most, but not all of them, spin webs.[1] Athena, in ancient Greco-Roman belief, is a perfect example of a secondary trickster: her association with the spider is strongly reinforced by Ovid in *Metamorphoses* VI.1-145, while Homer constantly reminds us throughout the Odyssey of Athena's support for Odysseus while the poet constantly uses the motifs of spinning and weaving, not only for the goddess herself but for each of the important ladies in Odysseus' personal life. Athena's birth advertises her ambiguity further: she wears battle-dress from the moment of her birth from the wrong gender of parent!

To the South of Mexico, in El Salvador, Panama, and beyond, the most popular trickster archetype is the snake (a difficult animal to categorize, since it does not move on legs even though it lives on land). The snake also symbolizes **immortality**, since people observe it shedding its skin when it appears to grow old.

In Africa, there are many tricksters depending on the locality. In addition to snakes and spiders, there is also the Hyena and the Monkey. Monkey tricksters are also found in many parts of Asia.

In Alaska, in the Canadian Rockies, and in Siberia the most commonly found trickster is the Raven. As a carrion bird, the raven is often encountered as representing the **psychopomp**, another important archetype who often overlaps with the trickster in role and function. The raven is also well known in Norse belief as Odin's shamanic bird. The Roman historian Tacitus observed that the Germanic tribes had an especially high regard for a god whom he identified as Mercury (*Germania* 9, see chapter 27, below). For more on this, see the next section, on the Psychopomp.

In early Greece the seal was clearly regarded as a trickster: it swims in the sea, it behaves like a fish and lives on sea food, but it has the head like that of a young dog

---

[1] Homeric Hymn XXVIII, *To Athena;* Hesiod, *Theogony* lines 886-900.

and barks like a dog. This perception led to belief in the monster Scylla, since *skylax* is Greek for a puppy, or young dog. For more on seals, see below under **shamanism**.

In Norse, the name of Loki is especially curious. Grimm and others have linked the name with *logi* (fire), concluding that Loki's presence in myths must derive from an early function as a fire-god. Comparison of this function with the role of Prometheus as fire-stealer led Grimm[2] to propose similar origins for both characters. While there is indeed an important parallel, we should also reflect that Grimm died before C.G. Jung was born and so did not live to hear the term *Archetypes of the Collective Unconscious*. If we apply what we know now to the picture, while also using some understanding of Germanic languages, we should remember the Norse word *lax* (cognate with American English *lox*), meaning salmon. When we fish, we select boats, equipment, and everything else on a basic binary polarization: saltwater fish versus freshwater. This polarization is valid for most species of fish but not the salmon, which is born in a river, swims out to sea where it reaches maturity, then returns upstream (with many other highly visible tricks on the way) to spawn and die. It cannot be a coincidence that Loki's most common transformation in Norse myths is into the shape of a salmon.

THE PSYCHOPOMP

This term *psychopomp* (*psyche* = soul/spirit; *pempein* = to send/escort) is normally indicative of the god or spirit who takes care of the souls of people when their bodies die. He is believed to send or escort them to their next destination. In Greek the most obvious psychopomp is Hermes. It is, in fact, probably one of his most fundamental & primary functions (hence his role by extension of messenger to the gods).

Psychopomps are very often also tricksters, a fact which is most clearly shown in the *Homeric Hymn to Hermes*, a poem in which Hermes' first achievement, when he is one day old, is to steal his older brother Apollo's cattle. The reason for the coincidence is obvious: psychopomps need, as part of their job, to be in more than one state of existence at the same time, so they cannot conform to category-divisions. Hermes is also the male god most closely associated in Greek myth with the workings of Sympathetic Magic. An extract from the *Homeric Hymn to Hermes* is provided below, chapter 15. Hermes can therefore be fairly called a secondary trickster. He shares this attribute with Athena, who also relies on her trickster attributes to accomplish her primary goal, that of cleaning out the old so that the newer or the more righteous order may be established. This function is clearly spelled out by Homer throughout the *Odyssey*.

---

[2]*Teutonic Mythology* p. 242 (1966 reprint of translation of Grimm's *Deutsche Mythologie*, 1835)

In Norse myths, the very reason for Oðin's supremacy over the Aesir gods is his combination of qualities as a god of Sympathetic Magic through the Runes (see Crossley Holland's Myth #4, which is based on the ancient Eddic poem *Havamal*, or Sayings of the High One, verses 138-164.) and his presidency over Valhalla as the Norse Psychopomp.

SHAMANISM

The word *shaman* is a very old term, possibly of mid-Asiatic origin. Shaman is normally translated as being roughly equivalent to *Medicine Man*. In fact, a shaman is a kind of human or living psychopomp. In some cultures such a person enters into a trance-state, either by ritual fasting, hallucination, or dancing, in order to communicate with and derive powers from the world of nature (see *Sun-Catcher* in chapter 11 of this textbook). A similar practice also explains the ancient rituals and beliefs associated with the *Pytho*, or Priestess of Apollo, at Delphi in Greece. Apollo and Dionysus were the gods most closely linked with shamanism by the ancient Greeks (see Herodotus, IV.13–16 and the beginning of Euripides' *Bacchae* chapter 22 below). The most obvious human shaman in Greek mythology was the Theban prophet Teiresias (below and in *Odyssey* XI). The various legends which were attached to him concerning changes of species and sex make it very obvious that he can best be summarized as a Shamanic Trickster. It is very noteworthy that he serves as a kind of psychopomp in *Odyssey* XI. Hermes, on the other hand, is not explicitly introduced as a psychopomp in Book XI, where Odysseus reaches the underworld simply by following Circe's directions. He does appear as a psychopomp in Book XXIV, a portion of the *Odyssey* which seems to have been added after the rest was composed.

Proteus was another shaman character mentioned by Homer. He is represented as a kind of human living on the Delta of Lower Egypt but living amongst seals and easily capable of shape-shifting. He is the prophet whom Menelaus encounters in *Odyssey* IV.384-570.

Homer's use of this shamanic consultation was later recycled by the Roman poet Vergil, in *Georgic* IV, lines 387-529. The culture-hero Aristaeus is told by his mother the goddess Cyrene to catch 'blue Proteus' in 'the Carpathian whirlpool,' an exotic place apparently unrelated to Egypt and where Proteus lives with his seals in a cave in the side of a rocky cliff.

Teiresias

Adapted principally from Apollodorus III.6–7

3 SHAMANIC PATTERNS:

A. born male

hunting on Mt. Cyllene or Mt. Kithairon, saw two snakes coupling
struck at with staff or killed female and became woman for seven, eight, or nine
    years
saw same or two other snakes coupling
struck at with staff or killed male and became man
quarrel of Zeus and Hera over pleasure of sex; chose woman
blinded by Hera; given prophecy and long life (seven generations) by Zeus

B. born male

hunting near Mt. Helicon
saw Athene bathing
blinded by Athene
through intercession of mother Khariclo, Athene gives:
knowledge of birds; staff; long life; intelligence after death
died after drinking of spring Telphusa in Theban war of Epigoni

C. born female to 7th year

loved by Apollo and taught music;
rejected Apollo and turned into—
male: judges Zeus and Hera; turned by Hera into—
female: has squint-eyed son through anger of Hera; mocks Hera's statue; turned
    into—
male: ugly, called Pithon (ape); turned by Zeus through pity into—
female: nubile; attacked by Glyphios, beloved of Poseidon, in bath; strangles
    Glyphios; Fates take away power of divination and turn into—
male: Teiresias, without divination; learns divination from Chiron; turned by
    Aphrodite in anger into—
female: old woman (to prevent from enjoying sex); Kalé

circumvents by endowing with beautiful hair and hiding in Crete; beloved by
    Arachnos; turned by Aphrodite into—
mouse (male): sacred to Apollo Smintheos; Arachnos turned into
weasel (female)

FURTHER READING

American Indian Myths and Legends (R. Erdoes and A. Ortiz) especially part 7.

The Trickster (Paul Radin, with additional material by K. Kerényi and C.G. Jung; Schocken Books, 1956–72): this book is in Library Reserve at MCC SC.

Myths of the Dog-Man (David Gordon White; Chicago 1991): a historical and geographical survey of Cynocephali and other mythical creatures, including some little-known medieval materials.

Hopi Coyote Tales (Ekkehart Malotki and Michael Lomatuway'ma, Bison Books/U. of Nebraska Press, 1984) gives the text of traditional Hopi myths with English translations on the facing pages.

Coyote Stories by Mourning Dove (Bison Books/U. of Nebraska Press, 1990) was originally written in 1933, mainly collected from Colville-Okanogan people in Washington State.

Raven Tales: Traditional Stories of Native Peoples (ed. Peter Goodchild; Chicago 1991) is a survey of North American (especially Tlingit) raven-trickster tales. Note fire theft story, p. 17.

American Indian Trickster Tales (selected and edited by Richard Erdoes and Alfonso Ortiz, Penguin Books, 1998) is a specialized sequel to the same editors' **American Indian Myths and Legends** but is much shorter as a result of one editor's untimely death.

Trickster Makes this World (Lewis Hyde, North Point Press New York, 1998, pb. 1999) is a comparative survey of trickster-myths worldwide, concentrating especially on the trickster's role in creation and in the arts.

Shamanism: Archaic Techniques of Ecstasy (Mircea Eliade; Princeton, 1972) especially pp. 392–7, with comments on Aristeas.

The Spirit of Shamanism (Roger N. Walsh, Tarcher Putnam, 1990) is a recent and popularized update of Eliade 1972.

Aristeas of Proconessus (J.D.P. Bolton; Oxford 1964) is an attempted reconstruction of all the available evidence for the life, deeds, and poetry of an ancient Greek shamanistic poet who may have visited Siberia.

The Medieval Outlaw (Maurice Keene) is a discussion of the historical aspects of the English trickster-bandit. ˙

CHAPTER 8

Myth and Language

A student background guide by J.G. Farrow

A. THE INDO-EUROPEAN LANGUAGES: GRIMM TO THE RESCUE!

Shortly before the birth of the brothers Grimm, European scholars became aware of a surprising fact about similarities and differences between groups of the world's languages. It had always been known, for example, that languages like Italian, French, Spanish, and Portuguese (those we call the Romance languages) are similar to each other because they are all based on Latin. They began their existence as different provincial dialects of Latin before, during, and immediately after the Roman Empire (roughly between 100 B.C. and 500 A.D.).

It was equally well known that another group, the Germanic languages (including Norse, Dutch, and Old English[1]), were also interrelated. Until the late 18th century scholars still debated whether two major groups (Romance and Germanic) could be traced back to earlier generations of languages and a link established between the two, or whether borrowing had occurred after the languages had formed independently but later established inter-communication. Likewise the Slavic languages (Russian, Polish, Czech, Slovak, Croatian, etc.) were obviously related to each other, but were they also linked to the other European groups? Or were they, as some argued at the time, simply from a "barbarian" group brought into Europe after the collapse of the Roman Empire? Likewise how many similarities between Greek and Latin words or grammatical rules could be explained simply by direct borrowing versus a common ancestry shared by these major languages?

Another puzzle was the Celtic group (Welsh, Irish, Gaelic, Breton, etc.). Some words resembled Latin or Greek equivalents slightly: was this a sign of kinship or simply of borrowing during the days from Greek colonization down to the Roman Empire?

---

[1]There is a separate section on the development of English later in this chapter.

The puzzle took on a new dimension during the 18th century when European traders and British administrators in India became aware of Sanskrit, a very ancient language which is still used in a written form for many of the oldest scriptural texts of the Hindu religion. While Sanskrit is considered a "dead" language for practical and conversational purposes (like Latin or Homeric Greek), it has many descendants in modern languages of India. Some of the grammatical rules and forms of Sanskrit resemble those of Homeric Greek (but not Modern Greek). Many individual words in Sanskrit resemble their equivalents in Latin, Greek, Slavic, Germanic, or even Celtic.

It became obvious that long ago (perhaps as much as 6,000 years ago) a parent language existed from which the above major groups are each descended. This parent language is the one we now call Indo-European. The actual Indo-European language, as such, has probably not existed in a pure form since the Bronze Age, but the presence of its descendants proves that it was once an actual language spoken by actual people. Who were they? Where did they live? What did they call themselves? We can still not answer any of these questions with any certainty, though scholars have been making well-supported suggestions for the last two centuries.

The next question is, how can we account for differences which, in some Indo-European language patterns, seem to contradict the similarities? If the differences are random, they probably reflect independent influences on each language. If the differences themselves follow a consistent pattern, then reasons probably exist as to why letter- sounds have evolved from a common ancestor but in different ways. This was the problem which Jacob Grimm set himself to solve in the early 1800s. His work led to what we still call **Grimm's Law**, a system of rules by which we can predict the phonic shifts which occur when languages break down into dialects and those former dialects then become languages in their own right.

Thanks to Grimm and other scholars of his generation, there is now a simple test to tell whether any new language we encounter is Indo-European or not: count from one to ten in the language. The word for *one* in the √IE (Indo-European) languages is always based on a nasalized vowel (with or without an inflexion indicating gender or grammatical function): *one, un (une), uno (una), ein (eine, einer)*, etc. The Slavic form *jedan* (pronounced "yedan") is slightly more complex. The word for *two* always seems to begin with a "d" (*deux, dos, duo, due, dyo*, etc.) or a "t" (*two*, and the German form *zwei*, which is pronounced "tsvey"). The list goes on. It makes a useful class exercise when people from different language backgrounds pool their knowledge to see which languages are from Indo-European groups and which are from entirely different families. A question arises when we reach four: *vier* to *four* is easy to understand, but how is this related to *quattuor* (Latin, hence *quatre, quattro, cuatro*, etc.) or to ancient Greek *tettares* (modern *tessara*), or to Welsh *pedwar*? Grimm's Law provides the clues linking **p** to **c**, to **t**, or to **f**, just as we can hear the mutation between **t** and **d** (or between either of them and the glottal stop sound) when an American speaker of English says "better," compared with either the standard British pronunciation or (more extreme) the Cockney or London street pronunciation.

B. MÜLLER'S JOKE

Max Müller made a famous joke, "Myth is a disease of language." In essence he was starting from Grimm's observation of Cinderella's glass slipper. There is no reference to a glass slipper, in spite of three occasions when an opportunity might have been offered, in Grimm's 1857 version of the story, given below in chapter 10. It is also absent from earlier Italian versions, usually entitled *La Cenerentola*. The motif first appeared in Perrault's collection (1697) where it is described as "une pantoufle de verre" (a slipper of glass). The French word *verre* sounds exactly like *vaire*, the cognate of English *fur*, a word which does not exist in English before the Norman period (1066-c.1200, when members of the ruling class spoke French). By Perrault's time, when the French had already been colonizing the Great Lakes area of North America

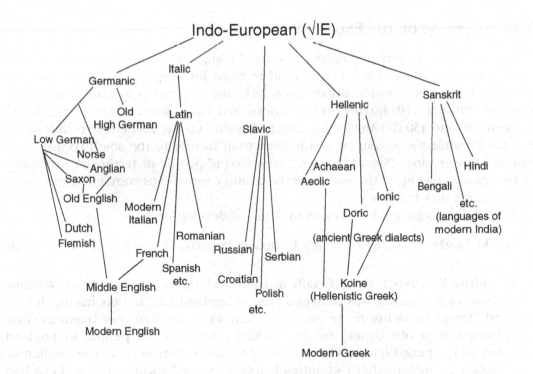

and had newer, more specialized terms for different types of more fashionable animal pelts, the word *vaire* indicated cheaper varieties, making *verre* (glass) more exotic in spite of the obvious safety risk implied. Both sound alike in French, and in no other language. Once we have decided which makes a more comfortable and practical dancing-shoe (and safer!) we know exactly in which language tradition the mistake occurred. Grimm used this as an equivalent, for his time, of modern DNA-tagging. Any version of the Cinderella story which has the glass slipper has obviously been "genetically" infected from Perrault, who must have been responsible for the change. In Müller's view of myths, far more stories than just Cinderella have suffered from similar infections, to the point that their original (etiological) purpose has been completely lost. In Müller's approach to the Troy story, for example, there is no need to search for an actual place or time in history for such a war. The whole story is merely an elaborate recollection of stories relating struggles of sky-gods between East and West. Helen's name, for instance (*Helene* in most ancient Greek dialects, or *Helana* in Doric) is merely a variant on *Selene*, the word for *moon*. Initial **s** and the aspirate **h** are often interchangeable (as with *seven* in English, *septem* in Latin, and *hepta* in ancient Greek). The language joke thus becomes an easy shortcut to classify a myth as a nature etiology.

C. DEVELOPMENT OF THE ENGLISH LANGUAGE

There was no such country as England or such a language as "English" before about 450 A.D. at the very earliest. *English* was another word for *Anglian*. The Angles were a Germanic tribe who invaded Britain soon after the occupying Romans moved out, between 390 and 410, leaving mainly Romanized Celts and non-Romanized Celts. Between 420 and 450 the Angles migrated to England via the East coast (mainly north of London) while the Saxons moved in somewhat further to the south (possibly via Kent and Sussex, since "Sussex" means "South Saxon" people or territory.). Eventually the two groups met up in the middle of the country, sometimes combining and sometimes creating new borders.

The English language has three main stages of development:

1. **Old English** (Anglo-Saxon) is a Germanic language. **Example**: the anonymous *Beowulf* poem.

2. **Middle English**: Starts officially in 1066 with the Norman invasion. William, Duke of Normandy, was crowned king of England 12.25.1066, having defeated Harold Godwinson the previous October at the Battle of Hastings (East Sussex, near the county border of Kent). Upper class people in England began to speak French, while the lower classes continued to use Anglian or Saxon. In the Northern counties Norse was used locally where there had

been Viking colonies. Celtic was still used in the West, where it continues today as the official language of Wales. Another Celtic language was Cornish, used in Cornwall until the 18th century. Over the next 500 years after the Norman Conquest the English county dialects gradually began to merge, but regional differences still made "English" hard to define. **Examples**: Geoffrey Chaucer, *Canterbury Tales* (Chaucer was from Kent in the southeastern corner of the country but worked in London for much of his adult life); see also the anonymous epic *Sir Gawain and the Green Knight*, composed in the Northwest Midlands dialect. In late Middle English, plural endings in –s start to appear (not used in Old English), a clear example of French (and to some extent Spanish) influence.

3. **Modern English**: Starts in the early 1500s with the printing industry. **William Caxton** published an English translation of Vergil's *Aeneid* soon after 1500 so that people who could not read Latin might enjoy this major epic poem. He prefaced the translation with a complaint over the difficulty of defining "English." The following extract from this complaint shows the difficulties in an amusing way while enabling us to see what a radical change to our language the printing industry must have made.

EXTRACT FROM CAXTON'S PREFACE TO HIS ENGLISH TRANSLATION OF VERGIL:

And certaynly our langage now vsed varyeth ferre from that whiche was vsed and spoken whan I was borne. For we Englyssche men ben borne vnder the domynacyon of the mone, which is neuer stedfaste but euer wauerynge, wexynge one season and waneth & dyscreseath another season. And that comyn englysshe that is spoken in one shyre² varyeth from a nother.

In so much that in my dayes happened that certayn marchauntes were in a shippe in tamyse³ for to haue sayled ouer the see into zelande,⁴ and for lacke of wynde thei taryed atte forlond,⁵ and wente to lande for to refreshe them. And one of theym named Sheffelde, a mercer,⁶ cam into an hows and axed for mete, and specyally he axyd after eggys.

---

²Shire (from Old English) = county (from French, *comté*)

³The river Thames, which flows eastwards through London and out into the North Sea.

⁴Zeeland = Holland.

⁵Foreland = in Kent.

⁶Mercer = merchant.

And the good wyf answerde that she coude speke no frenshe. And the marchaunt was angry, for he also coude speke no frenshe, but wold haue hadde egges, and she vnderstode hym not. And thenne at last a nother sayd that he wolde haue *eyren*.[7] Then the good wyf sayd that she vunderstod hym wel.

Loo, what sholde a man in thyse days now wryte, *egges* or *eyren*? Certaynly, it is harde to playse eurey man by cause of dyuersite & chaunge of langage. For in these dayes euery man that is in ony reputacyon in his countre wyll vtter his commynycacyon and matters in such maners & terms that fewe men shall vunderstonde theym.

By the early 1600's the compilation of the King James Bible and the publication of collected volumes of Shakespeare's plays created a standard form of accepted English.

D. SPELLING VARIANTS COMMONLY ENCOUNTERED IN MYTHOLOGY

When names from Greek or Roman myths and literature are transliterated into English, certain regular changes occur. The Greek alphabet, for instance, has seven vowels: alpha (short **a**), epsilon (short **e**), eta (long **a** or long **e**, but pronounced in modern Greek like English "ee" and often transcribed as **i**), iota (simple **i**, but see also below), omicron (short **o**), ypsilon (**u**, but also serves as **y**) and omega (long **o**). This means that there is more than one way to transcribe a Greek name or word into English (for example, Athena or Athene; hubris or hybris). The Greek alphabet has no **c** (**g** is the third letter) and uses **k** for the hard sound, **s** for the soft. Latin, on the other hand, has both **c** and **k** but Romans preferred to use **c**, which in ancient times was pronounced in its hard form.

The letter **j** is a relative newcomer to our alphabet. It began its life as an **i** with a tail, to show that it was doing the job of a consonant, more like a **y** sound. This is why its sound has unique values respectively in English, French, and Spanish, while other Germanic languages (and all the Slavic ones which use the Latin alphabet) consistently pronounce it as a **y**.

---

[7] A Germanic word for *eggs*. In modern German the word is **Ei**, plural **Eier**. Thus 'Eyren' is an ungrammatical double-plural form, as is the modern English *children*. In modern German the word for 'the child' is **das Kind**, pl. **die Kinder**. English doesn't need **..en** when it already has the **..er** plural ending. In the old dialect of Lancashire (NW England) the plural of *child* was pronounced "chilther" until the mid-20th century.

To add to the complexity for mythologists, some very influential artwork based on myths has been created in Italy over the centuries. Students often need a guide to reassure them that a certain name is or is not the one they want from a myth.

The following table is designed to help you decide whether a certain name may or may not be the same as the one you were looking for when researching a source taken from another language.

ANCIENT GREEK	LATIN	MODERN ITALIAN	MODERN ENGLISH
i- (+ vowel)	i-	gi-[8]	i- or j-
(= consonantal i)	j- (later sources)		
k-	c-	c-	c-
-a (fem. sg. noun)	-a	-a	-a
or -e			
-os (masc. sg. noun)	-us	-o	-us
-ai (fem. pl.)	-ae	-e	-ae
-oi (masc. pl.)	-i	-i	-i

---

[8]Jupiter's name in Latin (Iuppiter) can be broken down as "Iov-pater." When accusative (object of a verb) it becomes "Iovem." In Modern Italian his name is *Giove*.

PART 2

Short Examples

CHAPTER 9

Little Red Riding Hood
And Her Relatives

1. LITTLE RED RIDING-HOOD, FRENCH VERSION

From *Contes Moralisés* (1697) by Charles Perrault

Once upon a time there was a little village girl, the prettiest that had ever been seen. Her mother was obsessed with her and her grandmother was even more so. This good woman made her a little red hood, which suited her so well that everywhere she went people called her Little Red Riding Hood.

One day her mother, who had just been cooking and had baked some cakes, said to her: "Go and see how your grandmother is, for I have heard that she is ill. Take her a cake and this little pot of butter."

Little Red Riding Hood set off immediately for her grandmother's house: she lived in another village. On her way through a wood she met old Father Wolf. He would have very much liked to eat her, but dared not do so on account of some woodcutters who were in the forest. He asked her where she was going. The poor child, not knowing that it was dangerous to stop and listen to a wolf said: "I am going to see my grandmother, and am taking her a cake and a little pot of butter which my mother has sent to her."

"Does she live far away?" asked the Wolf.

"Oh yes," replied Little Red Riding Hood; "it is over there by the mill which you can see down there, the first house in the village."

"Good!" said the Wolf "I'd like to go and see her too. I will go by this path, and you by that path, and we will see who gets there first."

The Wolf set off running with all his might by the shorter track, and the little girl continued on her way by the longer road. As she went she amused herself by gathering nuts, chasing butterflies, and making bouquets of the wild flowers which she found.

The Wolf did not take long in reaching Grandmother's house. He knocked. "Toc Toc!"

"Who is there?"

"It is your little daughter, Red Riding Hood," said the Wolf disguising his voice, "I've brought you a cake and a little pot of butter that my mother sent."

The good grandmother, who was in bed and had not been very well, called out to him:

"Pull out the peg and the latch will fall."

The Wolf drew out the peg and the door flew open. Then he sprang upon the good lady and ate her up in less than no time, since he had not eaten for three days. After that he shut the door and went to lie down in Grandmother's bed, waiting for Little Red Riding Hood.

A little while afterwards she came and knocked. "Toc Toc!"

"Who is there?"

Now Little Red Riding Hood on hearing the Wolf's gruff voice was a little afraid at first but, believing that her grandmother had a bad cold, replied:

"It's your little girl, Red Riding Hood, bringing you a cake and a little pot of butter that my mother sent."

The Wolf called out to her, softening his voice:

"Pull out the peg and the latch will fall."

Little Red Riding Hood pulled the peg and the door flew open. The Wolf, when he saw her coming in, hid himself in the bed beneath the covers.

"Put the cake and the little pot of butter on the bin," he said. "Come and lie down with me."

Little Red Riding Hood took off her clothes, but when she climbed up on the bed she was surprised to see what her grandmother looked like in her nightgown.

"Grandmother!" she exclaimed, "what big arms you have!"

"All the better to hug you with, my girl!"

"Grandmother, what big legs you have!"

"All the better to run with, my child!"

"Grandmother, what big ears you have!"

"All the better to hear with, my child!"

"Grandmother, what big eyes you have!"

"The better to see you with, my child!"

"Grandmother, what big teeth you have!"

"All the better to eat you with!"

With these words the wicked Wolf jumped upon Little Red Riding Hood and ate her up.

Moral

Little girls, this seems to say,
Never stop upon your way.
Never trust a stranger-friend;
No one knows how it will end.
As you're pretty, so be wise;
Wolves may lurk in every guise.
Handsome they may be, and kind,
Bright, or charming never mind!
Now, as then, 'tis simple truth—
Sweetest tongue has sharpest tooth!

2. LITTLE RED RIDING-HOOD, GERMAN VERSION

from *Kinder-und Hausmärchen* (1812) by Jacob & Wilhelm Grimm

Once upon a time there was a sweet little girl, who had gained the love of everyone, even those who had only seen her once. She had an old grandmother, who could scarcely do enough for her, she loved her so much. Once she sent her a little cloak with a red velvet hood, which suited her so well that she obtained the name of Little Red Riding-Hood.

One day her mother said to her, "Come, Red Riding-hood, I want you to go and see your grandmother, and take her a piece of cake and a bottle of wine; for she is ill and weak, and this will do her good. Hurry up and get ready before the weather gets too hot, and go straight on your road while you are out, and behave prettily and modestly; and do not run, for fear you should fall and break the bottle, and then grandmother would have no wine. And when you pass through the village, do not forget to curtsy and say 'good-morning' to everyone who knows you."

"I will do everything you tell me, mother," said the child, as she wished her good-bye, and started for her long walk.

It was quite half an hour's walk through the wood from the village to the grand-mother's house, and no sooner had Red Riding-hood entered the wood than she met a wolf. Red Riding-hood did not know what a wicked animal he was, and wasn't a bit scared of him.

"Good-day, Red Riding-hood," he said.

"Good-morning, sir," replied the little girl, with a curtsy.

"Where are you going so early, Red Riding-hood?" he asked.

"To my grandmother, sir," she replied. "Mother baked yesterday, and she has sent me with a piece of cake and a bottle of wine to her because she is sick, and it will make her stronger and do her good."

"Where does your grandmother live, Red Riding-hood?"

"About half a mile from here through the woods; her house stands under three large oak-trees, near to the nut hedges; you would easily know it," said Red Riding-hood.

The wolf, when he heard this, thought to himself, "This little delicate thing would be a sweet morsel for me to last, and taste nicer than her old grandmother, but she would not satisfy my hunger; I must make a meal of them both."

Then he walked quietly on by the side of Red Riding-hood till he came to a part of the wood where a number of flowers grew.

"See, Red Riding-hood," he said, "what pretty flowers are growing here; wouldn't you like to rest and gather some? And don't you hear how sweetly the birds are singing? You are walking on as steadily as if you were going to school, and it is much more pleasant here in the wood."

Then Red Riding-hood looked up and saw the dancing sunbeams shining between the trees and lighting up the beautiful flowers that grew all around her, and she thought, "If I were to take my grandmother a fresh bouquet of flowers, it would make her so pleased; it is early yet, and I have plenty of time."

So she went out of her way into the wood to gather flowers. And when she had picked a few, she saw some more beautiful still at a little distance; so she walked on farther and farther, till she was quite deep in the wood.

Meanwhile the wolf went straight on to the grandmother's house, and knocked at the door.

"Who is there?"

"Little Red Riding-hood," replied the wolf, imitating the voice of the child. "Mother has sent me with a piece of cake and a bottle of wine for you. Open the door."

"Lift up the latch and come in," she replied; "I am too weak to get up."

So the wolf lifted the latch, and the door flew open; then he rushed in, sprang upon the poor old grandmother, and ate her up. Then he shut the door, dressed himself in the old woman's nightgown and nightcap, and laid down in the bed to wait for Red Riding-hood.

After Red Riding-hood had gathered as many flowers as she could carry, she found her way back quickly to the right path, and walked on very fast till she came to her grandmother's house, and knocked at the door.

"Who is there?" said the wolf, trying to imitate grandmother.

His voice was so gruff, however, that Little Red Riding-hood would have been frightened, only she thought her grandmother had a cold. So she replied,

"It's Little Red Riding-hood. Mother's sent you a piece of cake and a bottle of wine."

"Lift up the latch and come in," said the wolf.

So Red Riding-hood lifted the latch and went in. When she saw her grandmother, as she thought, lying in bed, she went up to her and drew back the curtains; but she could only see the head, for the wolf had pulled the nightcap as far over his face as he could.

"Good-morning," she said; but there was no answer. Then she got on the bed, and cried out, "Oh, grandmother, what great ears you have got!"

"All the better to hear with, my dear," he said.

"And what great eyes you have got!"

"All the better to see with, my dear."

"And, grandmother, what large hands you have got!"

"All the better to hold you, my dear."

"But, grandmother, what great teeth you have got!" cried Red Riding-hood, who began to be frightened.

"All the better to eat you with!" cried the wolf, jumping from the bed; and, seizing poor Red Riding-hood, he swallowed her up at one mouthful.

Now, as soon as the wolf had satisfied his hunger, he laid himself in the bed, and snored so loudly that he could be heard outside. A hunter, who was out with his gun, was passing by, and thought to himself.

"How the old woman snores; I must go in and see what is the matter."

Then he stepped into the room, and when he came to the bed he saw the wolf lying on it.

"Oh, you old sinner," said the hunter, "Have I found you at last? I have been seeking you a long time, Mr. Wolf."

He was just going to raise his gun when he noticed that old Grandmother was missing. Thinking that the wolf might have swallowed her, he remembered she might yet be saved. So he decided not to shoot, but, taking a pair of scissors, cut open the stomach of the sleeping wolf.

How surprised he was to see the smiling face of Red Riding-hood beaming out at the first snip; and as he cut further, she sprang out, exclaiming: "Oh, I have been so frightened; it was dreadfully dark in the wolf's stomach!"

Then they helped out the old grandmother, who was also unhurt and living, but she could scarcely breathe. Red Riding-hood, however, was sent out to pick up big stones, with which she filled the wolf's stomach. And so, when he woke up, he tried to jump at her again, but the stones were so heavy that he sank back on the bed and died.

And so the three of them celebrated: the hunter had the wolf's skin to take home with him. Grandmother drank the wine and ate the cake which Red Riding-hood had brought; and then the hunter took the little girl safely to her house.

"Ah," she thought, "I will never go out of my way to run in the wood again, when my mother has forbidden me."

⊗   ✂   Ψ   ⤬   ☠   ✂   Ψ

It is also told that once after this, when Little Red Riding-Hood was going again to her old grandmother with some of the nice things her mother had made, another wolf spoke to her, and wanted to entice her out of the way. But Red Riding-hood was on her guard, and went straight forward without stopping till she came to her grandmother's house.

"Oh, grandmother," she said, "I met a wolf, who wished me 'good-day'; but he looked at me with such wicked eyes, that if I had not been in the street I am sure he would have eaten me up."

"Perhaps he will come here," said the grandmother, "so we will lock the door and keep him out."

Sure enough, soon after the wolf came to the door and knocked, crying, "Open the door, grandmother; I am Red Riding-hood, and I have brought you some cake and wine." But all remained silent, and the door was not opened.

Then the sly old thief prowled round the house, and at last sprang on the roof to wait till Red Riding-hood went home in the evening, that he might seize her in the dark and devour her. But the grandmother knew what was in his mind. Now there stood near the house a large stone trough, and she said to the child: "Red Riding-hood, I cooked a large sausage yesterday; you can empty the water in which it was cooked into the stone trough."

Red Riding-hood drew off the water from the copper, and emptied it into the trough until it was quite full, and the smell of the sausage reached the wolf's nose. He sniffed, and sniffed, and looked down, till at last he stretched his neck out to such a distance that he lost his balance, and fell from the roof into the great trough full of water, and was drowned. Red Riding-hood went home that evening in happiness and safety, and no one attempted to hurt her on the road.

3. THE WOLF AND THE SEVEN YOUNG KIDS

from *Kinder-und Hausmärchen* (1812) by Jacob & Wilhelm Grimm

Once upon a time there was an old nanny-goat who had seven young kids. She loved them as much as any mother loves her children. One day she wanted to go into the woods to bring home food. She called all seven round her and said, "Dear children I must go out into the wood. In the meantime behave well, keep the door shut and watch out for the wolf! If he comes in he will eat you up, skin and hair! That wicked villain uses disguise a lot, but you can recognize him by his rough voice and black feet."

The kids said: "Dear mother, we'll take good care, you can go out without worry." The old goat grumbled and went confidently on her way.

She had not been gone long when a knock came at the door and a call: "Get up, dear children, your mother is here and has brought something for each of you!" But the kids heard the rough voice—it must be the wolf!

"We're not coming out!" they called, "You're not our mother! She has a soft, lovely voice, but your voice is rough. You're the wolf!"

So the wolf went off to a distant store and bought a big piece of chalk. He ate it to make his voice soft. He then came back, knocked on the house-door and called: "Get up, dear children, your mother is here and has brought something for each of you!"

But the wolf had set his black foot on the window-sill. The children saw it and called out, "We're not coming out! Our mother has no black foot like you. You're the wolf!"

So the wolf went to the baker and said: "I've bruised my foot. Put some dough over it for me."

When the baker had spread the dough over his foot, he went to the miller and said, "Spread some white flour over my foot." This scared the miller, so he made the foot white.

Now the villain went a third time to the house-door, knocked and said: "Get up, dear children, your dear mommy is home and has brought something from the wood for each of you!"

The kids called out: "Show us first your foot, so we know whether you're our dear mommy."

Then the wolf put his foot on the window-sill. When the kids saw that it was white, they believed that everything he said was true, and opened the door. But who's coming in but the wolf? The kids were terrified and went to hide. One jumped under the table, the second in the bed, the third in the oven, the fourth in the kitchen, the fifth in the closet, the sixth under the wash-bowl[1], the seventh in the case of the grandfather

---

1. Literally "wash-dish," the kind still displayed in old homes alongside a water-jug.

clock. But the wolf caught them and swallowed them, one after the other. Only the youngest, in the clock-case, did he not find.

As the wolf was full he trundled out, lay down outside in the green meadow, and went to sleep under a tree.

Not long afterwards the old nanny-goat came back home from the wood. Oh! What did she see? The house door was wide open! The table, chairs and benches were scattered. The wash-bowl lay in pieces, covers and pillows were pulled from the bed. She looked for her children, but nowhere could she find them. She called each one after the other by name, but none answered. Finally, as she called the youngest, a thin voice answered: "Dear mother, I'm stuck in the clock-case!"

The mother got her young kid out of the place where she was stuck. She told her mother how the wolf had come and eaten up all the others. Can you imagine how the old nanny-goat lamented her poor children?

At last in her grief she went outside and her youngest kid came with her. When she reached the meadow, the wolf was still lying under the tree and snoring so much that the branches were shaking. The old nanny-goat looked at him from all sides and saw that in his full belly something was moving and wriggling.

"Please, God," she thought, "could it be my poor children, that he scoffed down for supper, that are still alive?"

So the kid had to go back to the house and bring scissors, a needle and some thread. Then the old nanny-goat slit open the villain's belly. She had scarcely made the first cut when a little kid put his head out. As she cut further, all six came out one after the other. They were all safe and sound because the wolf in his hurry had swallowed them all whole.

What a joy! Their dear mother hugged them and danced like a tailor at a wedding. But the old lady said: "Go and look for some big stones to fill the evil beast's belly while he's still asleep."

The seven kids, all in a hurry, brought as many stones as they could carry and filled his belly. Then the old lady stitched him up with such speed that the wolf neither noticed anything nor moved once.

When he finally awoke he moved his legs. The stones in his belly made him very thirsty, so he decided to go to a stream and drink. But as he started to walk the stones in his belly rubbed against each other and rattled. So he said:

"What's rumbling and bumbling around in my belly?
I think instead of six kids it must be a mighty stone."

As he came to the stream and was leaning over the water, about to drink, the heavy stones pulled him over and in, so he drowned miserably.

As the seven kids saw this, they came up in a hurry and called out, "The wolf is dead! The wolf is dead!" They squeezed each other's hands and danced with their mother all along the stream.

Name: _____ Date: _____

QUESTIONS

1. Compare the structure of the two versions of Red Riding Hood. Why do they end differently?

2. Which version seems more familiar from your own childhood?

3. Perrault's little verse at the end shows that he did not want his readers to take the wolf character literally as a canine, but was using a moral allegory. How would you modernize Perrault's interpretation of the "wolf" archetype?

4. Grimm, in the early 1800s, believed that the German version of LRRH was older than the French even though Perrault had published his over a century earlier. What methods did Grimm use to try and prove this? Use the notes on Grimm in the **Modern Critics** section (Chapter 3, critic #1).

5. If Grimm was right in considering the German version (which he collected from oral sources) older than the French, then A) how might you explain the reference to the woodcutters early in the French version? B) why would Grimm include a reference to a gun?

6. The episode given by Grimm involving the sausage-water in the trough is clearly an alternate version of the story. What did Grimm hope this would tell his adult readers about the age of the story itself and its early circulation?

7. Given that (a) it was common in ancient Germanic culture to refer to the sun as the head or face in the sky, and that (b) many early Germanic (including Norse) myths represent a monstrous wolf in the sky as pursuer and would-be devourer of the sun, how might Max Müller and his followers have interpreted this story? Use the notes on Müller in the **Modern Critics** section (Chapter 3, critic #2).

8. How can you use Grimm's story of the Wolf and the Seven Little Kids, given here, to reinforce the view that the Little Red Riding Hood story might have originated as a solar myth?

9. In an interpretation based on a solar allegory or on a nature etiology, how might the Hunter in the German version be interpreted? When you have read the Sun Catcher story (later in this course) you should see that the Hunter has an interesting parallel in the Ojibwa culture of Northern Michigan.

CHAPTER 10

Aschenpüttel

from Jacob Grimm's *Kinder- und Hausmärchen,* 1857 edition

A rich man's wife, who fell sick, knew that her end was near. She called her only daughter to her bedside, and said, "Dear child, when I am gone continue good and pious, and God will be beside you and I will look down on you from heaven and be with you."

Soon after this the mother closed her eyes in death, and day after day the maiden went to her mother's grave to weep. But she never forgot her last words, and continued pious and gentle to all around her. Winter came and covered the grave with its dazzling drapery of snow; but when the bright sun of spring again warmed the earth, the husband had taken to himself another wife. This wife had been already married, and she brought with her two daughters who were fair and beautiful in appearance, while at heart they were evil-minded and malicious. It soon became a very sad time for their poor stepsister, of whom they were very envious, and at last persuaded their mother to send her to the kitchen.

"Is the stupid goose to sit in the parlour with us?" they said. "Those who eat ought to work. Send her into the kitchen with the kitchen-maid."

Then they took away all her nice clothes, and gave her an ugly old frock and wooden shoes, which she was obliged to put on.

"Look at our fine princess now! See how she has dressed herself!" they said, laughing, and driving her into the kitchen. And there she was obliged to remain doing hard work from morning till night; and she had to rise early to draw water, to light the fire, to cook, and to wash. Besides all this, her stepsisters invented all sorts of ways to make her more unhappy. They would either treat her with scorn or else push her out of their way so roughly that she sometimes fell among the pea shells and cabbage leaves that lay in the yard.

At night, when she was tired with her work, she had no bed to lie on, and when the weather was cold she would creep into the ashes on the warm hearth, and get so black and smutty that they gave her the name of Aschenpüttel.

It happened one day that the father was going to a fair, and he asked his two step-daughters what he should bring back for them as a present.

"A beautiful dress," said the eldest; "a pearl necklace," said her sister. "And, Aschenpüttel," asked her father, "what will you have?" "Father," she replied, "please bring me the first twig that strikes your hat on your way home."

So the father bought for his stepdaughters a beautiful dress and a pearl necklace, and, as he was returning home, he rode through a shrubbery, where the green bushes clustered thickly around him, and a hazel twig stretching across his path struck his hat. Then he stopped, broke off the twig, and carried it home with him.

As soon as he reached the house he gave his stepdaughters the presents they had wished for, and to Aschenpüttel the hazel twig from the hazel bush. She thanked him for it even more than her sisters had done for their beautiful presents, and went out immediately to her mother's grave, where she planted the hazel twig, and wept over it so much that her tears fell and softened the earth.

The twig grew and became a beautiful tree, and Aschenpüttel went three times every day to pray and weep at the grave; and on each visit a little white bird would perch on the tree, and when she expressed a wish, the bird would throw down whatever she wished for.

After a time the king of the country gave a grand ball, which was to continue for three days. All the beautiful young ladies in the land were invited to this ball, so that the king's son might make choice of a bride from amongst them. The two stepsisters, when they heard that they were invited, knew not how to contain themselves for joy. They called Aschenpüttel in haste, and said, "Come and dress our hair and trim our shoes with gold buckles, for we are going to the ball at the king's palace."

When Aschenpüttel heard this she began to cry, for she was fond of dancing, and she wanted to go with her stepsisters, so she went to her stepmother and begged to be allowed to accompany them.

"You, Aschenpüttel!" cried her stepmother, "so covered with dirt and smut as you are; you go to a ball! Besides, you have no dress nor dancing shoes."

Aschenpüttel, however, continued to beg for permission to go, till her stepmother said at last: "There, go away into the kitchen; I have just thrown a shovelful of linseed into the ashes; if you can pick these seeds all out and bring them to me in two hours you shall go."

Away went the girl through the back door into the garden, and called out:

> "Little tame pigeons, Turtle-doves, too,
> If you don't help me, What shall I do?
> Help me pick up the seeds, all the birds in the sky,
> The good stuff in the pot,
> The cheap stuff in your crops!"

Then came flying in at the kitchen window two pretty white doves, and they were followed by all the birds of the air, twittering in a swarm. Nodding their heads at Aschenpüttel, they began to pick, pick, and very quickly picked every seed from the ashes, till the shovel was full. It was all finished in one hour, and then the birds spread their wings and flew away.

Full of joy, the maiden carried the shovelful of seed to her stepmother, believing that now she was sure to go to the ball.

But her stepmother said: "No, Aschenpüttel, you have no dress, and you have not learnt to dance; you would only be laughed at."

Still she cried and begged so hard to be allowed to go that her stepmother, to keep her quiet, threw two shovelfuls of linseed in the ashes this time, and told her she should go if she picked all these out in two hours.

"She can never do that in the time," thought the cruel woman, as Aschenpüttel ran away to the kitchen; but the girl went again into the garden and called the birds:

> "Little tame pigeons, Turtle-doves, too,
> If you don't help me, What shall I do?
> Help me pick up the seeds, all the birds in the sky,
> The good stuff in the pot,
> The cheap stuff in your crops!"

Then the birds all came as before, and in less than an hour every seed was picked out and laid in the shovels. As soon as they had flown away Aschenpüttel carried the shovelfuls of seed to her stepmother, quite expecting now to go to the ball with her stepsisters. But she said again: "It is of no use to fret, Aschenpüttel; you have no dress, you cannot dance, and were you to go it would be a disgrace to us all."

Then she turned her back on the poor girl and hastened away with her two proud daughters to the ball. There was no one at home now but Aschenpüttel, so she went out to her mother's grave and stood under the hazel-tree and cried:

> "Shake and shiver, little tree,
> With gold and silver cover me."

Then the bird in the tree threw down a beautiful silk dress embroidered with gold and silver, and a new pair of glittering golden slippers. In great haste she dressed herself in these beautiful clothes and went to the ball. When she entered the ballroom, looking so beautiful in her rich dress and slippers, her stepmother and sisters did not know her; indeed, they took her for a foreign princess. The idea that it could be Aschenpüttel never entered their heads; they supposed she was safe at home picking linseed from the ashes.

The king's son took a great deal of notice of this unknown lady, and danced with her several times, till at last he would dance with no other, always saying, "This is my partner." So she danced all the evening till it was time to go home, and the prince said he would accompany her, for he wanted to discover where she lived. But she avoided him, and with one bound sprang into the pigeon-house. The prince was quite astonished, but waited till nearly all the company had left, and then told his father that the strange lady was in the pigeon-house.

"Could it be Aschenpüttel?" thought the stepmother, who would not leave till the last; "I must find out." So she advised the prince to send for workmen to pull down the pigeon-house. This was soon done, but they found no one there. When the stepmother and her daughters reached home, they found Aschenpüttel in her smutty dress, lying in the ashes, and a dingy little lamp burning on the chimney-piece. The truth was, Aschenpüttel had slipped out from the back of the pigeon-house even more quickly than she had jumped in, and had run to the hazel tree. Here she hastened to take off her beautiful clothes, and lay them on the grave while she put on her kitchen clothes, and the bird came down and carried the ball-dress away, while Aschenpüttel went home to lie in the ashes.

A short time after this the king gave another ball, to which her parents and step-sisters were invited. As soon as they were gone, Aschenpüttel went to the hazel-tree and said—

> "Shake and shiver, little tree,
> With gold and silver cover me."

Then the bird threw down a far more elegant dress than the first, and when she entered the ballroom in her rich apparel, everyone was astonished at her great beauty. The king's son, who refused to dance till she came, took her hand and led her to her seat, and during the whole evening he would dance with no one else, always saying, "This is my partner."

Again, when it was time to go, the prince wanted to accompany her and find out her home, but she managed to avoid him and rushed out into the garden behind the palace, in which grew a beautiful tree loaded with pears. She climbed like a squirrel between the branches, and the prince could not find her anywhere.

When his father came home they even ordered the tree to be cut down, but no one could be found among the branches. The stepmother still had a fear that it might be Aschenpüttel, but when they returned home, there she was in her kitchen dress lying among the ashes as usual. When they were looking for her, she had sprung down at the other side of the tree, and the bird in the hazel tree had brought her kitchen clothes and taken away the ball-dress.

A third fête took place, to which the stepmother and her daughters were invited, and Aschenpüttel again went to her mother's grave and said to the tree—

> "Shake and shiver, little tree,
> With gold and silver cover me."

Then the bird threw down a most magnificent dress, more glittering and elegant than ever, and the brightest pair of gilded slippers.

When she appeared at the fête in the dress, everyone was astonished at her beauty. The prince danced only with her, and to every other proposal replied, "This is my dance-partner" When the time came to leave, Aschenpüttel wanted to go, and the prince wished to accompany her, but she darted away from him and vanished so quickly that he could not follow her.

Now, the king's son had had recourse to stratagem in the hope of discovering the home of the lovely princess. He had ordered the steps of the castle to be strewed with pitch, so that as Aschenpüttel hurried away her left slipper stuck to the steps, and she was obliged to leave it behind. The prince himself picked it up; it was very small and elegant, and covered with gold.

The next morning he sent for one of his servants and said to him, "None other shall be my bride but the lady to whom that slipper belongs, and whose foot it shall fit."

When the stepsisters heard of this proclamation from the prince they were delighted, for they both had small feet. The messenger went with the slipper from house to house, and the young ladies who had been present at the ball tried to put it on, but it would fit none of them, and at last he came to the two sisters. The eldest tried it on first in another room, and her mother stood by. She could have worn it if her great toe had not been so large, so her mother offered her a knife, and told her to cut it off. "When you are a queen," she said, "you will not want to use your feet much."

The maiden cut the toe off and forced on the slipper in spite of the pain, and the messenger led her to the prince. But on their road they had to pass the grave of Aschenpüttel's mother, and on the hazel-tree sat two doves, who cried—

"That is not the right bride,
The slipper is much too small,
Blood is flowing inside,
The shoe does not fit her at all."

Then the messenger examined the slipper and found it full of blood. So he led her back and told the next sister to try. She also went into another room with her mother, and found that she could not get the slipper over her heel. "Cut a piece off," said her mother, offering her a knife; "when you are queen you will not have to use your feet much."

The maiden cut a piece off her heel, and fitted on the slipper in spite of the pain, and then went to the prince. They also had to pass the grave of Aschenpüttel's mother, in which the two doves still sat and cried:

"Go back, go back,
There is blood in the shoe,
The shoe is too small,
That bride will not do."

So the messenger examined the shoe, and found the white stocking quite red with blood. He took the false bride back to the house, and this time the king's son went with him.

"Hast thou not another daughter?" asked the prince of Aschenpüttel's father. "None," he said, "excepting the child of my first wife, a little Aschenpüttel; she could not possibly be your bride." "Send for her," said the prince.

But the stepmother answered, "Oh no! I dare not let you see her, she is much too dirty." But the prince insisted that Aschenpüttel should be sent for, so at last they called her in.

After washing her hands and face, she made her appearance, and bowed to the prince, who offered her the golden shoe. She seated herself on a footstool, took off the heavy wooden shoe from the left foot, and slipped on the golden slipper, which fitted her exactly. Then, as she lifted up her head and looked at the king, he recognized the beautiful maiden who had danced with him at the ball, and exclaimed, "That is the right bride!"

The stepmother and her two daughters were in a dreadful rage when they heard this, and turned white with anger. But the prince disregarded their anger, and taking Aschenpüttel on his horse, rode away with her. As they passed the hazel-tree on the grass, the two white doves cried:

> "Fair maid and true,
> No blood in her shoe;
> She is the bride,
> With the prince by her side."

As they rode by, the doves came and perched on Aschenpüttel's shoulders, one on the right, and the other on the left.

When the marriage-day came, the two stepsisters, wishing to share Aschenpüttel fortune, contrived to be present. As the bridal party walked to church, they placed themselves one on the right, and the other on the left of the bride. On the way, the doves picked out one eye from each of them. When returning, they changed places, and the doves picked out the other eye of each, so they were for their wickedness and falsehood both punished with blindness during the rest of their lives.

Name: _____ Date: _____

QUESTIONS

1. Is this the version with which you were familiar as a child? Can you name the source from which you knew the story? List below the main differences you observed and remembered between the two.

2. Read a good translation of the earlier French version of the story, written by Charles Perrault in 1697. There is a good English translation available online at D.L. Ashliman's folktexts, a library of folk tales, folklore, fairy tales, and mythology. http://www.pitt.edu/~dash/type0510a.html Is this French version any closer to your familiar story, or more radically different from it? Can you account for any of the similarities or differences?

3. Can you find any details or cultural references in the German version to explain:

   a) what kind of neighborhood or type of home the girl's family might occupy, or

   b) where the girl's mother might have been buried? Why are these details important to the later development of the story?

4. a) What was the most obvious structural difference you noticed between the central development part of this Grimm version of the traditional story (when preparations are being made for the ball) and other versions you have encountered?

   b) In chapter 5 of this book (Myth and Structure) there are some useful hints as to why the Grimm brothers preferred this version, assuming that they actually heard the story told "live" in this way. Why would they have chosen such a structural sequence over simpler versions which are normally regarded as more traditional?

CHAPTER 11

The Sun-Catcher
or Boy Who Set a Snare for the Sun

A Myth of the Origin of the Dormouse (from the Odjibwa)

At the time when the animals reigned in the earth, they had killed all but a girl, and her little brother, and these two were living in fear and seclusion. The boy was a perfect pygmy, and never grew beyond the stature of a small infant, but the girl increased with her years, so that the labor of providing food and lodging devolved wholly on her. She went out daily to get wood for their lodge-fire, and took her little brother along that no accident might happen to him; for he was too little to leave alone. A big bird might have flown away with him. She made him a bow and arrows, and said to him one day, "I will leave you behind where I have been chopping—you must hide yourself, and you will soon see the *Gitshee-gitshee-gaun-ia-see-ug*, or snow birds, come and pick the worms out of the wood, where I have been chopping" (for it was winter). "Shoot one of them and bring it home."

He obeyed her, and tried his best to kill one, but came home unsuccessful. She told him he must not despair, but try again the next day. She accordingly left him at the place she got wood, and returned. Towards nightfall, she heard his little footsteps on the snow, and he came in exultantly, and threw down one of the birds which he had killed.

"My sister," said he, "I wish you to skin it and stretch the skin, and when I have killed more, I will have a coat made out of them."

"But what shall we do with the body?" said she, for as yet men had not begun to eat animal food, but lived on vegetables alone.

"Cut it in two," he answered, "and season our pottage with one half of it at a time."

She did so. The boy, who was of a very small stature, continued his efforts, and succeeded in killing ten birds, out of the skins of which his sister made him a little coat.

"Sister," said he one day, "are we all alone in the world? Is there nobody else living?" She told him that those they feared and who had destroyed their relatives lived in a certain quarter, and that he must by no means go in that direction. This only served to inflame his curiosity and raise his ambition, and he soon after took his bow and arrows and went in that direction. After walking a long time and meeting nothing, he became tired, and lay down on a knoll, where the sun had melted the snow. He fell fast asleep; and while sleeping, the sun beat so hot upon him, that it singed and drew up his bird-skin coat, so that when he awoke and stretched himself, he felt bound in it, as it were. He looked down and saw the damage done to his coat. He flew into a passion, and upbraided the sun, and vowed vengeance against it. "Do not think you are too high," said he, "I shall revenge myself."

On coming home, he related his disaster to his sister, and lamented bitterly the spoiling of his coat. He would not eat. He lay down as one that fasts, and did not stir, or move his position for ten days, though she tried all she could to arouse him. At the end of ten days, he turned over, and then lay ten days on the other side. When he got up, he told his sister to make him a snare, for he meant to catch the sun. She said she had nothing; but finally recollected a little piece of dried deer's sinew, that her father had left, which she soon made into a string suitable for a noose. But the moment she showed it to him, he told her it would not do, and bid her get something else. She said she had nothing—nothing at all. At last she thought of her hair, and pulling some of it out of her head, made a string. But he instantly said it would not answer, and bid her, pettishly, and with authority, make him a noose. She told him there was nothing to make it of, and went out of the lodge. She said to herself, when she had got without the lodge, and while she was all alone, "*neow obewy indapin*."[1]

This she did, and twisting them into a tiny cord, she handed it to her brother. The moment he saw this curious braid, he was delighted. "This will do," he said, and immediately put it to his mouth and began pulling it through his lips; and as fast as he drew it changed it into a red metal cord, which he wound around his body and shoulders, till he had a large quantity. He then prepared himself, and set out a little after midnight, that he might catch the sun before it rose. He fixed his snare on a spot just where the sun would strike the land, as it rose above the earth's disk; and sure enough, he caught the sun, so that it was held fast in the cord, and did not rise.

The animals who ruled the earth were immediately put into a great commotion. They had no light. They called a council to debate upon the matter, and to appoint someone to go and cut the cord—for this was a very hazardous enterprise, as the rays

---

[1] "From my body, I shall take something." This third material is probably her umbilical cord, which according to a very ancient custom would have been preserved by her parents and passed on to her in a personal "medicine-pouch" as soon as she was old enough to take care of the contents. The pouch would be a very private possession, not to be opened in front of others. Umbilical cord is known to many tribes in the Great Lakes area as "Cord of Life."

of the sun would burn whoever came so near to them. At last the dormouse undertook it—for at this time the dormouse was the largest animal in the world. When it stood up it looked like a mountain. When it got to the place where the sun was snared, its back began to smoke and burn with the intensity of the heat, and the top of its carcass was reduced to enormous heaps of ashes. It succeeded, however, in cutting the cord with its teeth, and freeing the sun, but it was reduced to a very small size, and has remained so ever since. Men call it the *Kug-e-been-gwa-kwa*—the blind woman.

From *The Hiawatha Legends*, Henry R. Schoolcraft

Name: _____ Date: _____

QUESTIONS

1. At the beginning the boy and girl are "living in perfect seclusion." What does this mean? If it is not (and there is no reason to believe that it is) a myth about the repopulation of the world, it must mean that only their immediate area is deserted. Where might this be, given the girl's warning and what later happens to the boy? Schoolcraft clearly heard this story from Native Americans in the Upper Peninsula of Michigan. Use a map of Upper Michigan to consider this question.

2. Find two **etiologies** in this myth.

3. The references to the bird-skin coat and to the boy's ritual-like fasting are probably motifs associated with shamanism (see Chapter 7, above, **Tricksters, Psychopomps, and Shamans**). What might the original audience have understood to be happening to the "boy"?

4. The color red (that of blood) symbolizes life in many cultures. How is this symbolism used in this story?

5. Whom would you consider to be the main character of the story, given that the girl disappears from the narrative immediately after giving her brother the "curious braid" and that he also disappears as soon as he has trapped the sun, while the "Dormouse" only appears at the end?

6. If the "boy" is symbolic of an event in nature, what might this event be? Can you name a specific date on which he is meant to accomplish his trapping of the sun? If you can, then calculate the direction from which the sun would seem to rise on that date. This will help you answer question 1, above.

7. The actual *dormouse* is a European mammal which hibernates. It derives its name from the Latin *dormire* = to sleep. If Schoolcraft is translating an unfamiliar Ojibwa word, what are the necessary characteristics of any animal which might fit the narrative?

8. Can you now name a specific date on which this animal is understood to set the sun free? Do we still celebrate this date in modern American popular culture?

9. What might Max Müller (**Chapter 3 #2**) have said about this myth? Reread the questions on Little Red Riding-hood and consider the function of the Hunter in the German version of the story. Who is his parallel here?

CHAPTER 12

Swing on the Pictured Rocks of Lake Superior

A Tradition of the Odjibwa

An old woman lived with her daughter-in-law, and son, and a little orphan boy, whom she was bringing up. When her son came home from hunting, he would usually bring his wife the moose's lip, the kidney of the bear, or some other choice bits of different animals. These she would cook crisp, so as to make a sound with her teeth in eating them. This kind attention of the hunter to his wife at last excited the envy of the old woman. She wished to have the same luxuries, and in order to get them she finally resolved to get rid of her son's wife.

One day, she asked her to leave her infant son to the care of the orphan boy, and come out and swing with her. She took her to the shore of a lake, where there was a high range of rocks overhanging the water. Upon the top of this rock, she erected a swing. She then undressed, and fastened a piece of leather around her body, and commenced swinging, going over the precipice at every swing. She continued it but a short time, when she told her daughter-in-law to do the same. The daughter-in-law obeyed. She undressed, and tying the leather string as she was directed, began swinging. When the swing had got in full motion and well a-going, so that it went clear beyond the precipice at every sweep, the old woman slyly cut the cords and let her daughter-in-law drop into the lake. She then put on her daughter-in-law's clothing, and so disguised went home in the dusk of the evening and kept up a pretence of her appearance and duties. She found the child crying, and gave it the breast, but it would not draw. The orphan boy asked her where its mother was.

She answered, "She is still swinging."

He said, "I shall go and look for her."

"No!" said she, "you must not—what should you go for?"

When the husband came in, in the evening, he gave the coveted morsel to his supposed wife. He missed his mother, but said nothing. She eagerly ate the dainty, and tried to keep the child still. The husband looked rather astonished to see his wife carefully keeping her face away, and asked her why the child cried so much. She said, she did not know—that it would not feed.

In the meantime, the orphan boy went to the lake shores, and found no one. He mentioned his suspicions, and while the old woman was out getting wood, he told him all he had heard or seen. The man then painted his face black, and thrust his spear downwards into the ground, and requested the Great Spirit to send lightning, thunder, and rain, in the hope that the body of his wife might arise from the water. He then began to fast, and told the boy to take the child and play on the lake shore.

We must now go back to the swing. After the wife had plunged into the lake, she found herself taken hold of by a water-tiger, whose tail twisted itself round her body, and drew her to the bottom. There she found a fine lodge, and all things ready for her reception, and she became the wife of the water-tiger. Whilst the children were playing along the shore, and the boy was casting pebbles into the lake, he saw a gull coming from its centre, and flying towards the shore, and when on shore, the bird immediately assumed the human shape. When he looked again, he recognized the lost mother. She had a leather belt around her loins, and another belt of white metal, which was, in reality, the tail of the water-tiger, her husband. She suckled the babe, and said to the boy—"Come here with him, whenever he cries, and I will nurse him."

The boy carried the child home, and told these things to the father. When the child again cried, the father went also with the boy to the lake shore, and hid himself in a clump of trees. Soon the appearance of a gull was seen, with a long shining belt, or chain, and as soon as it came to the shore, it assumed the mother's shape, and she began to suckle the child. The husband had brought along his spear, and seeing the shining chain, he boldly struck it and broke the links apart. He then took his wife and child home, with the orphan boy. When they entered the lodge, the old woman looked up, but it was a look of despair; she instantly dropped her head.

A rustling was heard in the lodge, and the next moment she leaped up and flew out of the lodge, and was never heard of more.

From *The Hiawatha Legends*, Henry R. Schoolcraft

Tiger Muskellunge, a cross between the Muskellunge (Muskie) and the Northern Pike

QUESTIONS

1. Why does Schoolcraft specifically mention the Pictured Rocks of Lake Superior in the title but not in the body of the story?

   a. Find the area of the Pictured Rocks on a map of Upper Michigan.

   b. In what ways does the landscape suit the story's requirements?

2. Why does the man blacken his face and thrust his spear downwards into the ground?

   a. What kind of ritual is he performing?

   b. What does he hope to achieve?

3. The "belt of white metal" is not merely representative of the water-tiger's tail (not a particularly characteristic feature of this fish: check the picture). What else does it symbolize in holding the baby's mother to the lake? Schoolcraft is clearly trying to rationalize an indigenous motif for his English-speaking readers.

4. What is the woman's husband metaphorically doing when he cuts this "chain"?

5. What can you infer from the description of this chain as white, versus the red "cord" in the previous story?

6. What happens to the old woman? (**Clue**: some of the words used are reminiscent of phrases used by the Roman poet Ovid in some passages of his *Metamorphoses*.)

Hyginus: *Fabulae*

With notes by J.G. Farrow

These stories were compiled in Latin at some point between the second and fourth centuries A.D. The compiler of the text called himself "Hyginus." The first printed edition of the Latin text (Basle 1535) has the author's name in the heading, "*Caius Julius Hyginus, Augusti libertus,*" but the author could not have been the same Caius Julius Hyginus who was Augustus' (Emperor 28 B.C.–A.D. 14) freedman (ex-slave). A writer of Augustus' time and in the Imperial Court would have presented the myths in a more florid literary way. These myths are usually rationalized and are almost always presented as if the compiler did not take them literally. The plots are taken in many cases from Athenian tragedy (e.g., IV states in its title that the direct source is Euripides) but the events are stripped down to the bare essentials.

PREFACE

1. From Darkness was born Chaos. From Chaos and Darkness were born Night, Day, Erebus and Aether. From Night[1] and Erebus were born Fate, Old Age, Death, Letum, Contention,[2] Sleep, Dreams, [Love] that is the one who frees people from care, Epiphron, Hedymeles, Porphyrion, Epaphus, Discord, Misery, Petulance, Nemesis, Euphrosyne, Friendship, Pity, and Styx. There were also the Three Parcae (Fates)—that is, Clotho, Lachesis and Atropos and the Three Hesperides: Aegle, Hesperia, and Aerica.

---

[1] Compare the list of Night's children in Hesiod, *Theogony* 211ff.

[2] Readings of this name are very confused: P.K. Marshall's Teubner Latin text (Stuttgart & Leipzig 1993) reads *Continentia*, while manuscripts vary from *Incontinentia* (incontinence) to *Conscientia* (conscience). The name *Amor* (= Love) was added later in the line by H.J. Rose, although Dreams could equally be called *Lysimeles* (Gk., = "Freer(s) from care").

2. From Aether and Day were born Terra (Earth), Caelum (Sky), and Mare (Sea).

3. From Aether and Terra were born Pain, Trickery, Anger, Grief, Lies, Oath, Vengeance, Intemperance, Argument, Oblivion, Discord, Fear, Arrogance, Incest, Fight, Oceanus, Themis, Tartarus, and Pontus. There were also born the Titans: Briareus, Gyges, Steropes, Atlas, Hyperion and Polus,[3] Saturn, Ops, Moneta,[4] and Dione. There were also the Three Furies—that is, Alecto, Megaera and Tisiphone.

4. From Terra and Tartarus were born the Giants: Enceladus, Coeus[5] ... Astraeus, Pelorus, Pallas, Emphytus, Rhoecus ... Agrius ... Ephialtes, Eurytus .... Otus, Typhon, Polybotes, Menephiarus, Abseus, Colophomus, and Iapetus.

5. From Pontus and Mare were born the different kinds of fish.

6. From Oceanus and Tethys were born the Oceanitides—that is, Hestyaea, Melite, Ianthe, Admete[6] .... Eurynome .... Metis, Menippe, and Argia. From the same seed were born the Rivers—that is, Strymon,[7] Nile, Euphrates, Tanais,[8] Indus, Cephisus, Ismenus, Axenus, Achelous, Simois,[9] Inachus, Alpheus, Thermodon, Scamander, Tigris, Maeandrus, and Orontes.

---

[3]Probably the Pole Star. Saturn is normally equated with Cronus and Ops with Rhea.

[4]Since we later learn (#27) that Moneta becomes mother of the Muses, she must be Hyginus' equivalent of Mnemosyne (= Memory).

[5]Coeus is a Titan in Hesiod, *Theog*.130f. The next name on the list is corrupt and indecipherable in the manuscripts.

[6]Several of the names from this point are so varied in spelling and so obscure that they are impossible to reconstruct. I have omitted several of them.

[7]The Strymon flows into the Aegean Sea from Thrace (modern Bulgaria). It is most famous in myth from its association with the death of Orpheus, torn to pieces by Maenads (Bacchae) on its banks. His head floated down the river and was believed to have been washed up on a small island in the Northern Aegean. The myth is probably etiological for a local cult on the island centered around a preserved skull which was believed to give prophecies. Such head-cults were rare in Greek culture but much more common amongst Germanic and Celtic tribes (see Herodotus' comments, IV.26, about similar cults amongst the Issedones, whom he counted as a Scythian tribe), so the myth explains the importation of this particular head-cult into Greek territory.

[8]Tanais is the old name for the river Don, which flows through Russia. Sometimes it is also confused with the Danube.

[9]The Simois and Scamander rivers were described by Homer as meeting together at a confluence near Troy.

7. From Pontus and Terra were born Thaumas, Ceto, Nereus, and Phorcus.

8. From Nereus and Doris were born the fifty Nereids: Glauce, Thalia, Cymodoce.....
   Galatea, Nemertes,[10] Apseudes.... Arethusa, Clymene, Creneis, Eurydice, and
   Leucothoe.

9. From Phorcus and Ceto were born the Phorcides:[11] Pemphredo, Enyo, and
   Persis (some people put Dino in place of the last). From Gorgon[12] and Ceto
   were born Sthenno, Euryale, and Medusa.

10. From Polus and Phoebe were born Latona,[13] Asteria, Aphirape, Perses, and
    Pallas.

11. From Iapetus and Clymene were born Atlas, Epimetheus, and Prometheus.

12. From Hyperion and Aethra were born Sol (Sun), Luna (Moon), and Aurora
    (Dawn).

13. From Saturn and Ops[14] were born Vesta, Ceres, Juno, Jupiter, Pluto, and
    Neptune.

14. From Saturn and Philyra were born Chiron[15] and Dolops.

15. From Astraeus and Aurora were born Zephyrus (West Wind), Boreas
    (North Wind), Notus (South Wind), and Favorinus (East Wind).

---

[10]In Hesiod, *Theog.*235, *nemertes* is used as an adjective to describe Nereus. See notes *ad loc.*

[11]Hesiod (*Theog.* 270ff.) only names Pemphredo and Enyo as daughters of Phorcys and Ceto, calling these sisters collectively the "Graeae," or Gray Women.

[12]The oldest manuscript (now lost) was already corrupt and subsequently damaged so badly as to become almost illegible here. Editors have reconstructed "Gorgon" as Hyginus' name for the father of the three sisters, thus explaining their family name. Compare Hesiod, *Theog.* 276ff.

[13]Hyginus is clearly equating Latona with the Greek goddess Leto (see notes to Hesiod, *Theog.*404-406). He is also substituting Polus for the Titan Coeus, but his reason for doing so is not clear.

[14]Saturn and Ops were the Roman counterparts of Cronus and Rhea. Cronus, most popularly portrayed in ancient art as carrying a farmer's sickle, was an obvious choice as a harvest-god. The name *Saturnus* is probably derived from *satur* (full, plentiful, as in English "saturate"). *Ops* (plenty, abundance) is a natural Latin name for his wife.

[15]Chiron was the most famous of the Centaurs: *Theog.* 1001. The name Dolops in Greek means "Tricky-Face." *Ops* in Greek (= face/eye) must not be confused with the same word in Latin (= wealth/ plenty), used by Hyginus as equivalent of Rhea the second-generation Earth Mother.

16. From Atlas and Pleione were born Maia, Calypso,[16] Alcyone, Merope, Electra, and Celaeno.[17]

17. From Pallas the Giant and Styx were born Scylla, Vis[18] (Force), Envy, Power, Victory, the Springs, and the Lakes.

18. From Neptune and Amphitrite, Triton.

19. From Dione and Jupiter, Venus.

20. From Jupiter and Juno, Mars.

21. From Jupiter's head, Minerva.

22. From Juno without a father, Vulcan.

23. From Jupiter and Eurynome, the Graces.

24. From Jupiter again and Juno, Youth and Freedom.

25. From Jupiter and Themis, the Horae.

26. From Jupiter and Ceres, Proserpina.

27. From Jupiter and Moneta, the Muses.

28. From Jupiter and Luna, Pandia.

29. From Venus and Mars, Harmonia and Fear.[19]

30. From Achelous and Melpomene: the Sirens, Thelxiepia, Molpe, and Pisinoe.

31. From Jupiter and Clymene, Mnemosyne.

32. From Jupiter and Maia, Mercury.

33. From Jupiter and Latona, Apollo and Diana.

34. From Terra, Python[20] the divine dragon.

---

[16]The same Calypso who offers Odysseus immortality in the *Odyssey*. Alcyone

[17]Celaeno is also one of the Harpies: #35, below.

[18]Vis is the Latin counterpart of the Greek noun *Bia* (*Theog*.385); likewise *Potestas* (Power) equates to Hesiod's *Cratus* in the same line.

[19]*Formido* in Latin; presumably *Phobos* in Greek, while Deimos is not counted separately.

[20]This is probably a reference to the old myth of the Oracle at Delphi. *Pytho* was, in the Archaic and Classical periods, both the name of the Oracle itself (including its location: Hesiod, *Theog*. 499) and the title of the chief priestess. Traditionally the oracle was that of Gaea and subsequently of Themis before Apollo took control of it, presumably reflecting the different national and tribal groups which had controlled the site before it became a centre of Panhellenism.

35. From Thaumas and Electra: Iris and the Harpies, Celaeno, Ocypetes, and Podarces.[21]

36. From Sol and Persa: Circe, Pasiphae, Aeëtes, and Perses.

37. From Aeëtes and Clytia was born Medea.

38. From Sol and Clymene: Phaethon and the Phaethontides[22] (Merope, Helie, Aetherie, and Dioxippe).

39. From Typhon and Echidna: Gorgon, Cerberus, the dragon[23] who guarded the Golden Fleece in Colchis, Scylla who had the upper portion of a woman and lower parts of a dog (Hercules killed her), the Chimaera, the Boeotian Sphinx, the Hydra (a snake which had nine heads and was killed by Hercules), and the Snake of the Hesperides.

40. From Neptune and Medusa: Chrysaor and the horse Pegasus.

41. From Chrysaor and Callirhoe: three-limbed Geryon.[24]

---

[21]Hesiod (*Theog.* 267) lists two Harpies, Aello and Ocypetes. *Podarces* = "swift-footed."

[22]This name can mean either "Daughters of Phaethon" (actually they were his sisters) or "Phaethonesses."

[23]Even though Hyginus offers no distinct name for this *draco* (=dragon/serpent/snake) it must be a separate entry in the list.

[24]Compare Hesiod, *Theog.* 277-294.

I. THEMISTO

Athamas, son of Aeolus,[1] married Nebula.[2] They had a son Phrixus and a daughter Helle. Athamas also, by Themisto the daughter of Hypseus, had two sons, Sphincius and Orchomenus. By Ino the daughter of Cadmus he had two more sons, Learchus and Melicertes.[3]

Themisto, because Ino had ruined her marriage, wanted to kill Ino's children. So she hid in the palace and, siezing a suitable opportunity (thinking she was killing her rival's sons), she accidentally killed her own, tricked by the nurse who had switched their clothes. When Themisto discovered this, she killed herself.

II. INO

Ino, daughter of Cadmus and Harmonia, since she wanted to kill Phrixus and Helle (Nebula's children), formed a plan with the women of her whole tribe, and conspired to parch the seed grain to make it infertile. She intended that sterility and scarcity of grain would result and so the whole state would perish by a combination of starvation and sickness. To solve the problem Athamas sent a servant to Delphi, but Ino gave the slave instructions to bring back a false reply, saying that that the pestilence would end if Athamas sacrificed Phrixus to Jupiter. When Athamas refused to do this, Phrixus soon promised of his own free will that he would single-handedly free the state from its distress. And so he was led to the altar, wearing sacrificial garlands[4] but the slave, pitying the young man, revealed Ino's plans to Athamas. The king, informed of the crime, gave his own wife Ino and her son Melicertes to be put to death, but Father Liber put a cloud around her, saving Ino his nurse.[5] Later Athamas, driven mad

---

[1]This Aeolus is traditionally represented as a king in Thessaly (NE Greece) and founder of the Aeolic group of Greeks. He must not be confused with the wind-god encountered in *Odyssey* Bk. 10.

[2]Athamas' first wife is called *Nephele* in Greek; as a word, it means "Cloud," as does *nebula* in Latin.

[3]The name Melicertes is generally acknowledged to be a Greek adaptation of the Phoenician name *Melqarth*. In ancient Phoenician myth this character was the approximate equivalent of Hercules, but he was sometimes equated by epithet with Zeus in inscriptions.

[4]In ancient Greek and Roman religion sacrificial animals were decorated with garlands of flowers before being led to the altar for slaughter. Phrixus is offering himself in this way.

[5]The reference is to the story (Apollodorus 3.iv.3) that Zeus had entrusted the baby Dionysus, dressed as a girl, to Ino and Athamas in order to protect him from Hera's jealous anger.

by Jupiter, killed his own son Learchus. But Ino, together with Melicertes her son, threw herself into the sea.[6] She is the one whom Liber wanted to call Leucothea, and Melicertes (her son) the god Palaemon, but we call her Mater Matuta,[7] and him Portunus.[8] In his honor once every four years gymnastic contests are held, which are called Isthmian.[9]

III. PHRIXUS

While Phrixus and Helle were wandering in a forest afflicted by madness sent by Liber, Nebula their mother is said to have come there and to have brought with her a golden ram, the child of Neptune and Theophane. She told her children to ride it to Colchis, to King Aeëtes the son of the Sun,[10] and there sacrifice the ram to Mars. They are reported to have done this, but once they were on the ram's back and the ram had carried them over the sea,[11] Helle fell from the ram. In consequence the sea was called Hellespont.

---

[6]Compare Ovid, *Metamorphoses* IV.500ff.

[7]*Mater Matuta* was probably the Roman dawn-goddess in the early stages of Latin religion. By the time the Romans were absorbing Greek ideas they had probably lost sight of this early function and, because of the narrative details of her myth, identified her with Leucothea. She would have more accurately been linked with Eos. See Georges Dumézil, *Archaic Roman Religion* (Baltimore, 1996) I.338.

[8]"We" are, of course here, the Romans: Matuta and Portunus are the closest equivalents in Latin. The Greeks did, in fact, identify Ino the daughter of Cadmus and her son Melicertes with the nature-deities Leucothea (= *White Goddess*) and Palaemon. See notes on Xenophanes in **Ancient critics** (Chapter 2, above).

[9]This is a reference to the famous Isthmian Games, held every four years at Corinth. The Latin literally reads "Each fifth year." Ancient Greeks counted ordinal numbers inclusively, so the Olympiad years (now marking Leap Years) were termed "fifth" years. The Isthmian games were held in honor of Poseidon and the hero Palaemon. Palaemon is equated here with Melicertes, in Phoenician Melqarth, a sort of Hercules-figure worshipped by the Phoenicians who were expanding their colonies Westward in the early Iron Age and were a major factor in the growth of the Greek "orientalizing" style evident in art and pottery during the times of Homer and Hesiod. They were also responsible for the Greek adaptation of the Semitic alphabet, probably in the 8th century B.C. Palaemon/Melicertes was clearly celebrated at the festival in very much the same way as Hercules was (as founder, Zeus being the patron god) at the Olympics.

[10]Sol (Latin) = Sun, = *Helios* (Greek). Helios' famous children were Circe and Aeëtes; see Hesiod, *Theogony* 955f.

[11]The Hellespont is the western of two straits separating the Aegean Sea from the Black Sea.

Phrixus was carried to Colchis, where (according to his mother's instructions) he sacrificed the ram and set up its golden fleece in the temple of Mars. It is said that this same fleece, guarded by a dragon, was the object of Jason's quest (he was the son of Aeson and Alcimede). But Aeëtes gladly welcomed Phrixus, and gave him his daughter Chalciope in marriage. Later she became the mother of his children, but Aeëtes was afraid that they would expel him from his kingdom, because he had been warned by omens to beware of death at the hands of a foreigner, a son of Aeolus. So he killed Phrixus but Phrixus' sons (Argus, Phrontis, Melas, and Cylindrus) sailed off to go to their grandfather Athamas. They were shipwrecked, however, and Jason, while voyaging for the fleece, rescued them from the island of Dia,[12] and took them back to their mother Chalciope. By her favor he was recommended to her sister Medea.

IV. Ino of Euripides

When Athamas, king of Thessaly, thought that his wife Ino (mother of his two sons) had been killed, he married Themisto, the daughter of a nymph, and had twin sons by her. Later he discovered that Ino was on Parnassus, where she had gone for the Bacchic[13] revels. He sent someone to bring her home, and concealed her when she came. Themisto discovered she had been found, but didn't know her identity. She conceived the desire of killing Ino's sons, and made Ino herself, whom she believed to be a captive, a confidant of the plan, telling her to cover her children with white garments, but Ino's with black. Ino covered her own with white, and Themisto's with dark; then Themisto mistakenly killed her own sons.[14] When she discovered this, she committed suicide. Furthermore Athamas, while hunting, in a fit of madness killed his older son Learchus; but Ino with the younger, Melicertes, cast herself into the sea and was made a goddess.[15]

---

[12]Translated from Greek *Dia*, as a name, would mean "Zeus' [Island]." Dia was another name for the island of Naxos in the middle of the Aegean.

[13]The Dionysiac Mysteries; see Euripides, *Bacchae*. There was a tradition at Delphi that Apollo, the god of the oracle there, would leave to spend the three months of winter in Tempe, a memorial of his self-exile after killing the Python. During these times the oracle at Delphi was considered to be dedicated to Dionysus.

[14]The motif of the black vs. white clothing, leading to a fatal mistake, is similar to the story of Theseus forgetting to change the sails of his ship, thus unwittingly causing his father's suicide. See below, Fab. XLIII.

[15]This same goddess rescues Odysseus, *Od.* V.333-338. For Xenophanes' ridiculing of the myth of her suicide and deification, see **Ancient critics** (Ch. 2, above) **1c**.

V. ATHAMAS

Because of Semele's intercourse with Jupiter, Juno was hostile to her whole family.[16] So Athamas, son of Aeolus, in a fit of madness shot his own son dead with arrows while hunting.

VI. CADMUS

Cadmus, son of Agenor and Argiope, together with Harmonia his wife (daughter of Venus and Mars), after their children had been killed, were turned into snakes[17] in the district of Illyria[18] by the anger of Mars, because Cadmus had slain the dragon which had guarded the spring of Castalia.

VII. ANTIOPA

Antiopa, daughter of Nycteus, was treacherously raped by Ephaphus, and as a result was thrown out by her husband Lycus. So Jupiter embraced her in her abandonment. But Lycus married Dirce. She suspected that her husband had continued a secret affair with Antiopa, so she ordered her servants to keep Antiopa bound in a dark place. When her time was approaching, by the will of Jupiter she escaped from her chains to Mount Cithaeron, and when childbirth drew close and she was looking for a place to bear her child, pain compelled her to give birth at the very place where the roads cross. Shepherds reared her sons as their own, and called one Zetos, meaning "seeking a place,"[19] and the other Amphion, because "she gave birth at the crossroads," or "next to the road." When the sons found out who their mother was, they put Dirce to death by tying her to an untamed bull. From her body spring was formed on Mount Cithaeron, which was called Dirce. This was a gift from Liber, since she was one of his Bacchae.

---

[16]Ovid expands on this motif, *Met.* IV. 400ff.

[17]Compare Ovid *Met.* IV. 605ff. The motif of transformation into snakes clearly reflects an etiology for a cult of a hero as an "immortal" by comparison with the snake, apparently cheating death by shedding its skin. In Apollodorus (3.iv.1) the dragon guards Ares' stream. Castalia is the stream at Delphi, not Thebes where there is a river Dirce. But the etiology for Dirce follows in the next story (Antiopa).

[18]Modern Croatia, NW of Greece along the Adriatic coast.

[19]*Zêtein*, in Greek, means "to seek/search"

XII. PELIAS

An oracle instructed Pelias, son of Cretheus and Tyro, to sacrifice to Neptune. It told him his death was drawing near if a *monocrepis* (a man wearing only one sandal) should arrive. While he was making the annual offerings to Neptune, Jason (son of Aeson who was Pelias' brother), anxious to make sacrifice, lost his sandal as he was crossing the river Evenus, and in order to arrive promptly at the ceremonies, failed to recover it. When Pelias noticed this, remembering the warning of the oracle, he ordered him to fetch from King Aeëtes, his enemy, the golden fleece of the ram which Phrixus had dedicated to Mars at Colchis. Jason, after summoning Greek chieftains, set out for Colchis.

XIII. JUNO

When Juno was standing near the river Evenus, after taking on the form of an old woman, waiting to test men's minds to see if they would carry her across the river Evenus, nobody was willing to do so. Jason, son of Aeson and Alcimede, took her across. She, angry at Pelias for neglecting to sacrifice to her, caused Jason to leave one sandal in the mud.

XIV. ARGONAUTS ASSEMBLED

[The Argonauts were:]

- Jason, son of Aeson and Alcimede, Clymene's daughter, leader of the Thessalians.
- Orpheus, son of Oeagrus and the Muse Calliope, a Thracian from the city Flevia on Mount Olympus near the river Enipeus, prophet,[20] citharist.
- Asterion the son of Pyremus and Antigona (Pheres' daughter) from the city of Pellene. Some say he was Hyperasius' son from the city of Piresia at the foot of Mount Phylleus in Thessaly, the place toward which two rivers, Apidanus and Enipeus with their own separate origins, flow together.

---

[20]The Cithara gives its name to the guitar, but the instrument's shape has changed more substantially than its name. The original was a larger version of the lyre. Orpheus' appearance in the list of Argonauts, even though it appears traditional to us, is an unnecessary piece of doubling. The prophets Mopsus and Idmon were probably more authentic to the earliest traceable versions of the story. Orpheus simply appears because he fits approximately the right time (a generation or so before the Trojan Wars) and belongs ethnically to Northern Greece. His true home is actually closer to the Thracian border.

- Polyphemus, son of Elatus by Hippea, daughter of Antippus, a Thessalian from the city Larissa, with his lame feet.
- Iphiclus, son of Phylacus by Clymene, daughter of Minyas, from Thessaly, Jason's maternal uncle.
- Admetus, son of Pheres, by Periclymene, daughter of Minyas, from Mount Chalcodonius in Thessaly, whence both town and river derive their names. They say Apollo once pastured his sheep there.
- Eurytus and Echion, sons of Mercury and Antianira, daughter of Menetus, from the city Alope, which is now called Ephesus; some authors consider them Thessalians.
- Aethalides, son of Mercury and Eupolemia, daughter of Myrmidon; he was a Larissaean.
- Coronus, son of Caeneus, from the city Gyrton, which is in Thessaly. This Caeneus, son of Elatus, a Magnesian, proved that in no way could the Centaurs wound him with iron, but they did so with trunks of trees sharpened to a point. Some say that he was once a woman to whom, in answer to her prayer, Neptune for her favors granted transformation into the form of a young man who could be killed by no blow. This has never been done: it is impossible for any mortal to escape death by iron weapons, or to be changed from a woman into a man.[21]
- Mopsus, son of Ampycus and Chloris; taught augury by Apollo, he came from Oechalia, or, as some think, he was a Titarensian.
- Eurydamas, son of Irus and Temonassa; some say he was son of Ctimenus, who lived in the city Dolopeis near Lake Xynius.
- Theseus,[22] son of Aegeus and Aethra, daughter of Pittheus, from Troezen; others say from Athens.[23]

---

[21]This editorial comment sits awkwardly in the narrative. We may well take it as a piece of evidence that, if it does belong here in the text, the author cannot have been a court literary figure, but was probably a *grammaticus* (professor) with a simplistic rationalizing agenda. See the **Ancient Critics** section of this textbook, especially section 2 (Sophists and Logographers).

[22]Theseus is another hero who appears by courtesy of late approximations (he belongs to the time of a generation or so before the Trojan War according to the chronology of Hellanicus, who based his research in the 440s to c. 410 B.C. on legends linking Theseus and Helen) but is from the wrong part of Greece; Theseus was the legendary king of Athens and unifier of Attica, but legends linking Attica with Thessaly in the North probably did not begin to grow until the 560s B.C. at the earliest, when Peisistratus the Tyrant of Athens is known to have pursued close diplomatic relations with Thessaly.

[23]Troezen was traditionally Pittheus' kingdom and the place of Theseus' conception and birth; Plutarch, *Theseus* III-IV.

- Pirithous,[24] son of Ixion, brother of the Centaurs, a Thessalian.
- Menoetius, son of Actor, an Opuntian.
- Eribotes the son of Teleon, from Eleon.
- Eurytion son of Irus and Demonassa.
- Ixition from the town of Cerinthus.
- Oileus, son of Hodoedocus and Agrianome, daughter of Perseon, from the city Narycea.
- Clytius and Iphitus, sons of Eurytus and Antiope, daughter of Pylon, kings of Oechalia. Some say they were from Euboea. Eurytus, granted skill with the bow by Apollo, is said to have competed with the giver of the gift. His son Clytius was killed by Aeëtes.
- Peleus and Telamon, sons of Aeacus and Endeis daughter of Chiron, from the island of Aegina. These two left their country because of the murder of Phocus their brother, and went to live elsewhere; Peleus went to Phthia and Telamon went to Salamis (Apollonius of Rhodes calls it Atthis).
- Butes, son of Teleon and Zeuxippe, daughter of the river Eridanus, from Athens.
- Phaleros, son of Alcon, from Athens.
- Tiphys, son of Phorbas and Hyrmine, a Boeotian; he steered the ship Argo.
- Argus, son of Polybus and Argia; some say son of Danaus. He was an Argive, wearing a black-haired bull's hide. He was the builder of the ship Argo.
- Phliasus, son of Father Liber and Ariadne, daughter of Minos, from the city Phlius in the Peloponnese. Others call him a Theban.
- Hercules,[25] son of Jupiter and Alcimena, daughter of Electryon, a Theban.

---

[24]Pirithous was traditionally Theseus' companion on several adventures, including the abduction of Helen and the attempted abduction of Persephone (for an attempted rationalisation see Plut. *Thes.* XXXI). As a Thessalian he fits this list with a somewhat greater sense of authenticity than does Theseus (see above notes).

[25]Another famous and relatively late insertion. As Hyginus says, Hercules was more closely connected with Thebes, though he was also linked to Tiryns near Argos. His failure to reach Colchis (where there is obviously no place for him in the legend) had to be explained by the loss of his friend Hylas, possibly an etiological myth for a swamp beside a pond somewhere near the coast of the Hellespont.

- Hylas, son of Theodamas and the nymph Menodice, daughter of Orion, a teenager, from Oechalia; others say from Argos, a companion of Hercules.
- Nauplius, son of Neptune and Amymone, daughter of Danaus, an Argive.[26]
- Idmon, son of Apollo and the nymph Cyrene; some say [he was son] of Abas from Argos. He was skilled in prophecy, and though he knew that he would die because the birds had predicted it, he did not shirk military service.
- Castor and Pollux, sons of Jupiter and Leda, daughter of Thestius, Lacedaemonians[27] (some call them Spartans), both beardless youths. It is written that stars appeared simultaneously on both their heads,[28] having apparently fallen there.
- Lynceus and Idas,[29] sons of Aphareus and Arena, daughter of Oebalus, Messenians from the Peloponnese. They say that one of these, Lynceus, saw things hidden under the ground, not obstructed by any darkness. Some say that Lynceus saw nothing by night, but was regularly able to see underground because he knew of gold mines; when he went down and suddenly showed gold the rumor spread that he could see underneath the earth.[30] Idas, too, was keen and fierce.
- Periclymenus, son of Neleus and Chloris (daughter of Amphion and Niobe), was from Pylos.
- Amphidamas and Cepheus, sons of Aleus and Cleobule, from Arcadia.
- Ancaeus, son (some say grandson) of Lycurgus, from Tegea.

---

[26]Nauplius' name indicates his association with Nauplion (modern Nafplio), an ancient seaport on the East coast of the Argolid peninsula. His son Palamedes was a popular figure in non-Homeric accounts of the earlier part of the Trojan War.

[27]Lacedaemon, which traditionally includes the city of Sparta, is again in the wrong part of Greece (the South) for the homes of the Argonauts. Notice that Castor and Pollux appear at the head of a list of famous twins who were believed to have sailed in the Argo (see next two notes).

[28]Castor and Pollux were the twins believed to be depicted in the Gemini constellation. They were also closely identified with the electrical phenomenon now called St. Elmo's Fire, observed occasionally at sea. As traditional helpers and guides of sailors and horsemen, they were the closest Greek equivalent of the ancient Hindu *Asvins*. See *Fab*. XVII with notes, below, and my notes on the *Alcis*, in Tacitus, *Germania* 43.

[29]The tradition which puts Lynceus and Idas in the same crew as Castor and Pollux must be very late indeed. In the early epic poem *Cypria* the two pairs of twins were rivals.

[30]This rationalization is from Palaephatus, Myth IX.

- Augeas, son of Sol[31] and Nausidame, daughter of Amphidamas; he was an Elean.
- Asterion and Amphion, sons of Hyperasius (some say of Hippasus), from Pellene.
- Euphemus, son of Neptune and Europe, daughter of Tityus, a Taenarian. It is said he could run over water with dry feet.
- A second Ancaeus, son of Neptune by Althaea, daughter of Thestius, from the island Imbrasus, which was called Parthenia but is now called Samos.
- Erginus, son of Neptune (some say of Periclymenus), from Orchomenus.
- Meleager, son of Oeneus and Althaea, daughter of Thestius (some think he was the son of Mars), a Calydonian.
- Zetes and Calais, sons of the wind Aquilo[32] and Orithyia, daughter of Erechtheus. These are said to have had winged heads and feet and dark-blue hair, and traveled by air. They drove away the three Harpies, Aëllopous, Celaeno, and Ocypete,[33] daughters of Thaumas and Ozomene, from Phineus, son of Agenor, when Jason's crew were on their way to Colchis. The Harpies lived in the Strophades islands, now called the Plotae, in the Aegean Sea. They are said to have had heads and feathers like a rooster with wings and human arms, with great claws, chickens' feet, breasts, bellies, and female parts like a human. Zetes and Calais, however, were killed by the weapons of Hercules. The stones placed over their tombs are moved by their father's winds. These, too, are said to be from Thrace.
- Phocus and Priasus, sons of Caeneus, from Magnesia.
- Eurymedon, son of Father Liber and Ariadne, daughter of Minos, from Phlius.
- Hippalcimos son of Pelops and Hippodameia (Oenomaus' daughter) from Pisa in the Peloponnese.
- Asclepius the son of Apollo and Coronis, from Tricca. . . .
- Neleus, son of Hippocoon, from Pylos.[34]
- Iolaus, son of Iphiclus, an Argive.

---

[31]The sun-god, in Greek *Helios*.

[32]The North Wind.

[33]Hesiod (*Theog.* 267) lists only two Harpies, Aëllo and Ocypetes.

[34]Neleus was father of Nestor, senior officer in Agamemnon's army at Troy and a prominent character in both of Homer's epics.

- Deucalion, son of Minos and Pasiphaé (daughter of Sol), from Crete.
- Philoctetes, son of Poeas, from Meliboea.[35]
- Another Caeneus, son of Coronus, from Gortyn.
- Acastus, son of Pelias and Anaxibia, daughter of Bias, from Iolchus, wrapped in a double cloak. He joined the Argonauts as a volunteer,[36] a comrade of Jason by his own decision.

All of these were called Minyae, either because daughters of Minyas bore most of them, or because Jason's mother was a daughter of Clymene, daughter of Minyas. But not all of them reached Colchis nor did all return to their country. For in Moesia near Cios and the river Ascanius Hylas was abducted by the nymphs. While Hercules and Polyphemus were looking for him, they were left behind when a wind carried the ship on. Polyphemus, too, was left by Hercules. After founding a city in Moesia, he perished in the country of the Chalybes. Tiphys too became ill and died among the Mariandyni in Propontis where Lycus was king; in his place Ancaeus, Neptune's son, steered the ship to Colchis. Idmon, too, son of Apollo, died there at Lycus' court, savaged by a wild boar when he had gone out to fetch straw. He was avenged by Idas, son of Aphareus, who killed the boar. Butes, son of Teleon, though called back by the singing and cithara of Orpheus, nevertheless was overcome by the sweetness of the Sirens' song, and in an attempt to swim to them dived into the sea. Venus saved him at Lilybaeum, where he was carried along by the waves. These are the ones who did not reach Colchis.

On the return trip Eurybates, son of Teleon, died, as did Canthus. They were killed in Libya by the shepherd Cephalion, brother of Nasamon, son of the nymph Tritonis and Amphithemis, whose sheep they were rustling. Mopsus, too, son of Ampycus, died of a snake bite in Africa. He had joined the Argonauts on the trip after the killing of his father Ampycus. The sons of Phrixus and Chalciope (Medea's sister) joined them from the island of Dia: Argus, Melas, Phrontides, and Cylindrus. Others call them Phronius, Demoleon, Autolycus, and Phlogius. Hercules intended to take them as companions in his quest for the girdle of the Amazons, but left them behind stricken with terror by Dascylus the son of Lycus, king of the Mariandini.

---

[35]This is the famous companion of Hercules who inherited the latter's weapons after constructing and lighting a cremation pyre for the suffering hero. For a sequel, set during the last year of the Trojan War, see Sophocles' play *Philoctetes*.

[36]It is unclear why Acastus was chosen as a traitor-figure in the 1963 film *Jason and the Argonauts*. His present role as a volunteer casts him in an entirely honorable light.

When the crew left for Colchis, they wanted to have Hercules as leader. He refused, saying that Jason, on whose undertaking they all were leaving, should be the leader. So Jason was in charge. Argus, son of Danaus, was shipbuilder; Tiphys was pilot. After his death Ancaeus, son of Neptune, steered. Lynceus, son of Aphareus, who had keen sight, was the lookout man at the prow; helmsmen were Zetes and Calais, sons of the North Wind, who had wings on their heads and feet. At prow and oars sat Peleus and Telamon; at the mast Hercules and Idas. The rest were in order of rank. Orpheus, son of Oeagrus, called the beat. Later, when Hercules left his place, Peleus, son of Aeacus, sat there.

This is the ship Argo, which Minerva put in the starry zodiac because it was built at her behest. As soon as this ship was launched into the sea, it appeared among the stars from rudder to sail. Cicero[37] in his *Phaenomena* described its appearance and beauty in the following verses:

> But creeping near the Dog's tail the Argo glides along,
> Turned to carry her stern first, with its light;
> Not as other ships usually move bow-first on the deep
> Cutting Neptune's meadows with their figureheads,
>
> ....
>
> But Argo slips backwards as the ancient sky rotates.
> Her rudder, as it hangs from the flying stern,
> Touches the last footprints of the bright Dog.

This ship has four stars on her stern; to the starboard of the rudder there are five; four to port, all matching one another; in all, thirteen.

XV. WOMEN OF LEMNOS

On the island of Lemnos the women for several years did not sacrifice to Venus. Because of her anger their husbands married Thracian women and rejected their previous wives. But the Lemnian women, at the instigation of the same Venus, plotted to kill the whole generation of men who were there. They all did this except Hypsipyle, who secretly put her father Thoas on board a ship. A storm carried it to a Taurian

---

[37]The Roman orator Marcus Tullius Cicero made several attempts at epic poetry, including one on the subject of his own consulship. The *Phaenomena*, however, was not his own composition. It was in fact a Latin rendering of a Hellenistic Greek poem by Aratus. The whole poem is a collection of etiological myths for constellations. The dog here is, of course, *Canis Major*. In Aratus' zodiac the Argo clearly follows this dog.

island.[38] Meanwhile the Argonauts, as they sailed along, came to Lemnos. When Iphinoe, guardian of the harbor, saw them, she announced their arrival to Hypsipyle the queen. Polyxo, a senior woman and the queen's advisor, advised Hypsipyle to follow obligations to the gods of hospitality and treat them as guests.

Hypsipyle bore to Jason two sons, Euneus and Deipylus. When they were delayed there for many days, Hercules grew impatient and complained until finally they left. When the Lemnian women learned that Hypsipyle had saved her father, they tried to kill her. She escaped but pirates caught her, carried her off to Thebes, and sold her as a slave to King Lycus. The Lemnian women gave the names of the Argonauts (whose fathers they were) to their children.

XVI. Cyzicus

Cyzicus, son of Eusorus, was king in an island of the Propontis.[39] He received the Argonauts with generous hospitality, but when they had left him, and had sailed a whole day, a storm arose in the night which brought them unaware to the same island. Cyzicus, thinking they were Pelasgian enemies, attacked them on the shore at night, and was killed by Jason who, the next day when he approached the shore, saw that he had killed the king. He buried the king and handed over the kingdom to his sons.

XVII. Amycus

Amycus, son of Neptune and Melie, was king of Bebrycia. He forced whoever came to his kingdom to box with him and killed his defeated opponents. When he challenged the Argonauts to a boxing match, Pollux[40] took him on and killed him.

XVIII. Lycus

Lycus, king of an island on the Propontis, treated the Argonauts as guests of honor because they had killed Amycus, who had often raided him. While the Argonauts were staying with Lycus, and had gone out to gather straw, Idmon the son of Apollo was wounded by a wild boar and died.

---

[38]The Taurian district roughly corresponds to Crimea on the north side of the Black Sea.

[39]The Propontis is the stretch of water between the Aegean Sea and the Black Sea. See the earlier note on the Hellespont, *Fab.* III.

[40]Of these famous twins, Pollux excelled in boxing and Castor in horsemanship.

While they were waiting even longer for his burial, Tiphys the son of Phorbas died. Then the Argonauts gave charge of the Argo's steering to Ancaeus, son of Neptune.

XIX. PHINEUS

Phineus of Thrace, son of Agenor, had two sons by Cleopatra. Because of their stepmother's charges, they were both blinded by their father. Apollo is said to have given the gift of prophecy to this Phineus. But he, for having announced publicly the decisions of the gods, was blinded by Jupiter who then set the Harpies over him (they are called the Hounds of Jupiter) to take the food from his lips. When the Argonauts arrived and asked him to show them the way, he said he would show them if they would free him from the punishment.

Then Zetes and Calais, sons of the North Wind and Orithyia, who are said to have had wings on their heads and feet, drove the Harpies to the Strophades[41] Islands, and freed Phineus from the punishment. He showed them how to pass the Symplegades by sending out a dove. When the rocks rushed together, they would rebound.[42] By the help of Phineus the Argonauts passed the Symplegades.

XX. THE STYMPHALIAN BIRDS

Once the Argonauts had reached the island of Dia,[43] the birds were shooting them, using their feathers as arrows. So they were unable to deal with the great numbers of birds. Following Phineus' advice they took up shields and spears, putting them to flight by the noise, in the style of the Curetes.[44]

---

[41]*Strophades* means "turning places." Since Zetes and Calais then turned around and returned, we have an etiological myth for the naming of this group of islands.

[42]There is a lacuna in the text here. Clearly the rebounding and regrouping of the rocks would take time and thus enable the Argonauts to pass through.

[43]Compare Fab. XXX, where Hercules deals in a similar way with these birds on "the island of Mars." Dia here is clearly not Naxos, but is located by narrative sequence (and in the next story) just beyond the East end of the Propontis. It seems to be a purely mythical island.

[44]This is a reference to the ancient Dance of the Curetes, an initiatory dance performed as a kind of endurance test by teenagers in full armor, especially in Crete. An important part of the dance was to beat the shield and sword together, making as much noise as possible. The ritual was associated with the mythical young men who had protected the baby Zeus, using the noise to drive away Cronus. See Apollodorus I.i.6 (Chapter 16 below). The use of noise to drive away evil spirits is extremely ancient and widespread. It may be compared with the use of fireworks at the celebration of the new year in many cultures.

XXI. SONS OF PHRIXUS

When the Argonauts had sailed through the Cyanean Cliffs (also called Rocks of the Symplegades), they entered the sea called Euxine and were lost. By the will of Juno they were carried to the island of Dia. There they found shipwrecked men, naked and helpless. These were the sons of Phrixus and Chalciope (Argus, Phrontides, Melas, and Cylindrus). The men told their sad story to Jason, how they had suffered shipwreck and become castaways there while hurrying to go to their grandfather Athamas. Jason welcomed and gave them help. They led Jason to Colchis through the river Thermodoon, and when they were not far from Colchis, they told the Argonauts to hide the ship. They themselves went to their mother Chalciope, Medea's sister, and told of Jason's kindness explaining why they had come. Then Chalciope told them about Medea, and brought her with her own sons to Jason. When Medea saw him, she recognized him as the one to whom she had, at Juno's instigation, made love in dreams. She promised him everything and they brought him to the temple.

XXII. AEËTES

An oracle told Aeëtes, son of Sun,[45] that he would keep his kingdom as long as the fleece that Phrixus had dedicated should be in the shrine of Mars. So Aeëtes set this task for Jason, if he wished to take away the golden fleece: to harness together a pair of bronze-footed bulls breathing flames from their nostrils with a yoke of adamant. He was to plough and sow from a helmet the dragon's teeth, from which a species of armed men would rise up and kill each other. Juno, however, wished to save Jason. The reason was that once when she had come to a river and wanted to test the minds of men, she assumed the shape of an old woman and asked to be carried across. He had carried her across when others who had passed over despised her. And so, knowing that Jason could not perform the tasks without the help of Medea, she asked Venus to inspire Medea with love. At Venus' instigation,[46] Jason became the object of Medea's love. By her help he was freed from all danger, for when he had done his ploughing with the bulls the armed men were born. On Medea's advice he threw a stone amongst them, making them fight among themselves and kill one other. When the dragon was drugged to sleep, Jason took the fleece from the shrine and left for his own country with Medea.

---

[45]See Hesiod, *Theogony* 956ff.

[46]Traditionally Aphrodite used a magical charm involving the spinning of a wryneck (a type of sea bird) on a wheel; see Pindar, *Pythian* IV. 215-6.

XXIII. Absyrtus

When Aeëtes found out that Medea had escaped with Jason, he got a ship ready and sent his son Absyrtus with a retinue to pursue her. When he had caught up with her in the Adriatic Sea in Histria[47] at King Alcinous' court, he wanted to fight for her. Alcinous intervened to prevent their fighting. They accepted him as a judge and he put them off till the next day.

When he seemed sadder than usual, Arete, his wife, asked him the cause of his sadness. He said he had been taken on as a judge by two different states, to judge between Colchians and Argives. When Arete asked him what judgment he would give, Alcinous replied that if Medea were a virgin, he would return her to her father but, if no longer so, to her husband. When Arete heard this from her husband, she sent a message to Jason, and he took Medea's virginity by night in a cave. The next day when they came for the judgement and Medea was found to be a wife, she was given to her husband. Nevertheless, when they had left, Absyrtus, fearing his father's orders, pursued them to the island of Minerva.

Absyrtus came to Jason as he was sacrificing there to Minerva and was killed by Jason. Medea gave him burial and they left. The Colchians who had come with Absyrtus, fearing Aeëtes, stayed there and established a town which from Absyrtus' name they called Absoris. Now this island is located in Histria, opposite Pola, next to the island Canta.

XXIV. Jason: Daughters of Pelias

Since Jason had faced so many perils on the orders of his uncle Pelias, he began to plan a way to kill him without suspicion. Medea promised to accomplish this. And so, since they were now far from Colchis, she gave orders for the ship to be hidden in a secret place while she herself, disguised as a priestess of Diana, approached the daughters of Pelias. She promised to make their father Pelias young again[48] instead of an old man, but his eldest daughter Alcestis said this was impossible. To lead her on more easily, Medea cast a mist before them, and by use of drugs performed many

---

[47]Istria is at the northern end of the Adriatic. If Colchis is at the eastern end of the Black Sea, we have suddenly sailed over a thousand miles by the realistic route via the Hellespont and round the southern tip of Greece. Clearly Hyginus envisages a shortcut, following a version of the story popular since the version of Apollonius Rhodius (3rd century B.C.) that the Argo had traveled up the Danube and was carried across the Alps, being launched down another river (whose geography is, of course, confused) into the Mediterranean or the Adriatic.

[48]Compare Ovid, Met. VII.150ff.

miracles which seemed just like reality. She put an old ram in a bronze vessel, from which a very fine young lamb seemed to spring. In this way the daughters of Pelias—that is, Alcestis, Pelopia, Medusa, Pisidice, and Hippothoe—were driven on by Medea to kill their father and cook him in a bronze cauldron. When they realized they had been deceived, they fled the country. But Jason, picking up a signal given by Medea, took over the palace and handed over the rule to Acastus, son of Pelias, brother of the Peliades, because he had gone with him to Colchis. He himself left with Medea for Corinth.

XXV. MEDEA

When Medea, daughter of Aeëtes and Idyia, had already borne sons (Mermerus and Pheres[49]) to Jason and they were living in great harmony, it occurred to Jason that a man so brave, handsome, and noble should have as wife a foreigner and poisoner. Creon the son of Menoecus, king of Corinth, gave his younger daughter Glauce to Jason as wife. When Medea saw that she, who deserved so much good of Jason, was being so insulted, she made a golden crown [steeped] with poison and told her sons to give it as a gift to their stepmother. Creusa took the gift, and burst into flames along with Jason and Creon. When Medea saw that the palace was on fire, she killed Mermerus and Pheres, whom she had born to Jason, and escaped from Corinth.

XXVI. MEDEA IN EXILE

Medea, in exile from Corinth, reached Athens and was treated as a guest by Aegeus, son of Pandion, then married him; Medus[50] was their son. Later the priestess of Diana began to make trouble for Medea, telling the king that she could not perform sacrifices in ritual cleanliness because there was a woman in town who was a poisoner and a criminal. She was exiled then for a second time. Medea, however, drawn by a team of dragons, left Athens for Colchis. On the way she came to Absoros where her brother Absyrtus was buried. There the people of Absoros could not deal with an infestation of snakes. At their request Medea gathered them up and threw them into her brother's

---

[49]*Pheres* is a very old Greek word, later replaced by *Kentauros* (Centaur) meaning a mythical wild creature which was half human, half horse. The IE v*fer-* simply means "wild."

[50]Medus was the one who, in the earlier story given by a continuator of Hesiod (*Theog.* 998-1002), was raised by Cheiron the Centaur.

tomb. They are there to this day, but if one of them goes outside the tomb, it pays the debt to nature.[51]

XXVII. MEDUS

An oracle was given to Perses, son of the Sun, Aeëtes' brother, to beware of death from a descendant of Aeëtes. Medus, searching for his mother, was brought to Aeëtes' territory by a storm. Guards arrested him and brought him to King Perses. When Medus, son of Aegeus and Medea, saw that he had come under the power of an enemy, he claimed falsely that he was Hippotes, son of Creon. The king asked careful questions and had him thrown into prison. After this, there is said to have been sterility and famine. When Medea arrived there in her chariot with its team of dragons, she falsely claimed before the king that she was a priestess of Diana. She said she could make ritual atonement for the sterility. When she heard from the king that Hippotes, son of Creon, was being held under guard, she supposed he had come to avenge the injury to his father. At that point she unwittingly betrayed her son. For she persuaded the king that he was not Hippotes, but Medus, son of Aegeus, sent by his mother to kill the king, and asked for him to be handed over so that she could kill him (she thought he was Hippotes). And so when Medus was brought out to be executed for his lies, and she realized how different the situation was than she had thought, she said she wished to talk with him. She handed him a sword, and ordered him to avenge the wrongs done to his grandfather. Medus, on hearing this, killed Perses and took possession of his grandfather's kingdom. He called the country Media after himself.

XXVIII. OTOS AND EPHIALTES

Otos and Ephialtes, the sons of Aloeus and Iphimede (Neptune's daughter) are said to have been of a supernatural size. Growing up, they increased in size by nine inches every month, so when they were nine years old they tried to reach up to heaven. This is how they created access: they piled Mount Ossa on top of Mount Pelion[52] (and for this reason Pelion is also called Ossa) and started to add other mountains. They were caught by Apollo and killed.

---

[51]It dies, having outlived its natural span. The snake is, again, a symbol of immortality; see above, *Fab.* VI, with note.

[52]See Odyssey XI, 305ff., especially 314–320 for the piling of Pelion on Ossa and Apollo's foiling of the attempt. The myth is evidently an early etiology for the extraordinary height of Pelion, in Northern Greece.

Other authors, however, say that they were the invulnerable sons of Neptune and Iphimede. They tried to rape Diana and she was unable to resist their strength. But Apollo sent a deer in between them and, driven furious, they tried to kill it with their spears and so killed each other. This is the punishment they are said to suffer in the underworld: they were tied by means of serpents to a column, back to back with one another. There is an owl sitting on the column to which they are bound.

XXIX. ALCIMENA

When Amphitryon was away taking Oechalia by storm, Alcimena, thinking Jupiter was her husband, received him in her bedroom.[53] When he had entered her room and told her what he had done in Oechalia, she believed he was her husband and lay with him. He lay with her with so much pleasure that he used up one whole day and the two adjacent nights, so that Alcimena was amazed that the night was so long. Later when the word came to her that her husband coming home in victory, she showed no concern, because she thought she had already seen him. When Amphitryon reached the palace and noticed her lack of concern, he began to wonder and complained that she had not rushed to receive him on his arrival.

Alcimena answered, "You already came and lay with me, and told me your achievements in Oechalia."

When she had told him all these wonders, Amphitryon realized that some deity had stood in for him, and from that day did not lie with her. But she, after being embraced by Jupiter, bore Hercules.[54]

XXX. TWELVE LABORS OF HERCULES
ORDERED BY EURYSTEHEUS

When he was a baby, he killed with his two hands both the snakes which Juno had sent. This is why he is called Primigenius. He killed the Nemean Lion, an invulnerable monster which the Moon had nursed in a two-mouthed cave, and kept its skin to cover himself.

---

[53]This intrigue is the subject of Plautus' Roman comedy *Amphitruo.* For the story of Hercules' conception, see Apollodorus' account in this textbook, chapter 21.

[54]There is a more elaborate version of Hercules' nativity-story, given in the form of a reminiscence by Alcmene, in Ovid *Met.* IX. 280ff. See also the extract from Apollodorus in this textbook. Hyginus does not develop here the story of Iphicles, though he mentions him elsewhere.

At the spring of Lerna he killed the nine-headed Lernaean Hydra, daughter of Typhon. This monster was so poisonous that she could kill men with her breath, and if anyone passed by when she was sleeping, he breathed her tracks and died in the utmost agony. He killed this creature as Minerva showed him, disemboweled her, and dipped his arrows in her gall. This is why, later, whatever he hit with his arrows did not escape death, and later it was the cause of his own death in Phrygia.[55] He killed the Erymanthian Boar. The ferocious stag with golden horns in Arcadia he brought alive into full sight of king Eurystheus. With his arrows he killed the Stymphalian Birds on the island of Mars which shoot their feathers out like spears. In one day he cleaned out the manure of King Augeas' cattle, mainly with Jupiter's help. He washed out the manure by letting in a river.

He brought to Mycenae alive from the island of Crete the bull with which Pasiphaé had lain. He killed Diomedes the king of Thrace and his four horses that fed on human flesh, then he killed the slave Abderus. The horses' names were Podargus, Lampon, Xanthus, and Dinus. [He killed] Hippolyte, daughter of Mars and Queen Otrera, and took the belt from the Amazon Queen, then he presented Antiopa as captive to Theseus. The triple-bodied Geryon, son of Chrysaor, he killed with a single spear. He killed the huge dragon, Typhon's son, which used to guard the golden apples of the Hesperides, near Mount Atlas, and brought the apples to King Eurystheus. He brought from the underworld the dog Cerberus, offspring of Typhon, into the king's sight.

XXXI. Additional Labors of the Same Hercules

He killed Antaeus, son of Earth, in Libya. This man would force visitors to wrestle with him and when they were exhausted he would kill them. He killed them in wrestling. [He also killed] Busiris in Egypt, who made a practice of sacrificing guests. When Hercules heard of his practice, he allowed himself to be led to the altar wearing a sacrificial fillet, but when Busiris wanted to call upon the gods, Hercules killed him with his club together with the sacrificial assistants. He killed Cygnus, son of Mars, after defeating him with weapons. When Mars came there and wanted to have an armed contest with him because of his son, Jupiter sent his thunderbolt between them. At Troy he killed the sea-monster to whom Hesione had been offered. He shot Laomedon, Hesione's father, with arrows because he did not give

---

[55]Not Mount Oeta, near Thermopylae, as most Greek traditions maintain.

her back.[56]   He killed the shining eagle which was eating out the heart of Prometheus with arrows. He killed Lycus, son of Neptune, because he intended to kill Megara the daughter of Creon (Hercules' wife) and their sons Therimachus and Ophites. The River Achelous used to change himself into all shapes. This person, when he fought with Hercules to win Deianira in marriage, changed himself into a bull. Hercules tore off his horn and gave it to the Hesperides or Nymphs, the goddesses who filled it with apples and called it the Horn of Plenty, *Cornucopia*. He killed Neleus the son of Hippocoon and his ten sons for refusing to cleanse him or purify him when he had killed his wife Megara, daughter of Creon, and his sons Therimachus and Ophites. He killed Eurytus for refusing to give him his daughter Iole as a bride. He killed the centaur Nessus because he tried to violate Deianira. He killed Eurytion the Centaur because he wooed Deianira, daughter of Dexamenus, his hoped-for bride.

XXXII. Megara

When Hercules had been sent for, the three-headed dog by King Eurystheus, and Lycus, son of Neptune, thought he was dead. Lycus planned to kill Hercules' wife Megara, daughter of Creon, and their sons, Therimachus and Ophites, so as to usurp the kingdom. Hercules intervened and killed Lycus. Later, when Juno sent madness upon him, he killed Megara and his sons, Therimachus and Ophites. When he came to his senses, he requested an oracular statement from Apollo on how to cleanse himself of his crime. Because Apollo was unwilling to give back an answer Hercules, in a rage, carried off the tripod from his shrine. He later returned it, at the command of Jupiter, and ordered him to give the reply against his will. For doing this Hercules was given as a slave to Queen Omphale by Mercury.

XXXIII. Centaurs

When Hercules had come to the court of King Dexamenus and had taken the virginity of the king's daughter Deianira, he gave a pledge that he would marry her. After he had

---

[56]There are many references in antiquity to this story of an earlier Trojan War, in which Hercules, after killing a sea-monster and rescuing the princess Hesione, requested the princess as a bride in reward for his work. King Laomedon (Priam's father) refused and so Hercules laid siege to the city. In later sources he does this after returning to Greece and enlisting the help of several heroes including the fathers of some who later attacked Troy to reclaim Helen.

left, Eurytion the son of Ixion the centaur and Nubes,[57] asked for Deianira as a wife. Her father, fearing violence, promised to give her to him. On the arranged day he came with his brothers to the wedding. Hercules arrived in time, killed the centaur, and carried off his bride.

Likewise at another marriage, when Pirithous was marrying Hippodamia, daughter of Adrastus, centaurs, full of wine, attempted to carry off the wives of the Lapithae. The centaurs killed many of them, but were then killed by the Lapiths.

XXXIV. Nessus

Nessus the son of Ixion and Nubes, a centaur, was asked by Deianira[58] to carry her across the river Euhenus. As he was carrying her, he tried to rape her right in the river. When Hercules arrived and Deianira asked him to believe her, he shot Nessus with arrows. As he died, Nessus, knowing that they had been dipped in the poison of the Lernaean Hydra, took up some of his blood and gave it to Deianira, telling her it was a love-charm. If she wanted her husband not to desert her, she should make sure his clothing was steeped in this blood. Deianira, believing him, kept it carefully hidden.

XXXV. Iole

Hercules requested Iole, the daughter of Eurytus, as a bride. When Eurytus refused, Hercules attacked Oechalia. So that he would be asked by the girl, he threatened to kill her relatives in her presence. She, in her determination, suffered them to be killed before her eyes. When he had killed them all, he sent Iole ahead as a captured maid to Deianira.

XXXVI. Deianira

When Deianira, Hercules' wife and daughter of Oeneus, saw the captive Iole arrive, and noticed her outstanding beauty, she was afraid that she would steal her marriage. So,

---

[57]*Nubes* means "Cloud." The association between centaurs and clouds because a cloud shaped like such a monster was the only one to be seen in nature, is made by the philosopher Socrates in Aristophanes' *Clouds*.

[58]The material in this and the next two *Fabulae* serves as a background to Sophocles' tragedy *Trachiniae* (The Women of Trachis).

remembering the instructions of Nessus, she sent a servant named Lichas to bring to Hercules a robe dipped in the centaur's blood.

Then, when a little of it fell to the ground and the sun touched it, it began to burn. When Deianira saw this, she knew that Nessus had lied and sent a man to call back the one to whom she had given the robe. Hercules had already put it on, and immediately began to burn. When he jumped in the river to put out the fire, it burned still more fiercely. When he tried to take off the robe the flesh came off with it. Then Hercules spun Lichas, who had brought the robe, round and round, threw him into the sea. In the place where he fell a rock arose which is called Lichas.

Then Philoctetes, son of Poeas, is said to have built a pyre on Mount Oeta for Hercules. He mounted it and became immortal. For this service Hercules gave Philoctetes his bow and arrows. But Deianira killed herself because of what had happened to Hercules.

XXXVII. AETHRA

Neptune and Aegeus, son of Pandion, one night in the shrine of Minerva both lay with Aethra, daughter of Pittheus.[59] Neptune conceded the child to Aegeus. Now he, on the point of returning to Athens from Troezen, put his sword under a stone, and told Aethra that when the boy could lift the stone and take his father's sword, she should send him to him. He would recognize his son by that. And so later Aethra bore Theseus.[60] When he had reached young manhood, his mother told him Aegeus' instructions, showed him the stone so that he could get the sword, and bade him set out for Athens to Aegeus . . . and he killed all those who made the road unsafe.

XXXVIII. LABORS OF THESEUS

[Theseus] slew Corynetes, son of Neptune, by force of arms. He killed Pityocamptes, who forced travelers to help him bend a pine tree to the ground. When they had taken hold of it with him, he let it rebound suddenly with force. Thus they were dashed violently to the ground and died.[61] He killed Procrustes, son of Neptune. When a guest

---

[59]Troezen is on the eastern coast of the Isthmus of Corinth.

[60]There is a much fuller account of this hero's biography in the *Life of Theseus* by Plutarch (first in his series Parallel Lives).

[61]The myth of Pityocamptes (=Pine Bender) may have origins in a ritual of human sacrifice in which a young tree was bent downwards and one of the victim's limbs was attached to the top branch: compare Euripides, *Bacchae* 1043–1085.

came to visit him, if he was rather tall, he brought a shorter bed, and cut off the rest of his body; if rather short, he gave him a longer bed, and by hanging anvils to him stretched him to match the length of the bed. Sciron used to sit near the sea at a certain point, and compel those who passed by to wash his feet; then he kicked them into the sea. Theseus cast him into the sea by a similar death, and from this the rocks are called those of Sciron. He killed by force of arms Cercyon, son of Vulcan. He killed the boar which was at Cremyon. He killed the bull at Marathon, which Hercules had brought to Eurystheus from Crete. He killed the Minotaur in the town of Cnossus.

XXXIX. DAEDALUS

Daedalus, son of Eupalamus, who is said to have received the art of craftsmanship from Athena, threw down from the roof Perdix, son of his sister, envying his skill, because he first invented the saw. Because of this crime he went into exile from Athens to Crete to King Minos.

XL. PASIPHAÉ

Pasiphaé, daughter of Sol and wife of Minos, for several years did not make offerings to the goddess Venus. Because of this Venus inspired in her an unnatural love for a bull. At the time when Daedalus came there as an exile, he asked her to help him. For her he made a wooden heifer, and put in it the hide of a real heifer, and in this she lay with the bull. From this intercourse she bore the Minotaur, with bull's head but human body. Then Daedalus made for the Minotaur a labyrinth with an undiscoverable exit in which it was confined. When Minos found out the affair he cast Daedalus into prison, but Pasiphaé freed him from his chains. And so Daedalus made wings and fitted them to himself and to his son Icarus, and they flew away from that place. Icarus flew too high, and when the wax was melted by the sun, fell into the sea which was named Icarian for him. Daedalus flew on to King Cocalus in the island of Sicily. Others say that after Theseus killed the Minotaur he brought Daedalus back to Athens, his own country.

XLI. MINOS

When Minos, son of Jupiter and Europa, fought with the Athenians, his son Androgeus was killed in the fight. After he conquered the Athenians their revenues became his; he decreed, moreover, that each year they should send seven of their children as food for the Minotaur. After Theseus had come from Troezen, and had learned what a calamity afflicted the state, of his own accord he promised to go against the Minotaur. When his father sent him off, he charged him to have white sails for his ships if he came back as victor; those who were sent to the Minotaur journeyed with black sails.

XLII. THESEUS AND THE MINOTAUR

When Theseus came to Crete, Ariadne, Minos' daughter, loved him so much that she betrayed her brother and saved the stranger, for she showed Theseus the way out of the labyrinth. When Theseus had entered and killed the Minotaur, by Ariadne's advice he got out by unwinding the thread. Ariadne, because she had been loyal to him, he took away, intending to marry her.

XLIII. ARIADNE

Theseus, detained by a storm on the island of Dia,[62] thought it would be a reproach to him if he brought Ariadne to Athens, and so he left her asleep on the island of Dia.

Liber, falling in love with her, took her from there as his wife. However, when Theseus left, he forgot to change the black sails, and so his father Aegeus judged that he had been devoured by the Minotaur. He threw himself into the sea, which was called Aegean from this. But Theseus married Phaedra, Ariadne's sister.

XLIV. COCALUS

Minos, because many misfortunes had come to him through the agency of Daedalus, followed him to Sicily, and asked King Cocalus to surrender him. When Cocalus had promised this, and Daedalus found it out, he sought help from the daughters of the king, and they killed Minos.

XLVII. HIPPOLYTUS

Phaedra, daughter of Minos and wife of Theseus, fell in love with her stepson Hippolytus. When she could not bend him to her desire, she sent a letter to her husband saying that she had been attacked by Hippolytus, and slew herself by hanging.[63]

---

[62]Dia (=godly; divine) was another name for Naxos.
[63]Euripides' tragedy *Hippolytus* is based on this story.

Theseus, when he heard this, ordered his son to leave the city and prayed Neptune his father for his son's death. And so when Hippolytus was driving his team of horses, a bull suddenly appeared from the sea. The horses, terrified at its bellowing, dragged Hippolytus, rending him limb from limb, and caused his death.

XLVIII. KINGS OF THE ATHENIANS

Cecrops, son of Terra; Cephalus, son of Deione; Erichthonius, son of Vulcan; Pandion, son of Erichthonius; Erechtheus, son of Pandion; Aegeus, son of Pandion; Theseus, son of Aegeus; Demophoon, son of Theseus.

XLIX. AESCULAPIUS

Aesculapius the son of Apollo is said to have restored life to Glaucus the son of Minos, or to Hippolytus[64] and for this reason Jupiter is said to have struck him with a thunderbolt. Apollo, being unable to harm Jupiter, killed the Cyclopes who made Jupiter's thunderbolts. For this deed Apollo was handed over as a slave to Admetus the king of Thessaly.

LI. ALCESTIS

Several suitors sought marriage with Alcestis the daughter of Pelias and Anaxibia (daughter of Bias). Pelias avoided meeting their terms and set up his own conditions: he would give his daughter to whoever could yoke wild animals to a chariot and carry Alcestis off to marry her. And so Admetus asked Apollo to help him. Apollo, moreover (because he had been treated kindly in captivity by Admetus) gave him a wild boar and a lion yoked to a chariot. Admetus used these to carry off Alcestis.

Admetus also received this bounty from Apollo: another person might die (but voluntarily) in his place. Since neither his father nor his mother would volunteer to die for him, Admetus' wife Alcestis offered herself and died in his place. Hercules[65] later brought her back from the Underworld.

---

[64]See Fab. XLVII.

[65]The story of Hercules' visit to the Underworld to regain the soul of Alcestis is the subject of Euripides' play *Alcestis*. In the 18th century the myth was used as the basis of an opera, *Alceste*, by Christoph Willibald von Gluck.

LIV. THETIS

A prediction about Thetis, the Nereid, was that her son would be greater than his father.[66] Since no one but Prometheus knew this, and Jupiter wished to lie with her, Prometheus promised Jupiter that he would give a timely warning if he would free him from his chains. And so when the promise was given he advised Jupiter not to lie with Thetis, for if one greater than he were born he might drive Jupiter from his kingdom, as he himself had done to Saturn. And so Thetis was given in marriage to Peleus, son of Aeacus, and Hercules was sent to kill the eagle which was eating out Prometheus' heart. When it was killed, Prometheus after thirty thousand years was freed from Mount Caucasus.

LXIII. DANAÉ

Danaé was the daughter of Acrisius and Aganippe. A prophecy about her said that the child she bore would kill Acrisius, and Acrisius, fearing this, shut her in a stone-walled prison. But Jupiter, changing into a shower of gold, lay with Danaé and from this embrace Perseus was born. Because of her sin her father shut her up in a chest with Perseus and cast it into the sea. By Jupiter's will it was borne to the island Seriphus, and when the fisherman Dictys found it and broke it open, he discovered the mother and child. He took them to King Polydectes, who married Danaé and brought up Perseus in the temple of Minerva. When Acrisius discovered they were staying at Polydectes' court, he started out to get them, but at his arrival Polydectes interceded for them, and Perseus swore an oath to his grandfather that he would never kill him. When Acrisius was detained there by a storm, Polydectes died, and at his funeral games the wind blew a discus from Perseus' hand at Acrisius' head which killed him.

Thus what he did not do of his own will was accomplished by the gods. When Polydectes was buried, Perseus set out for Argos and took possession of his grandfather's kingdom.

---

[66]This prophecy seems to have been a well-established motif throughout ancient poetry. It had already been quoted by Pindar (*Isthmian* VIII.29) in the mid-5th century BC. The motif may have been attached to the story of Prometheus already by that time in the (now lost) epic *Cypria* two centuries earlier: it seems to have been used in this context by Aeschylus, from what we can gather of the fragments of his *Prometheus Freed*, written in Athens during Pindar's lifetime.

LXIV. ANDROMEDA

Cassiope[67] claimed that her daughter Andromeda's beauty excelled the Nereids'. Because of this, Neptune demanded that Andromeda, Cepheus' daughter, be offered to a sea-monster. When she was offered, Perseus, flying on Mercury's winged sandals, is said to have come there and freed her from danger. When he wanted to marry her, Cepheus, her father, along with Agenor, her betrothed, planned to kill him.[68] Perseus, discovering the plot, showed them the head of the Gorgon, and all were changed from human form into stone. Perseus with Andromeda returned to his country. When Polydectes[69] saw that Perseus was so courageous, he feared him and tried to kill him by treachery, but when Perseus discovered this he showed him the Gorgon's head, and he was changed from human form into stone.

LXXVII. LEDA

Jupiter, having transformed himself into the shape of a swan, seduced Leda the daughter of Thestius beside the river Eurotas. As a result she bore Pollux and Helen, but she bore Castor and Clytemnestra as Tyndareus' offspring.

CLXVII. LIBER

Liber, son of Jupiter and Proserpina,[70] was dismembered by the Titans, and Jupiter gave his heart, torn to bits, to Semele in a drink. When she was made pregnant by this, Juno, changing herself to look like Semele's nurse, Beroe, said to her: "Daughter, ask Jupiter to come to you as he comes to Juno, so you may know what pleasure it is to sleep with a god." At her suggestion Semele made this request of Jupiter, and was smitten by a thunderbolt. He took Liber from her womb, and gave

---

[67]Her name can also be spelled Cassiopeia, which is closer to the Greek.

[68]Compare Ovid, *Met.* IV-V.

[69]If this story is meant to be a continuation of its predecessor, Polydectes is already dead. Perhaps Proetus is meant.

[70]This reference is to Dionysus-Zagreus, whose cult and myths may have been imported into Greece in the late 6th or early 5th centuries BC. It is certainly out of keeping with the Dionysus/Bacchus who is the central character of Euripides' *Bacchae*. Aeschylus, who had been dead for at least forty years when Euripides wrote the *Bacchae*, composed a play called *Dionysus' Nurses*. If Hyginus' story is based in any way on Aeschylus' play, then Euripides must have rationalized the story somewhat in his own last tragedy. There is another version of this myth below, CLXXIX.

him to Nysus to be cared for. For this reason he is called Dionysus, and also "the one with two mothers."[71]

CLXXVIII. EUROPA

Europa was the daughter of Argiope and Agenor, a Sidonian. Jupiter, changing his form to that of a bull,[72] carried her from Sidon to Crete, and begat by her Minos, Sarpedon, and Rhadamanthus. Her father Agenor sent his sons to bring their sister back, or else not to return to his sight. Phoenix set out for Africa, and there remained. From this the Africans[73] are called Phoenicians. Cilix from his own name gave the name to Cilicia. Cadmus in his wanderings came to Delphi. There the oracle told him to buy from farmers an ox which had a moon-shaped mark on its side, and to drive it before him. Where it lay down it was fated that he found a town and rule. When Cadmus heard the oracle, he did as he was told. While seeking water he came to the fountain of Castalia, which a dragon, the offspring of Mars,[74] was guarding. It killed some comrades of Cadmus, but was killed by Cadmus with a stone. Under Minerva's instructions he sowed the teeth and plowed them under. From them sprang the Sparti. These fought among themselves, but from them five survived, namely, Chthonius, Udaeus, Hyperenor, Pelorus, and Echion. Moreover, Boeotia[75] was named from the ox Cadmus followed.

CLXXIX. SEMELE

Cadmus, son of Agenor and Argiope, married Harmonia (daughter of Mars and Venus) and begat four daughters—Semele, Ino, Agave, Autonoe—and a son, Polydorus. Jupiter desired to lie with Semele, and when Juno found out, she changed her form to that of the nurse Beroe, came to Semele, and suggested that she ask Jupiter to come to her as he came to Juno, "that you may know," she said, "what pleasure it is to lie with a god."

And so Semele asked Jupiter to come to her in this way. Her request was granted, and Jupiter, coming with lightning and thunder, burned Semele to death. From her

---

[71]An alternative explanation of this epithet, closer in spirit to Euripides' *Bacchae*, is that Zeus was Dionysus' second mother as well as being his father.

[72]Compare with this the closing lines of the second book of Ovid's *Metamorphoses*.

[73]Greeks and Romans normally used the name Africa to denote a specific part of the continent, in the area around the present Tunisia and Algeria. This includes the Phoenician colonies such as Carthage. When ancients wanted to indicate the whole African continent, they called it "Libya."

[74]See Ovid, *Met*. III.

[75]The name *Boeotia* means "Cow Country."

womb Liber was born. Mercury snatched him from the fire and gave him to Nysus to be reared. In Greek he is called Dionysus.

CLXXX. ACTAEON

Actaeon, son of Aristaeus and Autonoe, a shepherd, saw Diana bathing and desired to ravish her. Angry at this, Diana made horns grow on his head, and he was devoured by his own hounds.[76]

CLXXXI. DIANA

When Diana, wearied from constant hunting in the thickly shadowed valley of Gargaphia, in the summertime was bathing in the stream called Parthenius,[77] Actaeon, son of Aristaeus and Autonoe, grandson of Cadmus, sought the same place for cooling himself and the dogs which he had exercised in chasing wild beasts. He caught sight of the goddess, and to keep him from telling it, she changed him into a stag. As a stag, then, he was mangled by his own hounds.[78]

---

[76]This version of the story is, as it stands, a pale doublet of the next story. The only essential difference is that of Actaeon's intentions towards Diana/Artemis: compare Diodorus Siculus, IV.81.4-5.

[77]In Greek *parthenios* is an adjective, = "pertaining to the virgin."

[78]A rationalization of this version of the story (familiar from Callimachus, *Hymn* V.107-118; Ovid, Met.III.138-252; Nonnos Dionysiaca V.287-336) is given by Palaephatus, *On the Incredible* #6. An entirely different version of the story, easier to rationalize, is evident from some early treatments in art and can be detected from allusions in Euripides' *Bacchae*, Scene 2.

PART 3

Topics with extended selections from Primary Sources

Katabasis
with Homeric Hymn II, *to Demeter*

PART 1: WHAT IS A KATABASIS?

The word καταβασις is an ancient Greek term. *Κατά* in this context means "down," while *βάσις* is a noun derived from a verb meaning "to go." It can mean any kind of downhill voyage but in mythology it specifically refers to a journey to the underworld. By now you have probably realized that such stories are widespread throughout the world, but they can have many uses and applications that often overlap.

For our purposes we can consider two different ways in each of which a katabasis can be divided in terms of its meanings and applications.

1. THE NARRATIVE TYPE VERSUS THE RITUAL TYPE

Narrative: As the term suggests, a narrative katabasis takes the form of a story in which a character goes into an "underworld" kind of situation, either literally or figuratively. Epic poets such as Homer, Vergil, and Dante have created literary milestones in this genre. Recent fiction authors have exploited the theme to great effect, notably one author in a series of adventures of a student wizard, in which each volume includes at least one such episode.

The **ritual katabasis** is something performed by an actual person in a real place, in real time. It might involve going down a hole, into a cave, or to any place associated with death or the afterlife. Such rituals were extremely widespread among ancient and polytheistic religions but are not practiced very much in most organized religions today.

2. THE CHTHONIC VERSUS THE INITIATORY KATABASIS

The word chthonic is derived from the Greek χθῶν meaning ground, earth, or soil. A **chthonic katabasis** tends to focus on the world of nature, usually offering an explanation for seasonal decay of vegetation that in several months will lead to new growth of crops.

An **initiatory katabasis** illustrates the human individual, very often in the context of a quest, going to an intimidating underworld-like place either to learn something or to pass a test.

The *Homeric Hymn to Demeter* given below is an ancient poem that manages to achieve all four of the above goals at the same time without any apparent contradiction. It includes the story of Persephone's abduction, her mother's quest and the girl's return, but there is an important central section that portrays Demeter pausing on her search, in the little town of Eleusis. That episode was regarded by ancient Athenians as an etiology for the **Eleusinian Mysteries**, which were held twice a year. The Greater Mysteries were celebrated in the autumn, being "greater" because more time was spent at the celebration. The event was a kind of harvest thanksgiving (most of the intense farm-work was now done) but coupled with the fearful aspect of the girl's abduction by Hades. The Minor Mysteries were held in spring, a more obviously happy time, but were kept shorter because of the urgent need to prepare the fields for new crops. This was the **ritual** dimension of the hymn.

The hymn's **chthonic** function is obvious when we consider the identities of the characters involved. The hymn's **initiatory** dimension is seen when we remember that the girl was still regarded as a child, playing in the fields, at the beginning of the story. Her name at this point should be *Korê*, which simply means "Girl." It is only when she is in the underworld that she should really be Περσεφόνεια, as Homer calls her (*Odyssey* XI 635 and at several points late in the Hymn). Πέρσις (*persis*) means "destruction" and φόνος (*phonos*, (both o's pronounced short) means "murder". Both elements strongly indicate her gloomy side.

Other instances of initiatory katabasis

Homer: *Odyssey* XI

Odysseus' famous visit to the Underworld occurs in book XI, very close to the center of the *Odyssey*. The hero hears not just one but three pieces of prophecy from Teiresias (the explicit purpose of the visit) but, after much suspense, there is a crucial encounter with the ghost of Agamemnon. The dead king's advice draws attention to a key polarization between Odysseus and his late leader (noticeable in the *Iliad* as well as the *Odyssey*). This is the point at which the hero becomes aware that he must be sure to avoid Agamemnon's pitfalls. Over two millennia after Homer, Charles Dickens made similar use of Jacob Marley.

Vergil: *Aeneid* VI

Again at the central point of an epic, Vergil put his hero Aeneas into an underworld scenario closely modeled on *Odyssey* XI, but in place of a ritual at a blood-trench one needs a magic key (the famous Golden Bough) to enter the Underworld. This time the entrance is in western Italy, just a few miles outside Naples and the katabasis vision includes ghosts of famous Romans not yet born, a clever piece of prophecy after the event.

Hávamál

This Norse poem survives in a collection now called the Poetic Edda. The collection consists of assorted poems from between the ninth and twelfth centuries AD. The title *Hávamál* means the *Sayings of the High One* (a reference to Oðin). Verses 138–164 (end of the poem) recount Oðin's ritual suicide hanging from the great ash-tree Yggdrasill in order to take the secrets of runic spells from the underworld. According to the poem Oðin hung on the tree for nine days and nights, returning with eighteen spells. Complex multiples of three are very prominent and a modern reading of the poem reminds us of the ancient similarity between the two meanings (as a noun and as a verb) that we attach to the word "spell." Oðin is being initiated into his role as a god of sympathetic magic, while the tree becomes symbolically his steed as he rides it to Hell.

For more on the Eddic poems and Norse mythological sources see below, Chapter 28.

PART 2: HOMERIC HYMN II, *TO DEMETER*

📖 *This is one of the longest of the so-called **Homeric Hymns**. These are poems in honor of individual Greek deities, believed in ancient times to have been composed by Homer. This particular hymn is now thought to have been composed in the 6th century B.C. for use as a kind of "Catechism" for candidates who wished to be initiated into the Eleusinian Mysteries, held every year in Eleusis (modern Elevsini), a small agricultural town 14 miles from Athens. As a hymn of praise, the poem emphasizes Demeter's role as the Great Mother and Persephone's as the Divine Child. Here the girl is simply Kore, rather than Queen of the Underworld, the ominous background figure in* Odyssey *XI lines 47 and 635.*

Here begins my song of fair-haired Demeter, revered goddess. My song is of herself and of her long-ankled daughter, whom Hades snatched away (but heavily-thundering Zeus, who sees from afar, gave him permission) from golden-sworded Demeter, renowned for fruits. The girl was playing with the deep-bosomed daughters of Oceanus, and picking flowers trough the soft meadow: roses, and crocus, and beauteous violets, iris, and hyacinths, and narcissus, which Earth, upon Zeus' orders, brought forth as a trap to the virgin, favouring the Great Taker, wondrously flourishing, a marvel for all to see, both immortal gods and mortal men. And from its root a hundred heads sprang forth, and the sweetest smell poured out. The whole wide heaven above and the whole earth laughed; so too did the salty wave of the sea. But she, astonished, stretched out both her hands to seize the pretty plaything. The wide-wayed earth gaped in the Nysian plain, where the many-receiving king, the many-named son of Cronus, leaped forth with his immortal steeds. He snatched her away, unwilling though she was, in his golden chariot! He led her away weeping. She shrieked aloud, calling upon her supreme and excellent father, the son of Cronus. But no one of the immortals, nor any mortal person, heard her voice. Not even the olives with their rich fruit, only the daughter of Perses, mild in spirit, light-veiled Hecate, heard her from her cave, and king Helios, the glorious son of Hyperion, [heard] the girl calling on her father, Cronus' son. He, in fact, was sitting apart, away from the gods, in his well-built temple, receiving beauteous offerings from mortal men.

30. But her father's brother, the Great Taker, who rules over many, the many-named son of Cronus, bore her away against her will with his immortal steeds. Now as long as the goddess beheld the earth and the starry heaven, and the much-flowing fishy sea, and the rays of the sun, and still hoped to behold her careful mother, and the tribes of the gods who are forever, so long did hope soften her mighty mind, even in her grief. But the heights of the mountains and the depths of the sea resounded with her immortal voice, and her revered mother heard her.

40. Quickly grief seized [Demeter's] mind, and with her hands she tore the veil above her ambrosial locks, and cast the dark-blue robe from both her shoulders. She rushed, like a bird, over dry land and water, seeking her. None of the gods or mortal men was willing to tell her the truth, nor did any one of the birds [of omen] come to her as a true messenger. Then for nine days did hallowed Demeter wander over the earth carrying blazing torches in her hands. Grieving, she did not taste ambrosia or sweet-drinking nectar, nor did she wash her form in the bath. But when the tenth shining day dawned, Hecate met her, bearing a light in her hands, and bringing news, spoke to and addressed her:

"Revered Demeter, bearer of seasons, giver of glorious things, who of the heavenly gods or mortal men has snatched away Persephone, causing grief to your dear mind? For I heard her voice, but I didn't see with my eyes who it was."

59. Thus spoke Hecate, but the daughter of fair-haired Rhea gave her no answer in words. Quickly she sped forth with her, bearing lighted torches in her hands. They went to the Sun, the surveyor both of men and gods, stood in front of his steeds, and the divine one of goddesses asked [him]:

64. "O Sun, have pity on me as a goddess, if ever either by word or deed I have gratified your heart and mind. My daughter whom I bore, a sweet blossom, beauteous in form— I have heard her frequent cries through the unfruitful air, as though she were being forced away, but I have not seen her with my eyes. You, from the divine Aether, look down with your rays upon all the earth and sea. Tell me truly, dear son, if you have anywhere seen the man, whether a god or mortal, who without my consent has seized her by force and carried her off."

74. So she spoke, but the son of Hyperion answered her in words:

"Daughter of fair-haired Rhea, queen Demeter, you shall know; for I indeed grieve for you and pity you much, sorrowing for your slender-ankled daughter. But no other of the immortals is guilty, except only cloud-gathering Zeus, who has given her to his own brother Hades, to be called his wife in her bloom. And he, having snatched her away with his steeds, has led her, loudly shrieking, beneath the murky darkness. But come, O goddess, cease your great wrath. It in no wise suits you vainly to entertain boundless wrath. Pluto who rules over many, is by no means an unseemly kinsman [to have] among the immortals, your own brother and of the same seed. He has also obtained a prerogative, when division was first made threefold by lot; he dwells among those of whom he is appointed master by lot."

88. Thus having spoken, he cheered on his steeds, and they, at his exhortation, swiftly bore along the swift chariot, like wing-stretching birds. But upon her mind a more sad and ruder grief fell, and then, enraged at the dark-clouded son of Cronus, leaving the council of the gods and mighty Olympus, she went to the cities and rich fields of men, disguising her form for a long time. Not one of the men or deep-bosomed women, on seeing her, recognized her, before she came to the dwelling of prudent Celeus, who was at that time the ruler[1] of sweet-scented Eleusis. And she sat near the roadside, saddened at heart, by the Parthenian[2] well, whence the citizens drew their water (in the shade of the olive tree above) like an aged old woman, who is shut off both from child-birth, and from the gifts of crown-loving Aphrodite, such as are the nurses of the children of law-administering kings and housekeepers in their echoing dwellings. But the daughters of Eleusinian Celeus perceived her as they were coming for clear-flowing water, that they might bear it in golden pitchers to the beloved dwellings of their father, four [in number], like goddesses, possessing the flower of youth, Callidice, and Cleisidice, and lovely Demo, and Callithoe who was the eldest of them all. But they did not recognize her, for the gods are difficult for mortals to look at. Standing near, they addressed [to her] winged words:

113. "Who on earth are you, old woman? Why have you walked far away from the city, staying away from the dwellings, where there are women of your own age, in the shady homes, like yourself and younger ones too, who may even receive you kindly in word and deed?"

118. So they spoke, but she, hallowed one of goddesses, answered in words: "Dear children, whoever you are, women, hail! I will tell my story to you. It is by no means unfitting to tell the truth to you who ask. My name indeed is Dos,[3] for this my revered mother gave me. But now I have come unwillingly upon the wide back of the sea from Crete[4]. Pirates forced me away against my will. They then landed at Thorikos in their swift ship, where numerous women disembarked upon the mainland, and they themselves prepared supper near the hawsers of the ship. But my mind cared not for the pleasant feast, but I escaped secretly through the dark mainland. I fled from my overbearing masters, so they would not sell me at a profit after I had cost them nothing. Thus have I come here, wandering. I do not know what land this is, and who lives here. But to you, may all the Olympians grant you flourishing husbands, that you may bring forth children, as parents always wish.[5]

* * * * * * * *

[1]The poet is emphasizing that Eleusis, in the time when the narrative is set, was still an independent kingdom. It is unlikely to have been so when the poem was composed, even less so when the poem was put into writing.

[2]The Parthenian Well, or Well of the Virgin, is probably meant to be the one still visible today in the SE corner of the outer court of the complex at Eleusis. See G. Mylonas (*Eleusis*, p.97).

[3]*Dos* means "Gift."

[4]When the speaker describes himself or herself as being originally from Crete, it is often a sign to the audience that the following narrative is a fabrication to give the speaker a false identity. See Odyssey XIV.199. The stereotyping of Cretans as liars was very common in ancient Greece.

[5]There is a gap in the text here, since the surviving manuscripts are damaged.

138. "Take pity on me, ladies, kindly, dear children, until I reach the home of a man and woman, that I may willingly work for them in such thing as are the business of an aged woman. And truly I could nicely nurse a young baby, holding him in my arms. I could take care of the house, and could tidy my employers' bed in the well-built chambers, and could manage the works of a woman."

145. The goddess spoke, but the girl Callidice, most beautiful in form of the daughters of Celeus, answered her immediately:

"O nurse, we mortals must necessarily endure what the gods have allotted to us, even though we grieve, for they indeed are much more powerful [than we are]. But this will I clearly suggest to you, and will name the richer people of the city, those who by their advice and judgments guard the battlements of the city. There is shrewd-counseling Triptolemus, Diocles, and Polyxeines, and blameless Eumolpus, and Dolichus, and our noble father, all whose wives tend their houses; none of these would at first sight despise your appearance, or dismiss you from her dwellings. They will receive you, for truly you are godlike. But if you will stay a while, we will go to our father's home and tell all these matters thoroughly to our deep-bosomed mother Metaneira. Perhaps she will invite you to our home so that you need search no further. A quick son is now being nursed by her in the well-built house, a subject of many prayers and much love. If you could train him up, and he should reach his teenage years, you would certainly have reason to be envied. Such great rewards for your nursing would father give you."

169. So she spoke, but [the goddess] nodded assent. They filled the vessels with water and bore them rejoicing. Quickly they reached the great house of their father, and soon told their mother what they had both seen and heard. But she immediately bade them go and call her with [a promise of] boundless hire. And they, just as deer or heifers gambol through the meadow in the season of spring, having satisfied themselves with food, so they, lifted the folds of their beauteous robes and sped along the wagon-furrowed way. Around their shoulders their curls waved like the crocus flower.

179. On their return they found the renowned goddess, where they had left her near the road. They led her to their father's home. She, sorrowing at heart, followed behind them, with her head veiled as the dark robe shook loosely around her tender feet. They quickly reached the house of Zeus-nurtured Celeus, and went through the portico, where their hallowed mother awaited them by the lintel of the well-built homestead, holding her son, a young off-shoot, at her bosom. But they ran up to her, and she came to the threshold on her feet, and truly she reached the top of the dwellings and filled the doors with divine light. But admiration, and wonder, and pallid fear possessed the lady of the house, and she yielded up her seat, and bade the goddess be seated. But season-bearing Demeter, of glorious gifts, was not willing to be seated on the shining seat, but remained silent, casting down her beauteous eyes, until at length Iambe, remembering her manners, offered her a compact seat, and above it spread a silver-woven fleece. Here, sitting down, she stretched forth her veil [over her face] with her hands, and for a long time sat speechless, grieving, in her seat. Without any word or deed, without a smile, unfed or by food or drink, she sat, wasting away with longing for her deep-bosomed daughter; until well-mannered Iambe used jokes to cheer the holy [goddess] to smile, and to laugh, and to have an appeased mind. This is why, in after-times also she pleased her with humour. Metaneira gave her a cup of sweet wine, having filled it; but she refused it, for, said she, it was not lawful for her to drink the ruby wine.

210. Instead she told her to mix wheat and water with pounded pennyroyal and give it her to drink. The girl, having made the mixture, gave it to the goddess, as she commanded, and all hallowed Demeter, having received it, obtained the sacred honour. But well-dressed Metaneira began conversation:

"Hail! Lady, since I notice that you are not from mean parents, but good ones, since modesty and grace are conspicuous in your appearance, like [a descendant] of law-administering kings. But we humans must necessarily endure the lot given by the gods, even though we grieve; for the yoke lies upon our neck. And now, since you have come here, you shall share whatever is mine. But cherish for me this boy, whom born late, and unhoped-for, the immortals have bestowed [on us]. To me he is a subject of many prayers. If you will train him up and let him reach the measure of youth, with reason will **any** one of womankind, on seeing it, envy you. So great are the gifts I will give you for his nursing."

224. Well-crowned Demeter addressed her in reply: Hail to you too, lady! And may the gods grant you good things. But I will willingly receive your boy, as you command me, to nurture. No charms will ever harm him, nor [deadly] plant, through the carelessness of his nurse. For I know a remedy much more efficacious than wood cutting, and I know an excellent antidote for baleful spells."

Thus having spoken, she received him in her fragrant bosom and immortal hands, and his mother rejoiced in mind. Thus she indeed trained up in the palace Demophoon, the glorious son of prudent Celeus, whom well-girt Metaneira bore. But he grew up like a god, neither eating food nor sucking. But Demeter anointed him with ambrosia, as though sprung from a god, breathing sweetly upon him, and leaving him in her bosom. But at night she concealed him in the might of fire, like a brand, without the knowledge of his dear parents. But they were constantly surprised at the way he flourished, like the gods in person.

And truly she would have rendered him free from old age, and immortal, were it not for this: well-dressed Metaneira, in her folly, watching by night, had looked out from her perfumed chamber, and shrieked, striking both her thighs, fearing for her son. She was greatly disturbed in mind, and bewailing, she addressed winged words:

248. "My child Demophoon, the strange woman is immersing you in a great fire! She causes me groans and grievous sorrows." Thus she spoke, weeping, and the divine one of goddesses heard her.

But fair-crowned Demeter, enraged with her, put down from her hands to the ground the dear son, the one she had borne unexpectedly in the palace, having taken him out of the fire. Angry in her mind, she at once addressed well-dressed Metaneira:

256. "Ignorant and unwise humans, who neither foresee the destiny of coming good nor evil! You, too, by your stupidity, have made a big mistake! May the water of the Styx, binding oath of the gods that yields no forgiveness, bear witness—I would have made your dear son immortal and free from age for all days, and would have afforded him unperishing honour. But now it is not possible for him to escape death and the Fates; but unperishing honour shall always be his, because be has sat upon my knees, and slept in my arms. But when he is of age, as the years roll on, the sons of the Eleusinians will always throughout all days stir up battle and grievous conflict among each other. But I am honoured Demeter, who is the greatest benefit and joy to immortals and mortals. Come, let all the people build for me a great temple, and under it an altar, below the city and the lofty wall, above Callichorus, upon the jutting hill. But I myself will teach my rites, so that hereafter, performing them holily, you may appease my mind."

Having said this, the goddess changed her size and attitude. She put off old age, and beauty was breathed around her, and a pleasant odor was scattered from her scented robes. Far gleamed the light from the immortal flesh of the goddess, and her-yellow curls flourished on her shoulders, and the close dwelling was filled with the brightness of lightning. And she went out from the palace. But immediately the knees [of Metaneira] were relaxed, and for a long time she became speechless, nor did she at all think her of her darling son, to take him up from the ground. But his sisters heard his piteous voice, and they leaped up from their well-spread couches. One then, taking up the boy in her hands, placed him in her bosom, but another kindled the fire, and another ran with her tender feet to raise up her mother from the fragrant chamber. Gathering around him, they washed him, tending him as he still cried, for his mind was not comforted: inferior nurses and attendants now possessed him: They indeed, trembling with fear, kept appeasing the renowned goddess, throughout the night, but together with the dawn appearing they told the truth to Celeus the powerful, just as the goddess, fair-crowned Demeter, had commanded.

296. But he, having summoned the numerous people into council, ordered them to erect a rich temple[6] to fair-haired Demeter, and an altar on the jutting hill. But they immediately obeyed, listened to his words, and built as he commanded. The boy, in the meantime, kept growing by the will of the goddess. But when they had finished, and rested from their toil, they went each one homewards. But yellow-haired Demeter, sitting down here, far apart from all the blessed gods, remained, wasting away with longing for her deep-bosomed daughter. And she rendered that year a most grievous and cruel one for men upon the many-nurturing earth. The earth gave forth no seed, for well-crowned Demeter concealed it. And the steers dragged many bent ploughs over the fields to no purpose, and much white barley fell upon the earth in vain. She indeed would have destroyed the whole race of articulate-voiced men by grievous famine, and would have deprived those possessing the Olympian dwellings of the glorious honour of gifts and sacrifices, had not Zeus noticed it and taken counsel in his mind. And he first sent golden-winged Iris to call fair-haired Demeter, possessing a most lovely appearance. Thus he spoke; but she obeyed dark-clouded Zeus, the son of Saturn, and swiftly ran through the mid way with her feet. And she reached the city of incense-fraught Eleusis, and found dark-robed Demeter in the temple. She addressed her and spoke winged words:

321. "Demeter, your father Zeus, who knows imperishable [counsels], calls you to come to the tribes of the gods who are forever. But come, do not let my message from Zeus be unaccomplished. Thus she spoke; but Demeter's mind was not persuaded.

Again then Zeus sent on all the blessed immortal gods. And they, coming one after another, called her, and gave many beauteous gifts and honours, whatever she wished to choose among the immortals. But no one was able to persuade her mind and inclination, angry in mind as she was. She obstinately rejected their arguments.

"Never," said she, "Will I step upon incense-scented Olympus, nor let forth the fruit of the earth, before I see my fair-faced daughter with my eyes."

334. But when heavy-thundering, far-seeing Zeus heard this, he sent the golden-wanded slayer of Argus down into Erebus, to convince Hades by soft words, to lead away chaste Persephone from the murky darkness to the gods, that her mother might see her and cease from her wrath. But Hermes was not disobedient; he went

---

[6]This introduces the etiology for the Temple of Demeter at Eleusis, one of the main purposes of this hymn.

immediately beneath the earth, having left the dwellings of Olympus. And he found the king at home, sitting on a couch with his chaste spouse, who was grieving much through longing for her mother; but she, on account of the shameful deeds of the gods, devised a plan.[7]

* * * * * * * * * * * * *

346. Then the bold slayer of Argus, standing near, addressed him: "Dark-haired Hades, who rule over the dead, Father Zeus orders you to lead forth noble Persephone from Erebus to their company, that her mother may see her and from her wrath and bitter anger against the immortals. She is planning a dreadful deed, to destroy the weakly tribes of earth-born men, concealing the seed beneath the ground, and wasting away the honours of the immortals. But she cherishes grievous wrath, and does not associate with the gods, but sits afar off inside her incense-scented temple, possessing the rocky city of Eleusis."

357. Thus he spoke, but Aidoneus, king of the dead, smiled from beneath his eyebrows, not disobeying Zeus' command. Immediately he ordered Persephone:

"Go, Persephone, to your dark-robed mother, keeping a mild spirit and disposition in your breast. Do not give way to sadness excessively beyond others: In no way shall I be an unseemly husband among the immortals, being Zeus' own brother. When you come here you will be mistress of all beings, as many as live and walk, and you shall always possess the greatest honours among the immortals. And there will always be judgment upon those who have done injury, who do not appease your power with sacrifices, piously performing them, offering suitable gifts."

370. Thus he spoke, but prudent Persephone rejoiced, and quickly leaped forth in joy. But he had secretly given her the sweet grain of a pomegranate to eat, offering it to her in private, that she might not remain all days above with hallowed Demeter of dark robes. And Pluto, who rules over many, yoked his steeds in front beneath the golden chariot, and she mounted the chariot. Next to her the strong slayer of Argus, seizing the bridles and whip in his hands, drove straight out from Hades' home, and the two of them flew along willingly. And swiftly they passed over the long trail. Neither the sea, nor the water of rivers, not the grassy valleys, nor the heights, restrained the rush of the immortal steeds, but they cut through the deep darkness above them as they went. And he stopped driving them, where well-crowned Demeter stood, before the incense-scented temple. But she, as she saw them, jumped forward, like a maenad on a wood-shaded mountain.

---

[7]Some lines appear to be missing from the text here.

386. But Persephone . . . .

* * * * * *

395. "As for you,[8] you will live with me and your father, the dark-clouded son of Cronus, honoured by all the immortals. But if you ever tasted anything, you will have to go again beneath the hiding-places of the earth and spend a third part of the year there. But the [other] two [thirds] with me and the other immortals. But when the earth flourishes with all kinds of sweet-scented spring flowers, then again you will return from the murky darkness, a mighty marvel to gods and mortal men.

* * * * * *

404. "And by what trick did the Great Taker beguile you?"

Beautiful Persephone answered her in turn:

"I will tell you truly, mother. When kindly Hermes, the messenger, came from the Cronian father and the other gods, then he led me out from Erebus, so that you could see me with your own eyes and cease from your wrath and grievous anger against the immortals. I leaped forth for joy. But [my husband] secretly threw to me the grain of a pomegranate, pleasant to eat, and forced me against my will to taste it. He snatched me away through the cunning device of my father, the son of Cronus and kidnapped me beneath the hiding-places of the earth. How he did this I will speak out, and detail all things, as you ask.

418. "We indeed were all at play in the pleasant meadow: Leucippe, and Phoino, and Electra, Ianthe, Melite, Iacche, Rhaea, Callirrhoe, Melobate, Tyche, and rosy Ocyrrhoe, Chryseis, Ianeira, Acaste, Admeta, Rhodope, and Pluto, lovely Calypso, Styx, Urania, lovely Galaxaure, battle-rousing Pallas, and Artemis who enjoys archery. We were plucking the pleasant flowers with our hands, the beauteous crocus, and the iris, and hyacinth, and the rosebuds, and the lilies, a marvel to behold, and the narcissus, which, like the crocus, the wide earth produced. But I was plucking them with joy, when the earth yawned beneath and out leaped the strong king, the Great Taker. Off he went bearing me beneath the earth in his golden chariot as I grieved much, and I cried aloud with my voice. These things have I told you all truly, although they sadden me."

---

[8]Evidently Demeter is speaking to Persephone. Some of the text is missing here. The beginnings of some lines are legible, but for at least 10 lines there is not enough to make complete sentences.

434. In this way they embraced each other and greatly appeased each other's heart and mind; the mind [of both] was rested from sorrows. And they received and gave delights mutually. But near to them came delicately-veiled Hecate, and much she fondled the chaste daughter of Demeter, because the queen had been her attendant and servant. But to them loud-thundering far-seeing Zeus sent a messenger, fair-haired Rhea, to bring dark-robed Demeter to the tribes of the gods, and he pledged himself to give her honours, whatever she might choose among the immortal gods. And he granted to her that her daughter should pass the third part of the revolving year under the murky darkness, but the two [other parts] with her mother and the other immortals. Thus he spoke, nor did the goddess disobey the message of Zeus, but she quickly sprang forth from the heights of Olympus. She came to the Rarian [plain], which previously had been the life-bearing udder of corn-land, but then no longer affording sustenance: it remained idle and leafless, and concealed the white barley, by the contrivance of fair-ankled Demeter; but it was then destined forthwith to bloom with long ears, as the spring advanced, and the rich furrows to abound in ears, and there to be bound in bundles. Here she first descended from the unfruitful air. But gladly they beheld each other, and rejoiced in mind. Fair-veiled Rhea first addressed her:

460. "Come here, child! Loud-thundering, far-seeing Zeus calls you to come to the tribes of the gods, and he has pledged himself to give you honour, whatever you may choose amongst the immortal gods. And he has consented that your daughter shall pass the third part of the revolving year beneath the murky darkness, but the [other] two with you and the other immortals. But come, child, and obey. Do not be excessively angry against the dark-clouded son of Cronus. Now increase the life-bearing fruit for men."

470. Thus she spoke and Demeter did not disobey; but she straightway sent forth the fruit from the rich-soiled fields. And all the wide earth was weighed down with leaves and flowers. She went to the law-administering kings, Triptolemus, and horse-driving Diocles, the mighty Eumolpus, and Celeus, leader of the people, and showed [them] the performance of her sacred rites, and she appointed her hallowed rites for all, for Triptolemus, and Polyxenius, and moreover, Diocles, which it is in no wise lawful either to neglect, or to inquire into, or mention, for a mighty reverence of the gods restrains the voice. Blest is he of mortal men who has witnessed these, for he who is initiated, and he who does not partake in these rites have by no means the same fortune, even when they are dead, beneath the murky darkness.

483. But when the divine one of goddesses had issued all her instructions, they set out for Olympus, to the assembly of the other gods. And here they live by thunder-rejoicing

Zeus, both venerable and revered. Greatly blessed is he, whomsoever of mortal men, they love with a kindly mind, and straightway they send to the hearth of his noble home Plutus, who affords riches to mortal humans.

490. But come, you who possess the state of incense-breathing Eleusis, and sea-locked Paros, and rocky Antron, hallowed, giver of glorious gifts, bearer of seasons, queen Demeter, yourself, and your supremely beautiful daughter Persephone, willingly grant me a pleasant life for my song. Now I move on to the rest of my song.[9]

---

[9]This English translation of the last line is the suggestion of Gregory Nagy (*Greek Mythology and Poetics*, Cornell 1990, p. 54). The previous translation of the words usually ran, "But I will recall you and another song too." The original purpose of the line, as Nagy points out, was to furnish a prelude or link to another song or poem. Compare the final line of the *Theogony*, which served a similar function explained by my notes.

STUDENT EXERCISES

PART A: THE DEMETER HYMN AND COMPARABLE MYTHS

There is an ancient Mesopotamian myth called *The Descent of Ishtar to the Underworld* in its Akkadian sources. A similar myth in Sumerian sources is usually known as *The Descent of Inanna*. Seasonal etiologies and ritual associations of this myth have been widely discussed and published since modern knowledge of the source-texts became better understood in the 1960s. A good modern translation can be found in *Myths from Mesopotamia*, ed. Stephanie Dalley (*Oxford World Classics*, 1989). An older translation can be found free on the Sacred Texts website, at http://sacred-texts.com/ane/ishtar.htm.

1. What can you learn from comparison of such a text with the "Homeric Hymn to Demeter"?

2. What are the most important differences between Homer's telling of the Persephone myth and the version given by Ovid, in "Metamorphoses" V.332–678?

PART B: HOMER'S *ODYSSEY* X–XI

1. BOOK X

a) Who tells Odysseus to go to the Underworld?

b) Why?

c) Quality of directions: Are they convincing?

2. BOOK XI BEGINNING

a) Topography and landscape: Does it seem like a real place? What are the alternative interpretations?

b) At the entrance: What's the ritual? How is it supposed to work?

3. The Ghosts: Is there any logical order, sequence, or priority to the appearance of the spirits?

4. End of episode: Escape from the Underworld

The ending of Book XI seems abrupt and disorganized. Why?

5. Over the whole episode, who is in charge of the story?

CHAPTER 15

Homeric Hymn IV, *To Hermes* (extract)

📖 *The numbering sequence of the Homeric Hymns is the one assigned by T.W. Allen, in his Oxford Classical Texts edition of Homer's complete works, Vol. 5 (Oxford 1912, reprinted regularly ever since). Some manuscripts bear the title,* **Second Hymn to Hermes** *to distinguish it from a much shorter hymn to the same god (XVIII, consisting of only 12 lines). Scholars since the 19th century, long before the Jungian concept of archetypes was established, have noticed that this story is essentially a complex mass of trickster-adventures. The following extract is only the first quarter of the total poem.*

O Muse, praise Hermes (the son of Zeus and Maia) who rules over Cyllene and Arcadia with its plentiful sheep! Maia the hallowed bride with beautiful hair bore him, the sharp messenger of the immortals, when she lay with Zeus in love. And she avoided the company of the blessed gods, dwelling within a shady cave. That was where the son of Cronus lay with the fair-tressed nymph in the depth of night, unknown to the immortal gods and mortal men. Meanwhile sweet sleep held down white-armed Hera. But when the intention of mighty Zeus was already on the point of fulfillment, and when Maia's tenth month was now fixed in the heaven, she led him into the light. Remarkable deeds were wrought: there she brought forth her cunning son, a smart talker, a thief, a cattle-rustler, a presenter of dreams, a looker-out for night, a gate-keeper, who was quickly about to perform glorious deeds amongst the immortal gods.

17 Born at dawn, he played the lyre at mid-day, in the evening he stole the cows of far-shooting Apollo. He did this on the fourth day of the month on which his mother Maia had given him birth. He too, when he had leaped from the immortal thighs of his mother, did not long remain lying in the sacred basket. No! He indeed leapt forth to seek the cows of Apollo, crossing the threshold of the high-roofed cave. There he found a tortoise and acquired immense wealth. Hermes, you see, was the first to devise the musical tortoise, which caught his attention at the doors of his home, feeding on the well grown grass before the house, walking slowly on its feet. But the sharp son of Zeus noticed it and laughed. He immediately spoke thus:

30 "A great and useful god-send you are for me now, not something I refuse. Hello! Sweet-natured, choir-resounding, companion of the feast, you have appeared at a lucky time! Where did this beautiful plaything come from? You are the patterned-shelled tortoise that lives on the mountains. But I will pick you up and take you to my home; you will be of some use to me! I won't dishonour you, but you will first be of some profit to me. It is better to be at home, since out-of-doors is dangerous. Alive, you will certainly have protection against troublesome attack, but if you die, you will then sing very beautifully."

39 Thus then he spoke, and having taken [it] up in both hands, he promptly went back home carrying the pleasant plaything. Here he deceitfully scooped it out with a knife of grey steel—he extinguished the life of the mountain tortoise! Just as when a swift thought passes through the heart of a man preoccupied by frequent cares, or when flashes are rolled from the eyes, so fast did glorious Hermes devise both word and deed. He cut joints of reed and fixed them into holes he pierced through the back of the stony tortoise shell. And around it by his own skill he stretched the hide of a bull, and fixed in the arms, and upon both he fixed the bridge. Between them he stretched out seven concordant strings of sheep-gut.

52 But when he had formed it, he took up his pleasant plaything; with a plectrum he tried it note by note, and it rang out melodiously beneath his hands. Accompanied by it the god sang beautifully, improvising a song, just as teenage boys at feasts sing skits at each other in turn: [he sang] of Zeus the son of Cronus, and Maia with the beautiful sandals, telling of their old habit of dallying in companionship and love, and of his own birth, making play of his own name. And he celebrated the attendants and the glorious gifts of the bride, even the tripods and durable cauldrons in the house.

62 These, then, were the things of which he sang, but he planned others in his mind. Then he took his hollow lyre and put it down in the sacred cradle. Then, with an appetite for meat, he ran from the sweet-scented house to the mountain, devising a sharp trick in his mind, a trick such as thieves plan at the time of dark night.

68 The sun indeed was setting beneath the earth towards the ocean, with his horses and chariot, but Hermes came running to the shady mountains of Pieria where the immortal cattle of the blessed gods kept to their stalls, pasturing on pure, pleasant meadows. From this flock, then, the watchful son of Maia, the slayer of Argus, cut off fifty loud-lowing heifers, and drove them, wandering, through the sandy country, after turning their footsteps backwards. He did not forget his cunning art, driving them with the fore hooves behind and the back ones in front. He himself walked backwards! He immediately wove some sandals by the sandy sea. He devised an unspeakable and unimaginably marvelous work, stitching together tamarisks and tamarisk-like twigs: he then bound together a small bundle of leafy wood, and [thus] avoided hurting himself by binding the light sandals beneath his feet, leaves and all. The renowned slayer of Argus had plucked them as rough-and-ready equipment for his journey from Pieria.

87 But then an old man, who was tending a flourishing vineyard, noticed him heading for the plain through grassy Onchestus. The son of glorious Maia spoke to him first:

> "Old man, grubbing these stumps with bent shoulders, you'll certainly have a plentiful harvest when all these plants shall bear fruit. But don't look too closely at what you see, and keep quiet about what you hear! No damage is being done to anything of yours."

94 Having said this, he prodded on the cattle (each head was valuable), and glorious Hermes drove them through many shadowy mountains, and echoing ravines, and flowering plains. But gloomy divine night, his ally, had almost passed away, and morning, who wakes people to work, chanced to be arising; but the divine moon, the daughter of king Pallas, son of Megamedes, had just gone into her watchtowers. Then the valiant son of Zeus drove the wide-browed cows of Phoebus Apollo to the river Alpheus.

103 Unimpeded they came into the high-roofed hall, and to the water troughs in front of the beautiful meadow. Here when he had fed the loud-lowing cows well with grass, and had herded them together, he fenced them in as they chewed the lush and dewy rush-grass. Then he collected plenty of wood, and devised a way of [producing] fire: taking a splendid branch of laurel, he pared it down with steel, rubbed it in his hand, and the heat burst upwards. Hermes, you see, was the first to give us fire-implements and fire. And having taken together many dry twigs, he placed them in a heap in a low trench, and the flame shone forth, sending afar the crackling of a strongly burning fire.

115 But while the might of glorious Hephaestus was kindling, he meanwhile drew two lowing heifers with curly horns out of doors, near to the fire, for mighty was his power. He threw them both panting to the ground, on their backs, and he rolled them over and over, bending down, and squeezed out their lives. And he accomplished toil upon toil, cutting their flesh together with the rich fat, and he roasted it after piercing it through with wooden spits, both the flesh and the valuable backs, and the black blood stored within the intestines: these things lay there upon the ground. And he stretched out the skins upon a rough rock. So they stay there even to this day, still cut up as they were left, a long and incalculable time after this. But then rejoicing, Hermes drew off the fat spoils on a smooth, flat stone and cut the meat into twelve parts, divided by lot, and he offered the perfect honour to each [of the twelve gods].

130 Then glorious Hermes longed for the sacrifice of flesh. His appetite made him hungry and weary, even though he was immortal, but not even then did his noble mind give way, as he was to convey [the meal] down his sacred throat! He made a pile of the fat and abundant flesh and he stacked them up as a sign of the recent slaughters. He put the piles over dry firewood and consumed the whole feet and heads in the vapour of fire. But when the gods had accomplished all things rightly, he threw his sandals into eddying Alpheus. Then he spent the whole night quenching the coals, and trampled them to black dust; but beauteous shone the light of the moon. The next morning he went again to the divine heights of Cyllene, at dawn, making sure that no one met him during the long journey, neither of the blessed gods, nor of mortal men, nor did the dogs bark. But Hermes, the tricky son of Zeus, twisted himself up and slipped through the keyhole of the house, just like an autumnal breeze, or a wisp of smoke. He came straight into the rich temple of the cave, stepping onwards on tip-toe, for he made no noise, as if [he were walking] on the earth. And glorious Hermes came hastily to his cradle, having wrapped his swaddling-clothes around his shoulders, like an infant child, playing with the coverlet with his [right] hand on his knees, and holding his beloved lyre in the left.

Name: _____ Date: _____

STUDENT EXERCISES

1. What qualities of Hermes are stressed in the first paragraph of this Hymn?

2. In the paragraph beginning at line 17 we are given Hermes' accomplishments completed on his very first day of existence.

   a. What does baby Hermes accomplish?

   b. What date does the poet give as Hermes' birthday?

3. The poet Hesiod in his *Theogony* (chapter 18, below) introduces us to the goddess Hecate (lines 411–452). Locate these lines and read them. What does Hesiod tell us about the shared features of Hecate and Hermes as deities?

4. Another character discussed in detail by Hesiod is Prometheus. The passage in the *Theogony* covers from lines 507–615 and Prometheus reappears in the *Works and Days* (chapter 19, below) between lines 42 and 105. What do these two passages tell you about the way ancients Greeks regarded Hermes and how he differed from Prometheus in ancient belief?

CHAPTER 16

Greek Creation Myth (from Apollodorus, *Library*)

from The Library of Mythology

*Attributed to Apollodorus of Athens,
translated & annotated by J.G. Farrow*

📖 *The following extract is from a Greek mythological textbook of the first or second century A.D. As it stands, it cannot strictly be considered a primary source, since belief in the ancient gods was beginning to be questioned increasingly by that time (see Chapter 2, Ancient Critics). Apollodorus himself, from what we know otherwise of his work, usually gave rationalized or allegorical explanations with myths. The Library, as we now have it, does not do this, which leads us to suspect that the present author was merely a grammatikos, or schoolmaster, and not the more famous Apollodorus of Athens. Sometimes, however, our author (especially in later sections on hero myths) gives details on source-criticism.*

The creation myth as it is given below bears only a superficial resemblance to the one in Hesiod's Theogony. Many details are different, as a careful reading will show. Many modern scholars think the following version is based on a prose summary of an anonymous "Cyclic" Theogony, originally conceived as a poem in the days of Homer and Hesiod, but changed and re-edited to fit a larger-scale composition during the following centuries; eventually it was reduced to the prose summary we have before us now.

I.

1. Uranus was the first ruler over the whole universe. He married Gê and begat, as his first children, the so-called Hecatoncheires:[1] Briareus, Gyes, and Cottus. They were unsurpassed in size and power, having a hundred hands and fifty heads each.

2. After this Gê bore to Uranus the Cyclopes: Arges, Steropes, and Brontes, each of whom had a single eye in his forehead. But Uranus tied them up and threw them into Tartarus. It is a gloomy[2] place in Hades' realm, as far distant from Earth as Earth is from the Sky.

3. He then had some more children by Gê, the so-called Titans: Oceanus, Coeus, Hyperion, Crius, Iapetus, and the youngest of them all Cronus. He also had daughters, the so-called Titanesses: Tethys, Rhea, Themis, Mnemosyne, Phoebe, Dione, and Theia.

4. When Gê was upset at the loss of her children who had been thrown into Tartarus, she persuaded the Titans to turn against their father, and she gave an adamantine sickle to Cronus. All of them except Oceanus attacked him. Cronus cut off his father's genitals and threw them into the sea. From the drops of blood that flowed from them were born the Erinyes (Furies) Alecto, Tisiphone, and Megaera. They cast their father from his position of power, brought up from below their brothers who had earlier been imprisoned, and handed over control to Cronus.

5. But he bound them all over again and cast them down into Tartarus. After he married his sister Rhea, and because Gê and Uranus kept foretelling him that he would be expelled from his rule by his own son, he began to swallow his own offspring. He swallowed his firstborn child Hestia, then Demeter and Hera, and after them Pluto[3] and Poseidon.

6. Rhea grew angry at this treatment and went to Crete when she was pregnant with Zeus. She gave birth to Zeus in a cave in Mount Dicte.[4] She gave him to the Curetes and to the nymphs Adrasteia and Ida, the daughters of Melisseus, to be raised.

---

[1]*Hekaton* = a hundred, *cheir* = hand/arm. Compare Hesiod, *Theog.* 147f. The spelling "Gyes" is also used in some manuscripts of Hesiod where modern critical texts read Gyges.

[2]The word for "gloomy" is *erebódes*, meaning "Looking like Erebus." See Hesiod *Theog.* 123-5.

[3]*Pluto* means "the rich man." This god's alternate name Hades, originally *a-widês*, means "invisible."

[4]Hesiod calls the mountain *Aigaion* (Latinized into *Aegeum*), or "goat-mountain." Diodorus of Sicily variously uses Dicte or Ida as the name of the mountain where Zeus grew up in a cave.

7. These nymphs nursedz the child with the milk of Amalthea,[5] while the armed Curetes[6] guarded the child in the cave, banging their spears on their shields so that Cronus should not hear the baby's voice. But Rhea wrapped a stone in baby clothes and gave it to Cronus to swallow, as if it were the newborn child.

II.

1. When Zeus was fully grown he took Metis the daughter of Oceanus as his accomplice. She gave Cronus a drug to drink: he was forced by it to vomit up first the stone, then the children whom he had swallowed. Along with these children Zeus waged war against Cronus and the Titans. When the war went on for ten years Gê prophesied victory to Zeus if he should have as his allies those who had been thrown down into Tartarus. Zeus then killed Campe (who was guarding their jail) and freed them. And the Cyclopes at that time gave thunder, lightning, and the thunderbolt to Zeus, the helmet to Pluto, and the trident to Poseidon. These three gods, armed with these weapons, overthrew the Titans, cast them down into Tartarus, and put the Hecatoncheires there as guards. The (three) gods then cast lots for rule. Zeus drew power in the sky, Poseidon power in the sea, and Pluto power in Hades' place.

2. These were the offspring of the Titans: the children of Oceanus and Tethys were the Oceanides, that is, Asia, Styx, Electra, Doris (Eurynome), Amphitrite, Metis. The children of Coeus and Phoebe were Asteria and Leto. The children of Hyperion and Theia were Eos, Helios, and Selene. The children of Crius and Eurybia (the daughter of Pontus) were Astraeus, Pallas, and Perses.

3. The children of Iapetus and Asia were Atlas (who holds the sky on his shoulders), Prometheus, Epimetheus, and Menoetius (whom Zeus hit with a thunderbolt and threw into Tartarus in the Titan War).

4. The son of Cronus and Philyra was Chiron (a Centaur of two species). The children of Eos and Astraeus were the Winds and the Stars. Hecate was the daughter

---

[5]Amalthea was traditionally a female goat. For more on this myth, see Hyginus, *Fab.* CXXXIX.

[6]The word *Curetes* is probably derived from *kouros* = "boy." In real life amongst Dorian Greeks the Curetes were army cadets; there was a famous Dance of the Curetes, a kind of endurance test performed in full military gear, described by Lucian in his essay *On the Dance.*

of Perses and Asteria. The children of Pallas and Styx were Nike, Cratus, Zelus, and Bia.

5. As for the water of Styx, which flows from a rock in Hades' place, Zeus made it the oath of the gods, giving it this honor because Styx, along with her children, had been his allies against the Titans.

6. The children of Pontus and Gê were Phorcus, Thaumas, Nereus, Eurybia, and Ceto. The children of Thaumas and Electra were Iris and the Harpies Aello and Ocypete. The children of Phorcus and Ceto were the Phorcides and the Gorgons (whom we shall describe when we speak below about Perseus).

7. The children of Nereus and Doris were the Nereids, whose names were Cymothoe. . . .Amphitrite, Eunice, Thetis, ... Galatea, ... Calypso, ... Dione, ... Ceto, and Limnoreia.

III.

1. Zeus married Hera and begat Hebe, Eileithyia, and Ares. But he also had affairs with many women, both mortal and immortal. By Themis, the daughter of Uranus, he had as daughters the Horae (Eirene, Eunomia, and Dike) and the Fates (Clotho, Lachesis, and Atropos). By Dione he begat Aphrodite. By Eurynome, the daughter of Oceanus, he begat the Graces (Aglaea, Euphrosyne, and Thaleia). By Styx he begat Persephone. By Mnemosyne (Memory) he begat the Muses: first Calliope, then Clio, Melpomene, Euterpe, Erato, Terpsichore, Urania, Thaleia, and Polymnia.

2. Calliope and Oeagrus (or, as the myth goes, Apollo[7]) had a son Linus,[8] whom Hercules killed. They had another son, Orpheus, who played and sang to the lyre: with his singing he moved rocks and trees. When this man's wife Eurydice died (bitten by a snake), he went down to Hades with the intention of bringing her back up and persuaded Pluto to send her up. The latter promised to do this on condition that Orpheus did not turn back on his way until

---

[7]This is rather vague; Apollodorus is probably summarizing the work of an earlier mythographer of the 5th century B.C. who, in turn, was compiling information from "cyclic" poems (see introduction). He is giving the account from a written source (probably rationalized—Oeagrus was a kind of early folk-hero) and comparing it with a version more popular in his own time.

[8]Linus was a famous musician. His death at the hands of Hercules was traditionally the first instance of the latter's destructive madness, sent upon him by Hera.

he reached his own house. But he disobeyed and turned around to look at his wife and she went back down. Orpheus also invented the Mysteries of Dionysus. He is buried in Pieria,[9] where he was torn to pieces by the Maenads.

---

[9]Pieria is in Northern Greece, near Mount Olympus.

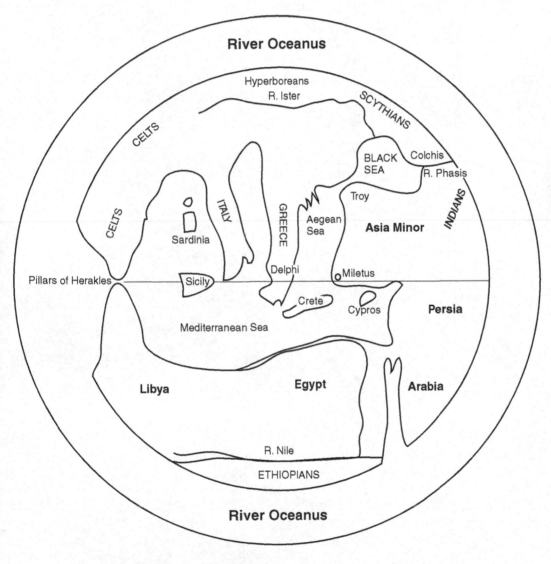

Map of the World, as it might be understood by Greeks of the fifth century B.C., such as Sophocles, Euripides, or Socrates

CHAPTER 17

Early Greek Creation Myths

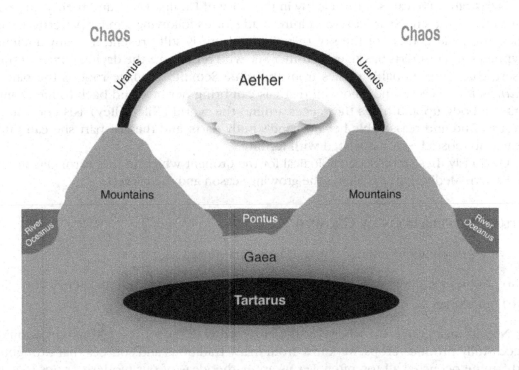

The single most popular type of Creation Myth current in classical Greece was the type we call **The Sacred Marriage of Earth and Sky**. This type of creation myth recurs frequently in animistic and polytheistic cultures throughout the world. Instances of the "Sacred Marriage" creation story occur in sources as far apart as the ancient Near East and in Native American myths.

This type of myth follows its own pattern, a sex-act between the two most primeval gods, Earth and Sky. In most instances throughout the world, Sky is male and Earth female (still referred to as "Mother Earth").

The single most notable exceptions are to be found in Egypt, where a male earth-god (Geb) mates with a sky-goddess (Nut). Osiris and Isis may also be considered an instance of the same union. The etiology is quite obvious: the mating

171

of the two is etiological for the planting and growing seasons. In most parts of the world crops grow after it rains. In Egypt rain is seldom seen at all, so the soil of the Nile valley is fertilized after the flooding of the river (fluid of fertility rises upward from below).

A VIOLENT SEQUEL

The "Sacred Marriage" story is often followed by a brutal act of violence: the male partner is castrated. We can see this clearly in the story of Uranus, Gaea, and their youngest son Cronus. Ancient Near Eastern cultures had stories following similar patterns. Even when the male god is not the sky, this violent motif is still present. In many ancient Egyptian sources Osiris has an evil brother Set, who represents the drying power of the desert. His name probably comes from the same Semitic language root as the name *Satan*. Set kills Osiris and, knowing that Isis can bring her husband back to life again, cuts the body up and hides the pieces around the world (Nile valley). Isis goes on a quest to find and reassemble her husband's body parts, and the last part she can find is the one most closely associated with fertility.

Obviously these motifs are etiological for the drought which, in the warm climate of the Eastern Mediterranean, follows the growing season and the harvest.

RITUAL CELEBRATIONS OF GROWTH

The views of creation outlined above clearly served two purposes:

(a) a one-time-fits-all explanation of how our universe came into existence and

(b) an explanation for the seasons.

Not all springtimes (or whenever the crops grew in the local environment) would successfully produce crops. We know from many traditions and sources that droughts and famine occurred all too often. Let us apply the ideas of our modern critics to see what sense we can make of the Greek creation myth, both in Hesiod and in Apollodorus.

1. Nature etiology (especially studied in the time of Max Müller and his followers): both the explanations listed as (a) and (b) above were valid for the seasonal growth phenomena and would also explain why the ancients took the castration myth so seriously as a sequel.

2. Ritual etiology (suggested by William Robertson Smith and developed by several of his followers, known to the outside world as the "Cambridge Ritualists"):

According to these scholars the "sacred marriage" would have been enacted in the form of processions in the fields, carrying of effigies representing fertility gods, and sometimes even a sex-act between the representatives of the two main deities involved. In Greece we do not know how the marriage of Gaea and Uranus would have been celebrated in any particular region because their respective cults had become almost obsolete by the Classical period when the sources were put into writing. In the case of Cronus, Rhea, and baby Zeus it is clear (especially from Apollodorus' account) that the enactment was a kind of New Year's ritual connected with the ceremonial "birth" of a new sacral king. Questions set below will help the student to see this. In ancient Mesopotamia (Iraq) the epic *Enuma Elish* ("When on high . . .") seems to have been recited at the New Year's festival.

3. Psychoanalytical interpretations: for Freud's views, see above (Chapter 1, definition 12).

IDENTITY OF APHRODITE

In ancient Phoenician belief (Phoenicia corresponds roughly to modern Lebanon and nearby parts of Syria) the sex-goddess Ashtaroth, or Astarte as she was often called in Hellenistic Greek, seems to have been born in a similar way to Hesiod's account of *Aphrodite's birth.* For Herodotus' observations on this, see chapter 18, footnote 18, below. Clearly this *Aphrodite Ourania* (Aphrodite from the sky) spread in Greek belief alongside the Phoenician copper trade, since Homer acknowledges the Eastern influence by having Aphrodite married to Hephaestus (an otherwise unlikely choice) making her relationship with Ares extra-marital and a source of comic relief.

In the *Iliad* (V.166-359) Homer presents a version of Aphrodite in which her mother is Dione. Aphrodite is thus a "junior" Olympian, probably reflecting an older belief from the Greek mainland. It has been well recognized since the time of Max Müller that Zeus' name in the late Bronze Age would have been pronounced "Di-waus" and that "Di-Wône," the female counterpart form, makes her "Zeus-ess."

---

2 translations of this ancient document are available online:
Links
http://www.etana.org/node/581
and
http://www.sacred-texts.com/ane/stc/index.htm

Homer, then, keeps the early name for Aphrodite's mother while making her marriage a concession to the imported Phoenician version. Hesiod's observation of the more indigenously Greek Aphrodite is to keep her married to Ares. Cyprus and Cythera are still her alternate birthplaces in both sources: both islands were extremely important to the Phoenician copper trade, especially during the early iron age. Both their names begin with the same pair of letters: the cy- in English (via Latin) was Ku- or Ky- in classical Greek but in the earliest alphabetic Greek (adapted from Phoenician script) it was ϙ or in Latin / English QU. The letter koppa (ϙ) fell out of use for spelling purposes in classical Greek but survived as a numeral sign and for certain branding purposes. In the modern world it still represents the female gender. In Latin, on the other hand, it survived in the Q form. In Latin the word *cyprium* is the ancestor of our word "copper."

Name: _____ Date: _____

Using the resources given, answer the following questions.

1. In the opening verses of the *Theogony*, lines 1-22, Hesiod includes a list of gods and goddesses whom he obviously considers important. One of these is the goddess Dione. Find out what you can about Dione from other mythological references. Which online sources do you find most helpful?

2. How many instances of "Sacred Marriage of Earth and Sky" can you identify in Hesiod's *Theogony* (Chapter 18, below)?

3. Read Freud's statements, given in the **Definitions** section of chapter 1, above, outlining why Freud believed that tensions between parent and child of the same sex are so common. Do you think that these views are still valid in terms of modern science as an explanation for the antiquity of rules against incest? Give your reasons for or against Freud's arguments.

4. List the number of phrases used by Hesiod that would, at first glance, support Freud's arguments.

5. **a)** How might a ritualist explain the castration story as Hesiod (*Theog.* 154-187) gives it?

   b) Find out what is meant by the term *apotropaic gesture*. Do you see any reference to one in this part of Hesiod?

6. **a)** Use footnote 18 to Hesiod (at *Theog.* Lines 192-3) to reconstruct the reason why Aphrodite had two "birthplaces." Remember that the Phoenicians had been active in the Eastern Mediterranean long before Hesiod's time and, probably during his lifetime, were responsible for bringing alphabetic writing to Greece.

   b) What was the commodity which the Phoenicians had originally been looking for in Cyprus? (Clue: the commodity had the same name as the island.) What was its symbol in alchemy? What does that symbol usually mean now?

7. Compare Apollodorus' account of Zeus' birth (I.1.6-7) carefully with the one given by Hesiod (*Theog.* 453-506). What are the main differences?

8. In almost all ancient sources Crete was Zeus' birthplace. During the middle bronze age this island and the surrounding area were dominated by people we can only call "the Minoans." This is by reference to their mythical king Minos. Unfortunately we do not know the language of these Bronze-age people, even though we have some examples of their writing. One theory is that *Minos* was the title for the local sacral king. Starting in the 16th or 15th centuries B.C. Crete was taken over by Greek warlords, possibly from Mycenae. The local ritual for the regular (either annual or every four years) "rebirth" of the sacral king did not lose its popularity, but it would have to have been renamed to keep its relevance to the new government and language. In the 10th century B.C. the Dorian Greeks took over large areas of the island. How does Apollodorus help us to see how each successive wave of cultural change shaped the "mainstream" nativity story he gives us?

9. If Apollodorus represents the "mainstream" nativity story of Zeus, why does Hesiod go off on a tangent immediately following the trick with the stone? (**Clues**: To see the tangent, check your answer to question 5. Also, check the map of Greece and the photo given below.)

A conical stone found by French archaeologists during a 19th century excavation at Delphi, just below the Manteion (main oracle building). Its shape may be based of that of the holy stone described by Hesiod (*Theogony* 497-500).

CHAPTER 18

Hesiod's *Theogony*

Translated and edited by C.S. Mayes and J.G. Farrow

Composed, according to ancient belief, in Ascra (a village in the Greek state of Boeotia) around 700 or 650 B.C. Hesiod, according both to this poem and to his **Works and Days,** *was a farmer.*

Let us start singing with the Heliconian Muses, who live on the great and very holy mountain of Helicon, and dance with light feet around the violet spring[1] and the altar of the mighty son of Cronus.[2] They bathe their smooth skin in the Permessus or the spring of Hippus[3] or very holy Olmeius, and commence their beautiful dances on highest Helicon with nimble feet. They start from there, hidden in dense mist, and go forward in the night, singing out beautifully, to hymn aegis-bearing Zeus and Hera the Lady of Argos who wears golden sandals. They also hymn Phoebus

---

[1]The ancient Greek tradition of round-dances, performed by groups of women around wells and natural springs, has survived into surprisingly modern times. It may have originated in antiquity as a form of sympathetic magic to prompt the flowing (movement) of the water.

[2]The modern name for Mt. Helicon is Zagara. On its summit, and now surrounded by fir trees, is the remaining shell of the Greek Orthodox chapel of St. Elias. This Saint (= the Old Testament prophet Elijah) was commonly named, because of his association with the sky, as the dedicatee of shrines previously consecrated to Zeus. See Sir James Frazer's commentary on Pausanias IX (Boeotia) 31.3.

[3]In Greek, the noun *hippos* means "horse." Natural springs were often associated in ancient Greece with the god Poseidon. He was also, in turn, associated with bulls and horses (earth-shaking animals). It was very common for stories of a supernaturally strong horse kicking the ground and puncturing it to be used as etiological myths for natural springs in a hillside.

Apollo and Artemis who showers arrows, Poseidon who upholds and shakes the earth, and august Themis, Aphrodite with her fluttering eyes, golden-crowned Hebe, beautiful Dione,[4] and Eos, great Helios and bright Selene; Leto, Iapetus, and crafty Cronus; Gaea and great Oceanus; black Nyx and the rest of the holy race of immortals who live forever.

22 The Olympian Muses, daughters of aegis-bearing Zeus, once taught Hesiod the art of beautiful singing while he was tending his sheep in the shadow of very holy Helicon. The goddesses first made this speech to me: "Field-dwelling shepherds, lowly disgraces to your name, nothing but bellies, we know how to tell many lies resembling truth; and when we wish, we know how to sing the truth."

29 So spoke the glib daughters of great Zeus, and plucked a striking branch from the lush bay tree and gave it to me as a staff. Then they breathed inspired speech into me, that I might tell of the future and of the past, and they ordered me to hymn the great ones who live forever, and always to sing of the Muses themselves first and last. So what am I waiting for?

36 Come on, let us start with the Muses, who sing for father Zeus and delight his great mind within Olympus, telling in harmony of the present, the future, and the past.

42 Sending forth their immortal voice, the Muses sing first of the distinguished race of the gods whom Gaea and wide-ranging Uranus were bringing forth from the beginning, and of those gods who, in turn, were born of them. Second, they hymn Zeus, father of gods and of humans, both at the beginning and at the end of their song, telling how far he excels the rest of the gods in greatness and in strength. Finally the Muses sing of the race of men and of the mighty Giants, delighting the mind of Zeus on Olympus.

53 Memory, who reigns over the hills of Eleuther, bore them (the Muses) in Pieria to the Father, Cronus' son, as a means of forgetting ills and resting from sorrow. Zeus lay with her for nine nights, entering her holy bed away from the immortals. And when a year had passed and the days were accomplished, she bore nine daughters, all of one mind,[5] whose carefree hearts are set on song, not far from the highest peak of snowy

---

[4]Dione is mentioned by Hesiod here the *Theogony* without any indication of who she is or why she is important. In Homer's *Iliad* she is Aphrodite's mother (A's father in the Homeric version is Zeus). Since Hesiod prefers an entirely different version of Aphrodite's origin (188–206), it is obvious why he never explains Dione.

Olympus. There they have their splendid dance-sites and lovely house; beside them live the Graces and Desire amongst festivities. They dance and sing with lovely voice, telling of the customs and cares of all the immortals.

75 So the Muses who inhabit the Olympian house were singing thus, the nine daughters born of great Zeus: Clio, Euterpe, Thalia, Melpomene, Terpsichore, Erato, Polymnia, Urania, and Calliope. The last is the most excellent of all, for she attends both kings and dignitaries. When the daughters of great Zeus look favorably at birth on a Zeus-cherished king[6] and honor him, upon this man's tongue they pour sweet dew; gentle words flow from his mouth. All the people watch him faithfully rendering justice; he, speaking confidently, stops a fierce quarrel quickly and skillfully. For kings must be sensible for this reason; that with gentle encouragement they may easily render justice for those wronged in the marketplace. The people greet such a king with quiet respect when he enters the assembly, as if he were a god, and he stands out amongst those gathered. This is the nature of the Muses' holy gift to men.

94 The earth gets her singers and cithara-players from the Muses, and her kings from Zeus. Happy is he whom the Muses love: sweet speech flows from his mouth. For if someone is consuming his own heart out in grief at a recent misfortune, and a singer of the Muses' guild begins to hymn the glories of the men of old and the blessed gods of Olympus, he suddenly forgets his cares and remembers nothing of his troubles. The gifts of the goddesses quickly distract him.

104 Greetings, daughters of Zeus! Grant me a lovely song and tell of the holy race of immortals who live forever, who were born of Gé and starry Uranus, of dark Nyx, and the offspring of salty Pontus. Tell how the gods and Earth and Rivers and boundless, swelling Sea and shining Stars and wide Heaven above first came into being. As for the

---

[5]There is no suggestion in Hesiod of demarcation amongst the Muses, as one finds in later literature and art, such as their being allocated individual responsibilities amongst the arts. For Hesiod, all the Muses act together and share responsibility for all the arts.

[6]In Hesiod's time most Greek city-states were ruled by a *basileus*, or hereditary king of a relatively minor, or local type. There were no large empires that might be ruled by an *anax*, of the sort that Agamemnon had been during the Trojan Wars. Some states were moving toward oligarchic systems in which local landowners ruled by assembly, but there was not yet even the beginning of a concept of democracy in our modern sense.

gods who were born from them, givers of good things, tell how they shared wealth among themselves, allotted the prerogatives, and how first they occupied Olympus with its many dells. Tell me these things from the beginning, O Olympian Muses, and tell who came into being first.

116 Truly Chaos[7] was first. Then was[8] broad-breasted Gaea, the firm, eternal foundation for all the immortals who live on Olympus' snowy peak; and murky Tartarus in the heart of the broad earth; and Eros, most attractive of immortal gods, the hypnotist who conquers mind and prudent counsel in the heart of every god and every man.

123 Erebus[9] and black Nyx were born from Chaos; Aether[10] and Hemera[11] in turn from Nyx (who slept with Erebus in love, conceived, and gave birth).

126 Gaea first gave birth to starry Uranus, her mate, to enclose her on all sides so that she could be a firm, eternal foundation for all the blessed gods. Then she bore the Mountains, lovely haunts of the nymph-goddesses who inhabit their wooded slopes. She also bore the cropless, swelling sea, Pontus, without using sweet love.

---

[7]*Chaos* is related to a verb, *cha'ein*, meaning "to lie open." *Chaos* therefore means openness, emptiness, or space. Thus there is no need to account for anyone or anything existing earlier.

[8]There is no separate verb in the Greek original to go with Gaea as its subject. We must therefore assume that the same verb that went with Chaos is repeated. This verb actually means, "became," "came into existence," or "was born." The assumption is that Gaea, Tartarus, and Eros, like Erebus and Nyx in line 123, are also born from Chaos.

[9]*Erebos* is a masculine noun in Greek, *Nux* feminine. The two nouns therefore signify male and female aspects of darkness. Erebus is normally associated with the underworld or with something like the Biblical concept of "outer darkness," whereas *nyx* = night.

[10]*Aither*, in Greek, signified the bright layer of upper air; the bright (or daylight) sky.

[11]*Hemera* = "Day." Note that daylight does not seem to come entirely from the sun, which does not exist yet. Aether, her brother, hung above the earth and illuminated it in a generalized way. Many Greeks of Hesiod's time and afterward understood the sun to rise in response to the daylight, not as its cause.

But then[12] she slept with Uranus and bore deep-whirling Oceanus,[13] Coeus, Crius,[14] Hyperion, and Iapetus; Theia, Rhea, Themis, Memory, gold-crowned Phoebe, and lovely Tethys. Lastly the youngest, crafty Cronus, was born, the most awesome of the children. He hated his virile father.

139 Next she bore the Cyclopes with their overbearing hearts: Brontes,[15] Steropes, and willful Arges, who made thunder for Zeus and gave him the thunderbolt. These were like the gods in other respects, but one single eye lay in their brow. They were given the name "Cyclopes"[16] because one round eye was in the middle of their brow. Strength, might, and stratagem characterized their deeds.

147 Gaea and Uranus had three more children, mighty and unspeakable: arrogant sons Cottus, Briareus, and Gyges. A hundred terrible arms sprung from their shoulders and fifty heads sprouted from their sturdy bodies. Mighty strength was in their huge form.

154 All the awe-inspiring children of Gaea and Uranus were hated by their father from the start. He hid them all away in the depths of Gaea as soon as each was born and would not let them see the light of day. Uranus was pleased with his wicked deed but huge Gaea, cramped for room, groaned within and planned a wicked trick. She quickly

---

[12]Hesiod seems to have made a break in sequence here; I have indicated it by beginning a new paragraph. He probably means to include all the gods down to, and including, Pontus (= the salt sea) in a first generation, whereas all those born to Gaea as a result of sex with Uranus constitute the second generation, loosely referred to as Titans.

[13]Oceanus (*Okeanos*) meant, to Homer and Hesiod alike, a river surrounding a more-or-less circular world. The mountains therefore exist to enclose Pontus and form a kind of cosmic salt-bowl. Ancient Greeks did not fully understand the laws of evaporation and condensation, but they certainly knew that sea-water, left in an open dish, dries up to leave salt. See diagrams in chapters 16 & 17.

[14]Some manuscripts spell this name *Kreios*, meaning "mighty"; others spell it *Krios*, meaning "fleece," the skin and wool of a sheep or goat.

[15]*Brontes* = Thunder-man; *Steropes* = Thunderbolt-man; *Arges* = Flashing/Shining.

[16]*Kyklos* = round, *ops* = face/eye. It is perhaps a mistake to envisage Hesiod's Cyclopes in a completely anthropomorphic form. Hesiod casts them in the role of an etiological motif, partly explaining volcanic phenomena and partly, as their names suggest, stormy weather. They become, as he tells us, makers of Zeus' thunder-weapons. The Cyclopes described by Homer in *Odyssey* IX are quite different, being closer to primitive farmers, little advanced beyond the hunter-gatherer stage, living like cavemen. Polyphemus, the most famous of the latter, is introduced as son of Poseidon. Later authors usually associated the Cyclopes, especially those of Homer, with Sicily.

made the gray substance adamant, made from it a great scythe and addressed her children. Though it grieved her own heart, she encouraged them thus:

"My children by an arrogant father, if you can be persuaded, we might repay your father's outrageous conduct. For earlier he made shameful plans."

167 So she spoke, but fear seized them all and none replied. Yet great, crafty Cronus found courage and quickly told his dear mother:

"Mother, I will undertake and accomplish this deed, since I do not respect our ill-named father." So he spoke, and huge Gaea rejoiced greatly in her heart. She hid Cronus and laid an ambush; she put the jagged-toothed sickle in his hands and explained the whole scheme. Great Uranus came, bringing on night, and stretched himself round Gaea, longing for love, fully extended. Then his son put out his left hand from ambush, holding the sickle in his right. Hurriedly he cropped the genitals from his own father and threw them backwards. They did not fly from his hand uselessly, for Gaea received all the splattering drops of blood. When a year was over she gave birth to the strong Furies and the huge Giants, resplendent in armour, holding long spears in their hands, and the nymphs called the Meliae[17] over the boundless earth.

188 As at first he cut off the genitals with the adamant and threw them from the land into the crashing sea, so they drifted upon the deep for a long time. White foam appeared about them from the immortal flesh, and a maiden grew up within it. First she approached very holy Cythera,[18] then from there she came to waterlocked Cyprus. The esteemed, beautiful goddess debarked, and grass grew up around her slender feet. Both gods and men call her Aphrodite, foam-born goddess, and well-crowned Cythereia; the former because she grew up in the foam, but the latter because she

---

[17]The Meliae are the Nymphs, or goddesses, of ash-trees. There was evidently a very ancient superstition that humans were born from ash-trees. In Hesiod (*Works & Days* 145) it is the people of the Age of Bronze who are so born. There is also a rationalization of this Greek myth in Palaephatus 35. Snorri Sturluson (*Prose Edda*) refers to "*Ask and Embla*" (Ash & Elm) as the first parents of humanity, animated by the gods Oðin, Vili, and Vé from driftwood.

[18]There was an ancient shrine of Aphrodite at Cythera. By mentioning the island at this stage in the goddess's hatching-out process, Hesiod may have been paying tribute to an old etiological myth for the shrine. *Aphrodite Ourania* (Aph. from the Sky) is cited as an ancient cult-name for the goddess by Herodotus (I.104-5), who tells us that her oldest shrine was the one at Ascalon in Syria. He adds, "*The Cyprians themselves admit that the one in Cyprus was derived from it. The Phoenicians built one in Cythera: they came from this part of Syria.*" Herodotus is clearly referring to the cult of the Syro-Phoenician fertility goddess Ashtaroth.

stopped at Cythera. They also call her Cyprus-born, because she was "born" on sea-washed Cyprus; and genital-loving, because she came forth from the genitals. Eros attended her and fair Desire accompanied her, first at her birth and then at her going into the family of the gods. She has had this prerogative from the beginning and has obtained this lot among men and the immortal gods: girl talk, smiles, thorough deceits, sweet delight, love, and gentleness.

207 Great Uranus surnamed the children whom he himself fathered *Titans,* a term of reproach. For he said they *strained arrogantly*[19] to do a mighty deed for which they would afterward receive retribution.

211 Nyx gave birth to hateful Doom and black Ker[20] and Thanatos, as well as Hypnos and the whole Dream race. Next dark Nyx, painful goddess, having slept with no one, gave birth to Momus,[21] painful Misery and the Hesperides,[22] who care for the beautiful golden apples and the fruit-bearing trees on the far side of glorious Oceanus. She also bore the Moirai and Keres who punish without pity, who hound men and gods for their transgressions. These goddesses never abandon their terrible wrath until they render ugly vengeance on the sinner. Deadly Nux also gave birth to Nemesis,[23] a bane to mortal men, and then Deceit, Love, destructive Old Age, and strong-willed Eris.[24]

---

[19]This pun, on the Greek word which Hesiod believed to be the origin of the name *Titans,* does not work in English.

[20]*Ker* is another Greek word for "doom." I have kept it in Greek, (a) to avoid confusion with the first name, and (b) to show that its plural form, *Keres,* occurs later in the same passage.

[21]*Momos* means "Blame." He seems to have been more than a personification of an abstract concept in early epic; in the lost poem the *Cypria,* for example, Momus apparently prevented Zeus from drastically reducing the human population to relieve pressure on Gaea (the *"A"* Scholia to the Iliad at I.5 = *Cypria* fragment 1 in the collections of Allen, Davies, Bernabé, Farrow).

[22]Pindar and other Greek lyric poets, several centuries after Hesiod's time, continued to refer to the islands of the Hesperides as a kind of paradise for dead heroes. This belief in an afterlife other than Hades, reserved for those who had died a heroic death, was not common to all Greeks and is totally absent from the *Odyssey.*

[23]*Nemesis* does not = destruction itself, but rather the path to it, or Machinery of Destruction. Very often in tragedy, *Nemesis* is caused by *Hubris,* which means an insult (lowering another person in general esteem), especially when that insult is directed against the gods. See note on *Ate,* below.

[24]*Eris* = discord/quarreling. Note the much later myth of Eris making an apple inscribed "to the fairest" and throwing it into the banquet of the gods, to which she had deliberately not been invited, at the wedding of Peleus and Thetis. The motif of the apple here is not attested in literary sources before the Hellenistic period.

226 Hateful Eris gave birth to painful Toil, Lethe,[25] Hunger; and tear-causing Pains, Fights, Battles, Murders, Slaughters; and Quarrels, Lies, Words, Disputes; and Lawlessness and Ate,[26] who live together; and Oath, who utterly ruins earth-bound men whenever one of them willingly swears falsely.

233 Pontus fathered truthful, reliable Nereus, the eldest of his children. People call him "Old Man," and "Trusty One," because he *ne'er fails*.[27]

240 Children, most lovely of the goddesses in the cropless sea, were born of Nereus and fair-haired Doris, daughter of Oceanus the encircling river: Amphitrite . . . Thetis,[28] . . . good-looking Galatea.[29] These fifty maidens, expert at perfect deeds, were born of blameless Nereus.

 265 Thaumas married Electra,[30] daughter of deep-flowing Oceanus, and she gave birth to swift Iris[31] and the fair-haired Harpies[32] Aello and Ocypetes, who by their swift wings keep company with gusts of wind and with birds, for they fly high in the air.

---

[25]*Lethe* = forgetfulness/oblivion/negligence. Hesiod would not have included, as later authors did, Lethe as a river round the underworld. Hesiod's only such river was Styx. It is possible that the idea of Lethe as another river of death arose in response to the Pythagorean doctrine of Metempsychosis (reincarnation of souls), to explain why we cannot remember past lives. Pythagoras died shortly before 500 B.C.; he thus lived at a time more than a century later than Hesiod.

[26]*Ate* is a very difficult word to translate into English. It can be treated as yet another word for "fate" or "doom," but perhaps the best translation is "built-in self-destruct mechanism," used in a psychological sense. Sometimes *Ate* is used by poets to indicate the working of *Nemesis*.

[27]This attempt to translate Hesiod's pun on the name *Nereus* into English is the idea of Prof. M.L. West. Hesiod equates the name with the word *nêmertês*, meaning kind or gentle.

[28]Thetis was the Nereid who was fated to bear a son who would become greater than his father. Zeus, in order to avoid becoming a displaced father, married her off to Peleus the Northern hero (see note on *Eris*, above).

[29]There are many poetic treatments of Polyphemus and his love for Galatea. The fullest is in Ovid's *Metamorphoses*, XIII.750-897.

[30]*Elektron* = amber. This substance (which can be rubbed to produce static *electricity*, hence the origin of the term) was prized by the Greeks and other Mediterranean peoples. The best types of amber, hard enough to be used as jewelry, were and still are found on the Baltic coast. The Greeks purchased amber from the Celts who then inhabited the Northern "edge of the world," hence the myth that Electra was daughter of Oceanus. See Herodotus, III.115.

[31]Iris, the rainbow goddess, was represented either as Hera's special messenger or as female messenger to the gods generally. See lines 775–80.

[32]The feminine noun *harpyia* in Greek is derived from the verb *harpazein* = to snatch/grab. *Aëllo* = whirlwind; *Okypetes* = fast-flying.

270 Ceto[33] bore to Phorcys the beautiful-cheeked Graeae, gray from birth, which is why the immortal gods and earth-bound men call them Graeae: well-dressed Pemphredo and Enyo wearing yellow. She also gave birth to the Gorgons, who live[34] on the far side of glorious Oceanus near the edge of Nyx, where the clear-voiced Hesperides live. Of the Gorgons, Sthenno and Euryale are immortal and unaging; Medusa, who suffered severely, was mortal. Dark-haired Poseidon lay beside her in a soft meadow among the spring flowers. When Perseus cut off her head, great Chrysaor[35] and the horse Pegasus leapt out. The latter was so named because he was born beside the *streams*[36] of Oceanus; the former holds a golden sword in his hands. Pegasus flew off, leaving behind the earth, mother of sheep, and came to the immortals. He lives in the house of Zeus, bringing thunder and lightning to the wise god. Chrysaor slept with Callirhoe, daughter of glorious Oceanus, and fathered three-headed Geryon. Mighty Heracles killed him beside his moseying cattle on waterlocked Erytheia;[37] the same day he drove the broad-browed cattle to holy Tiryns, after he passed over the ford

---

[33]*Kêtos* = whale. Phorcys' name is harder to explain, but it might possibly be a corrupted form of *phôkos* = seal.

[34]Hesiod does not name the island of the Gorgons. One of his contemporary poets, the obscure author of the *Cypria*, called the island "Sarpedon" and may have lived in the time when the islands of Sardinia and Corsica were first being explored and colonized by the Greeks.

[35]*Chrysaor* = Golden Sword. We do not hear much of him in Greek myths, apart from his being Geryon's father.

[36]In ancient Greek, *pêga* = stream.

[37]Erytheia must be the name of an island, since Hesiod calls it "waterlocked." He seems to think of it as being located some distance from the Greek coast. Hecataeus of Miletus, one of the earliest Greek historians, argued that Erytheia was actually part of the North-Western Greek mainland (Epirus, near modern Albania) but Hecataeus was rationalizing the myth and his views should not be considered part of the mainstream (see **Ancient Critics** part 2). The myth of Hercules stealing Geryon's cattle can be fairly classified as a kind of initiatory myth, since its form is very close to the kind of cattle-rustling story which in old Irish was called a *Táin Bó*. Most treatments of the myth locate the adventure to the West of Greece: Stesichorus, a lyric poet who lived in Sicily about a century or more after Hesiod's time, told the story of Hercules borrowing the cup of Helios to reach Erytheia. This would not have been Stesichorus' invention, but evidence of an old solar myth. For references & discussion see Walter Burkert, *Structure & History in Greek Mythology & Ritual* (1979) pp. 83–85. In Stesichorus' time popular imagination seems to have located the story in Italy (a later tradition linked it with the Phlegrean Fields, near Mount Vesuvius), but Herodotus (IV.8) equated it with an island near Cadiz in Spain. Hesiod surprises us by having Hercules bring the cattle home to Tiryns (on the Eastern side of Greece) by sunset, presumably on the same day as the theft. This would add to the "miraculous" element of the myth.

of Oceanus and killed Orthus and the cowherd Eurytion in the murky stable on the far side of glorious Oceanus.

295 She gave birth to another invincible monster in a hollow cave, a goddess nothing like mortal men and immortal gods, dauntless Echidna.[38] She is half nymph, with fluttering eyes and beautiful cheeks, and half monstrous snake, terrible, huge, slithering, eating raw flesh in the depths of the very holy earth. Her cave is down there in the hollow rock far from the immortal gods and mortal men. There the gods assigned her to inhabit a glorious house.

304 Baneful Echidna, the immortal and forever unaging nymph, stands guard among the Arimoi under the earth. They say that Typhaon slept with her in love, a terrible, proud, and lawless monster with a flutter-eyed maiden. She conceived and gave birth to dauntless children. First she bore Geryon's dog Orthus; second came the invincible, unspeakable one, Cerberus who eats raw flesh, the bronze-voiced dog of Hades, with fifty heads, impudent and strong; third she gave birth to the Lernaean Hydra, expert in destruction, whom the goddess white-armed Hera reared in her terrible resentment of mighty Heracles. He, son of Zeus, son of Amphitryon, killed the Hydra with merciless bronze, helped by Iolaus, a favorite of Ares, and the advice of Athena the despoiler.

319 She gave birth to the Chimaera who breathes invincible fire, a terrible, great, swift-footed and strong creature. She had three heads: one that of a lively-eyed lion, another of a nanny goat, and the last of a snake, a mighty serpent. With the lion in front, the serpent in back, and the nanny in the middle, she breathed forth a terrible blast of blazing fire. Pegasus and brave Bellerophon[39] killed her.

326 Then Orthus had his way with her and she gave birth to the murderous Sphinx, destruction for the Cadmeians,[40] and the Nemean lion, which Hera, Zeus' illustrious wife, reared and settled in the hills of Nemea as a bane to men. While he lived there he destroyed the tribes of man, mastering Tretus, Apesas, and Nemea. But the strength of mighty Hercules overpowered him.

333 Ceto slept with Phorcys in love and bore her youngest, a terrible snake who guards the all-golden apples in the depths of the black earth at its utter ends. This is the family of Ceto and Phorcys.

---

[38]*Echidna* = viper. Compare Herodotus, IV.8 ff.

[39]The hero Bellerophon was traditionally associated with Lycia, in southwest Asia Minor (Turkey).

[40]The Cadmeians are the people of Thebes in Greece. The reference here is to the story of Oedipus.

337 Tethys bore to Oceanus the whirling Rivers: Neilos,[41] Alpheius, ... divine Simoeis and Peneius ... and divine Scamander.

346 She gave birth to a holy race of daughters[42] who, with lord Apollo and the Rivers, raise boys to manhood throughout the earth. Zeus assigned this responsibility to them. There are three thousand slender-ankled Oceanids, splendid goddesses who busy themselves in every way with the broad earth and the depths of the sea. August Tethys bore just as many thundering Rivers, sons of Oceanus. It is difficult for a mortal man to tell the names of all of them, but they who live nearby know each and every one.

371 Hyperion had his way with Theia in love, and she gave birth to great Helius, bright Selene, and Eos who gives light to earth-bound humans and to the immortal gods who live in wide heaven.

375 Eurybia, goddess of goddesses, slept with Crius in love and bore great Astraeus, Pallas,[43] and Perses who eclipsed all in knowledge. To Astraeus Eos bore the strong-willed winds: sky-clearing Zephyrus, swift-flying Boreas and Notos. These were born when goddess slept with god in love. After them early-born Eos gave birth to the star Eosphorus and the shining stars with which heaven is wreathed.

383 Styx, daughter of Oceanus, slept with Pallas and gave birth in her house to Zelus and beautiful-ankled Nike,[44] as well as her famous sons Cratus and Bia. Their home is not separate from that of Zeus, nor do they have any seat or journey apart from his command. But they ever sit beside loud-thundering Zeus. For thus Styx, the immortal Oceanid, advised them on the day when the Olympian god of lightning summoned all the immortal gods to high Olympus. He told them that whoever of the gods should fight with him against the Titans would not be stripped of his prerogatives, but each would have the honor which he formerly had among the

---

[41]*Neilos* is the River Nile in Egypt. Alpheius and Peneius are rivers in southern Greece. Simoeis and Scamander are the two rivers which meet just below Troy.

[42]These daughters usually are called collectively the Oceanides.

[43]Pallas is a classic example of the *deus otiosus*, or obsolete god. There may have been an obscure myth circulated at one time to explain the absorption of his divine essence into that of Athena, who bore his name as her epithet. If so, such a myth would have had the practical function of explaining encroachment of a temple or other religious property dedicated to Athena upon adjacent land previously dedicated to an older cult.

[44]*Nikê* = victory; *Kratos* = power/strength; *Bia* = force/violence. The last two appear as Zeus' enforcers in Aeschylus' tragedy *Prometheus Bound*.

immortal gods. And he said that whoever had been unhonored and unrewarded by Cronus would obtain honor and privilege from him, as is right. So immortal Styx was the first to come to Olympus, bringing her children because of the counsels of her father. Zeus honored her and gave her extraordinary gifts. For he made her the great oath of the gods,[45] and her children his constant companions. And so in this manner he did for all as he had promised, without exception. He himself rules mightily and is lord.

404 Phoebe entered the much-desired bed of Coeus. Then in love the goddess conceived by the god and gave birth to dark-robed Leto.[46] She is always gentle, kind to men and to the immortal gods, gracious from birth, mildest within Olympus. Phoebe also bore honored Asteria,[47] whom Perses once brought into his great house to be his wife. She conceived and gave birth to Hecate, whom Zeus, the son of Cronus, honored above all and presented with splendid gifts. Both earth and cropless sea are hers, and she also has her share of honor from starry heaven, being especially honored by the immortal gods. For even now, whenever any earth-bound man makes propitiation by offering good sacrifices as prescribed, he invokes Hecate. Much honor quite effortlessly accompanies him whose prayers the agreeable goddess receives, and she gives him wealth, since she has this power. For she has a share of all those prerogatives which the children of Gaea and Uranus obtained. The son of Cronus did not force her in any way, nor did he take away whatever she obtained among the former gods, the Titans. No, she has the same honors first allotted to her in the beginning. Neither does the goddess have a lesser share of honor, even honors in earth, heaven, and sea, because she is an only child. Rather, she has much more since Zeus honors her.

429 She visits and helps greatly whom she wishes: in court she sits beside august kings, and in assembly whomever she wishes distinguishes himself among the people. Whenever men arm themselves for war the man-killer, then the goddess comes to aid the man to whom she zealously wishes to give victory and hold out glory.

---

[45]The significance of this "great oath" is explained later, in lines 775–819.

[46]Leto, the mother of the twins Apollo and Artemis, was later identified (wrongly) by the Romans with Latona, the goddess of childbirth. The latter is closer to the Greek goddess Eileithyia. Leto's name is more properly to be explained by association with the verb-stem v Lêth- , meaning "to lie hidden." The same verb-stem is also the root of the name *Lethe*, explained above. Leto was probably identified originally as the goddess of the night sky.

[47]Asteria = Starry Woman/Lady of the Stars, an appropriate sister for Leto.

Whenever men compete in contest, then the good goddess stands beside them and helps them, and by force and might the victor easily carries off a good prize with joy and brings honor to his parents. She is a boon to those horsemen she chooses to stand beside, and to those who work the rough and stormy sea, who pray to Hecate and loud-crashing Earthshaker. The noble goddess readily grants a big catch, readily whisks it from sight, as her heart desires. She is also handy in the stables, along with Hermes,[48] for enlarging the stock, whether herds of cattle, swine, wide herds of goats, or flocks of woolly sheep. As her heart desires she strengthens a meager herd and weakens a large one.

449 Thus she has been honored among all the immortals with these prerogatives, although she is her mother's only child. The son of Cronus made her nursemaid to those who after that day saw with their own eyes the light of watchful Eos. Thus from the beginning she has had this honor as well as the others.

453 Cronus had his way with Rhea and she bore glorious children: Hestia,[49] Demeter, and gold-sandaled Hera; and strong Hades[50] who lives in the house under the earth, his heart devoid of pity; and loud-crashing Earthshaker, and sagacious Zeus, father of gods and of men, whose thunder shakes the wide earth. Great Cronus gulped them down as each arrived at Rhea's knees from her holy womb, thinking thereby to ensure that no other of Uranus' illustrious descendants should be king among the immortals. For he had learned from Gaea and starry Uranus that he was destined to be overpowered by his son, by the plans of great Zeus, in spite of his own strength. Therefore he did not watch in vain, but paid close attention and gulped down his children; and unending grief held Rhea in its grip. But when she was about to give birth to Zeus, father of gods and of men, then she began entreating her own parents, Gaea and starry Uranus, to contrive a plan that she might bear her son unnoticed, and that Erinys might punish

---

[48]Hesiod seems here to be recommending that farmers who wish their animals to breed successfully should put male and female fertility fetishes in a prominent place overlooking the stable-yard during the breeding season. Hesiod is drawing attention here to the fact that Hermes and Hecate were regarded in his time as the god and goddess, respectively, of the workings of sympathetic magic. The use of fertility fetishes is still observed in some parts of the world.

[49]Hestia's name, like its Latin equivalent *Vesta*, is cognate with the Sanskrit name *Yavishta*, the Hindu fire-god. In Sanskrit *Yavishta* can be read as either male or female; in the European versions there was usually a division of functions between the male version (as in Greek *Hephaistos*) who represented volcanic and industrial fires, and the female counterpart, who represented domestic fire and thus came to be worshipped as a goddess of domestic life.

[50]Hesiod clearly indicates here that Hades is to be listed in the "Olympian" generation. Where this god chooses to live is irrelevant.

Cronus for what he did to his father, and for the children whom great, crafty Cronus gulped down. They listened well to their daughter, applied themselves to the task, and told her all that was destined to happen regarding king Cronus and this strong-willed son. They sent her into Lyctus, into the rich land of Crete, when she was about to bear the youngest of her children, great Zeus. Huge Gaea received him in broad Crete to nourish and raise.[51] Rhea went there, first into Lyctus, carrying him through the fleeting, dark night. She seized the child and hid him in a deep cave, in the depths of very holy Gaea, within heavily wooded Mount Aegeum. Then she wrapped a great stone in swaddling clothes and put it into the hands of the son of Uranus, the great lord, king of the former gods. He seized and swallowed it—the wretch!—and did not realize that his son was left behind unbeaten and untroubled, replaced by a stone. He would soon overpower his father with forceful hand, drive him from his position, and rule himself among the immortals.

492 Swiftly then the strength and shining limbs of the lord advanced. After some time great, crafty Cronus, beguiled by Gaea's shrewd suggestion, regurgitated his offspring. (He was conquered by the schemes and might of his son.) First he disgorged the stone which he had swallowed last. Zeus anchored it in the broad earth in most holy Pytho,[52] in the hollows of Parnassus, as a permanent sign, a marvel to mortal men.

501 Zeus released his uncles from their destructive bonds: Brontes, Steropes, and strong-willed Arges, sons of Uranus. Their father had enchained them in his folly. They remembered Zeus' favor with good deeds of their own; they gave him thunder and burning thunderbolt and lightning. Before this time huge Gaea kept these weapons concealed; now Zeus relies on them in his rule of mortals and immortals.

---

[51]This is Hesiod's only attempt to explain the childhood survival of Zeus. For references to the Curetes/Corybantes in this context and in association with Rhea/Cybele, see Euripides, *Bacchae*, antistrophe #3 of the first chorus.

[52]The shrine of the *Pytho* (pythoness/prophetess) was at Delphi. The Omphalos stone was exhibited as the center of the world, but there was also another stone which (Pausanias X, *Phocis*, 25) was respected as the one vomited by Cronus.

507 Iapetus[53] married a maiden, Clymene, a beautiful-ankled daughter of Oceanus, and shared her bed. She gave birth to a son, stout-hearted Atlas.[54] She also bore renowned Menoetius, shifty Prometheus with his bag of tricks, and simple-minded Epimetheus, who was trouble from the beginning for working men. For he first welcomed as wife the maiden[55] fashioned by Zeus. But far-seeing Zeus sent insolent Menoetius down into Erebus, after blasting him with a smoking thunderbolt because of his presumption and defiant manhood. Atlas upholds wide heaven against his will at the ends of the earth, before the clear-voiced Hesperides, with his head and tireless hands. For sagacious Zeus allotted this fate to him. And he bound wily-minded Prometheus with unpleasant shackles, with painful bonds, after driving a shaft through his middle, and sent a long-winged eagle upon him. It would eat his immortal liver, which would regenerate during the night as much as the long-winged bird ate all day. Heracles, the strong son of beautiful-ankled Alcmene, killed it, warded off evil suffering for the son of Iapetus, and freed him from his sorrows. This was not against the will of high-ruling, Olympian Zeus, who intended that the fame of Theban-born Heracles be greater even than before upon the all-nourishing earth. He was impressed by these things, and honored his famous son. He put aside his anger, although he was still riled at Prometheus for contending with him, the exceedingly strong son of Cronus, in wits.

---

[53]Whereas all of Iapetus' sons have names that can be translated from Greek to mean something, the name *Iapetos* is not a Greek word. Eusebius and later Christian chronographers throughout the middle ages decided that Iapetus was simply the Greek form of the Hebrew name Japhet(h), Noah's third son who migrated West and became the ancestor of the Greeks and other Europeans. Thus, the chronographers reasoned, Iapetus is simply another character whose deeds became so exaggerated by story-telling that he came to be regarded as a god (see *Euhemerism*, under **Ancient Critics, Chapter 2 #7**). It is not unreasonable to suggest, as a modern interpretation, that Iaphet was originally the name of a near-Eastern god, perhaps proto-Phoenician or Hittite, whose name was retained in the Greek tradition as that of a *deus otiosus*, and euhemerized in the Biblical tradition as that of a human pioneer.

[54]The name Atlas is derived from the negative prefix **a-** (corresponding to **un-**) and √ tla- , a verb stem meaning to tire out or exhaust.

[55]This "maiden" must be Pandora: see Hesiod's *Works and Days*, lines 45–100.

535 For indeed, when the gods and mortal men were deciding an issue[56] at Mekone, then Prometheus boldly divided a great ox and laid it out, thinking to deceive the mind of Zeus. For he set down for men the meat and fatty entrails in the hide, covered with the ox's stomach. For the gods he set down the ox's white bones, deceitfully well arranged and covered with shining fat. Then Zeus said to him,

"Son of Iapetus, most renowned of all lords, O friend, how unfairly you have allotted the portions!" So spoke unerring Zeus, taunting him.

546 Wily Prometheus smiled slightly and answered him, not forgetting the art of deceit, "O Zeus, most glorious and greatest of the eternal gods, choose from these two portions whichever your heart urges you." He spoke with treachery on his mind.

But Zeus, whose counsels never fail, knew it and was not unaware of the trick. He saw in his heart evils for mortal man, evils to be soon accomplished. With both hands he picked up the white fat. Anger filled his mind; anger entered his heart when he saw the white bones of the ox and the cunning trick. Because of this the tribes of earthbound men burn the white bones on smoking altars for the immortals.

558 Cloud-gathering Zeus furiously said to him, "Son of Iapetus, cunning above all others, O friend, you have not yet forgotten the art of deceit." He always remembered the trick, and because of it would not grant the power of inexhaustible fire to ash trees and benefit humans on earth. But Iapetus' noble son thoroughly deceived him, stealing the far-seen light of inexhaustible fire in a hollow stalk. It stung high-thundering Zeus to the bottom of his heart and infuriated him, when he saw among men the far-seen light of fire.

570 Immediately he made an evil for men in return for the fire. Famous, lame Hephaestus made something from earth, like a tender maiden,[57] at Zeus' instructions.

---

[56]This phrase can also mean *"were differing."* It seems to refer here to some kind of dispute, but it could equally mean that the essential difference between gods and human mortals was beginning to become apparent. The latter accords well with Hesiod's usual conception of a devolutionary pattern from gods to mortals: he never speaks of the actual creation of mortals, unless we count the creation of Pandora described below, from line 570. Mekone is an old name for Sicyon, in the northern Peloponnese near Corinth and Argos.

[57]For the reference to Pandora, see notes above. This statement is the closest Hesiod ever approaches to the making of a human by a god. Note that it does not necessarily refer to all women.

Athena the bright-eyed goddess dressed and adorned her with silver-white clothing. She held fast in her hands an embellished veil hanging down from her head, a marvelous sight. Pallas Athena put around her head lovely garlands blooming with fresh flowers of the field. The renowned lame god put a golden diadem around her head, made by his own hands, obliging father Zeus. He embellished it amply, marvelously, with all the terrible, dangerous animals which earth and sea nurture. He put many kinds of them on it, each imbued with grace, marvelous—one could almost hear them roar.

585 But after he had made this lovely evil in return for the good, he brought her out where the other gods and men were. She exulted in the adornment provided by the bright-eyed daughter of a mighty father. Amazement gripped both immortal gods and mortal men when they saw the utter fraud, irresistible to men. For from her is the race of female women; of her is the destructive race and tribe of women. They live with mortal men as a great bane, companions not of destructive poverty but of abundance. As when in covered hives bees feed the drones, their wicked partners, the former daily laboring all day long to sundown to make white honeycombs, the latter remaining within the covered hives and gathering into their stomachs the fruit of others' labor; just so high-thundering Zeus made women as an evil for mortal men, as troublesome partners. And he provided another evil in return for the good: **(a)** Whoever decides not to marry, avoiding matrimony and the distressful behavior of women, arrives at destructive old age in need of someone to care for him. He does not indeed experience any lack of money during his life, but after his death his relatives divide the estate among themselves. **(b)** On the other hand, the one whose lot is marriage, and who has a diligent wife endowed with intelligence, finds that evil continually offsets good throughout his life. And whoever has mischievous offspring lives with incessant grief in his breast, mind, and heart. This evil has no remedy.

So it is not possible to deceive or outwit the mind of Zeus, for not even the son of Iapetus, innocent Prometheus, avoided his heavy anger. In spite of his great intellect a mighty bond forcefully restrains him.

616 Now when their father first found hate in his heart for Briareus, Cottus, and Gyges, he bound them with strong bonds. Admiring their defiant manhood, appearance, and size, he trampled them down under the broad-pathed earth. Then they, in pain, living under the earth, were sitting at the edge, at the ends of great Earth, grieving heavily for a long time with great sorrow in their hearts. But the son of Cronus, and the other immortal gods whom fair-haired Rhea bore in love to Cronus, brought them up again into the light through Gaea's shrewdness. For the Titan gods and the children of Cronus had been fighting for a long time, with heart-straining effort, opposing one another in mighty battles. The illustrious Titans fought from high Othrys; the gods, givers of good things, to whom fair-haired Rhea gave birth after sleeping with Cronus, from Olympus. At that time they had been fighting continually with one another for ten full years in heart-straining battle. There was no release from hard conflict, no end for either side; the two had equal chance to win.

639 But when Zeus offered the Hecatoncheires[58] all the foods, both nectar and ambrosia, which the gods themselves eat, then the father of men and of gods addressed them: "Listen to me, splendid sons of Gaea and Uranus, that I may say the things my own heart commands. For we—the Titan gods and all those born of Cronus—have already been fighting for a very long time, face to face, every day, for victory and power. Now show your great strength and invincible hands against the Titans in severe battle, remembering our kind friendship—how you once suffered but have returned to the light from nightmarish bonds, from the murky undergloom, through our plans." Thus he spoke, and blameless Cottus answered him in turn:

"Noble sir, you are not speaking of things unknown to us. Rather, we ourselves know that your mind is superior and your understanding is unsurpassed. You protected the immortals from a chilling doom, and by your thoughtfulness we have come back from the murky undergloom, from cruel bonds, O lord Zeus, after suffering unexpectedly. And now with intent mind and thoughtful counsel we shall rescue your might in grim battle, fighting with the Titans in heavy combat."

664 Thus he spoke; and the gods, givers of good things, heard his speech and applauded him. Their hearts longed for battle even more than before, and on that day all the gods—males and females, Titans, children of Cronus, those whom Zeus sent to the light from Erebus under the earth, terrible and strong with defiant might—all raised a dire battle.[59] The Hecatoncheires each had a hundred arms springing from their shoulders

---

[58]Hesiod does not use this term as a proper name, in the way we have here. He simply calls them the "Hundred-Handers." The term became commonly used as a name by much later poets. The following description of Zeus "deals" with the enemies of his arch-rivals Uranus and Cronus, accounts for his weapon makers and the common belief in his skill as a patron god of politicians and leaders (see lines 75–93 for more on this in the context of the Muses).

[59]It is unclear why Hesiod structured the events of the *Theogony* in such a way as to put the War of the Titans after the episode of Prometheus and his brothers. Perhaps we are to envisage a gradual development of hostility.

and fifty heads sprouting from their sturdy bodies. They stood against the Titans in severe battle with enormous boulders in their stout hands. On the other side the Titans strengthened their ranks in earnest. Both sides showed at once what their strong hands could do. The boundless sea began reverberating terribly, the earth boomed deafeningly, wide heaven groaned in response to the shaking, high Olympus shuddered from the ground up under the impetus of the immortals; and the heavy shaking from their feet, as well as the sharp noise of horrendous charges and powerful throws, reached murky Tartarus.

687 Zeus did not continue to restrain his might, but now at once his heart was filled with rage, and he showed all his power. Leaving heaven he came from Olympus hurling lightning continually. The thunderbolts were flying from his stout hand, one after another, rolling along thickly in a holy flame, with thunder and lightning. The life-giving earth was roaring on all sides as it burned, and the unspeaking forest crackled all around with fire. The whole earth was boiling, and the streams of Oceanus and the cropless sea. A hot wind encompassed the earth-born Titans, a horrible flame reached the divine upper air, and the gleaming flash of thunderbolt and lightning deprived the eyes, however strong, of sight. Unspeakable burning heat restrained Chaos. To see the spectacle and hear the din it seemed just as if Gaea and wide Uranus above were about to collide. For so great a sound would have arisen, from Uranus tumbling down from above and Gaea being thus dashed down herself, as arose from the gods meeting in battle. The winds did their part, stirring up tremor and dust, and thunder and Zeus' lightning and burning thunderbolt, and carrying shout and war cry into the midst of both armies. A repellent din arose from the dreadful struggle. Mighty deeds were displayed, and the war was decided. Up to this time they had been continually attacking one another and fighting in mighty battles.

713 Cottus, Briareus and Gyges, insatiable in war, especially made the battle sharp. They kept throwing three hundred rocks from their stout hands one after another, and covered the Titans with their projectiles. They sent them under the broad-pathed earth and bound them in grievous bonds, after conquering them with force in spite of their proud hearts. As far under the earth as heaven is above it they sent them, for it is that far from earth to murky Tartarus. A bronze anvil falling from heaven for nine nights and days would reach the earth on the tenth, and it is the same from earth into murky Tartarus. A bronze anvil falling from earth for nine nights and days would reach Tartarus on the tenth.

726 A wall has been beaten out of bronze around Tartarus, and around this a triple necklace of night has been poured. Above it grow the roots of earth and cropless sea.

There by the counsels of cloud-gathering Zeus the Titan gods have been buried under the murky gloom in the dank ground, at the ends of the huge earth. For them there is no escape; Poseidon put bronze doors on the place, and the wall surrounds it. Gyges, Cottus, and greathearted Briareus live there, the faithful guards of aegis-bearing Zeus.

736 There in order are the streams and boundaries of all: dark earth and murky Tartarus, cropless sea and starry heaven. Distressing and dank, even the gods hate it. If someone should come inside the gates of this great chasm, he would not reach the ground in a whole year; but storm after miserable storm would carry him here and there. This wonder is terrifying even to the immortal gods. The dread dwelling of black Nyx also stands here, covered with dark blue clouds.

746 In front of these things the son of Iapetus stands unmoving and upholds wide heaven with his head and tireless hands, where Nyx and Hemera approach and speak to one another as they cross the great, bronze threshold. One goes inside and the other comes out the door; the house never contains both within. One of the two always leaves the house and wanders over the earth while the other goes inside and waits until the hour of her next journey arrives. The one has far-seeing light for earth-bound men; the other (destructive Nyx, covered with dark clouds) has in her hands Hypnos, brother of Thanatos.

758 There the children of black Nyx have their house: Hypnos and Thanatos, awesome gods; shining Helius never looks upon them with his rays as he goes up into heaven and comes down out of it. One of them travels about the earth and the wide back of the sea, gentle and kind to men. The other has an iron heart, a pitiless, bronze heart in his breast: once he takes a man he keeps him. Even the immortal gods hate him.

767 There in front stands the echoing house of strong Hades, god of the underworld, and dread Persephone. A terrible, pitiless dog stands guard in front in a wicked fashion; he moves tail and ears for those entering, but does not permit them to come back out. Keeping close watch he eats whomever he catches going out the gates.

775 There the goddess hated by the immortals lives, terrible Styx, eldest daughter of encircling Oceanus. She lives in a glorious house apart from the gods, a house covered over with large rocks and all around firmly fixed unto heaven with silver pillars. Seldom does swift-footed Iris, daughter of Thaumas, come upon the wide back of the sea with a message. But whenever strife and quarrel arise among the immortals and someone of those living in the Olympian house lies, Zeus sends Iris to carry from afar in a golden vessel the great oath of the gods, the famous cold water which pours down out of a high, precipitous crag. Far under the broad-pathed earth a branch of Oceanus flows through black night from the holy river; a tenth part is allotted to it. Nine parts wind around the earth and the wide back of the sea in silver eddies, and fall into the brine; but one part flows forth from the crag, a great bane to the gods.

793 If any of the immortals who inhabit the peak of snowy Olympus forsakes Styx and swears falsely, he lies breathless for a complete year. The nourishment of ambrosia and nectar never comes near him, but he lies unbreathing and unspeaking, covered in bed, and an unnatural coma shrouds him. But when he completes his long year of suffering, another, more difficult task awaits him: for nine years he is cut off from the eternal gods. He never mixes with them in council or at the feasts the whole nine years. In the tenth year he again participates in the assemblies of the immortals who live in the Olympian house. Such an oath the gods have made for themselves of the imperishable, primeval water of Styx, which she sends through the rock-hard earth.

820 When Zeus drove the Titans out of heaven, huge Gaea bore in love to Tartarus her youngest child, Typhoeus, through golden Aphrodite. His hands were capable of mighty deeds and he had the untiring feet of a strong god. From his shoulders grew a hundred snaky heads, the heads of a terrible serpent, with dark tongues flickering. Fire flashed from his eyes beneath the brows of those unspeakable heads; fire burned from all the heads as he glared. There were voices in all the terrible heads uttering varied, indescribable speech. At one time they spoke as the gods understand, at another with the forceful voice of a loud-bellowing bull, irrepressible and haughty, or of a lion with its proud heart; sometimes with a sound resembling young dogs, amazing to hear, sometimes with a hiss causing the high mountains to echo underneath.

836 And now there would have been an irreversible deed done on that day, and he would have been lord among mortals and immortals, if the father of men and of gods had not been sharply observant. He thundered harshly and mightily, and the earth resounded terribly all around, as did wide heaven above, the sea, the streams of Oceanus, and Tartarus below. Hades, who is lord among the dead below, fled in fear, as did the Titans under Tartarus who live around Cronus, from the ceaseless din and grim battle.

853 When Zeus had intensified his rage and seized his weapons, thunder and lightning and burning thunderbolt, he leapt upon and struck Typhoeus from Olympus, and burned all the unspeakable heads of the terrible monster. When he had subdued him by flogging him with blows, the beast fell down lame, and huge earth groaned. A flame sprang from the thunderbolted lord after he was struck in the dark, rugged glens of the mountain.[60] Much of huge earth was burning with unspeakable fire and melting away like tin skillfully heated by strong men in a well-formed crucible; or as iron (which is the strongest metal), overpowered by burning fire in the glens of a mountain, melts away in the sacred earth at the hands of Hephaestus. In the same way the earth was melting away in the flame of blazing fire. And Zeus, vexed in his heart, threw him into wide Tartarus.

869 From Typhoeus blow the strong, rain-laden winds—not Notos, Boreas, Argestes, and Zephyrus, who are a race from the gods and a great help to mortals. But these other winds blow upon the sea to no good. When they fall on the dark sea they are a great bane to mortals as they rush on in wicked storm. Blowing now this way, now that way, they scatter ships and destroy sailors; there is no defense against this evil for those men who meet with them at sea. Blasting also against the boundless, flowery earth they destroy the lovely works of earth-born men, filling them full of dust and distressing tumult.

881 When the blessed gods had finished their toil and forcibly decided the issue of honors with the Titans, then by Gaea's shrewdness they encouraged far-seeing, Olympian Zeus to be king and lord among the immortals; and he in turn skillfully distributed honors among them.

886 Zeus, king of the gods, made his first wife Metis,[61] who knew the most among gods and mortal men. But when she was about to give birth to the bright-eyed goddess Athena, then he quite deceived her wits with a trick, with flattering words, and swallowed her, by the shrewd suggestion of Gaea and starry Uranus. For thus they advised him, in order that no other of the eternal gods should be king in Zeus' place; for it had been decreed that notable children would be born from her, first the maiden bright-eyed Tritogeneia, equal to her father in might and thoughtful counsel. But then she would give birth to a child, king of gods and of men, with an arrogant heart. Zeus, however, swallowed her beforehand, that the goddess might advise him in good and evil.[62]

---

[60]At this point Typhoeus' punishment seems to double as an etiological myth for the formation and power of a volcano. Hesiod may have been thinking of Mount Etna, in Sicily. But, from line 869, Hesiod appears to be giving an etiology for certain storm-laden winds. It is not certain which winds he was trying to describe.

[61]*Metis* = Thought.

901 Second he married shining Themis who bore the Horae:[63] Eunomia, Dike, and Eirene in bloom, who care for the works of mortal men; and the Moirai to whom sagacious Zeus gave the most honor: Clotho, Lachesis, and Atropos, who give to mortal men both good and evil.

907 Eurynome,[64] daughter of Oceanus and very lovely in appearance, gave birth to the three beautiful-cheeked Graces: Aglaea, Euphrosyne, and lovely Thalie.[65]

912 Zeus entered the bed of bountiful Demeter, who gave birth to white-armed Persephone. Aidoneus[66] seized her from her mother's side, and sagacious Zeus allowed it.

Next he loved Mnemosyne with her beautiful hair, from whom the nine gold-filleted Muses were born; festivities and the pleasure of song delight them.

918 Leto slept in love with aegis-bearing Zeus and gave birth to Apollo, and Artemis who showers arrows, offspring lovely beyond all the descendants of Uranus.

Last of all he made Hera his wife in her bloom. She bore Hebe, Ares, and Eileithyia,[67] after sleeping in love with the king of gods and of men.

---

[62]This point, according to Prof. M.L. West, marks the limit of Hesiod's authentic work. The rest from here to the end of the present text must therefore be the work of continuator-poets.

[63]*Horae* = Hours. *Eunomia* = Sharing Well (Fair Shares) or Good Pasture. *Dike* = Justice. *Eirene* = Peace.

[64]Since we are clearly in the process of listing Zeus' wives, Eurynome must be Wife Number Three.

[65]Lines 910–11 are bracketed by several editors of the text. They add nothing to the meaning.

[66]Aidoneus, like the same god's alternative name Hades, is derived from the negative prefix **a-** before $\sqrt{(w)id—}$, = to see. Thus his name means "Invisible One." The full story of Demeter, Hades, and Persephone is told in the *Homeric Hymn to Demeter*.

[67]Eileithyia was the Greek goddess of childbirth. In early art she is often portrayed standing by during Athena's birth: clearly the sequential chronology outlined by Hesiod above was not taken literally by artists.

924 He himself gave birth to bright-eyed Athena from his head—the terrible, din-of-battle-rousing, army-leading, untiring queen—dins, wars, and battles please her. Hera slept in love with no one and bore famous Hephaestus, who surpassed all the descendants of Uranus in handiwork. In this she held back nothing and vied with her husband.

930 From Amphitrite[68] and loud-crashing Earthshaker great and mighty Triton was born, an awesome god who lives in the depths of the sea beside his mother and lordly father in a golden house.

Cythereia bore to shield-piercing Ares terrible gods: Phobus and Deimus,[69] who with city-wasting Ares drive in confusion the compact ranks of men in chilling war; and Harmonia, whom high-spirited Cadmus made his wife.

938 Maia, daughter of Atlas, entered the holy bed of Zeus and bore to him Hermes, herald of the immortals.

Semele, daughter of Cadmus, slept with Zeus in love and gave birth to a splendid son, pleasurable Dionysus.[70] She was mortal, her son immortal, but now they both are gods. Alcmene slept in love with cloud-gathering Zeus and bore mighty Heracles.

Very glorious, lame Hephaestus made Aglaea,[71] youngest of the Graces, his wife in her bloom. Golden-haired Dionysus made golden Ariadne, daughter of Minos, his wife in her bloom. For him the son of Cronus made her undying and unaging.

---

[68]Amphitrite was one of the Nereids, listed above. Lines 930 to 1022 are bracketed by several editors as being inauthentic (see note on line 900, above). We have retained them simply because of the information they contain.

[69]*Phobos* = Fear, *Deimos* = Panic. In the *Iliad* and in later poetry they accompany Ares into battle. Harmonia takes after her mother, but is usually depicted as only a demi-goddess; after marrying Cadmus and living as his wife in Thebes, the pair is immortalized by being turned into snakes. Such a myth normally reinforced the hallowing of sacred land (snakes being linked both to the earth and to the concept of immortality).

[70]For the full story of Zeus, Semele, and Dionysus, see Euripides' tragedy *The Bacchae*.

[71]In Homer, Hephaestus is married to Aphrodite who is constantly unfaithful to him; Ares is still the father of her children!

950 The strong son of beautiful-ankled Alcmene, powerful Heracles, after finishing his laborious tasks made Hebe, daughter of great Zeus and gold-sandaled Hera, his honored wife on snowy Olympus. The happy one has finished his great work and lives among the immortals untroubled and unaging forever.[72]

Perseis, glorious daughter of Oceanus, bore to tireless Helius Circe and king Aeëtes.[73] And Aeëtes, the son of Helius who brings light to mortals, married a daughter of the encompassing river Oceanus, beautiful-cheeked Idyia, by the will of the gods. Through golden Aphrodite he had his way with her, and she gave birth in love to beautiful-ankled Medea.

963 Farewell now, you who live in the Olympian house; farewell, islands and lands and salty sea between. Sing now of the tribe of goddesses, O sweet-voiced Olympian Muses, daughters of aegis-bearing Zeus; sing of all those immortal goddesses who slept with mortal men and gave birth to god-like children. Demeter, goddess of goddesses, bore Plutus after sleeping in dear love with the hero Iasion in thrice-plowed fallow, in the rich land of Crete. The wealthy god travels the whole earth and the wide back of the sea; he makes rich, he gives great wealth to, the mean who meets with him and lays hands on him.

975 Harmonia, daughter of golden Aphrodite, bore to Cadmus in well-crowned Thebes Ino, Semele, beautiful-cheeked Agave and Autonoe, whom thick-haired Aristaeus married, and Polydorus.

Callirhoe, daughter of Oceanus, slept in love with valiant Chrysaor through very golden Aphrodite and gave birth to a son, strongest of all mortals—Geryon, whom mighty Heracles killed for his moseying cattle in waterlocked Erytheia.

---

[72]This is a much more positive testimony to a belief in Herakles' immortality than we find at the end of *Odyssey* XI, where Odysseus first claims to have seen the hero's ghost, then in an afterthought concedes that it must have been a phantom double, because Herakles was already with the gods. Such a self-contradiction may be taken as indicating the uncertainty with which ancient Greeks viewed the immortality of heroes.

[73]At this point the end of Hesiod's *Theogony* starts to merge with other stories: Circe will be recognized from the *Odyssey*, Aeëtes from the legend of the Argonauts (Pindar, *Pythian* IV, 212ff.).

984 Eos bore to Tithonus[74] bronze-armored Memnon,[75] king of the Ethiopians, and lord Emathion; yet she bore to Cephalus a glorious son, strong Phaethon, a man like the gods. Laughter-loving Aphrodite seized and carried him off in the fresh, smooth bloom of glorious youth, when he was still a child thinking childish thoughts, and made him a keeper within her very holy temples, a divine daimon.[76]

992 The son of Aeson,[77] by the will of the eternal gods, took the daughter of Aeëtes, a king cherished by Zeus, from his side after he finished the laborious tasks, the many tasks which the great, overbearing king Pelias enjoined. Pelias was insolent and arrogant, a violent man. Having completed the tasks and having suffered much on his swift ship, the son of Aeson came to Iolcus bringing the maiden with fluttering eyes; he made her his wife in her bloom. Jason, shepherd of his people, had his way with her

---

[74]There have been several theories advanced since ancient times as to who exactly Tithonus may have been. Various kings and local rulers of Egypt had names that included the element *Thoth* (the name of the psychopomp god usually represented in the form of an ibis); Philo of Byblos, around 100 A.D., wrote a history of Phoenicia which he claimed to have translated from a much earlier work in the ancient Phoenician language by one Sanchouniaton. We don't know how much of the book was Philo's own creation, but it seems from extant fragments to have been mostly euhemerized myths of creation and exploration: one of the main characters was an explorer-king called Ta-autes. Diodorus of Sicily, in the first century B.C., identified Tithonus with an early Assyrian or Babylonian king called Tautanes.

[75]Memnon's death was described in the now-lost epic *Aethiopis* by Arctinus of Miletus. According to the poem's surviving summary, attributed to Proclus, Memnon came to Troy as an ally of King Priam. In the Hellenistic period Memnon's name was confused with Amunhotep III, of the Egyptian XVIIIth Dynasty. The latter's colossal statue, which had by then become a tourist attraction, was believed to sing a hymn to the sun every morning. The phenomenon was probably caused by convection-currents, but it reinforced the popular conception of Egyptian kings as solar gods in a human form.

[76]This strange reference to Phaethon as "a divine daimon" (spirit) can best be explained as originating with travelers' tales from Egypt, about a haunted temple, being promulgated in Greece. This Phaethon is clearly not the same one whose adventures with the Solar Chariot are described by Ovid, *Met.* I-II. The only factors they share are **a)** the solar association and **b)** that both died young.

[77]This reference is to Jason. Lines 992–1002 give us the earliest explicit outline of the quest for the Golden Fleece and its outcome.

and she gave birth to the child Medus,[78] whom Cheiron, son of Philyra, reared in the mountains. The purpose of great Zeus was accomplished.

1003 Two daughters of Nereus, old man of the sea, bore children: Psamathe, goddess of goddesses, in love gave birth by Aeacus to Phocus through golden Aphrodite; Peleus had his way with silver-footed goddess Thetis, and she gave birth to Achilles, the lion-hearted man-breaker.

1008 Well-crowned Cythereia[79] bore Aeneas after sleeping in dear love with the hero Anchises on the peaks of pleated, windy Ida.

1011 Circe, daughter of Hyperion's son Helius, in love gave birth by long-suffering Odysseus to Agrius, and blameless and strong Latinus;[80] and she bore Telegonus[81] through golden Aphrodite. Quite far away in the heart of holy islands they ruled all the very glorious Tyrsenians.[82]

---

[78]Very little can be said about Medus except that he seems to have been considered an eponymous king of the Medes, who inhabited ancient Iran. The ancient epic poet Cinaethon of Lacedaemon (quoted by Pausanias, II.3.9) mentioned *Medeios* and his sister Eriope. He is usually called *Mêdos*: Apollodorus I.9.28, Hyginus Fab. 27 (possibly based on a lost tragedy about Medea).

[79]For a full account of this story see the *Homeric Hymn to Aphrodite.*

[80]*Agrios* = Wild Man. Some scholars think this is a Greek reference to an ancient Italian woodland god such as Faunus or Silvius. *Latinus* = the Latin Man/Italian. M.L. West, in his 1966 notes to the *Theog.*, p. 434, argues that these lines must have been added to the *Theogony* after 600 B.C., when the Greeks had begun to colonize Italy and trade with both Latins and Etruscans, but before about 520, by which time they could have told the difference between the two nations.

[81]Telegonus was the son who tracked down Odysseus in Ithaca and killed him, according to a lost epic poem the *Telegonia*, by Eugammon of Cyrene. A summary of this poem is virtually all that survives; it was probably composed in the 6th century B.C.. See note on Calypso's sons, below.

[82]The "Tyrsenians" are Etruscans, the ancient inhabitants of central Italy. These references to Odysseus' travels in Italy are quite foreign, in every sense, to the *Odyssey*. Yet there were popular stories about Odysseus' travels in Italy. Ptolemy Chennos, who composed his New History in about 100 A.D., mentions one anecdote about Odysseus winning a musical contest in Italy by performing Demodocus' *Sack of Troy*. This poem and its author were probably fictional details in the *Odyssey*, made up by Homer to project sympathetic images of himself and his craft.

1017 Calypso, goddess of goddesses, bore to Odysseus Nausithous and Nausinous,[83] after sleeping with him in dear love. These immortal goddesses slept beside mortal men and gave birth to god-like children. Now sing of the tribe of women,[84] O sweet-voiced Olympian Muses, daughters of aegis-bearing Zeus!

* * * * * * * *

Nota Bene:

For the most part we have spelled proper names so that they may be looked up in Tripp's **Handbook** (*The Meridian Handbook of Classical Mythology*, by Edward Tripp: Meridian Books, 1970) or in any other standard reference-work without difficulty. Most modern dictionaries of myth or of classical antiquities tend to Latinize names (e.g., "Gaia" becomes "Gaea," and "Kronos" becomes "Cronus"). Where the name has no separate entry there and/or where the meaning is more important than the name-form we have simply transliterated or in some cases translated (e.g., "Mnemosyne" becomes "Memory").

---

[83]These names appear to be very generic. They mean "Fast-Sailing and Ship-Minded." Nausithous is mentioned in the *Odyssey* (VI.7, VII.55ff.) as first king of the Phaeacians, son of Poseidon and Periboea. The names, like those of Circe's children given above, probably reflect Greek colonizing interest in Italy: Iamblichus (*Life of Pythagoras* 127, 267) mentions a Nausithous as an early Pythagorean disciple. The Pythagorean College began in Southern Italy at about the same time as this continuation of Hesiod was added. The same approximate date can also be assigned to the *Telegonia*, a short epic poem by Eugammon of Cyrene which tried to furnish a continuation of the *Odyssey*.

[84]This new invocation to the Muses clearly indicates the beginning of the *Catalogue of Women*, also known as the *Ehoeae*. The text of the poem is now lost (it once existed in five books and after about the third century A.D. was considered too long and cumbersome to deserve copying out in full) but many fragments of it survive. They are collected and discussed by M.L. West, in *The Hesiodic Catalogue of Women* (Oxford 1986).

CHAPTER 19

Hesiod's *Works and Days*

☞ The following is a short selection from the beginning of Hesiod's short epic poem **Works and Days**. The whole poem is only 828 lines long. It is basically a farmer's calendar or almanac, giving the seasons of the year and listing the agricultural chores which should be done in due season. Hesiod also gives lists of auspicious or "lucky" days (and their opposites) with recommendations as to what should be done and what should be avoided at certain times of the month.

The extracts chosen are from the beginning of the poem, where Hesiod poses the question, **"Why is a farmer's work never done?"** and tries to come up with some answers. The etiologies he provides are, of course, based on familiar myths.

42. The gods keep the means of livelihood hidden away from men; otherwise you could easily do in one day enough work to keep you provided for a year at leisure. You would soon store away the rudder above the smoke,[1] and the work of oxen and long-toiling mules would be wasted. But Zeus in his anger hid it away in his mind because crafty Prometheus had tricked him. This is the reason why he planned hateful cares for humans and hid fire. This is what the son of Iapetus stole back for mortals from Zeus the planner, hiding it in a hollow stalk from Zeus who enjoys thunderbolts.

53. Cloud-gathering Zeus in anger addressed him: "Son of Iapetus, cunning above all others, you are pleased to have stolen fire and put my plans to the test, but great pain will come to you and to men yet to be born. I shall give them something evil instead of the fire, something that all may love at heart even though they embrace their own evil."

59. So he spoke, but the father of gods and men laughed out loud. He ordered famous Hephaestus to mix earth with water as quickly as possible, putting in it human voice and strength, making its face like those of the immortal goddesses, the lovely beauty

---

[1]The rudder, more like a kind of steering-oar, of a Greek ship was easily detachable (see Teireias' speech in Od. XI, 121–129). Storing it above the smoke of a domestic fire was a good way to prevent rot or parasites when it was not in use.

of a girlish face. Then he ordered Athena to teach her work, to weave at the highly complex loom. He ordered Aphrodite to pour golden grace around her head, painful desire too, and cares that waste away the limbs. But he charged Hermes the leader-across,[2] killer of Argus, with putting a shameless spirit in her mind and stealthy ways.

69. So he spoke, and they obeyed Lord Zeus the son of Cronus. Immediately the god with the twisted limbs fashioned from earth the likeness of a modest maiden, according to the plans of Cronus' son. The grey-eyed goddess Athena girdled her and made her up.[3] Around her skin the Graces and goddesses and lady Peitho[4] hung golden chains, while the fair-haired Hours crowned her with spring flowers. Pallas Athena made every ornament fit her. But in her heart Hermes the leader-across put falsehoods and tricky speech and stealthy ways, following the plans of deep-thundering Zeus. The herald of the gods put a voice in her and called this woman Pandora, because all those who live in Olympus had brought her gifts, a pain to bread-eating men.

83. When he had effected this terrible inescapable trap, the Father sent the famous Argus-slayer, swift messenger of the gods, to Epimetheus, bringing her as a gift. Epimetheus did not think on how Prometheus had told him never to accept a gift from Olympian Zeus, but to send it right back, lest some evil should happen to mortals. But once he had received it, he sensed the evil that was in his possession.

90. For the tribes of men previously used to live on earth free and remote from evil and from difficult work; from painful diseases, too, which have brought doom to men. As for now, mortals grow old in wretchedness. But once the woman, with her hand, removed the cover from the container, she scattered them,[5] contriving grievous cares for mortals. Alone Hope remained in there, in its undamaged home under the lip of the jar, nor did it fly outside. Prior to that she had been stuck to the lid of the jar, by the plans of Aegis-bearing Zeus the cloud-gatherer. But tens of thousands of other ills escaped amongst humanity, for the earth is full of evils; full too is the sea. Diseases haunt men by day, and come by themselves at night too, bringing evils to mortals in silence, since Zeus the planner has taken away their voice. This is how impossible it is to escape the mind of Zeus.

---

[2]Gk. *diáktoron*, clearly a reference to Hermes' function as psychopomp. "Killer of Argos" refers to the myth in which Hermes kills the hundred-eyed guard Argos: see *Homeric Hymn to Hermes* and Aeschylus' *Prometheus Bound*.

[3]Usually translated "decked her out" or "arranged" or "decorated." The actual verb used in Greek is the one which gives us the word "cosmetic."

[4]Persuasion, here personified as a goddess.

[5]The evils imprisoned in the container.

106. But, if you wish, I will tell you well and knowingly another story (keep it in your mind!) how gods and mortal men are from like origins.

109. First of all the immortals, who keep their homes on Olympus, made a race of articulate men of gold. These were in the time when Cronus ruled over heaven. They lived like gods with a carefree existence, keeping their minds free of labour and trouble, nor did wretched old age press upon them, but for ever they stayed the same in [respect of] their feet and hands, enjoying banquets, out of reach of all evils. They died as if overpowered by sleep, and all good things were theirs. The life-giving soil bore fruit of its own free will, much and plentiful. Gladly in peace they reaped the rewards of their labours with their fortunate communities.

121. But now that earth has covered this generation, they exist as spirits[6] by the will of great Zeus: kindly, living in the earth, guardians of mortals. They watch over judgments and wicked deeds, going everywhere over the world wrapped in mist, givers of wealth. This is the royal distinction that they have.

127. The inhabitants of Olympus next created a second generation much inferior to the first, one of silver, resembling the golden one neither in shape nor in mind. A boy was reared beside his wise mother for a hundred years, skipping around at home like a great baby. But whenever one came of age and reached the measure of maturity, they[7] would only live for a short time, suffering pains for their thoughtlessness. For they could not refrain from rashly insulting one another, nor did they willingly worship the gods, nor did they practice rituals at the holy altars of the blessed ones, as is right for men by custom. Zeus the son of Cronus buried these too in his anger, because they did not give honour to the blessed gods who hold Olympus. But when the earth had hidden this generation too, they are indeed called blessed underworld mortals, second in rank, yet honour attends these too.

143. But father Zeus created another, third generation of articulate men: bronze, in no way equal to the silver, terrible and mighty by reason of their ash-wood spears. Their concern was the mournful work and the insults of Ares; they did not just eat cereal food, but had a formidable spirit of adamant. Great violence and unconquered hands grew from their shoulders on strong limbs. These men had bronze armour, bronze houses too, and they worked with bronze. Dark iron did not exist yet. Conquered by

---

[6]Hesiod uses the term *daimones*, from which we get the word *demons*. He is using it in a good sense here, as can be seen from the context.

[7]The apparently illogical switch from singular to plural in the subject of this sentence reflects Hesiod's words exactly.

each other's hands they entered the mouldy home of chill Hades without glory. Dark death seized them, terrible though they were, and they left the bright light of the sun.

156. But when earth had covered [the third] generation too, Cronus' son Zeus made yet another one, the fourth, upon the fruitful ground, a more righteous one and warlike, a godlike race of hero-men, who are called demigods, the previous race [to ours] throughout the boundless earth. Some of them did evil war and dread battle destroy; some under seven-gated Thebes, Cadmus' land, when they struggled for the flocks of Oedipus. Others when it[8] had driven them in their ships over the sea's great expanse to Troy for the sake of beautiful-haired Helen. There death's end covered some of them over, but to some of them Cronus' son, father Zeus, gave a lifestyle and home apart from men, settling them at earth's ends. There they dwell with carefree heart in the Isles of the Blessed beside deep-whirling Oceanus—the lucky heroes, for whom the fertile soil bears tasty food three times a year.

174. I wish I had not been part of the fifth generation of men, but had either died before or been born afterwards. For now is the race of iron! They will never stop their toil or wretchedness by day or night, being worn out. The gods will give them hard problems. But Zeus will also destroy this generation of articulate men—they will die as soon as they become grey-haired.

> ☞ From this point onwards Hesiod laments his own "iron age" (not to be confused with the modern archaeological concept, even though Hesiod did in fact live in the archaeological Iron Age) as a time of corruption, depravity, dishonesty, and crime. Hesiod urges his naïve brother Perses to do what is right, both in terms of honesty and of agriculture. Thus Hesiod sets the stage for his little manual of instruction on farming in Iron Age Greece.

---

[8]"It" here is clearly war. Evidently Hesiod knew the basic story of the Trojan War in a form which generally resembled the accounts we still have. Most familiar accounts are ultimately based on poems such as those of Homer and his followers (see textbook Appendix on the Troy-Cycle), but Hesiod does not go into any further detail here. Later in the poem (651–3) Hesiod mentions Aulis, the Boeotian harbour facing Euboea, as the traditional port from which the Greeks sailed for Troy. He mentions the crossing simply in the context of being his own sole experience of sailing, even though he only went as far as Euboea, a crossing of barely one mile!

CHAPTER 20

Cadmus: Foundation of Thebes; Aristaeus; Actaeon (from Nonnos)

From Nonnos of Panoplis, Dionysiaca Bk. V

Translated and edited by J.G. Farrow

☞ Nonnos of Panoplis was a Greek-speaking epic poet who lived in Egypt during the late Roman Empire. We do not know his exact dates, but he flourished at some point between 390 and 550 AD. His poem *Dionysiaca* (epic of the god Dionysus) in 48 books is the longest ancient Greek poem to survive today.

In the following extracts Cadmus, a prince from the coast of SW Syria, has landed in Greece after failing to find his lost sister Europa. Unknown to him she had been abducted by Zeus (who had taken on the form of a bull). Cadmus is lost, but an oracle tells him to build a settlement in a prophecied place (later to become Thebes) since he has found the new Europa. Eventually Cadmus will raise a family, not only becoming the founder of the city and its first kings but also father of Semele, who is to be mother of Dionysus.

But when Cadmus had harvested the snaky crop of tooth-planted battles and had cut the stubble of the Giants,[1] pouring the blood-libation to Ares as the first offering of harvest-slaughter, he washed his body in dragon-breeding Dirce and sacrificed a Delphian[2] cow on the god-built altar as a fair sacrifice for Pallas (Athena). To begin the sacrifice he sprinkled both horns with grains of barley; drawing the bare knife which hung

---

[1]Cadmus had already landed in his new Western country and, in accordance with the gods' instructions, named it Europa after his sister. His first task was to kill a dragon (or serpent), after which he extracted its teeth and planted them in the ground to produce a fine crop of fully-armed soldiers.

[2]Delphi is in Phocis, the next state to Boeotia. The cow must be sacrificed because the gods had *prophesied* it, and the ancient shrine at Delphi was always associated with prophecy. The area in which Cadmus saw the cow must be called *Boeotia*, or, "Cow Country." This particular cow had a moon-shaped mark on one side of its body (Hyginus, *Fab.* CLXXVIII).

along his thigh from its Assyrian strap and cut the top hairs of the long-horned head with the handled blade.

11. Theoclymenus held the heifer's horns and drew back its throat, Thyestes cut through the sinews of the neck with a double-edged axe, the stone altar of Athena Onca[3] was reddened with the smear of the blood.

17. Cutting through the ribs they carved her up with the knife, stripped off the hide and stretched it out. Cadmus himself was busy, after folding his bright cloak and laying it on the ground. He cut off raw slices of the strong thighs, cut them small and placed them between two layers of fat.

29. The fragrant smoke of Assyrian incense spread around, curling through the air. After the sacrifice there was a feast. Cadmus took, offered and served to each an equal portion of choice food. The lines of guests at the well-rounded table were soon filled and sated their appetites.

35. The death of the dragon was not the last of Cadmus' labors. After the dragon and the wild tribes of giants, he fought the Ectenes and the Aonian hordes, reaping a barbarian harvest of Ares, and fell upon the neighboring Temmicans. When he summoned soldiers a motley swarm of neighbors came to help him.

49. After the bloody slaughter and confusion Cadmus laid the foundations of Thebes, which had not yet been fortified.

51. Here and there many dividing spaces and furrows were cut, the beds of many branching roads were dug by the sharp-toothed iron of the ox-plough; many streets were measured at right angles to the four opposing winds to share out the grassland. Then the Aonian city was decorated with the stony beauty of Tyrian art: then all were busy, one workman on another's heels, cutting under the Boeotian slopes with earth-cutting pick the many-folded rock which the hills near the thick forest of tree-covered Teumessos produce, which Helicon grew and Cithaeron brought forth. He built temples for the gods and houses for the people, planning with measurements. He plotted the shape of a city surrounded by walls on unbreakable foundation-stones, with seven gates, his design copying heaven with its seven yokes,[4] leaving the future wall for Amphion[5] to make for the inhabitants and to protect for them with his tower-building harp.

---

[3]Athena was worshipped with the epithet *Onca* at Thebes and only a small number of other cities. The cult was not at all like that of Athene Promachos (First in the Battle Line) or any other of this goddess' cults at Athens.

[4]The "Yokes of the Sky" were the courses of the planets. Ancient people frequently counted Venus twice, since its orbit (revere of the earth's) causes its apparent position in the sky to change depending on whether one sees it in the morning or evening, hence "Morning Star" and "Evening Star."

[5]Amphion was the legendary builder of the walls of Thebes.

67. He consecrated the seven gates, equal in number to the planets; first towards the sunset he dedicated the Oncaian Gate to Mene Bright-eyes, taking its name from the honk of cattle, because the Moon herself, ox-shaped, horned, driver of cattle, having three shapes is Tritonis Athena.

85. This was the seat he created; and after founding the sacred city he called it by the name of Thebes in Egypt, fashioning a shape in its decoration like an earthly (version of) Olympus.

88. The daughters of the Aonians struck up Harmonia's wedding-song with dances; the dancing girls sang the name of the Thracian bride in the palace with its fine bridal chamber. Her lovely mother too, she of Paphos, decorated her daughter's newly-built bower for Cadmus while she sang of the divinely-arranged marriage. Her father[6] danced with joy for his daughter, his armor stripped away—Ares was tamed!

121. And now bringing the nuptial hour to the bridal halls came the Serpent (the constellation Draco), neighbor of the Northern Wain, a messenger with news of the future: for Harmonia's bridegroom along with his bride was destined to change his shape for that of a serpent. The Blessed in turn brought their gifts to honor Cadmus as he hurried to his chamber. Zeus gave every success. Poseidon brought the gifts of the sea in honor to his famous sister Hera, since she was Ares' mother.

135. Aphrodite, wishing in her mind to please Ares, clasped round the girl's neck a golden necklace that shone bright, a clever work of Hephaistos set with sparkling jewels in fine craftsmanship. He had made this for his Cyprian bride, a gift for his first glimpse of Eros the Archer. For Hephaistos as a heavy-kneed bridegroom had always expected that Aphrodite would bear him a limping son, carrying the image of his father in his feet. But he was mistaken in this thought; and when he saw a whole-footed son shining with wings like Maia's son Hermes, he made this decorative necklace, shaped like a serpent with star-spangled back in twists and turns, . . . a two-headed serpent like the Amphisbaina.

190. And Harmonia, yoked by the Cestus-girdle[7] that provokes marriage's desire, conceived and bore many children one by one. First Autonoé, then Ino[8] who was to bear Athamas two children, third Agaué, who later married Echion of the Giant-breed and

---

[6]Nonnos is here following Homer's theme, representing Aphrodite as being married to Hephaestus but enjoying an occasional relationship with Ares, who is subsequently the father of her children. Compare Hesiod, *Theogony* 945–9.

[7]The Cestus, or Kestos, was Aphrodite's magical garment.

[8]For the myth of Ino, see Hyginus, *Fabulae* i–v.

bore a son like her husband who sprang from the dragon's teeth; fourth Semele,[9] like the Graces, to be preserved for Zeus. Although the youngest of the sisters, she alone received from nature the gift of unsurpassed beauty. Finally Harmonia bore a little son to add to his sisters and make Cadmus happy: Polydorus the Morning Star of his Aonian homeland, younger than rosy-cheeked Semele. But the lawless lord Pentheus[10] pushed him aside and assumed the scepter in Thebes. Eventually Old Father Time was to accomplish these things.

212. Cadmus selected husbands for his daughters and settled their four successive weddings one by one. First Aristaeus came with gifts, he of the herds and the wilds, son of Apollo and Cyrene the crafty huntress, married Autonoé according to the marriage-ritual. Cadmus did not refuse his daughter to a man so skilled in feeding many, but gave her to a clever husband, a life-saving son of Apollo who had calmed the disease-bearing Dog Star[11] of pestilential Maira by the healthy breezes of heaven-sent winds. He gave the girl unyoked oxen as a bridal-gift; he gave goats and mountain-bred sheep. Many was the line of porters that he forced to carry the weight of huge jars full of olive oil, much too of the work of the honey-bee that he brought in the complex comb that the bee had created.

229. Aristaeus ranging the mountains on his springing feet first discovered hunting in the wild among the rocks; how the hound scents the invisible prey with clever nose on the foothills, pricking up his ears on the twisting course. He learnt how to stake a net and (to recognize) the morning track of animals over the sand and the spoor pressed into the untrodden earth. He taught the huntsman how to use high boots in following the hounds in pursuit and the advantage of the shorter shirt so that the tunic should not trip the wearer.

242. Aristaeus also invented the hive riddled with many rows of cells and made a fixed place for the wandering bees when they fly from flower to flower over the meadows and land on clusters of fruit-bearing plants, sucking dew from the ends with the tip of their lips. He covered his whole body from toenails to hair with a fine-woven cloth of linen to protect himself from the terrible stings of the quarrelsome bees, and with the crafty trick of choking smoke he tamed their anger. He waved a torch in the air to threaten the hive-loving bee. Lifting two metal plates he banged the cymbals together

---

[9]For more on Semele, see the opening scenes of Euripides' *Bacchae.*

[10]Euripides, in the *Bacchae*, represents Pentheus as a typical *tyrannos.*

[11]Sirius, believed in ancient times to be responsible for the "Dog Days" of late summer. Aristaeus was traditionally the hero who had passed on to humanity a special ritual (revealed to him by his father Apollo) for producing the Etesian Winds, which would compensate to some extent for the late-year drought.

over the swarm in the hive while they buzzed and bumbled in never-ending noise. Then, cutting away the wax cover with its many-angled cells he drained from the comb its shining treasure of honey-dripping produce.

258. He was the first to discover the dew of slickly oozing oil when he cut into the fruit of the juicy olive with the heavy stone of a press and squeezed out the rich yield. From the richly wooded pasture under the shady forest-slopes he brought the shepherds to the meadow; he taught them to graze their flocks from the appearance of the sun to its setting. When the sheep strayed in lines on a wandering hoof, hesitating on ways they could not trace or trust, he joined them on a single path to the flowery pasture, sending a goat forward to lead the united trek. He too invented Pan's mountain-dwelling pastoral tune.[12] He lulled Maira's scorching Dog-star to sleep. Having lit the fragrant altar of Zeus Ikmaios he poured a libation with a bull's blood and the glistening gifts of the busy bee upon the altar, filling his elegant cups with a sweet mixture of honey. But father Zeus heard him and, honoring his grandson sent a counter-blast of winds, fending off evil, to restrain Seirios of the burning fevers. Even to the present time the Etesian Winds from Zeus proclaim the sacrifice of Aristaeus and cool the land when the ripening vine grows in dappled clusters.

280. Eros escorted Aristaeus, the Ceian son of Phoebus Apollo, to the Aonian wedding.

287. Later from the union of Aristaeus and Autonoé sprang up Actaeon.[13] With his passion for the rocky places and bearing the blood of the Hunter (Apollo) he followed his ancestral huntsmanship and became a mountain-ranging attendant of Artemis. Nor was it a miracle that unfortunate Actaeon learnt the tricks of the chase having been born grandson to Cyrene[14] the lion-killer! No bear ever escaped him on the hills; not even the lethal eye of the lioness with her litter could startle him. Often did he lie in wait for the panther and struck her down as she leapt at him from above.

Always would Pan the shepherd stare at him with wondering eyes over the bushes while he overtook the swift stag on his course. But the running of his feet gave him no profit, his quiver was useless, nor of use was the straightness of his aim or his cunning in the chase. But fate destroyed him, him the fleet fawn torn apart by dogs while still

---

[12]This is a reference to the *pastoral mode*, a kind of ancient music traditionally linked to life in the countryside. This mode is, in modern terms, mid-way between g minor and d minor: it runs from D to D, but F is sometimes sharp and B usually flat. Pastoral tunes are usually in 6/8 time.

[13]For more on the myth of Actaeon (Greek spelling *Aktaion*), see Ovid, *Metamorphoses* III.138-255; Hyginus Fabulae clxxx; clxxxi; ccxlvii.

[14]Cyrene was an important Greek farming colony in North Africa.

breathing destruction after the Indian war. For as he sat among the tall branches of a spreading oak tree, he had seen the entire body of the Archeress as she bathed.

Scanning avidly the goddess whom none may see, he studied inch by inch the sacred body of the unmarried virgin from a hide nearby.

An uncovered Naiad Nymph saw him from the distance with a sideways glance as he stared furtively at the unclothed shape of her queen and wailed with horror as she told her Lady the wild audacity of a love-maddened male. Half-exposed, Artemis snatched up her dress and wrapped her cloak around her, covering her modest breasts with her maiden's girdle in outrage. Sinking with gliding limbs into the water, by gradual degrees she hid all her shape.

316. Your fate weighs you down, Actaeon! Immediately your human shape left you; four feet had cloven hooves and long cheeks stretched out on your jawbones. Your legs became thinner, there grew two long bunches of spreading antlers curving over your forehead; a wrong shape, its body covered over with hair, every limb dappled with colored spots! There alone remained to the wind-running fawn your mind! With nimble leap of the hoof he ran through the hostile forest, a hunter dreading hunters. But his dogs no longer recognized their master in his new shape. The Archeress in her angry resentment nodded to them as they could not be escaped. Panting furiously in wild frenzy they whetted the double row of their deer-killing teeth and, tricked by the false appearance of a stag they tore apart the dappled changed shape in mad fury. But the goddess meant more; that the dogs should slowly tear Actaeon apart with their jaws while he was still breathing, and thinking in his brain, that she might still torture his mind further with more bitter pains. With human feeling he lamented his own fate, crying aloud in a pitiful voice;

337. "O happy Teiresias! You saw without being destroyed the naked form of Athena, not willingly but still to be pitied. You did not die, you were not apportioned a deer's hide, no projecting antlers raised themselves on your forehead. You live, having lost only the light of your eyes. Yours are now the brilliant eyes Athena substituted within your mind. The Archeress is more evil than Tritogeneia. Would that she had given me similar suffering, would that she had attacked me too in the eyes as Athena did! Would that she had transformed my mind as she did my body! For the foreign shape of a wild animal holds me, yet I have the mind of a man! Do animals ever bewail their own deaths? They live unthinking and do not consider their deaths. I alone keep a thinking mind as I perish; I pour tears from a mind under a beast's brow as I die. Now, hounds, you are fully wild as never before, for never before have you hunted lions with a leap as frenzied as this!"

CHAPTER 21

The Development of Greek Drama

J.G. Farrow

525 B.C.: Thespis, a poet, is said to have written and produced the first stage-play in Athens. What distinguished his play from the existing tradition of *choral lyric poetry* was that a solo singer was now to stand out as one of the characters in the story being treated in the poem. Variety was added to the performance of the poem by the fact that some passages were sung by the chorus, others by the soloist, and some were dialogues between the two.

Athens already had a number of traditional dances in which songs or hymns were sung by the chorus or solo singers. Most of these were ritualistic dances associated with religious or fertility festivals. At an early stage in the establishment of this new tradition which combined poetry, music, dance, and story-line, the practice grew of having judgments pronounced at the end of the whole festival to decide whose was the best production. After the Persian wars (491–478 B.C.) it became customary for each production not to be just a single play but a whole day's entertainment consisting of three or four plays altogether. A *trilogy* was usually a set of three tragedies in sequence. A *tetralogy* was a set of four plays: three tragedies and a Satyr-play for light relief at the end.

Aeschylus (525–456 B.C.) wrote at least 72 plays, most of them tragedies, but only 7 survive as scripts from which a performance might be constructed. One of these is the controversial *Persians*, a play about recent events (not a mythological plot). Another is the *Prometheus Bound*, in which it is suggested that Fate had a power superior even to the will of Zeus (king of the gods).

Aeschylus' largest surviving work is a complete trilogy, the *Oresteia* (story of Orestes). Each play depicts a sequence of events as a stage in a long-term pile-up of tragedy. The sequence is as follows:

1. *Agamemnon*: Agamemnon, king of Argos and Mycenae, returns home victorious from the Trojan War. He has been away for ten years and does not know what has been going on at home. He is murdered by his wife and her lover.

2. *The Offering-Bearers (Choephoroi)*: Several years later, Agamemnon's son Orestes, now grown up, returns home to avenge his father's murder.

3. *The Kindly Ones (Eumenides):* Orestes, now guilty of his own mother's murder, is haunted by the Furies and can only regain his sanity if he can be tried by a court which has the power to judge crimes against nature. He has to go to Athens to be tried by the Areopagus, a court which was believed to have had such a jurisdiction _____ granted by the gods.

Sophocles (496–406 B.C.) wrote between 70 and 123 plays, winning 24 first prizes and never being judged less than second throughout his long career. Performable copies of seven scripts survive. Although none of the surviving plays constitute trilogies as Sophocles intended them, three scripts deal with the story of Thebes and can be grouped together (as they often are by modern editors) as an "artificial trilogy." They are as follows:

1. *King Oedipus (Oedipus Rex):* Oedipus has been king of Thebes for 10 years and learns the terrible secret which accounts for the plague that has troubled the city.

2. *Oedipus at Colonus*: Oedipus, now blind and approaching death, knows that he cannot be laid to rest in a "normal" way. At Colonus, a border village of Attica, he is prevented by a group of "concerned citizens" from entering their state. He finally disappears mysteriously.

3. *Antigone*: Oedipus' sons have quarreled and finally killed one another in a civil war. Antigone insists on burying her brother in spite of a prohibition by Creon, the new king.

Euripides (485–406 B.C.) wrote 92 plays altogether, of which 19 survive as performable scripts. All but one of the surviving plays are tragedies. Euripides only won five major prizes in his life, showing that his plays were not popular at the time. They are, however, strikingly original; to us, quite "modernistic," since many of them show a preoccupation with human psychology, especially in portraying characters in the process of mental breakdown on stage.

The following are Euripides' best known plays:

Iphigenia in Aulis, a tragedy in which Agamemnon is told that he must sacrifice his daughter to the goddess Artemis, whom he had insulted, in order to regain the winds which will take his fleet and army to Troy. There are two versions of the play, in the longer of which Iphigenia vanishes mysteriously as she is about to be slaughtered at the altar.

Iphigenia in Tauris, a sequel to the above, shows how Iphigenia meets her long-lost brother Orestes, who is now in exile from Greece. Iphigenia has been in Tauris (on the coast of the Black Sea) for many years by this time, since she was transported there by the goddess Artemis, who saved her in Aulis. Now saved from being sacrificed, Iphigenia must serve the goddess by preparing strangers who arrive in the Northern land. She does not recognize Orestes at first. The plot makes full use of suspense in the build-up of the recognition and escape scenes.

The Bacchae, Euripides' last play, is about religious and psychological repression. The title refers to the women in the chorus, who have come under the intoxicating spell of Dionysus, a "new" god who has returned to his birthplace in Thebes. Pentheus, the conservative king of Thebes, tries to suppress the practices of the new cult. What happens to Pentheus from this point is shown to be a product not only of the god's wrath but also of the king's own mental preoccupations.

The Cyclops is the only complete **satyr-play** script to survive from classical antiquity. It is a stage rendering, often featuring crude slapstick, of the story of Odysseus and his men trapped in the one-eyed giant's cave.

Aristophanes (c. 450–386 B.C.) was the greets writer of Athenian **Old Comedy**. Eleven of his plays survive, and none by any other poet of Old Comedy. Most of his plays, typical of the genre, were based on absurd plots and derived their humor from political lampooning. Besides politicians, Aristophanes poked merciless fun at philosophers and sophists, especially in *The Clouds*. In this play Strepsiades, an old citizen driven to debt by his son's expensive habits, decides to send his son to the "Thinking Shop," a sort of college run by the philosopher Socrates. One highlight of the play is a guided tour of the college given by a student, showing the outrageous research projects being undertaken by self-confessed "searchers for truth." The real-life Socrates did not involve himself in scientific research, nor did he make claims to be a specialist of any subject.

In his late plays, such as the *Plutus* (The Rich Man), Aristophanes toned down the topical jokes and addressed the conditions of human life and different characteristics of individuals as the main humorous issue. This is a characteristic of **Middle Comedy**, a form which uses generalized human attitudes rather than attacking public figures by name. Much of this change was a result of Athens' losing the Peloponnesian War in 403 B.C., after which the city was ruled for a while by a military junta enforcing strict censorship.

Menander (342–289 B.C.) wrote approximately a hundred plays in the **New Comedy** genre. Five performable scripts now survive, including the *Dyskolos* (Disagreeable Man) and *the Rape of the Locks*. The tendency which grew in the Middle Comedy period toward character stereotyping becomes fully fledged in Menander: we regularly meet the young (often extravagant) hero, his girlfriend (who often seems to belong to a social class unacceptable to the hero's family until events prove otherwise), the mean father of one or other, and the hero's slave, often a character who extracts the hero from difficult circumstances and is shown to be the smartest person on stage.

CHAPTER 22

Euripides' *Bacchae*

Translated and edited by J.G. Farrow

This play was written late in Euripides' life, after he had emigrated from Athens to Macedonia. It is believed to have been produced in 406 B.C., the year of the poet's death.

CHARACTERS:

DIONYSUS: God of Moisture in Nature, also called Bacchus, Iacchus, or Bromius; he is son of Zeus

CHORUS of BACCHAE: Oriental women who have followed Dionysus to Greece

TEIRESIAS: The blind Theban prophet

CADMUS: Founder of Thebes; he has now handed over the power of king to his grandson Pentheus

PENTHEUS: Son of Cadmus' daughter Agave and of Echion, one of the Dragon's Teeth Soldiers

GUARD: Attending Pentheus

HERDSMAN: Attending Pentheus

MESSENGER AGAVE: Pentheus' mother and eldest of Cadmus' daughters

****

SCENE 1

The front of the Royal Palace in Thebes. The Palace occupies one side of the stage, while the other represents a road going up toward the mountains. In the middle background a smaller building is in ruins; it is the place where Cadmus' fourth daughter Semele lived. A shrine stands amongst the ruins, centre-stage, containing a constantly-burning flame. The stage is otherwise empty and the Chorus members are not yet seen in the Orchestra.

> *DIONYSUS enters the stage alone. He has an ivy crown on his head and is wearing a deerskin cloak. He holds a thyrsus, symbol of fertility, in his hand.*

DIONYSUS: Here I am—Dionysus, son of Zeus! My mother Semele, Cadmus' daughter, gave birth to me by the fire of lightning. I have come here to Thebes with its two rivers (Dirce and Ismenus) disguising my divine identity in a mortal shape. I see here, near the palace, my mother's memorial, recording her death by lightning.

Here her house stood. Its ruins smoulder with the still living fire of Zeus—the undying insult of Hera against my mother. I commend Cadmus for keeping this ground sanctified, a precinct consecrated to his daughter's name. I have decorated it all round with greenery of vine-leaves.

From the fields of Lydia and Phrygia, fertile in gold, I first travelled to the sun-baked plains of Persia, the walled cities of Bactria, the harsh land of the Medians, wealthy Arabia, and the whole stretch of the Asian coast where swarms of Greeks and Orientals live, mixed in vast, magnificent cities. Before I arrived here (the first Greek city I have visited), I had already throughout the East performed my dances and set forth my ritual to make my divine power recognized by mortal humanity. The reason why I have chosen Thebes as first place to raise the cry of Bacchus, to dress all who respond in deerskin clothing, and to put my ivy-wrapped thyrsus in their hands, is this: my mother's sisters, who should have been the last to say anything of the kind, said that I, Dionysus, was not Semele's son; that Semele, pregnant (according to them) by some mortal, was prompted by her father to claim that Zeus had taken her virginity and that for this lie Zeus had taken her life.

Therefore I have driven these same sisters mad, turned them all, raving, out of doors. They live now on the mountain, their wits gone. I have made them bear the symbol of my mysteries. I have sent the whole female population of Thebes out of their minds and out of their homes. Now they sit beside Cadmus' daughters, unprotected on the rocks under the silver pines. For the Thebans, though against their will, must learn this lesson in full, that my Bacchic worship is still a matter beyond their experience and understanding. I must also vindicate my mother Semele by revealing myself to humanity as the divine son she bore to immortal Zeus.

Now Cadmus has handed over his throne and royal honours to Pentheus, his grandson, an enemy of gods: that man defies me, excludes me from libations, omits my name from prayers. I shall therefore prove to him and to all Thebes that I am a god. When I have set everything in order here, I shall pass on and reveal myself somewhere else. Meanwhile if the Thebans try in anger to bring the Bacchants home from the mountain by force, I myself shall join that army of possessed women and bring them to battle. That is why I have changed my shape to that of a mortal man.

Come, my band of worshippers! Women I have brought from the East, from Tmolus the mountain of Lydia! Join me and share my travels! Raise the music of your own country, the Phrygian drums invented by Rhea the great Mother and by me! Fill Pentheus' palace with a noise to make Cadmus' citizens see!

I will go to the glens of Mount Cithaeron, where the Bacchants are, to join them in the holy dance.

> *Exit Dionysus towards the mountain. The Chorus members enter the Orchestra on the same side of the theatre.*

CHORUS:[1]

Strophe 1: From distant lands of Asia, from Tmolus the holy mountain,
    We run with Bromius, whose work is joy,
    Weariness sweet, to whom our Bacchic hymn resounds!

Antistrophe 1: Who stands in our path? Make way! Make way!
    Who is indoors? Close every mouth, keep holy silence,
    While we sing Bacchus' own hymn!

Str 2: Blessed, blessed is he who knows the mysteries the gods ordain,
    Who sanctifies his life, joins soul with soul in mystic unity,
    And, duly purified, enters the ecstasy of mountain retreats,
    Who observes the rites consecrated by Cybele the Great Mother,

---

[1]The Chorus, performing in the Orchestra below the stage and closer to the audience, customarily sang their songs in a form of highly ritualized dance routine. **Strophe** (literally "turn") was a single verse, sung by either a group of chorus members or by the Choregos (leader). It was followed by an **Antistrophe** which had a similar metrical structure to the immediately preceding Strophe, sung usually by an antiphonal group. An **Epode**, sung by the whole chorus, could either follow each pair of verses or could be reserved to the end of the song.

Who crowns his head with ivy, and waves his thyrsus in Dionysus' worship.
Run on! Dance on! Raving, possessed, Dionysus visits his own!
Bring to the wide streets of Hellas from Phrygia's mountains
The god, son of a god, spirit of ecstasy, Dionysus!

Ant 2: Once the thunderbolt from Zeus' hand delivered him,
   The pains of childbirth held his mother fast.
   But she delivered him prematurely, dying under the lightning's blast.
   But Cronus' son contained him instantly, pocketing him
   Inside the secret womb within his thigh;
   With golden pins he locked him, hidden from Hera's sight.
   So, when the fates had made the baby ready for birth,
   Zeus bore the bull-horned god, wrapping his head
   In wreaths of writhing snakes. So the Maenads too
   Catch wild snakes, nurse them, and twine them in their hair.

Str. 3: O Thebes, Semele's nurse of old, wear ivy garlands!
   Burst into flower with wreaths of lush, bright-berried bryony,
   Bring sprays of fir, green branches torn from oaks,
   Fill spirit and body with Bacchus' mystic power.
   Trim and cover your dappled fawn skin cloaks
   With locks of purest, whitest wool.
   Wild is the power of the fennel-wand: treat it with respect!
   Soon the whole land will dance,
   When the god with wild shout leads his company out
   To the mountain's towering height, swarming, rioting,
   Theban women leaving their spinning and weaving,
   Stung with the maddening trance of Dionysus!

Ant 3: O secret chamber of the Curetes, Zeus-cradling
   In the Cretan[2] glade, where, for our delight,
   The three-crested Corybantes tightened their round drumskin
   Till its wild beat made rapturous rhythm to the sweet breath
   Of Phrygian flutes! Rhea[3] the goddess found completion

---

[2]For the myth of Zeus' nativity, see Hesiod *Theogony* 480-506. Hesiod does not include the story of how Zeus was protected by the Corybantes (Helmeted Men), also known as the Curetes. The myth was associated with an ancient ritual of initiatory dancing, performed traditionally by teenage males in full armor.

[3]Rhea, as Zeus' mother, is being equated here with Cybele, the mother-goddess of Phrygia (now northwest Turkey).

In the drum with her Bacchic tunes!
From her, mother of all, very soon,
The crazy Satyrs in their festival of alternate years
Took the instruments' tune to play the leading part
In feasts delighting Dionysus' heart.

Epode: O what delight is in the mountains!
The celebrant in his sacred fawnskin
Throws himself on the ground in surrender,
While the swift company streams on!
There he hunts for blood, and rapturously
Eats the raw flesh of a slaughtered goat.
Possessed, ecstatic, he leads their cries
Over the Lydian or Phrygian mountain heights.
The earth flows with milk, flows with wine,
Flows with nectar of bees.
The air is thick with the scent of Syrian myrrh.
The celebrant runs on in a trance, whirling the torch
Blazing red from the fennel-wand in his grasp.
Shouting, he starts the scattered groups dancing,
As he shakes his delicate locks to the wild wind.
In the frenzy of song he shouts like thunder,
"On, on, run, dance, rave!
You, the gracious beauty of golden Tmolus, Sing for joy
To the rattle of thunderous drums,
Praise Dionysus the god of Joy!
Shout like Phrygians, sing out your familiar tunes,
While the sacred, pure-toned flute makes the air vibrate
With holy celebration in time with the rhythm
Of the feet that flock to the mountains, to the mountains!"
Like a foal with its mother at pasture,
Every Bacchant runs and leaps for joy.

SCENE 2

> *Members of the Chorus remain quietly in the Orchestra. Enter* **Teiresias**. *He knows where the door is, though he cannot see it, and knocks.*

TEIRESIAS: Who mans the gates? Call Cadmus, Agenor's son, out of his house, the man who left Sidon to build this city of Thebes. Go, someone! Tell him Teiresias is looking for him! He knows what I have come about, what I, an old man, agreed with him, an even older man: to twine our thyrsi and put on deerskins, to crown our heads with ivy shoots.

> *Enter **Cadmus**.*

CADMUS: My dear friend, I heard your voice though I was indoors. How glad I was to hear the wise voice of a wise man! I am here ready with the god's equipment. For we should glorify as much as we can the god Dionysus, who is my own daughter's son and has shown himself. Where should we direct our dance? Shake our silvery head? Teach me, Teiresias, old as we are (for you are wise) so that I may not grow weary night nor day, beating my thyrsus on the ground. Let us pleasantly forget how old we are.

TEIRESIAS: You feel as I do! I too am young and will try the dance!

CADMUS: So shall we take a ride to the mountain?

TEIRESIAS: No—the god would receive less respect.

CADMUS: Old as I am, I shall be your guide and instructor.

TEIRESIAS: The god will lead us there without tiring us.

CADMUS: Shall we alone of the city dance to Bacchus?

TEIRESIAS: For we alone are in our right mind: the rest are crazy.

CADMUS: Too much delay! Take my hand!

TEIRESIAS: Look, join hands, and lead on!

CADMUS: I, a mortal, do not despise the gods.

TEIRESIAS: Let us not be too clever in dealing with the gods. We have inherited traditions of our ancestors, as old as time, and no reasoning will overthrow them, not even if the ultimate peak of wisdom[4] be found in the mind. Someone may accuse me of having no respect for age, in wanting to dance and crown my head with ivy. But the god does not discriminate between older and younger in the dance; he wants to have like honours from all, and does not want his worship to be a matter of figures.

CADMUS: Since you, Teiresias, don't see the daylight, I shall become your prophet. Here comes Pentheus, hurrying to the palace, Echion's son, to whom I give kingship. How flustered he is! What news will he tell?

> *Enter **Pentheus**, officiously.*

PENTHEUS: While I happened to be out of the country, I have just heard evil news of the city, that our women have left home on a pretence of Bacchic worship, and are wandering in the wooded mountains, honouring Dionysus (whoever he is) with their

---

[4]The Greek word for wisdom is *sophia*. Euripides, through the stage-character of Teiresias, is using this speech and its sequel on the next page to make a public comment on the Sophists who were notorious in Athens at the time. For Sophist rationalizations of myth, see Chapter 2, Ancient Critics, #2.

dances. In the middle of their parties stand full cups, and they slink off in private, each in a different direction, giving themselves to men, on the excuse that they are Maenads celebrating rituals.

But they prefer Aphrodite to Bacchus! As many as I have caught, my servants are keeping manacled in the public prison. But those still at large I shall hunt out of the mountains, even Ino and Agave who bore me to Echion, and Actaeon's mother—Autonoe, too, I mean. I'll soon stop them from this Bacchic business when I have them caught in an iron trap.

They also tell me a foreigner has arrived, a singer of magic from Lydia, with blond hair dressed in scented locks, wine-complexioned with the bloom of Aphrodite on his cheeks. He spends days and nights pretending Bacchic celebrations with girls. If I catch him inside my home, I'll stop him beating his thyrsus and shaking his hair, by cutting his neck from his body! They say this man is the god Dionysus, that he was once stitched up in Zeus' thigh, he—who was once burned up by a thunderbolt along with his mother, because she lied of a union with Zeus. Isn't this a crime worthy of hanging—passing off these insolent statements—whoever the foreigner may be?

But look—another marvel! I see the prophet Teiresias dressed in a dappled deerskin, and my mother's father, a laughing-stock, waving a fennel-wand around! I'm ashamed, old man, to see you so senseless in your old age. Won't you take that ivy off? Won't you let go the thyrsus from your hand, grandfather?

You put him up to this, Teiresias! You want to introduce this new god to the people so that you can take pay for more augury and divination. If your grey age didn't protect you, you'd be sitting amongst the Bacchanal women in jail for introducing this troublemaking religion. I tell you: whenever the grape's produce has a place at a women's gathering, nothing healthy will come of their party.

Chorus: What blasphemy! Stranger, do you not respect the gods, nor Cadmus who sowed the earth-born crop? Are you ashamed of your birth, you who are a son of Echion?

Teiresias: Whenever a wise man finds a distinguished subject for a speech, it isn't difficult to be eloquent. You have a fluent tongue, as if you were in your right mind, but there is no sense to be found in your words. But a bold man, capable of speech and ready, becomes a bad citizen if he is not in command of his wits. But this new god, at whom you poke fun, I cannot explain how great he will become throughout Greece. For there are two things, young man, that come first in humanity: the goddess Demeter, she is the earth, call her by what name you like, she feeds mortals with dry food. The one who follows as her counterpart is Semele's son, who discovered the moist drink of the grape and introduced it to mortals, the remover of grief from wretched men as soon as they are filled with the grape's juice. He also gives sleep as forgetfulness from daily ills, and there is no other medicine for troubles. He, a god, is poured as a libation to gods, so that men can have what is good through him.

And do you mock the notion that he was sewn in Zeus' thigh? I shall show you that this makes good sense. When Zeus snatched him from the fire of the thunder-bolt, and carried the baby to Olympus, Hera would have liked to throw this god from heaven. But Zeus hatched a counter-plan, as a god can: he broke off a piece of the Aether that surrounds the world, and made it a hostage,[5] giving it to Hera for her spite against Dionysus. And in time mortals told how he was put in the thigh of Zeus, changing the name. And so the story grew, because a god was hostage once to the goddess Hera.

This god is also a prophet. For the Bacchic ecstasy and frenzy contain much prophecy: whenever the god comes, as often he does, into the body, he makes his initiates tell the future. He also, in turn, has some share of Ares' powers; for whenev-er fear comes down upon an army that is fully weaponed and in its ranks, before a spear is touched, this too is madness[6] from Dionysus. You will also see him leaping over the rocks of Delphi, with pine torches over a double hill, tossing and waving Bacchus' branch, great throughout Greece. But believe me, Pentheus: do not boast that force holds power over people; if you think it does, your own opinion is dis-eased. Welcome the god into your land, pour offerings, worship Bacchus, and crown your head.

Dionysus will not force women to be chaste, but chastity is always a power in their own nature. You must note this. For in Bacchic revels a chaste person will not be corrupted.

See, you rejoice whenever a crowd stands at the gates, and the city glorifies Pentheus' name. He too, I think, rejoices in being honoured. I therefore, and Cadmus whom you ridicule, will crown our heads with ivy and dance, a grey-haired team, but still we must dance. I will not fight gods under your persuasion, for you are mad in the sorriest way, and can take no cure with medicines, even though your sickness is not drug-free.

Chorus: Old man, you do not shame Phoebus with your speech, but you are wise in honouring Bromius as a great god.

---

[5]The word here for "hostage" is *homêros*. In the next sentence "the thigh" is *ho mêros*. The play on word-sounds obviously appealed to some real-life sophists in Euripides' own time as a legitimate tool in rationalizing myths.

[6]Euripides must be referring to *panic*, a condition which ancient Greeks attributed to the god Pan (hence the origin of the word). Pan was believed to be one of Dionysus' associates, or sometimes even an alternate form of the same god.

Cadmus: Child, Teiresias has given you good advice. Settle with us; do not live outside prevailing custom. For now you are in the clouds, there is no sense in your thoughts. For if this is no god, as you say, let him at least be called such by you. Tell a good lie that he is a god, so that Semele may be thought mother of a god, and honour may come to us all and to our family. Look at Actaeon's wretched fate, whom the hounds (that he himself had raised on raw meat[7]) tore apart in the fields, when he boasted that he was a better hunter than Artemis. Don't let this happen to you, but let me crown your head. Give honour with us to the god.

Pentheus: Take your hand away! Go away and play at Bacchants! Don't wipe off your folly on me! I shall exact a penalty from your teacher in stupidity. Will someone go quickly, to the place where this man does his bird-watching, uproot it with crowbars and turn it upside down? Throw his garlands to the winds and storms! In doing this I shall especially upset him. The rest of you, go through the city, root out the girl-faced foreigner, who brings strange sickness on our wives and defiles our beds. If you catch him, drag him here in chains, so that he may pay the penalty by stoning, and die on seeing his cruel revelry in Thebes.

Teiresias: Poor man, you don't know what you are saying! You are quite mad now; just out of your mind before. Let's go, Cadmus, and offer up prayers on this man's behalf, savage though he is, and on behalf of the city, that the god may do nothing terrible.

Follow me with your ivy-covered wand. Help support my body, as I shall yours. It would be a shame for two old men to fall. Let's go, for we must serve Bacchus the son of Zeus.

Cadmus, make sure Pentheus does not bring grief upon your house. I am not speaking in prophecy, but in reality. For, as a fool, he says foolish things.

SCENE 3

> *Re-enter* **Pentheus** *at one side, a* **servant** *at the other, with* **Dionysus** *in handcuffs.*

Servant: Pentheus, we are here as hunters who have caught this prey after which you sent us. We did not set out in vain. We found the beast tame; he didn't run away, but held out his hands willingly, didn't even turn pale, nor change his wine-coloured complexion, but laughed and let us tie him and bring him here. He even waited, and made

---

[7]Compare this account of Actaeon with sources from art in Euripides' time and earlier. It is not the same version as the one given by Ovid (*Metamorphoses*) and Nonnos (*Dionysiaca* V).

my job easy. Embarrassed, I told him, "Stranger, I'm not arresting you willingly, but by order of Pentheus who sent me."

As for the Bacchanal women you locked up in the public prison with chains, they are gone—freed!—to the meadows, where they dance and call on Bromius their god. Of their own accord the chains fell off their feet, locks unfastened themselves, doors flew open, without mortal hand.

This man came here full of many wonders to Thebes. The rest is up to you.

Pentheus: You are mad! Once he is within the trap of my hands, there is no way he can be fast enough to escape me. You are not without shape, stranger—for women's purposes, at least. That's why you came to Thebes. Your hair is long—no good for wrestling! You have a pale complexion from care, not from the sun's rays. You keep to the shade, pursuing Aphrodite with your looks. First tell me your nationality.

Dionysus: That's no boast, but easy to tell. I suppose you know by hearsay of flowery Tmolus?

Pentheus: I know—it surrounds the town of Sardis.

Dionysus: I am from there—Lydia is my homeland.

Pentheus: On what authority do you bring these rituals to Greece?

Dionysus: Dionysus, the son of Zeus, came to me.

Pentheus: Is there a Zeus over there too, who begets new gods?

Dionysus: No, but the same one who married Semele here.

Pentheus: Did he take control of you by night or in daylight?

Dionysus: I saw him as he saw me, and he gave me the rites.

Pentheus: What is the appearance of these mysteries of yours?

Dionysus: It is unspeakable for uninitiated mortals to know.

Pentheus: What profit do they bring to those who sacrifice?

Dionysus: It is not lawful that you should hear, but it is worth knowing.

Pentheus: You bait your answers well, that I should want to hear.

Dionysus: The god's rites are hostile to the man who practices impiety.

Pentheus: You say you saw the god; what was he like?

Dionysus: As he wanted. I didn't control that.

Pentheus: You have dodged the question again and said nothing.

Dionysus: Wise speech seems unwise to a fool.

Pentheus: Is this the first place you have come to, introducing your god?

Dionysus: All Asians dance these mystic rites.

Pentheus: They are far inferior to Greeks in their thinking.

Dionysus: Better in this respect, but their customs are different.

Pentheus: Do you conduct your rites by night or by day?

Dionysus: Mainly by night; darkness has solemnity.

Pentheus: This is an immoral trick when dealing with women.

Dionysus: A person can devise filth in daylight too.

Pentheus: You must be punished for the evil of your smart answers.

Dionysus: You too, for your ignorance and impiety towards the god.

Pentheus: How bold the Bacchant is, lacking no skill in words!

Dionysus: What must happen to me? What terrible thing will you do?

Pentheus: First I shall cut your dainty hair from you.

Dionysus: My hair is sacred. I grow it for the god.

Pentheus: Next, give me the thyrsus from your hand.

Dionysus: Take it from me yourself. I carry it as Dionysus' wand.

Pentheus: We will guard your body inside my prison.

Dionysus: The god himself will set me free whenever I want.

Pentheus: Yes—whenever you call upon him standing among your Bacchanal women!

Dionysus: He stands nearby and sees what is happening to me now.

Pentheus: Where is he? He's not apparent to my eyes!

Dionysus: Near me. You, being impious yourself, don't see him.

Pentheus: Seize him! He's laughing at me and at Thebes!

Dionysus: I warn you not to bind me: I'm in my right mind and you are not.

Pentheus: I, who am more in charge than you are, order you to be bound.

Dionysus: You don't know why you are alive, what you are doing, or who you are.

Pentheus: Pentheus, son of Agave and of my father Echion.

Dionysus: You are suited, according to your name, for ill fortune.[8]

Pentheus: Away! Lock him up nearby in the horses' stables, so that he can see dark gloom. Dance there! As for the women you have brought with you, accomplices in your mischief, we shall either sell them off as slaves or keep them as maids at the loom, and so occupy their hands away from cymbals and drums.

Dionysus: I go. But what cannot be cannot happen to me. But Dionysus will take from you compensation for these insults, the one you say doesn't exist. For when you injure me you put him in prison.

[A Choral Hymn has been omitted here.]

---

[8]*Penthos*, in Greek, means "grief."

SCENE 4

> *The **Chorus members** are in the orchestra at the conclusion of the hymn omitted above. **Dionysus** is heard off-stage.*

Dionysus: Yo! Listen to my voice! Yo, Bacchae! Yo, Bacchae!

Chorus: Who is here? From where did the voice of Evios call upon me?

Dionysus: Yo! Yo! Again I call, I, Semele's son, Zeus' son.

Chorus: Yo! Master, Master! Come now to our revel, Bromius, Bromius!

Dionysus: Shake, floor, shake, ground in mighty earthquake!

Chorus A:[9] Ah, ah, soon will Pentheus' palace be shaken in its fall!

Chorus B: Dionysus is in the hall! Worship him!

Chorus C: We worship him! See how the stone lintels over those pillars are moving! Bromius is raising his shout inside the palace!

Dionysus: Kindle the lightning-red torch! Burn, burn the palace of Pentheus!

> *Flame and earthquake effects: the fire on Semele's tomb blazes much higher*

Chorus A: Ah! Ah! Don't you see the fire around Semele's holy tomb, left once as a lightning-stricken memorial to the thunder of Zeus?

Chorus B: Throw to the earth your bodies, throw them, Maenads, trembling! For the King is coming, to put this palace in confusion and turn it upside-down.

> Enter **Dionysus**

Dionysus: Women of Asia, are you so stricken with fear that you have fallen to the ground? It seems you saw Pentheus' palace shaken down to the ground. But get yourselves up, take courage, be rid of the fear from your bodies.

Cho: O greatest light of our Bacchic revels! How glad I am to see you after being so lonely!

Dionysus: Did you enter into despair when I was put inside, thinking that I was sunk into darkness in Pentheus' prison?

Chorus: Of course! Who would protect me, if disaster befell you? But how did you escape the clutches of such a wicked man?

Dionysus: I freed myself easily, without any trouble.

Chorus: Didn't he tie your hands with chains and handcuffs?

---

[9]The Chorus now seems to have split into three groups for a general effect of mass hysteria.

Dionysus: I insulted him in this too, so that he thought he was tying me, but didn't lay a finger on me; he was fed on hopes. Near the stall where he wanted to tie me, he found a bull and tied the chains and handcuffs round its feet and knees, breathing his fury, the sweat pouring from him, chewing his lips. I just stood by and watched quietly. Meanwhile Bacchus came and shook the house, lit a flame on his mother's tomb. Pentheus, when he saw it, thought his house was on fire; he rushed here and there, calling on his slaves to bring river-water. Every slave was kept busy, working in vain.

Then he abandoned this job, thinking I had escaped. He drew his sword and rushed inside the house. And then Bromius (I suppose, for I'm telling what I could see) created a ghost in the courtyard. He rushed at this immediately, lunging at air as if he were stabbing at me. And Bacchus created more madness than this, for he threw the building to the ground. It's all ruined, to remind him of my cruel chains. Pentheus dropped his sword, fainting. For he, a man, dared to take up arms against a god. But I leave the palace and come to you, thinking nothing of Pentheus.

It seems to me, for I hear a footstep outside, that he will soon be here. What will he say to this? I shall treat it lightly, even if he breathes a lot of hot air. It's a wise man's job to contain his anger soberly.

> *Enter Pentheus*

Pentheus: I have suffered terrible things! The foreigner has escaped me, though I recently had him caught in chains.

Ahah! There's the man! What's this? How did you get out and appear in front of my home?

Dionysus: Stay there and keep your anger under control.

Pentheus: How did you escape and get out here?

Dionysus: Didn't I say, or didn't you hear me—that someone would free me?

Pentheus: Who? You are always coming up with new answers.

Dionysus: The one who makes the vine grow fruitful for mankind.

Pentheus: And drives women mad from their homes?

Dionysus: In insulting Dionysus you praise him.

Pentheus: I order every tower-gate around to be closed!

Dionysus: Why? Can't gods climb walls?

Pentheus: You are wise—wise except where you should be wise.

Dionysus: I certainly am wise[10] where wisdom is needed. But listen first to this man, who has just from the mountains to tell you something. I shall wait here for you— I won't run away.

> *Enter* **Herdsman**

---

[10]See note 4, above.

Herdsman: Pentheus, king of this Theban land, I have just left Cithaeron, where the arrows of white snow never fail, to come here.

Pentheus: What urgent message have you brought here?

Herdsman: I saw the lady Bacchae, who have left this land with their white feet stung by frenzy. I have come to tell you, my master, and Thebes, what strange and wonderful things they are doing. But I want to hear first whether I may speak freely of what went on up there, or edit my story. For I am afraid of your passion's quickness, Lord, and your over-royal anger.

Pentheus: Speak on. You will not be punished by me. For I shall not be angry with just men. The more terrible your stories about the Bacchae, the harsher will be the punishment I inflict on the man who taught the women these ways.

Herdsman: The herds of grazing cattle were just climbing the hillside as the sun was sending out his rays to warm the earth. I saw three groups of Bacchant women; of these, Autonoé was leader of the first, your mother Agave of the second, and Ino of the third group. All lay asleep, their bodies at rest, some leaning back on piles of pine-needles, some with oak-leaves for pillows, but lying modestly on the ground; not, as you claim, drunk with wine amongst the sound of flute-music or hunting Aphrodite alone through the woods. Then your mother stood up amongst the Bacchae and called out, "Shake off sleep!" as she heard the lowing of our horned cattle. The women, casting restful sleep from their eyes, stood upright, a wonder to see for their good order, young and old, even unmarried girls. First they let their hair fall down over their shoulders, then hitched up their fawnskins where the straps were loose, and wrapped around themselves snakes that licked their cheeks.

Some, cradling fawns or wolf cubs in their arms, fed the wild animals on their own white milk, if they were young mothers who had left their children at home. They wreathed their heads with leaves of ivy, oak, and flowery bryony. One took her thyrsus, hit a rock, and out came a spring of running water. Another planted her thyrsus in the ground, and through this the god sent a fountain of wine. Whoever had a thirst for white milk, scratched the ground with her finger-nails, and milk poured up for her. From their ivy-clad wands dripped streams of honey. So, if you had been there and seen it, you would be praising the god you now curse.

We cattle-men and shepherds got together, to confer with one another, to confer about these terrible deeds deserving of wonder. One of us, a streetwise town man with ready tongue, said to us all,

"You who live on the holy mountain sides, let us hunt Pentheus' mother Agave from her Bacchic revels, and do the king a favour!"

This seemed to us a good idea, so we hid ourselves in ambush amongst the leaves. At the appointed time they waved the thyrsus for their celebration, calling with collective voice on Iacchus, son of Zeus, Bromius. The whole mountain and its wild animals joined in the celebration, and nothing kept still as they ran.

Agave happened to dance around near me, so I jumped out, intending to seize her, leaving empty the cover where I had lain. She shouted out, "O my running hounds, we are chased by these men! Follow me! Follow with your thyrsus as a weapon!"

We then ran away and just escaped being torn apart by the Bacchae, but they descended on our grazing cattle without swords. Then you could have seen one take in her two hands a deep-uddered heifer, bellowing loud; others tore apart calves. You would have seen a rib or a cloven hoof thrown up and down. Shreds of flesh hung and dripped with blood under the pines. Challenging bulls showing their anger by the horns were tripped headlong to the earth, brought down by countless hands of maidens. The flesh was stripped from the bones sooner than you could blink your royal eyes.

They moved on, swooping like birds down to the lowland plain that raises crops for the Thebans along the stream of Asopus. Like enemies they attacked Hysiae and Erythrae that lie below Cithaeron. They turned everything upside down, snatched children from homes! Whatever they put on their shoulders stayed there without straps; nothing fell to the ground, whether bronze or iron. They carried fire on their heads, but it did not burn them.

The people, angry at being robbed by Bacchae, took up arms—and then, your majesty, something happened terrible to see. While they were unharmed by the steel-tipped spear, the thyrsus-darts thrown from their hands made wounds, and women turned back men in flight; not without some divine help. Then they went back where they had come from, to the streams the god had set up for them, and washed the blood, while snakes licked their faces clean with their tongues.

So whoever this god is, your majesty, receive him into this city. In addition to his other greatness, I hear, he sent the vine that ends cares for mortals. Where there is no wine, there is no Aphrodite, nor is there any other joy for humanity.

> *Exit Herdsman*

Chorus: I am afraid to speak words of freedom to the king, but I shall speak all the same: Dionysus is not inferior to any god!

Pentheus: The insolence of the Bacchae has come here like a flame, a great curse throughout Greece. We must not hold back. Go to the Electran Gate! Tell all my shieldbearers, all my fast cavalry and all my bowmen and light-armed troops to meet me there, so we may march against the Bacchae. For has this not gone too far, that we should endure what we have suffered from our women?

Dionysus: Even though you have heard me, Pentheus, you have not listened to a word. Though I have suffered ill at your hands, I still warn you not to bear arms against a god. Hold your peace. Bromius will not permit you to drive his Bacchae from the hills of their ceremonies.

Pentheus: Don't give me instructions, but be content with your escape. Shall I punish you again?

Dionysus: Better to sacrifice to him than to be angry with him and kick against the goad, a man fighting a god.

Pentheus: I'll sacrifice all right, a slaughter of women, as they deserve, creating all that trouble in the valleys of Cithaeron!

Dionysus: You will all run away. It would be a shame for bronze shields to be turned away by the thyrsi of women.

Pentheus: I'm tired of doing battle with this foreigner; whatever we do to him or he to us, he won't be quiet.

Dionysus: Sir, we can still turn this disaster round.

Pentheus: Doing what? Being a slave to my slave-women?

Dionysus: I shall bring the women here without arms.

Pentheus: Aha! Are you plotting a trick against me?

Dionysus: What trick, if I save you by my skill?

Pentheus: You have plotted to keep your revels going for ever.

Dionysus: Know this: my covenant is with the god.

Pentheus: Bring out my weapons! As for you, stop talking.

Dionysus: Wait! Do you want to see them sitting together on the hills?

Pentheus: Indeed I would give countless gold for that.

Dionysus: How did you fall into so great a desire for this?

Pentheus: It would grieve me very much to see them so drunk.

Dionysus: But you would gladly see a bitter sight?

Pentheus: Yes, if I could sit quietly under the pines.

Dionysus: But they will track you out if you come secretly.

Pentheus: Openly then! You are right in saying this.

Dionysus: If I lead you, will you try the road?

Pentheus: Lead on as quickly as possible; I begrudge you the delay.

Dionysus: We must now get you dressed in robes of fine linen.

Pentheus: What's this? Should I turn from man to woman?

Dionysus: But they'll kill you if they see a man there.

Pentheus: You're right again, as you were before.

Dionysus: Dionysus taught me this.

Pentheus: How shall we make your plan work?

Dionysus: I shall go into your house and dress you there.
Pentheus: What dress? A woman's? Shame seizes me!
Dionysus: Do you no longer want to watch the Maeneads?
Pentheus: What dress did you say I should wear?
Dionysus: I shall arrange long hair on your head.
Pentheus: What is the next detail of my dress?
Dionysus: Ankle-length robes, and a mitre[11] on your head.
Pentheus: Would you put anything else on me as well as these?
Dionysus: A thyrsus in your hand, and a covering of fawnskin.
Pentheus: I can't dress up as a woman!
Dionysus: But you'll shed blood if you come to blows with the Bacchae.
Pentheus: You're right. I must first go and spy them out.
Dionysus: Wiser than hunting evils with evils.
Pentheus: How should I walk through Cadmus' city unseen?
Dionysus: We shall go by empty streets. I'll lead the way.
Pentheus: Anything would be better than being ridiculed by the Bacchae. We shall go in the house and plan what seems best.
Dionysus: So be it; I am at your disposal in every way.
Pentheus: I go. I shall either march sword in hand, or obey your advice.

> *Exit Pentheus.*

Dionysus: Women, the man is stepping into the trap. He will find the Bacchae and will pay the death-penalty. Dionysus, it's your turn now, you are not far away. We shall be avenged: first he will lose his wits, sudden madness coming upon him. In his right mind he will never willingly put on women's clothes. Driven out of his mind he will put them on. I would like to make him a laughing-stock for Thebes, leading him in female attire through the city's streets, after the earlier threats in which he was so terrifying.

But now I go to put upon Pentheus the costume he will wear to Hades, slaughtered at his mother's hands. He will recognize Dionysus as Zeus' son, grown terrible at last, yet kindest to mankind.

>*Exit Dionysus*

* * * *Choral Hymn* * * * *(omitted).*

---

[11]The mitre was the traditional hat of ancient Phrygian religious ceremonies. It fits tightly round the head. In this scene one of its functions must have been to hold on Pentheus' blond wig (the "long hair" just mentioned; see also below, lines 1117 ff.).

SCENE 5

>*Re-enter Dionysus*

Dionysus: You who burn up to see forbidden things, eager for what should not be desired, Pentheus, I mean, come out before your palace! Let me see you dressed as a female reveler, a Bacchant, ready to spy on your mother and her group.

>*Enter Pentheus*

You look like one of Cadmus' daughters!

Pentheus: I think I see two suns, a double Thebes with twice its seven gates. You look like a bull leading me onwards; horns have sprouted forth on your head. Were you an animal before? You have certainly turned into a bull now!

Dionysus: The god leads us on, not in the kind form he had before, but now on our side. Now you see what you should see.

Pentheus: What do I look like? Have I the posture of Ino, or of my mother Agave?

Dionysus: I think I see their very selves reflected in you. But your hair slipped out of place, not the way I fixed it under the mitre.

Pentheus: Indoors I loosened it, shaking my head and practicing the Bacchic frenzy.

Dionysus: I'll put it right again for you, since I have taken the job of handmaid. Hold up your head.

Pentheus: See, straighten it out. I'm entirely in your hands.

Dionysus: Your girdle is loose now: the folds of your dress don't hang down evenly to your ankles.

Pentheus: That seems the case by my right foot. The robe hangs straight on the left side.

Dionysus: You'll certainly consider me your closest friend when you see the Bacchae unexpectedly sober.

Pentheus: Should I hold my thyrsus in my right hand or in this one, to look most like a Bacchant?

Dionysus: You must hold it in your right hand and raise your right foot in time with it. I congratulate you on your change of heart.

Pentheus: Would I be able to lift the mountain valleys on my shoulders, and the Bacchae themselves with them?

Dionysus: You would if you wanted. Your mind was not healthy before, but now it's as it should be.

Pentheus: Shall we use crowbars? Or shall I put my arm, or shoulder, under the cliffs and tear them up?

Dionysus: Don't destroy the shrines of the Nymphs and haunts of Pan, where he plays his pipes.

Pentheus: You are right. We should not overcome the women by force. I shall hide my body in the pine-trees.

Dionysus: You will hide in your fated hiding-place, when you come in treachery as a spy on the Maeneads.

Pentheus: I see them like birds caught in the bushes, caught in the closest nets of their couplings.

Dionysus: So you are sent forth as guardian for this purpose. Perhaps you will catch them, if you are not yourself caught first.

Pentheus: Take me through the middle of Thebes! For I alone am man enough to do this!

Dionysus: Alone and unassisted you endure this toil for the city. The contests you must face await you. Follow on. I shall go as your guide for safety, but another will bring you back.

Pentheus: My mother . . .?

Dionysus: A sight for all to watch.

Pentheus: I am going for this!

Dionysus: You will come back carried . . .

Pentheus: You talk of luxury for me!

Dionysus: In your mother's hands.

Pentheus: You are forcing pomp on me!

Dionysus: It's only the sort of pomp . . .

Pentheus: As I deserve.

Dionysus: You are strange, strange! And strange things will happen to you. You will win fame that soars to heaven.

>*Exit Pentheus*

Reach out your hands, Agave, and her sisters too, Cadmus' daughters! I am bringing the young man to this great confrontation, in which I shall be the winner, and Bromius too. The affair itself will explain the rest.

>*Exit Dionysus*

Choral Hymn (omitted)

SCENE 6

> *Enter another Messenger*

Messenger: O house once prosperous in the sight of all Greece,   1024
 Home of the old Sidonian who once sowed the wild offspring
 Of the snaky dragon in the soil, how I weep for you!
 Though I am a slave, nevertheless a slave shares his master's misfortunes.

Chorus: What is it? What news are you bringing from the Bacchae?
Messenger: Pentheus, the son of father Echion, is dead!
Chorus: Lord Bromius, you are clearly a great god!
Messenger: What do you mean? What did you just say? Do you rejoice at my master's
 misfortunes, woman?
Chorus: Being a foreigner, I sing a hymn in a foreign mode. For I no longer cringe
 in fear of chains.
Messenger Do you think Thebes is so unmanned?
Chorus: Dionysus, not Thebes, Dionysus has power over me.
Messenger: I excuse you, but it is not good to rejoice at evils that have happened
 to someone, women.
Chorus: Tell me, tell me, in what way did the unjust man who does unfair
 things die?
Messenger: When we had left the homesteads of this Theban soil,
 And had reached the streams of Asopus, we began to
 Push out into the hill-country around Cithaeron,
 Pentheus and I—for I was following my master—
 And the stranger who was our escort to the spectacle.
 First, then, we settled in a grassy glen,
 Keeping quiet every trace of movement from foot   1050
 Or tongue, so we could see and not be seen.
 There was a ravine, edged by cliffs, with waters
 Bubbling through it, shaded over by pines, where the maenads
 Sat down, occupying their hands in pleasant tasks.
 For some of them were re-crowning with ivy
 A thyrsus that had lost its headgear,
 Others, like fillies freed from a painted harness,
 Were singing to one another Bacchic antiphonal songs in turn.
 But Pentheus the bold, not seeing the crowd of women,
 Spoke thus: "Stranger, from where we are standing
 I cannot reach with my eyes these fake maenads.

But, if I climbed a fir tree up on the embankment,
I'd be able to see rightly the maenads' wrong-doing."

Then, indeed, I saw the stranger's marvelous power,
For, taking the sky-high topmost branch of the fir,
He pulled it, pulled it, pulled it down, to the dark ground.
So it was bent like a bow, or as a circular wheel
Is dragged when being marked out with peg on its course.
So the stranger took in his hands the mountain-tree stem
And bent it down to the ground, a deed no mortal could do.
He let Pentheus go, sitting on the fir-branch, carefully
Letting the stem go straight, upwards, through his hands,
Taking care not to shake him off.
The tree towered upwards, straight up to the sky,
Holding my master as he sat on its back.
He was clearly visible to the maenads, clearer than he could
See them; but just as he was coming up into sight
It was no longer possible to see the stranger,
But some kind of voice from the sky, I suppose
It was Dionysus, called out: "Young women,
I bring you the man who made a mockery
Of you, me, and of my rites. Avenge yourselves on him!"
As he said this a light of holy fire flashed
Both heavenwards and to earth.
The air was silent. Silent too, the wooded valley held   1085
Its leaves. You could not have heard the cry of any beast.
But the women, not hearing clearly what the voice proclaimed,
Stood upright and stared around them.
He called to them again; when Cadmus' daughters
Distinctly heard Bacchus' call, they came
Running no less swiftly than doves,
Mother Agave and all her sisters and relatives,
All the Bacchae too. Through the torrent-washed glen
They leapt onwards in a column, raging with the god's breath.   1095
But when they saw my master sitting up in the pine-tree,
First they started throwing broken pieces of rock at him,
As they perched on a facing cliff,
Then they started throwing pine-branches.
Others threw their thyrsi through the air at Pentheus,   1100
An ill-fated target. But they could not reach him.

For the wretched man sat beyond their aim,
A seat too high, yet trapped with no escape.
At last, with lightning speed tearing down
Oak branches, they tried to force up the roots
With levers not of iron.
But when they could achieve no end of their toils,
Agave spoke:
"Come, stand in a circle, take hold of the tree!
Maenads, seize the climbing creature we have trapped!
Don't let him disclose the secret dances of the god!"

They laid ten thousand hands on the pine tree
And wrenched it from the ground.
Sitting in the top, from on high he fell to the ground,
To the earth fell Pentheus with ten thousand groans!
For he had realized his end was near.
First his mother started, as priestess of the slaughter,
And fell upon him. But he tore the mitre from his hair,
So that wretched Agave should recognize and not kill him.
Touching her cheek, he said,
"It is I, mother, Pentheus, your child!
The one you bore in Echion's house! Have pity on me,
Mother, don't kill your own child because of my sins!"

She, raging wildly and rolling round her eyes,
Not thinking as her mind should have been thinking,
Was possessed by Bacchus and did not listen to him.   1125
Taking his left arm below the elbow, and
Putting her foot firmly against the doomed man's ribs,
She wrenched it out at the shoulder,
Not by her own strength, but the god put force in her hands.
Ino was working away on the other side,
Tearing at his flesh, while Autonoe
And the whole crowd of Bacchae joined in.
There was shouting all around every side, while he
Groaned as long as he had breath. One of them carried an arm,
Another, a foot with the boot still laced on it.
His ribs were laid bare with their tearing. Every one of them
Bloodied her hands as she played ball with Pentheus' flesh.
His body now lies strewn around, some bits under hard rocks,
Some in the deep woody shade of the trees,
No easy thing to find. As for his poor head,

His mother who took it holds it in her hands.
She carries it, brandishing it on the end of her thyrsus
As if it were a lion's head, caught in the middle
Of Cithaeron's mountain range. She has now left her sisters
At the dance of the Maenads. She herself is now coming
Within these walls, rejoicing in her ill-fated hunt.
She calls on Bacchus her huntsman comrade,
Her companion of the wild, bringing glorious victory,
Who will make her weep at her conquest.
I am now departing from this tragic scene,
Before Agave gets inside the palace.   1150
It is best to be prudent and revere the gods.
I think this is also the wisest piece of advice
For those who deal with mortals.

SCENE 7

>*The Chorus members are parading around the Orchestra as if they have just returned from the mountain*

Chorus: We dance to Bacchus, we shout aloud
   The disaster that has befallen Pentheus
   Of the dragon's blood.   1165
   But I see Agave, Pentheus' mother,
   Rolling her eyes wildly.
   Welcome the company of the god who shouts "Yo!"

>*Enter Agave*

Agave: Women of Asia . . .
Chorus: Why do you pester me? Ugh!
Agave: We are bringing to the palace a vine-branch,
   Freshly cut from the mountains, a blessed hunting-trophy.
Chorus: I see it, and shall welcome you in fellowship.
Agave: I caught it without a noose, the young offspring of a wild lion.
   So, . . . you can see it!
Chorus: In what wild place did you catch it?
Agave: Cithaeron . . .
Chorus: Cithaeron?
Agave: Was his killing-place.
Chorus: Who shot him?

Agave: The first honour is mine! We shall be called Blessed Agave at the victory
    party!
Chorus: Who else?
Agave: Cadmus' . . .
Chorus: Cadmus?
Agave: His daughters laid hold of this prey after me! Yes, after me!
    This was a splendid hunt, so come and share the feast.
Chorus: What . . .? Have a share in it? Wretch!
Agave: The calf is young. There's a thick crop of hair
    Growing up to the crest of his head.
Chorus: The thickness of his hair certainly makes him look like a wild animal.
Agave: Bacchus, our wise leader in the hunt, wisely
    Led the Maenads on to catch this animal.
Chorus: Our master is a hunter!
Agave: Do you praise me?
Chorus: I praise you!
Agave: Cadmus' children will too . . .
Chorus: And your son Pentheus . . .?
Agave: Will praise his mother for killing this lion cub!
Chorus: A strange prize!
Agave: Yes, strange!
Chorus: Are you happy?
Agave: I rejoice greatly! And evidently great
    Is this, the hunt I have seen to its fulfillment!
Chorus: Show now, wretched woman, the victory spoil   1200
    Which you have carried home.
Agave: You who live in Thebes' land
    With its fair-towered city,
    Come and see this wild catch which we,
    Cadmus' daughters, have tracked down!
    We didn't use strap-thrown Thessalian spears,
    Or nets, but the white fingernails
    Of our hands. After this, will huntsmen brag,
    Buying unnecessarily the armourers' instruments?
    We have caught this with our very own hands,
    Then tore the beast's limbs apart.
    Where is my father, the old man?
    Let him come quickly! Pentheus, my son—
    Where is he? Let him take a step-ladder, climb
    Up against the palace front wall,

And nail to the triglyphs this lion's head,
The one I've caught and stand here holding.

[Enter Cadmus, followed by servants with a covered stretcher]

Cadmus: Follow me bearing the sad weight of Pentheus,
Follow, servants, to the palace entrance.
Toiling over ten thousand quests I found his body
And bring it here—what I found
Scattered over Cithaeron's glens,
Finding no two parts in one place;
Difficult to find what lay in the bushes.
I heard too of my daughters' daring deeds,
As I came here within the town walls
From the Bacchic dance with Teiresias.
After struggling back up the mountain
I now bring the boy killed by the Maenads.
I saw Autonoe, who once bore Actaeon to Aristaeus,
And Ino with her, still suffering frenzy
Amongst the trees. But someone told me
That Agave had already set out here
With Bacchic foot—we did not hear wrongly,
For I see her, and not a pleasant sight!

Agave: Father, it's now possible for you to make
The greatest of boasts, to have fathered
Daughters the best by far of all mortals!
I mean all of them, but myself especially!
I have left weaving at the loom, and have
Arrived at greater things, hunting animals
With my bare hands! I now carry in my arms,
As you can see, this best of trophies,
To be fixed to the front of your palace.
As for you, father, take it in your hands,
And call your friends to a banquet
To celebrate my hunting! For you are blessed,
Blessed for what we have achieved here!

Cadmus: O grief immeasurable, impossible to behold!
Murder which made its perpetrators' hands wretched!
A fine sacrifice you have thrown down
Before the gods, inviting the citizens and me
To a banquet! Alas! I grieve for your evils first,

Then for my own. How rightly, too much so,
Has the god exacted justice! Lord Bromios,
Even though he is a relative, has destroyed us!

Agave: How disagreeable old age makes people!
What a scowl on his face! I wish my son
Could be a great hunter like his mother,
Going on hunts alongside the young men of Thebes.
The only thing he can do is fight against gods.
Father, you must sort him out. Who will call him
Out here, before my sight, to see how happy I am?
Cadmus: Alas! Alas! You will lament with a great grief
When you realize what you have done.
If you remain in the state you are now in
Until the bitter end, you will have
The good fortune not to know how unfortunate you are.
Agave: What is wrong? Why are you upset?
Cadmus: First turn your eye up here to the sky.
Agave: There? Why do you want me to look at it?
Cadmus: Does it look the same to you, or is it changed?
Agave: Brighter than before and more translucent.
Cadmus: And is this disturbance of your mind still there?
Agave: I don't know what you mean. But somehow I'm growing
Clear-minded, changing my mind from its previous state.
Cadmus: Can you hear me and answer clearly?
Agave: I've forgotten what we just said, father.
Cadmus: To whose home did you go after your wedding?
Agave: You gave me to a Sown Man, as they said, Echion.
Cadmus: Who was the child you then bore to him at home?
Agave: Pentheus, the son I shared with his father.
Cadmus: Whose face do you now hold in your arms?
Agave: A lion's! So they said on the hunt.
Cadmus: Now look straight at it. It's a quick job to look.
Agave: Oh! What do I see? What am I carrying in my hands?
Cadmus: Look closely at it and learn more clearly.
Agave: Wretched as I am, I see the utmost grief!
Cadmus: Does it still look to you like a lion?
Agave: No! I—wretched one—am holding Pentheus' head!
Cadmus: He was an object of mourning before you even realized it.
Agave: Who killed him? How did he come into my hands?
Cadmus: Wretched truth, at what an inopportune time have you come!

Agave: Tell me! My heart throbs to know the rest.
Cadmus: You killed him—you and your sisters.
Agave: Where did he die? At home? Or in what place?
Cadmus: The place where hounds tore up Actaeon before.
Agave: Why did the ill-starred man go to Cithaeron?
Cadmus: He went there to insult the gods and your Bacchic rites.
Agave: In what way did we get there?
Cadmus: You were mad, and the whole city was on a Bacchic riot along with you.
Agave: Dionysus has destroyed us, as I just now learn.
Cadmus: He was offensively insulted. You didn't believe he was a god.
Agave: Where is the dearest body of my son, father?
Cadmus: After a difficult search I am bringing it home.
Agave: Is limb decently laid to limb?   1300

[Lines missing in manuscripts]

What part did Pentheus have in my madness?
Cadmus: He became like you, not respecting the gods.
For this reason the god has joined us all to
One punishment, you and this man here,
So as to destroy the household and me,
Leaving me childless as regards male offspring.
Now I see this son of yours, wretched woman,
Killed by a most evil and disgraceful death.
By him the house had recovered sight.
You, my child, held the house together,
Son of my daughter, you were a source
Of fear to the city. No one, seeing your face,
Wanted to insult the old man. You would have
Demanded a penalty. But now I, Cadmus the Great,
Shall be cast from the palace dishonoured,
I, who sowed the race of the Thebans
And reaped the finest harvest.
O dearest of men, no longer will you be
Counted amongst my dearest, child,
No longer touch my beard with your hand
And call me father of your mother, or say,
"Who wrongs you? Who dishonours you, old man?
     What troublemaker is bothering you?
     Tell me, so that I can punish the one
     Who wrongs you, granddad."

But now I am in grief, and you too are wretched,
Your mother is pitiful! Miserable are your relatives!
If a person exists who despises the divine,
Let him look at this man's death and then believe in the gods.

CHAPTER 23

Greek Hero-Saga

Selected from Apollodorus, Library [of Mythology]

Translation & footnotes by JGF

📖 *For basic information on Apollodorus, see the introduction to Chapter 16. In the following extracts Apollodorus quotes not only poetic sources we still have, such as Hesiod, Homer, and Pindar, but also early historians such as Pherecydes and Acusilaus. These historians' works do not survive as actual texts in full, but only in quotations such as these. Such historians needed information on events before living memory and so used epic poems as their sources. Apollodorus was therefore a valuable "study guide" in late antiquity and is sometimes our only link to these otherwise lost sources.*

1. BELLEROPHON: APOLLODORUS, BOOK II, CHAPTER 3

Bellerophon, son of Glaucus and grandson of Sisyphus, came to Proetus and was purified after accidentally killing his brother Deliades. Some say this brother was called Peiren, others call him Alkimenes. Stheneboea fell in love with him and sent him messages about getting together with her. When he refused, she told Proetus that Bellerophon had been sending word to her intending seduction. Proetus believed her and gave him a message[1] to deliver to Iobates: in it was the instruction to kill Bellerophon. When Iobates read it he gave him the job of killing the Chimaera, thinking that he would be destroyed by the monster, since it was difficult for many men to

---

[1]The story of Proetus' message delivered by Bellerophon is recounted in *Iliad* VI. 150-214, where Homer treats the art of writing as a strange and potentially dangerous skill: in this early version Bellerophon seems unable to read the message himself. The passage has often been cited in opposition to the idea that Homer himself used writing. Apollodorus here seem to envision a sealed message.

catch, not just one: it had the front parts of a lion, a snake's tail,[2] and its third head in the middle was that of a goat, with fire breathing from it. It was destroying the countryside and injuring the cattle. One creature, it had the power of three wild beasts. It is said that this Chimaera had been raised by Amisodaros, as Homer[3] has also said, and was born from Typhon and Echidna as Hesiod tells.

So Bellerophon, having mounted Pegasus (the winged horse that was born from Medusa[4] and Poseidon), flew up high and shot down at the Chimaera. After this contest Iobates gave him the job of fighting the Solymoi.[5] When he had completed this too, he sent him to take on the Amazons. When he had also killed them, Iobates picked out those Lycian youths who had the best reputations, to ambush and kill him. When he had killed all of these, Iobates was amazed at his power and showed him the letter, demanding that he should stay with him. He gave him his daughter Philonoe and, after he died, left him his kingdom.

2. PERSEUS: APOLLODORUS BOOK II. CHAPTER 4.1 (DIRECTLY FOLLOWING FROM THE ABOVE EXTRACT)

When Acrisius asked the oracle about having male heirs, the god said that from his daughter would be born a son who would kill him. Acrisius, fearing this, built a bronze underground chamber and kept her guarded there. But, as some say, Proetus seduced her,[6] which caused a quarrel between the men. But some say Zeus turned himself into gold and poured down through the roof to fill her lap. Acrisius, finding out later that her baby Perseus had been born, did not believe that Zeus had seduced her, threw his daughter with her baby into a casket and launched it into the sea. When the casket drifted ashore at Seriphus, Dictys took the boy and raised him.

2. At that time Polydectes, brother of Dictys, was king of Seriphus. He fell in love with Danaé but, because Perseus was grown up, had no opportunity to consummate his desire for her. He called his friends together (Perseus was one of them) claiming

---

[2]Usually translated, "of a dragon," *drakontos* more commonly refers to a snake, just as *ormr* in Norse (cognate with Latin *vermis*, from which we get *vermin*) can mean snake, dragon or (its direct English counterpart) *worm*.

[3]*Iliad* XVI. 328f. For Hesiod's account, see *Theog.* 319f.

[4]Hesiod, *Theog.* 278 f.

[5]The Solymoi were an ancient people in Lycia (now SW Turkey). Herodotus (I.173) describes their origins.

[6]Apollodorus is clearly referring to a rationalized tradition here. Robin Hard, in his notes to his translation (Oxford World's Classics series, 1997, p. 200) attributes this version to Pindar on the authority of a scholion on *Iliad* XIV, 319. The shower of gold story, given next, was popular in ancient times as a poetic motif and was used by many artists in the renaissance and baroque periods.

that he was collecting for a wedding-dowry[7] to marry Hippodameia the daughter of Oenomaus. When Perseus said that he would not even stop at the Gorgon's head, Polydectes only asked the others to donate horses, but not taking any horses from Perseus he gave him the job of bringing the Gorgon's head.

Perseus, guided by Hermes and Athena, reached [the home of] Phorcys' daughters Enyo, Pephredo and Deino. These were the daughters of Ceto and Phorcys, sisters of the Gorgons, grey from birth. The three had only one eye and one tooth, which they shared between them. Perseus got control of these and, when they asked for them back, said he would give them back if they would direct him to the road that led to the nymphs. These nymphs had winged sandals and the kibisis, which people say was a wallet. But Pindar and Hesiod (in the *Shield*[8]) say this about Perseus:

> "All over his back he had the head of Gorgo, a terrible
> Monster, and round him was the kibisis."

They had also Hades' cap. When the daughters of Phorcys had shown him the way, he gave them back the tooth and the eye, approached the nymphs got what he wanted: he tied the *kibisis* around himself, strapped the sandals to his ankles, and put the cap on his head. As long as he wore it, he saw whom he pleased, but was not seen by others. On receiving also from Hermes a sickle of adamant, he reached the ocean by flying and caught the Gorgons asleep. They were Stheno, Euryale, and Medusa. Medusa alone was mortal; this was why Perseus was sent to fetch her head. The Gorgons' heads were entwined with the scales of snakes, huge tusks like those of pigs, bronze hands and golden wings, by which they could fly. They turned anyone who saw them to stone. Perseus, standing over them as they slept, while Athena guided his hand, turned away and looked at a bronze shield.[9] Through it he saw the image of the Gorgon and beheaded her. When her head was cut off, out of the Gorgon leaped the winged horse Pegasus and Chrysaor the father of Geryon.

3. They were her children by Poseidon. So Perseus put the head of Medusa in the *kibisis* and started to go back again; but the Gorgons started to wake up and chase Perseus, but they could not see him because of the cap, since he was concealed by it.

---

[7]It was traditional in early Greece for a prospective bridegroom to offer a bride-price to the girl's father.
[8]The *Shield of Herakles* is a miniature epic, 480 lines long in current editions. At one time in the poem's history in was included in Hesiod's *Catalogue of Women*, but it may have had an independent existence before that. This fragment is a garbled version of lines 223-225. NOTE: this is just Apollodorus' attempt at a source-citation and has nothing to do with Perseus' shield (see next footnote).
[9]References to this bronze shield do not occur in the earliest references to the Medusa story. As Apollodorus tells it, Perseus does not seem to have been carrying the shield on arrival, but it was already inside Medusa's lair. The three things he was already carrying, according to the tradition which Apollodorus followed, were the *kibisis* (a kind of bag), the cap of invisibility and the sickle of adamant.

On arriving in Ethiopia, where the king was Cepheus, he found the king's daughter Andromeda put out as prey for a sea monster.[10] For Cassiepeia,[11] the wife of Cepheus, competed with the daughters of Nereus in beauty and boasted that she was superior to all of them. So the Nereids were angry, and Poseidon, sharing their anger, sent a flood and a sea-monster against the land. Since Ammon[12] had predicted deliverance from the calamity if Cassiepeia's daughter Andromeda should be offered as a prey to the monster, Cepheus did this under compulsion by the Ethiopians, and chained his daughter to a rock. When Perseus caught sight of her, he fell I love and promised Cepheus that he would kill the monster, if he would give him the girl as a wife. Oaths were sworn on these terms, so Perseus stood up to the monster, killed it and freed Andromeda. But Phineus, who was Cepheus' brother, and to whom Andromeda had been first engaged, plotted against him. But Perseus learned of the plot, and by showing the Gorgon on the spot turned him and his fellow conspirators into stone. On arriving in Seriphus he found that his mother, along with Dictys, taking refuge at the altars for fear of violence from Polydectes. He went into the palace where Polydectes had gathered his friends, and with his face turned away he showed the Gorgon's head. Each person who looked at it was turned to stone in the attitude in which he was standing at the time. He appointed Dictys king of Seriphus, gave back the sandals, *kibisis* and cap to Hermes, but gave the Gorgon's head to Athena. Hermes returned these items to the nymphs, but Athena set the Gorgon's head in the middle of her shield. But some sources say that Medusa was beheaded through Athena's agency, claiming that the Gorgon wanted to compete with the goddess even in beauty.

📖 *Students researching Perseus for essay material should also read Ovid,* Metamorphoses IV, 605–803, *where interesting etiologies are developed.* http://www.theoi.com/Text/OvidMetamorphoses4.html#8

3. HERAKLES' PARENTAGE AND CONCEPTION: APOLLODORUS BOOK II. CHAPTER 4.5

When Herakles was about to be born Zeus declared amongst the gods that the descendant of Perseus[13] who would be born would reign over Mycenae. Hera, acting out of jealousy, persuaded the Eileithyiae to delay Alcmene's delivery,

---

[10]The Greek word here is *kêtos,* from which we derive the word *cetacean.*
[11]Cassiopeia in most of the later sources.
[12]Oracle in Egypt, associated by ancient Greeks with Zeus.
[13]Perseus traditionally came to Greece from the Middle East and founded the ruling dynasty of Mycenae, the fortified castle which controlled the region of Argos during the late Bronze Age.

arranging that Eurystheus, the son of Sthenelus,[14] would be born at seven months' gestation.

6. When Electryon[15] was king of Mycenae the sons of Pterelaos came there with Taphios[16] to demand the kingdom of their maternal grandfather Méstor. Since Electryon paid no attention to their claim they rustled his cattle away. When Electryon's sons put up a resistance they challenged and killed each other. Only one of Electryon's sons survived, Lykimnios, who happened to be too young.[17] Of Pterelaos' sons only Everes survived, because he was guarding the ships. The surviving Taphians sailed away taking the cattle they had rustled and left them in the protection of Polyxenus the king of the Eleans.[18] Amphitryon then ransomed the cattle and brought them back to Mycenae.

Wishing to avenge the death of his sons, Electryon planned a war against the Teleboans and first entrusted his kingdom to Amphitryon. He also entrusted his daughter Alkmene making Amphitryon swear an oath to preserve her virginity until he should return. As he was taking his cattle back one of them charged and Amphitryon hit out at her with a club he was carrying. The club rebounded from the cow's horns and hit Electryon, killing him. Sthenelus used this as an excuse to banish Amphitryon from the whole of Argos, seizing the throne of Mycenae and Tiryns for himself. He sent for Atreus and Thyestes, the sons of Pelops, and entrusted Midea[19] to them.

Amphitryon went with Alkmene and Likymnios to Thebes and was purified by Creon.[20] He gave his sister Perimede [as a wife] to Likymnios. As Alkmene had said she would marry him when he avenged her brothers' death, he promised to do so and undertook an expedition against the Teleboans with the help of Creon. The latter said

---

[14]Sthenelus was one of Perseus' sons born after the hero settled in Argos. Eurystheus was the king who sent Herakles on many of his famous labours. The motif of Hera's support for Eurystheus over Herakles is a common denominator in most early sources. He is often shown in vase-paintings, cringing in a pot, when Herakles brings back Cerberus or the Erymanthian Boar.

[15]Electryon and Méstor were two of the sons of Perseus and Andromeda born as princes of Mycenae. The myth seems to reflect a sentiment passed on in various traditions at Mycenae and at Thebes that the descendants of Perseus fell into a dynastic decline after the latter's death. Electryon was father of Alkmene and thus Herakles' maternal grandfather.

[16]The Taphian islands are a small group off the west coast of Greece, between Ithaca and Leucas (Lefkadi). Taphios, the son of Poseidon, was Pterelaus' father and the founder of the Teleboans who inhabited the islands. Pterelaus was fated to be immortal as long as he had a golden hair on his head.

[17]Presumably he was too young to have gone out to fight.

[18]Elis is on the west coast of the Peloponnesus (southern Greece).

[19]Midea was Electryon's widow.

[20]Creon was Oedipus' brother-in-law, ruling Thebes when the latter was banished and again when the latter's sons had killed each other in a civil war. See Sophocles' play *Antigone*.

he would join the expedition if Amphitryon would first raid the Cadmeia[21] of the vixen which was then terrorizing the area. Although Amphitryon undertook to do it, there was a divine fate that nobody would catch her.

7. The countryside was being so badly damaged by her that each month the Thebans exposed one of their babies to the animal, otherwise she would have carried off many of them. Amphitryon left and went to Kephalos the son of Deioneos at Athens and promised him a share of the spoils from the Teleboan expedition if he would bring to the hunt the hound that Procris had brought from Crete as a gift from Minos. The dog was fated to catch whatever it chased. When the vixen was chased by this hound, Zeus turned them both into stone.[22]

With the help of his allies (Kephalos from Thorikos in Attica, Panopeos from Phocis, Heleus the son of Perseus from Helos in the Argolid, and Creon from Thebes) Amphitryon ravaged the Taphian islands. As long as Pterelaos was alive, Amphitryon could not take the Taphian islands, but when Komaitho (Pterelaus' daughter, who had fallen in love with Amphitryon) pulled the golden hair from her father's head he died and Amphitryon took control of the whole group of islands. He killed Komaitho and sailed off with the plunder to Thebes, giving the islands to Heleios and Kephalos who established cities in their own names and settled there.

8. Before Amphitryon reached Thebes, Zeus visited the town by night, multiplied the single night's length three times, took on Amphitryon's appearance, went to bed with Alkmene and told her the whole story of the Teleboan expedition. When Amphitryon arrived home he noticed that his wife did not seem particularly excited and asked her the reason. When she replied that he had already come home the previous night and slept with her, he found out from Teiresias how Zeus had spent the night with her. Alkmene bore two sons: Herakles, who was Zeus' son and was older by one night, and Iphikles, who was Amphitryon's son.

When the baby was eight months old Hera wanted to destroy him and sent two snakes of unusual size to his bed. Alkmene screamed to Amphitryon for help, Herakles

---

[21]The area round Thebes, named after the city's legendary founder Cadmus. The vixen was the Teumessian Fox, subject of several primitive hunting-legends and heroic poems. A reference to the story forms one of the very few surviving fragments of a lost epic, *The Epigonoi,* or "Those born afterwards," the epic of the generation after the Theban civil war between the sons of Oedipus.

[22]The motif is obviously the resolution of two mutually contradictory fates. The story of the Teumessian Fox was also in ancient Greek culture an etiology for the constellation *Canis maior* as well as for a rock formation on a hillside near Thebes.

got up, grabbed a snake in each hand, and strangled them both. Pherecydes[23] says it was Amphitryon who put the snakes in the bed because he wanted to know which of the two babies was his own; when Iphikles ran away and Herakles stood up to them he found out that Iphikles was his own son.

📖 *The rest of Hercules' biography is covered by Apollodorus in great detail, so students researching the labors or other incidents should read from II.4.9 to II.7.8. Sir James Frazer's translation, originally published for the Loeb edition in 1921, is now available online at www.perseus.tufts.edu or at theoi.com. http://www.theoi.com/Text/Apollodorus2.html*

4. THESEUS

📖 *A short summary of Theseus' life is given by Hyginus XXXVII—XLIII, given in Chapter 13, above. Theseus is also covered in great detail by Apollodorus at the end of Book III, up to the point where the main manuscript breaks off and the continuation is derived from an* Epitome. *http://www.theoi.com/Text/Apollodorus3.html#16 http://www.theoi.com/Text/ApollodorusE.html*

Frazer's translation is again available at www.perseus.tufts.edu or at www.theoi.com. The most important biography of Theseus is that by Plutarch in his Parallel Lives. *It is available in English translations on several sites including those mentioned above. http://www.theoi.com/Text/PlutarchTheseus.html*

---

[23]A historian who flourished around 500 BC. His works are now lost, but we know from many fragments and references that he tried to compile national and heroic histories from earlier epic poetry.

Pindar: *Pythian Ode IV*

Translated and edited by J.G. Farrow

This is the earliest surviving literary source on the journey of the Argonauts. It was composed as a victory hymn in honour of Arcesilaus IV, king of Cyrene, who had won a chariot race at the Pythian Games in 462 B.C. Pindar was commissioned to write this hymn by Damophilus, a nobleman who was staying in Thebes while in exile from Cyrene for political offenses. Cyrene was the largest and most important Greek colony in Libya (North Africa). It had been founded, according to legend, by Battus I, who had gone there from Thera (probably before 600 B.C.: Thera is the "holy island" mentioned in lines 7-8) and established his family as the colony's rulers. Arcesilaus, the dedicatee of this poem, was son of Battus IV.

Early in the poem Pindar explains the relevance of the Argonaut story by stating that Battus I, in founding the colony of Cyrene, was fulfilling a prophecy made centuries earlier (17 generations earlier, according to the poet) by Medea when she had travelled to Greece with the Argonauts after they had captured the Golden Fleece.

Lines 13-56 are typical of mantic *poetry: this section is supposedly a report of Medea's words when she went into a prophetic trance on the way to Greece. Don't worry about the time-sequence, which can be very confusing.*

Choral lyric poetry was traditionally composed and performed in the Doric dialect, which tended to avoid diphthongs and used shorter vowel-sounds than other dialects of Classical Greece. For instance, the name arcesilaus *becomes* arcesilas. *The poem is divided into alternating verses, each called either a* **strophe**, **antistrophe**, *or an* **epode**.

Strophe α' Today you, my Muse, must stand up in the presence
   Of a dear friend, the king of Cyrene with its fine horses,
   So that alongside Arcesilas you may swell the heavens
   With your hymn of honour to Leto's children[1] and to Pytho too,

---

[1]Apollo and Artemis. The Pythian games were held at Delphi, the location of Apollo's sacred shrine.

In the place where once, when Apollo was not far away, 5
The priestess enthroned beside Zeus' golden eagles prophesied,
That Battus would colonize fruitful Libya, that immediately
He would leave the holy island and build upon a silvery peak
A city thronged with noble chariots.

Antistrophe α' And so he would, in the seventeenth generation, fulfill Medea's words
  Spoken at Thera,[2] when Aeëtes' brave daughter,[3] lady of Colchis, 10
  Uttered them from her immortal mouth. Thus she spoke
  To the warrior Jason's demigod[4] crew:
  "Hear ye, sons of high-spirited men and of gods,
  For I say that some time Epaphus' daughter[5] from this salt-washed land
  Will have, planted in her, a root of human-nourished cities 15
  At the foundations of Zeus Ammon.[6]

Epode α': They will take fast horses instead of short-finned dolphins.
  Instead of oars they will ply chariots that race the wind.
  That omen-bird will make it happen, that Thera will be a mother of great cities,
  The omen which Euphamus one day, at Tritonis' estuary, 20
  Received, as he landed from the Argo's prow,
  As a hospitality-gift from a god disguised as a man.
  Immediately Cronus' son, father Zeus, rang out a peal of thunder.

Strophe β': This was when the stranger met us, as we slung the bronze anchor,
  The swift Argo's bridle, alongside the ship. 25
  At that time we had already left the Ocean and, by my advice,
  Had carried the ship twelve days over desert lands.
  Then it was that the lonely god [Triton] came to us
  In the splendid appearance of a distinguished man;
  He began his friendly words, such as kindly hosts use 30
  When they invite newly arrived guests to dinner.

---

[2]Thera is a small island to the Northeast of Crete. It was known in the Argonaut story as a stopping-off place on the return journey: Apollonius of Rhodes, *Argonautica* IV. 1762-4.

[3]Medea

[4]Many of the Argonauts were traditionally the sons of gods. See the list that follows.

[5]Libya. Epaphus was a mythical Egyptian god-king, perhaps to be identified with the bull-god Apis.

[6]The oracle of Ammon (Egyptian Amun, whom the Greeks identified with Zeus) was in Northwestern Egypt.

Antistrophe β': But the excuse of a sweet return home kept us from staying.
  He said he was Eurypylus the son of the immortal Earthshaker
  Poseidon. He realized we were about to leave, and immediately
  He seized in his right hand some of the soil and offered   35
  To give it to Euphamus as a hospitality-gift.
  Nor did the latter refuse; the hero, jumping down to the shore,
  Took his host's hand and received from him the fateful soil.
  But, I believe, it was washed out of the ship into the sea

Epode β': At evening, following the watery tide.
  Often did I warn the forgetful sailors on watch to guard it,
  but it slipped their minds.   40
  Now the imperishable seed of broad Libya is washed ashore
  Before its time on the island [Thera]. For if lord Euphamus,
  Horse-ruling Poseidon's son, whom Europa daughter of Tityos once bore
  By the banks of Caphisus, had hurried home to holy Taenarus[7]   45
  And thrown the lump down beside the mouth of Hades,

Strophe γ: Then the blood of his descendants of the fourth generation
  Would, with the Danaoi, have taken possession of the wide continent.
  Thereupon people would have left great Lacedaemon and the Argive Gulf and
      Mycenae.
  But now Euphamus will find his chosen race in marriages with foreign wives, 50
  Descendants who, with the honour of the gods, will come to Thera
  And there beget the lord of the plains mantled in the dark cloud.
  This man will Phoebus mention in oracles within his golden home

Antistrophe γ: When later he goes down from the threshold into the
      Pythian shrine,
  Telling how he will carry many people in his ships   55
  To the fertile precinct of Cronus' son beside the Nile."
  So were the verses of Medea's words. But the godlike heroes
  Bowed down in silence as they heard her deep advice.
  O blessed son of Battus! In this speech the oracle pointed to you
  By the unprompted utterance of the Delphic bee!   60
  Three times it greeted you as destined king of Cyrene!

********* *(verses omitted)* * * ** * * * * * * *

---

[7]Taenarus (Tainaros) is the western of the two most southerly promontories of mainland Greece.
It was locally believed to be the location of an entrance to the underworld.

Strophe δ': How did they start their voyage? What danger bound them 70
  With strong bonds of adamant? The oracle had foretold
  Pelias' death at the hands of Aeolus' proud sons, or
  By their unopposeable plans. But the oracle came to him
  Shaking his spirit, spoken at tree-clad Mother Earth's
  central navel,[8] telling him to be on his utmost guard 75
  Against the single-sandalled man, who, whether citizen or foreigner,
  Would descend from the mountain homesteads to the sunny soil
  Of famous Iolcus.

Antistrophe δ': At last he came, an outstanding hero brandishing twin spears.
  He wore two kinds of clothing, in that round his limbs
  The close-fitting tunic of the Magnesians fit, but 80
  A leopard skin protected him from shivering rains.
  Nor were the splendid locks of his hair cut back,
  But they rolled gleaming down his back. Immediately he went
  To try his fearless spirit, and stood
  In the thickly-crowded market place. 85

Epode δ': They did not recognize him. But one of the impressed onlookers said:
  "I suppose this can't be Apollo, nor is he Aphrodite's bronze-armed charioteer.
  They say Iphimedia's sons, Otus and warlike lord Ephialtes,[9]
  Died in shining Naxos. And a swift arrow, they say,
  Hunted down Tityos,[10] the arrow Artemis shot 90
  From her unconquerable quiver, as a warning
  To humans, only to aim at objects of desire within their reach."

Strophe ε': Thus they conversed with one another in turn.
  Meanwhile, driving his mules and polished chariot with headlong speed,
  Pelias arrived in haste. He looked, and saw the single sandal 95
  Unmistakable on the stranger's right foot. But hiding in his heart
  His fear, he spoke: "What country, O stranger, do you claim
  To be your fatherland? And who, of earth-born humanity,

---

[8]The Oracle at Delphi was believed to have been occupied by Gaea at first, then taken over by Themis and finally by Apollo. The myth indicates Greek occupation of a site held sacred by previous inhabitants, possibly because of subterranean gases which once came out of the ground at that part of central Greece. The myth is also etiological for the *Omphalos* stone, believed to be the Earth's navel. See notes to Hesiod, *Theog.* 500.

[9]Two giants who rebelled against the gods, attempting to draw level with Olympus by piling Mount Pelium on top of Mt. Ossa (2 mountains in Thessaly).

[10]Tityos tried to rape Leto (*Odyssey* XI.576-581) and was punished by having his liver eaten by a pair of vultures in the Underworld. The story, like that of Otus and Ephialtes, is a generic instance of *Hybris.*

Brought you forth from her ancient womb? Tell me your family
And do not contaminate it with most hateful lies!"   100

Antistrophe ε': Then the stranger answered him thus with brave, gentle words:
"I shall reveal Chiron's training,[11] for I have come from his cave,
From beside Chariclo and Philyra, where the Centaur's
Holy daughters raised me. After completing twenty years,
Uttering nothing unbecoming to them in deed or in word,   105
I have come home bearing the ancient honour of my father, now being
Controlled in no rightful way, the ancient honour which
Zeus granted Aeolus and his sons.

Epode ε': For I hear that lawless Pelias,[12] obeying his frantic passions,
Stole by force from my parents the primal right of kingship.   110
As soon as I first saw daylight, fearing the overbearing king's
Insolence, they made gloomy mourning in their home as though
A person had died, with wailing of women, while secretly
They sent me away, wrapped in purple with night as companion
On my way, and gave me to Cronus' son Chiron.   115

Strophe F': But you already know the gist of this story.
And now, noble citizens, please show me clearly
The palace of my ancestors who rode white horses.
For, as native-born son of Aeson, I have come to my own land,
Not a foreigner's. The divine centaur usually called me Jason."   120
So he spoke. And as he entered his father's eyes recognized him.
Tears broke from the old man's eyelids, and he rejoiced in his heart
On seeing his son, the choicest and finest of men.

Antistrophe F': And both his father's brothers came, as soon as they heard tell of him.
Nearby Pheres left the Hypereian[13] spring, while from Messene   125
Came Amythaon.[14] Admetus[15] too and Melampus[16] came, with good intention

---

[11]Chiron the Centaur was traditionally believed to have raised Jason and, at a later time, Achilles.

[12]Pelias and Neleus were the sons of Poseidon and Tyro (Apollodorus, *Library* I.9.8). Neleus became father of Nestor (famous in Homer's poems as king of Pylos). Tyro then married Cretheus; they had three sons including Aeson the father of Jason (Apollodorus I.9.12, Homer, *Odyssey* XI.258ff; Hyginus *Fab.* XII).

[13]In Thessaly. Pheres was founder of Pherae and father of Admetus (next line).

[14]Amythaon was son of Cretheus (n.10) and father of Melampus (n.14).

[15]Admetus was a hero from Pherae in Thessaly. Apollodorus (I.8.2) lists him as one of the heroes who joined in the Calydonian Boar Hunt.

[16]Melampus was a famous prophet from Southern Greece.

Towards their cousin. Jason, welcoming them in their share
With gentle words offered fitting hospitality at the feast,
Held out all good cheer, for five full nights together
And for as many days trimming the sacred choice cuts of good life.   130

Epode F': But on the sixth day, setting forth his serious words,
The hero shared the whole story with his relatives.
And they followed him. At once he started out with them
From the tents, and they came to Pelias' palace.
They hastened and stood inside. And Pelias himself,   135
Son of Tyro with the beautiful hair, when he heard them
Came out to meet them. And Jason, speaking gently with soothing voice,
Thus laid a foundation of wise words: "Son of rocky Poseidon,

Strophe ζ': The sons of mortals are only too quick
To praise crafty profit instead of justice, even as they move on   140
Just the same towards the consequences. But you and I
Must rule our grievances by the law of right, creating future well-being.
For you know what I shall say. One heifer was mother
To Cretheus and bold-minded Salmoneus.[17] In the third generation
We, in turn, who now look at the sun's golden light, were born.   145
But the fates, should any hostility befall men of the same kin, hold back in shame.

Antistrophe ζ': It does not befit us two to resort to bronze swords
Nor to spears, in sharing the great honour of our ancestors.
As for the sheep, . . . the cattle . . . I leave all to you.   151
But, as for the royal sceptre and throne, on which
Aeson once sat, while making laws for his horse-riding people,
Let me have them without trouble on either side,

Epode ζ': That no new ill should arise from them."   155
So he spoke, and Pelias in turn answered him:
"I shall concur with you. But old age is already surrounding me.
But the bloom of youth is fresh upon you;
You are able to remove the resentment of the chthonic gods.
For Phrixus orders us to bring his spirit home,[18] by going to Aeëtes' halls   160

---

[17]Enarete married Aeolus and became mother of Cretheus, Sisyphus, Athamas, Salmoneus, and several other children. See Apollodorus I.7.3, Diodorus Siculus IV.67, 2-7.

[18]Phrixus and Helle were the two Greek children who had travelled to Colchis many years earlier on the golden ram (Hyginus *Fab.* III). This reference to bringing Phrixus' "spirit home" may have been intended by Pindar as a command from Pelias that Jason bring home the bones of Phrixus. The retrieval of heroes' bones, in the belief that they held talismanic power, was a frequently used political issue in Pindar's time. The Scholiast explains this line as a reference to a mourning ritual for those killed in foreign lands, quoting *Odyssey* IX.65: *"The ships did not leave the land until we had called out three times for each of our comrades who had died in the plain."*

And recovering the thick-fleeced wool of the ram, on which
He was once rescued from the sea....[19]

Strophe η': ... and from his stepmother's ungodly weapons.
A wonderful dream came and told me this. I have asked
The oracle at Castalia if further quest is needed. The oracle tells me to
Equip a ship to bring him home again with full speed.   165
I would have you accomplish this promptly; I promise
To let you rule in sovereignty. As common pledge
May Zeus our joint ancestor be witness!"
They approved and sealed this agreement; and Jason immediately

Antistrophe η': Sent messengers that a sea-voyage would really take place.   170
And soon there came Cronus-born Zeus' three sons unwearied in war,
Whom bright-eyed Alcmene[20] and Leda bore, and twin heroes with high crests,
Sons of Poseidon, their souls inspired by courage,
Both from Pylos and from Taenarus; outstanding fame belonged
To Euphemus and to Periclymenus, whose power extends far and wide.   175
Apollo's son came too, that father of lyre and song,
The famous Orpheus.[21]

Epode η': Hermes of the golden wand sent twin sons to join the never-ending toil,
Both Echion and Eurytus, rejoicing in their youth.
Swiftly came they who live around the foothills of Pangaeus,   180
For gladly did their father Boreas, king of the winds,
Send Zetes and Calaïs, heroes both with purple wings
Spreading down their backs. All-persuading Hera
Inspired sweet kindness amongst the gods,

Strophe θ': Towards the ship Argo, that no-one should be left behind,   185
Staying for ever free from danger by his mother's side,
But, even to the point of death, should find with his comrades
The ultimate drug of his own courage. But when this
Pick of voyagers came to Iolcus, Jason praised them all
And counted them. To help him Mopsus, after checking the gods' will   190
By means of bird-flight and by drawing lots, gave favourable signs

---

[19]The vocal exchange between the *Strophe* and *Antistrophe* groups occurs here in mid-sentence.

[20]Alcmene's son here is obviously Herakles. Leda's twins, sons of Zeus, are Castor and Polydeuces (the famous Dioscuri, or Gemini).

[21]Many scholars have noticed that Orpheus does not really belong amongst the Argonauts, yet he was included in the traditional lists from a very early date. He was probably included because he was associated with Northern Greece. This is a good illustration of how important the earliest traditions were in forming ideas which had already become accepted as basic by the time of our surviving poetry.

To the army. And, when they had slung the anchor
Over the ship's prow,

Antistrophe θ': . . . the leader took in his hands a golden cup
And, standing at the stern, called on Zeus father of the Heaven-dwellers,
Whose weapon is lightning, on the rushing powers of waves and winds,
To speed the journey; on the nights and on the seaways,   195
That the days would be favourable and the fortune
Of their homeward return might be friendly. From the clouds
An auspicious answer of thunder came. Bright flashes of lightning
burst forth, and the heroes took fresh courage on believing
The signs of a god. The prophet inspired them with sweet hopes   200

Epode θ': While loudly he urged them to ply their hands to the oars.
The rowing built up speed, insatiable under their swift palms.
The breezes from the South in their favour, they reached the mouth
Of the Inhospitable Sea, where they established a plot of holy ground
In honour of salty Poseidon. There was found a red herd   205
Of Thracian bulls, and a new stone hollow on top of an altar.
Rushing on into deep danger they prayed to the Lord of Ships,

Strophe ι': That they might escape the irresistible attack
Of the Clashing Rocks. These were living twins,
Rolling forward more swiftly than the battle-lines of the loud-roaring winds.   210
But that voyage of demigods was already bringing their end.
On they went to Phasis, where they mixed in battle
With the dark-skinned Colchians in Aeëtes' own home.
Then for the first time from Olympus the Cyprus-born
Lady of swiftest darts tied a speckled wryneck[22]   215
To the four spokes of an endless wheel, brought to men the maddening bird,

Antistrophe ι': And taught the wise son of Aeson the hymns of offering,
So that he could take away Medea's respect for her parents,
So that longing for Greece might beat her with Persuasion's whip,
Burning in her mind. But she soon explained the means of accomplishing   220
The tasks set by her father. With oil she mixed antidotes

---

[22]The wryneck is a sea-bird. It was associated by some ancient Greeks with Aphrodite. This is a
reference to a kind of sympathetic magic spell, performed by tying the bird to a wheel and spinning it.

To take away pains, and gave them as ointment to Jason.
They promised mutual wedlock, sweet union with one another.

Epode ι': But when Aeëtes had placed in midfield the adamantine plough
　　And the oxen, which breathed from their tawny jaws the flame　　225
　　Of burning fire, and kept pawing the ground in response to one another
　　With their bronze hooves, Aeëtes alone brought them out
　　And tied them to the yoke. Straight he stretched the furrows as he drove,
　　And split a ridge of earth a fathom deep. Thus he spoke:
　　"May the king, whoever commands the ship, once he has completed　　230
　　This task for me, carry off the unaging skin,

Strophe ια': The shining fleece with its golden fringe." When Aeëtes had said this,
　　Jason flung off his saffron robe and, trusting the god,
　　Began the task. The fire did not harm him, by the savage girl's tricks.
　　But seizing the plough, and binding the necks of the oxen　　235
　　In unbreakable harness, and poking the persistent goad
　　Into their strong-ribbed frame, the hero accomplished
　　The allotted measure of his task. But Aeëtes, his grief inexpressible,
　　Cried in amazement at the stranger's strength.

Antistrophe ια':
　　His comrades too in turn stretched out their hands to the conquering hero,　　240
　　Crowned him with garlands of greenery and hailed him with gentle words.
　　Immediately the miraculous son of Helios spoke of the shining fleece,
　　Telling where it had been stretched out under Phrixus' blade.
　　He hoped this would no more be a labour that Jason could complete.
　　For the fleece lay in a thick bush, held by the devouring jaws of a dragon,　　245
　　Which in thickness and length exceeded a ship of fifty oars, made by blows of iron.

Epode ια': It is too long a journey for me along the road, for time presses on.
　　I also know a short cut. To many others I am held high in my craft.
　　Jason killed the glaring-eyed, speckle-backed serpent (you know this, Arcesilas).
　　He stole Medea away, with her own connivance, to be Pelias' death.[23]　　250

---

[23]There are several different traditions on the death of Pelias, but in the one to which Pindar is referring, Medea induced Pelias to climb into a cauldron, having convinced him that he would be participating in a magical process to make him young again. See Apollodorus, I.9.27, with Frazer's notes and cross-references.

They joined the waters of Ocean and the Red Sea,[24]
And the generation of husband-killing Lemnian women.[25]
There they proved their excellence in athletic contests, competing for clothes,

Strophe ιβ': And got themselves wives. And then the fated day,
Or night, received in a foreign land the seed of your bright prosperity-glow.   255
There the race of Euphemus was planted, to prosper evermore.
Later, after mixing with the people of Lacedaemon, they went
To settle in the island once called Calliste.[26] From there it was
That Leto's son provided you with the plains of Libya,
To help you with God-given honours, and to rule   260
Over golden-throned Cyrene, so that you could discover awareness of right thinking.

[24]In order to make sense of this line we must first understand Pindar's concept of the world, surrounded by the River Oceanus, with Colchis situated on the river Phasis at the eastern end of the Black Sea, the Phasis acting as some kind of Eastern counterpart to the Pillars of Herakles (Straits of Gibraltar). Jason does not head West from Colchis, as we would now automatically suppose, but East into Oceanus and South round the world's outer perimeter. Pindar's account of the clockwise return of the Argonauts, via the River Oceanus, is of course physically impossible. The motif was used about 40 or 50 years before Pindar by Hecataeus of Miletus, but shortly after Pindar's death the Greeks began to realize that there is no River Ocean, and that the River Phasis (which flows into the Black Sea at its Eastern end) does not connect with any kind of outer sea or other major waterway. The first historian to question Pindar and Hecataeus in this was probably Herodotus (II.23): *I know of no River Oceanus surrounding the Earth. I think it's the invention of Homer or some earlier poet.* Herodotus had the support of a slightly younger Northern contemporary, Herodorus of Heraclea, who died around 400 B.C.

[25]The daughters of Thoas, king of Lemnos, had been put under a curse by Aphrodite for killing their husbands. The Argonauts impregnated the daughters and thus relieved the curse before leaving the island. Apollonius of Rhodes (Argonautica I.600-900) and Apollodorus (I.9.17) both put this episode in the outward journey.

[26]Calliste was another name for the island of Thera (note 2, above). We have thus come full circle in Pindar's reason for telling this story.

CHAPTER 25

Extracts from Herodotus

Translated and edited by J.G. Farrow

   📖 *Herodotus was writing in Ionian Greek between about 450 and 410 B.C. His great work (from which the following extracts are taken) is a nine-book history of the Persian Wars (494–478 B.C.). He simply called the work "Historiai," which we would naturally translate as "Histories," but the term really meant "Researches." Even If Herodotus had been born before the end of the wars (the last stage was Xerxes' great invasion of Greece, 482–478), he would have been too young to remember much of it himself. Many of his sources of information were war-veterans and people who had traveled all around the eastern Mediterranean. In Book II Herodotus claims to have visited Egypt personally, but it is very unlikely that he would have sailed more than the first 50 miles up the Nile.*

   *The first four books are about the cultural and geographical background of the wars, putting them into a larger perspective as part of a world-scale struggle between the polarized cultures of East and West. The first extract shows Herodotus' attempts to use scientific criticism to explain phenomena which were normally accepted as due to supernatural causes. Even if his understanding of climate and the world's shape are faulty by modern standards, we can still see his first glimmer of critical thinking. Compare this extract with those in the **Ancient Critics** section at the beginning of this book, especially the second entry, **"Logographers and Sophists."** The extracts in the second group are all taken from the parts describing lands to the north of the world as it was known to the ancient Greeks. The term "Scythia" is really a generic term covering a vast tract of unknown land, from Poland, the Baltic coast, and East Germany across through Russia and the Ukraine to Armenia and Siberia.*

1. HERODOTUS' EXPLANATION OF WHY THE NILE FLOODS

(Book II, 19ff)

As to why the Nile behaves the way it does I could get no answers from the priests or from anyone else. I especially wanted to know why the water begins to rise at the summer solstice, continues to do so for a hundred days, and then falls again at the end of that period, so that it remains low throughout the winter until the summer solstice begins again the next year. Nobody in Egypt could explain this to me, in spite of my constant attempts to find what was causing the Nile act in a way directly opposite that of other rivers, and why it was the only river to cause no breezes.

Certain Greeks, hoping to advertise their own cleverness, have tried to explain the flooding of the Nile in three different ways. Two of the explanations are not worth dwelling upon, except to say what they are; one is that the Etesian[1] winds cause the water to rise by checking the flow of the current towards the sea. In fact, however, these winds have often failed to blow but the Nile has risen as usual. Besides, if the Etesian winds were responsible, other rivers affected by them would behave in the same way as the Nile; in fact, they would do this the more so in that they are smaller and have a weaker current.

The second explanation is less rational, being of a more legendary character: it is, that the Nile behaves as it does because it flows from the Ocean, the stream of which encircles the world. The third theory is by far the most plausible, though even further from the truth: according to this, the water of the Nile comes from melting snow . . . but as it flows through Ethiopia into Egypt, that is from a very hot into a cooler climate, how could it possibly originate in snow? Obviously this view is as worthless as the other two. Anyone of intelligence will find lots of arguments to prove how unlikely it is that snow is the cause of the river-floods. The strongest is provided by the winds, which blow from those regions; secondly rain and frost are unknown there, and after snow rain is certain to fall within five days. So if there were snow in that region, there would be rain too. Again, kites and swallows remain there throughout the year, and cranes migrate there in winter to escape the cold climate of Scythia. Therefore it makes no sense for snow to fall in that region through which the Nile flows. As to the writer who mentions Ocean in this context, his account is based on a myth meant to explain an unknown factor and cannot be

---

[1]The Etesian Winds blew on the north coast of Egypt in late summer, tempering what would otherwise have been intense heat and drought. They were often regarded as God-given. This wind-pattern, already unreliable in Herodotus' own time, declined severely during the Roman Empire.

disproved by argument. I know of no River Oceanus surrounding the Earth. I think it is the invention of Homer or some earlier poet. If I were to express my own opinion, I would say briefly that during winter the sun is driven out of his course by storms towards the upper parts of Libya (i.e., the African continent). It stands to reason that the country closest to and therefore most directly under the sun should be most short of water, and that the streams which feed the rivers in that neighborhood should dry up the soonest.

In the upper parts of Libya the atmosphere is always clear and there are no cold winds to temper the heat. As a result the sun, when it passes over, has the same effect that it normally has elsewhere in summer on its passage through the middle of the sky; namely, it draws the water towards itself and then thrusts it into those parts of the country which are still further inland, where it comes under the influence of the winds which scatter and disperse it in vapor, so naturally the south and southwest winds which blow from this region are the most rainy. It seems to me that not all the moisture drawn each year from the Nile is dispersed but that a certain amount is retained, as it were, in the vicinity of the sun. When winter storms are over, the sun resumes its normal course in mid-heaven, and from that point onwards exercises an equal attraction on all rivers.

2. ON THE SCYTHIANS AND ARIMASPIANS

A) III. 115–116

As to the part of Europe which is furthest to the west, I cannot speak accurately. For I cannot accept that a river, called Eridanus[2] by the barbarians, flows out into the sea towards the north, where the popular story says that amber comes from, nor do I know of the existence of the Cassiterides[3] islands, from which we obtain tin. This name *Eridanus* is clearly Greek, not barbarian, and must have been made up by some poet. Secondly, in spite of careful research, I am still unable to hear at first hand that there is

---

[2]The Eridanus has been variously identified as the Dnieper, the Volga, and the Rhine. Herodotus' vagueness as to the northern and western shores of Europe shows that he had absolutely no notion as to the continent's shape or size in those directions.

[3]The "Cassiterides" or "Tin Islands" are probably the Scilly Isles. Even if they are not, they must be somewhere in Britain or the Channel Islands. There is no evidence that tin deposits ever existed in the Scillies, but there have been deposits mined in Cornwall from a very early date. Phoenicians had begun to exploit these mines by the time of the Roman invasions of Britain, and are known to have discouraged competition. The geographer Strabo (Ch. 176) tells how a Phoenician merchant tried to cause a whole Roman fleet to run aground in these waters.

a sea on the other side of Europe.[4] Yet tin and amber do come to us from the ends of the earth.

116. Most of the gold seems to come from the Northern side of Europe, but how we get it I cannot say accurately. It is said that the Arimaspians,[5] single-eyed men, steal it from the griffins. I don't believe that single-eyed men exist who are like regular human beings in all other respects except that they only have one eye. But countries which are at the ends of the earth, being farthest-flung from the rest of the world, produce things which seem to us the most beautiful and expensive.

B) IV.5–36

5. As the Scythians claim, they are youngest of all nations; they give the following account of their origin. The first man to live in their country, which before his birth was uninhabited, was a certain Targitaus, the son of Zeus and of a daughter of the river Borysthenes—I merely repeat the tradition, and do not myself believe it.

Targitaus had three sons, Lipoxais, Arpoxais, and Colaxais, the youngest; and during their reign in Scythia there fell from the sky a golden plough, a golden yoke, a golden battle-axe, and a golden cup. The eldest of the three was the first to see these treasures, and as he went to pick them up the gold caught fire. At this he withdrew, and the second of the brothers approached; but the gold caught fire and blazed, just as before. Lastly, when the two elder brothers had been kept off by the flames, the youngest came along, and this time the fire went out, so that he was able to pick up the golden implements and carry them home. The elder brothers accepted this as a sign from heaven and made over the whole kingdom to Colaxais.[6]

6. The descendants of Lipoxais were those Scythians now known as Auchatae; those of the second brother, Arpoxais, are the Catiari and Traspies; those of the youngest brother

---

[4]That is, to the northwest coast

[5]The Arimaspians may well have been the Arimoi under the earth, neighbors of the monster called Echidna, in Hesiod's Theogony, 295-305. Whatever their unlikely physical characteristics (see further below), they must have been a nation of miners who had a vested interest in discouraging visitors. It is unlikely that any of the travelers who had furnished stories of these ancient gold-miners had envisaged them in northern Europe (in terms of our present knowledge of geography) unless it had been a deliberate attempt to put potential prospectors off the scent.

[6]This motif, in which the youngest brother is the most successful, is still very popular in *skazki* (traditional Russian folk tales). Some of the best examples are found in the *Ivan* cycle, the collection which was systematically studied in the 1920s and 1930s by Vladimir Propp.

are the Royal Scythians, now called Paralatae. They are known indiscriminately under the general name of Scoloti, after one of their kings; it is the Greeks who call them Scythians.

7. Such is the Scythians' account of their origin, and they add that the period from Targitaus, their first king, to Darius' crossing of the Hellespont[7] to attack them, is just a thousand years. The "gold which fell from heaven" is guarded by the kings with the utmost care, and every year they visit it and offer it magnificent sacrifices. There is a legend in the country that any guardian of the gold who falls asleep in the open air during the festival will die within the year, and when this occurs the person concerned is given as much land as he can ride round in a day. In view of the great size of Scythia, Colaxais split it up into three separate kingdoms for his sons, making the one where the gold was kept larger than the other two. It is said to be impossible to travel through the region which lies further north, or even to see it, because of falling feathers—both earth and air are thick with them and they shut out the view.

8. The above is what the Scythians themselves say about themselves and the land beyond their own country. But the Greeks of Pontus[8] give a different account. According to them, Hercules came into this part of the world, which was then uninhabited, with the oxen of Geryon. His home was far away, on an island which the Greeks call Erythea, near Gades,[9] which lies on the Ocean beyond the Pillars of Hercules. People pass on the story that Ocean is a great river running from the east all around the world; but there is nothing to prove this. When Hercules reached the country which is now Scythia, the weather was bad and it was bitterly cold, so he drew his lion's skin over him and went to sleep. While he slept, the horses which he had unharnessed from his chariot and turned loose to graze mysteriously disappeared.

9. As soon as he awoke Hercules began to look for them, and roamed all over the country until he came at last to a place called Hylaea, or the Woodland, where in a cave he found a viper-girl—a creature which from the buttocks upwards was a woman, but below them a snake.[10] For a moment he looked at her in astonishment; then asked if

---

[7]Approximately 500 B.C.

[8]Herodotus may have been referring to a specific Greek author, who had a name very similar to his own but came from this Northern colony: Herodorus, of Heraclea in Pontus, had compiled an enormous collection of Herakles stories. Examples are given in **Ancient Critics**, above #2b.

[9]Gades is Cadiz, on the southwest coast of Spain.

[10]The Greek word for "viper" (adder) is *echidna*.

she had seen his mares straying around. She replied that they were in her own keeping; she would return them to him on condition that he lay with her.

Hercules complied. The viper-girl, however, did not at once give him back the mares, but put off the fulfillment of her bargain in order to keep Hercules as long as possible for her lover, though all he wanted himself was to get the horses and go. At last she let him have them, and said: 'I kept these horses safe for you, when I found them here; and you have given me my reward, for I have three sons by you. Now tell me what I am to do with them: when they grow up, shall I settle them here in this country, of which I am mistress, or send them to you?'

'When the boys are grown to be men,' Hercules answered, 'you will not be far wrong if you do what I will now tell you. Whichever of them you find can draw this bow as I do, and put on this belt in the way I will show you, should be settled here in this country; but any of them who fail to do these two things must be sent away. Do this, and you will not only show proper obedience to me but find happiness for yourself as well.'

10. Hercules then strung one of his bows—up to that time he always carried two—and showed her how to put on the belt, after which he put into her hands both bow and belt, and went away. The belt had a little gold cup attached to the clasp. When the boys grew up, their mother named the eldest Agathyrsus, the next Gelonus, and the youngest Scythes, and carried out the instructions which she remembered Hercules had given her. Two of the young men, Agathyrsus and Gelonus, failed to accomplish the task assigned them and were therefore banished from the country by their mother; but the youngest brother, Scythes, succeeded and was allowed to remain. In this way Scythes, the son of Hercules, became father of the line of Scythian kings; and to this day the Scythians wear belts with little cups attached to the clasp, in memory of the belt of their ancestor Hercules. This was the only thing the mother of Scythes did for him.

12. There are still traces of the Cimmerians in Scythia: one finds, for instance, remains of fortifications, a Cimmerian strait, a Cimmerian Bosphorus, and a tract of land called Cimmeria. It is clear that the Cimmerians entered Asia to escape the Scythians, and built settlements on the peninsula where the Greek town of Sinope now stands; and there is no doubt that the reason why the Scythians in the course of their pursuit entered Median territory was that they took the wrong route by mistake; for whereas the Cimmerians kept along the coast, the Scythians took the inland road, keeping the Causcasus on their right, until they found themselves in Media. These facts are admitted by Greeks and foreigners alike.

13. Aristeas, son of Caystrobius, a native of Marmora, tells us more information about this part of the world in a poem he wrote; he claims that "under the inspiration of Phoebus" he journeyed to the country of the Issedones, and that beyond the Issedones live the one-eyed Arimaspians, and beyond them the griffins which guard the gold, and beyond the griffins the Hyperboreans, whose land comes down to the sea. All these, except the Hyperboreans, were continually encroaching upon one another's territory, beginning with the Arimaspians, so that the Issedones were expelled by the Arimaspians, the Scythians by the Issedones, and the Cimmerians by the Scythians, who forced them from their homes along the shores of the Black Sea. Here, then, is further evidence against the Scythians' account of this region.

14. I have mentioned the birthplace of Aristeas, the author of this poem; now here is a story I heard about him in Marmora and Cyzicus. He belonged to one of the first families in his home town, and one day, upon entering a laundry shop, he fell down dead. The fuller closed his shop and hurried out to inform his relatives of what had occurred, but no sooner had the news of Aristeas' death got about, than a person from Cyzicus, who had just arrived from the town of Artaca, contradicted the rumor and declared that he had met him going toward Cyzicus and had talked to him. He was absolutely certain of this and would take no denial. Meanwhile, Aristeas' relatives were on their way to the shop with what was necessary for the funeral, intending to take the body away; they opened the door, and the room was empty—Aristeas was not there, either dead or alive. Seven years later he reappeared in Marmora, wrote the poem we now call *The Arimaspia*,[11] and again vanished.

15. I will add something which I know happened to the people of Metapontum in Italy two hundred and forty years (as I found by computation) after the second disappearance of Aristeas. There the story goes that the ghost of Aristeas appeared and told them to erect an altar to Apollo, with a statue beside it bearing the name of Aristeas of Marmora; then, after explaining that they were the only people in Italy whom Apollo had visited, and that he himself on the occasion of his visit had accompanied the god in the form of a raven, the phantom vanished. The Metapontines sent to Delphi to ask the oracle what the apparition signified, and were advised that they had better do what it rec-

---

[11]These references in Herodotus furnish most of what we now know about Aristeas and his poem the *Arimaspia*. How much geographical fact the poem contained we can never know, since it is lost and only a few other fragments remain. As for Aristeas himself, it would be fair to assume that he was a sort of **Shaman** of the 7th or 6th century B.C. (we don't even know how reliable are the dates estimated by Herodotus). For a full collection of all available information on this strange topic, see *Aristeas of Proconessus* by J.D.P. Bolton (Oxford 1966).

ommended. This advice they took, with the result that in the market-square of the town a statue inscribed with the name of Aristeas stands today by the side of the image of Apollo, surrounded by myrtle bushes.

16. No one has any accurate information about what lies beyond the region I am now discussing, and I have never met anyone who claims first-hand acquaintance with it. Even Aristeas, whom I have just mentioned, does not pretend in his poem to have gone further than the country of the Issedones, and admits that his account of what lies beyond is mere hearsay, founded on tales which the Issedones told him. I will, nevertheless, put down everything which careful inquiry about these remote parts has brought to my notice.

26. Some knowledge of the practices of the Issedones[12] has come through to us: for instance, when a man's father dies, his kinsmen bring sheep to his house as a sacrificial offering; the sheep and the body of the dead man are cut into joints and sliced up, and the two sorts of meat, mixed together, are served and eaten. The dead man's head, however, they gild, after stripping off the hair and cleaning out the inside, and then preserve it as a sort of sacred image, to which they offer sacrifice.

In other respects the Issedones appear to have a sound enough sense of the difference between right and wrong, and a remarkable thing about them is that men and women have equal authority.

27. It is amongst the Issedones themselves that the strange tales of the distant north originate—tales of the one-eyed men and the griffins which guard the gold—and the Scythians have passed them on to the rest of us, which explains why we call the one-eyed men by the Scythian name of Arimaspians—*arima* being the Scythian word for 'one', and *spu* for 'eye.'

31. As for the feathers which the Scythians say fill the air, and make it impossible to traverse, or even to see, the more northerly parts of the continent—I think myself that it must be always snowing in these northerly regions, though less, of course, in summer than in winter. Anyone who has seen heavy snow at close quarters will know what I mean—it is very like feathers; and it is because of the severity of these northern winters that the country is uninhabited. No doubt the Scythians and their neighbors when they talk of the feathers really mean snow—because of the likeness between the two. I have now related the utmost which can be gathered from report.

---

[12]A Scythian tribe which Herodotus seems to locate in a poorly specified area of what is now Russia or northern Ukraine

32. We get no information from the Scythians or anyone else in that part of the world about Hyperboreans, except, perhaps, from the Issedones. Not that the Issedones really tell us anything; for if they did, we should have it from the Scythians too, like the story of the one-eyed men. There is, however, a mention of the Hyperboreans in Hesiod,[13] and in Homer's *Epigoni*[14]—if, indeed, Homer was the composer of that poem.

36. I laugh when I see the great number and the stupidity of all the map-makers. They show Ocean running like a river round the world (which is as circular as if it were drawn with a compass!) and make Asia the same size as Europe.

C) IV. 64–67

In the matter of warfare, the arrangement is thus: when a Scythian man kills his first enemy, he drinks of the blood; as many as he kills in battle, he takes off their heads for the king. Having taken a head, he gets a share in the captured loot, but gets no share without a head.

He skins the head in this way: he makes a circular cut around the ears and shakes it off the head, then after scraping it with an ox's rib-bone, he softens it with his hands. Once it is supple he uses it as a kind of handkerchief; he fixes it to the driving-rein of his horse and takes great pride in it. The man who has the biggest number of skin handkerchieves is judged to be the greatest man.

Many of the Scythians also make cloaks from scalps and wear them as overcoats, sewing them together like a shepherd's cloak. There are also many Scythians who skin the right hands of their dead enemies, including the nails, to make covers for their quivers.

65. There is one custom in particular which prevails amongst them: it is their way of treating skulls; not generally, but specifically those of their worst enemies. What they do is this: after sawing off the whole part below the eyebrows, they clean out what is left. If a man is poor, he just stretches a piece of untanned ox-hide round it and uses it the way it is. If, however, the man is rich, he stretches the hide round the outside but gilds the inside and uses it in this form for a drinking-cup.

---

[13]Hesiod (?) mentioned the Hyperboreans in the *Catalogue of Women* (*Eboeae*); Merkelbach and West fragment 150 (= Oxyrhynchus Papyri #1358 fr.2). All that can be seen of the context of this reference is a list of Northern tribes "Who dwell around the Hyperboreans with their good horses." It is tempting to interpret this as a reference to the horse-breeding tribes of the Ukraine and of central Russia.

[14]The *Epigonoi* (Tale of the Men born Afterwards) was the epic poem about the sons of the Seven Against Thebes. The poem has been lost since ancient times and we do not know the poetic context of this citation.

They also do this to the skulls of relatives with whom they have quarrelled, and in cases where one man has defeated another in the presence of the king. When guests visit them, the host tells the story of these skulls as he passes them round: that these were his relatives who once waged war against him; how he got the better of them. These anecdotes illustrate his courage.

66. Once a year each local governor mixes a cup of wine from which those Scythians drink who have killed a man in war. Those who have not achieved this are excluded from tasting the wine, but sit separately without honour. This is the worst disgrace that can happen to them. But, as for the man who has killed the biggest number of enemies, sure enough he gets two cups! Holding both of them together, he drinks from both of them at once!

67. The Scythians have a lot of prophets, who make their prophecies with a large number of willow twigs in this way: when they gather together large bundles of twigs, they put them on the ground, untie them, put out each twig separately,[15] and prophecy. While they are speaking they collect the twigs back up again and lay them out all over again. This is their ancestral form of divination.

---

[15]If Herodotus is trying to describe the process of prophecy by runes, he cannot have seen it being done. He may, on the other hand, be describing an entirely different process of divination used by a Scythian tribe quite unrelated to any proto-Germanic group.

CHAPTER 26

Chronological Guide to Greek Cultural Background

J.G. Farrow

DATE (approx.) B.C.

3000–2000:   **Early Bronze Age:** Aegean: Cycladic

Mainland Greece: Early Helladic

Egypt: Dynasties I–XII

Crete: Early Minoan

2000–1900:   In early Minoan are found the first stages in the development of Cretan palaces, showing parallels with Egyptian and Sumerian civilizations. During the Early Helladic period Greek-speaking people began to migrate into the Southern Balkan peninsula.

2000–1600:   **Middle Bronze Age:** Minoan/Middle Helladic

Egypt: Dynasties XII–XVII

c.1800   Spread of Early Assyrian merchant colonies westward toward Asia Minor.

1600   "Minoan" naval power, centered on Crete, reached a peak. Use of linear scripts spread through Crete, some islands, and coastal settlements on the Greek mainland. We do not yet know the language represented by linear "A," except that it was an early form of Cretan. Linear "B" has been identified as an early written form of the Greek language; most surviving samples of "B" are from a later date than "A," but there is substantial overlapping in probable dates of samples depending on locations where they were found. Between the 1650's and 1400 there were 2 major disasters in Crete, apparently caused by seismic phenomena (Crete is situated on a major fault line). Between & after these events there is evidence of growing Greek influence in Crete, e.g. the transition from Linear A to Linear B as a writing system. This would have accompanied a shift in language from Eteo-Cretan to Greek.

1600–1100:   **Late Bronze Age:** Late Minoan/Helladic

Late Helladic is also termed the "Mycenaean Age."

Egypt: Dynasties XVII–IX

During the 16th century were constructed the shaft graves found by Schliemann at Mycenae; the contents and structure of these graves and absences of them from earlier levels show the sudden rise of this civilization's wealth. Perhaps the Perseid dynasty, according to Argive legend the founders of Mycenae, dates from this time.

1648   Probable date of volcanic activity on Thera (Santorini), destroying home bases of Cretan naval power.

1450/1300 ?   In Athenian chronology, approximate date range of King Theseus, apparently pre-supposing the existence of a Cretan empire and taxation-system as circumstantial background to the hero-myth.

1400–1300 ?   Growth of Troy VI, "Laomedon's Troy," coinciding with some incidents in the Argonautica and Hercules cycles of legend. The site of Troy has, since its discovery in the late 19th century by Heinrich Schliemann, been found to have been settled on many different levels at nine main periods.

c. 1250   The settlement at Troy, Level VI was destroyed by earthquakes and/or tidal waves, the smaller town built later within its ruins (Level VII) by fire. In central Asia Minor at this time the Hittite empire was growing substantially.

📖 *Cautionary Note:* Blegen found most Trojan pottery of this period to have more in common with the "Minyan Ware" of the Greek mainland than with Anatolian styles. Also during this same time period, Greek genealogies record a series of dynastic marriages which may be at least partially accounted for by historical intermarriages between mainland aristocracy (Achaean/Mycenaean royalty) and descendants of the Minoans who still held respect in areas once controlled by Crete. The Atreids, who traditionally superseded the Perseids as kings of Mycenae after arriving from Lydia in Asia Minor, raised Mycenae to dominance on the Greek mainland. They used tombs of the "tholos" type.

1208 "Fall of Troy" (defeat of Priam's city by an Achaean alliance under Agamemnon, dynastic head of a Mycenaean empire) according to Athenian chronological tradition.

1184 "Fall of Troy" according to Eusebius' chronicle, derived from Eratosthenes (a Hellenistic chronographer). This "fall" is traditionally associated with the *Iliad* and *Odyssey* of Homer and with the "Wooden Horse" motif. Troy VII was destroyed by fire, but very few possible traces of violence are now in evidence. References in the *Iliad* and in later tradition to widespread coastal raids support a view expressed by many modern archaeologists and historians that the siege of a single site in the northeastern Aegean was just a single manifestation of friction involving Achaean and Hittite powers, sometimes in direct conflict with one another, at other times against island powers more difficult to identify in modern terms.

1200–1100 Decline of Mycenaean civilization in Greece, traditionally attributed to an over-expensive overseas campaign (Trojan War: compare the domestic situation resulting in Greece as seen in Homer's *Odyssey* with that in Aeschylus' "Oresteia" Trilogy). Archaeological evidence indicates that the Bronze Age "palace" or castle at Mycenae, was suddenly abandoned during this period.

1100–1000 *"Return of the Sons of Hercules,"* the mythic context of the Dorian invasion of southern and central Greece. During this period literacy became almost extinct as far as we know in the Greek-speaking world, to be revived after the old syllabic linear scripts had long been forgotten. Stories of Achaean and Ionic achievement from earlier generations survived in orally-transmitted heroic poetry sung to instrumental accompaniment for the entertainment and glorification of surviving descendants of the old Achaean and Ionian nobility. On mainland Greece, only Athens claimed to have remained unaffected by the Dorian invasion.

900–600   Phoenician traders and colonists introduced alphabetic script to Attica, Boeotia, Euboea, and Corinth. Use of coinage began to spread; early period of Greek colonization.

800–500   Stories featured in the Epic Cycles started to take on their present forms as they were "frozen" in writing. The term **primary epic** will here be used to describe poems essentially composed in oral form and subsequently written down.

Secondary epic describes poems composed in writing, usually at a time when written source-materials were available (though obviously this was not possible in the earliest days of secondary epic).

The heroic poetry of Ionian Greece is preserved in an intrinsically primary form in the *Iliad* and **Odyssey** attributed to **Homer.** This poet was believed to have been born on the island of Chios in the eighth century B.C. and to have been blind. Modern knowledge of oral composition in an illiterate society offers few objections to these possibilities. Speculations as to Homer's identity and methods of composition were rife in the ancient world and the "Homeric Question" in all its ramifications is still far from settled.

There is also a substantial corpus of *Homeric Hymns*, poems of varying length, glorifying not only the deities to whom they are addressed, but also human families claiming descent from them. All these poems share a common feature of reflecting an Ionian/Achaean world struggling to remind itself of past glories.

700-500   Just as Homeric poetry as a genre was peculiar to the Achaean/Ionian tradition, so "Hesiodic" covers a corpus of poems composed in Boeotia and attributed to **Hesiod**. These poems were chiefly of a **didactic** nature (especially the *Works and Days*). The **Theogony** has a conclusion (lines 900–1020) which may have been composed in its present form much later than the rest of the poem (i.e., after 560 B.C.). Compare the debate over the origin of the "Catalogue of Ships" in Book II of Homer's *Iliad*, a section of the poem which many scholars have thought to have been an interpolation.

The "Hesiodic Catalogues" were doubted even by the ancients as being Hesiod's work, as the priests at Ascra told Pausanias. The fact that some of the Hesiodic corpus, at least, was said to have been inscribed on metal shows an early dependence on writing, at least for transmission of the poems if not their composition.

560–514   Athens was ruled by Peisistratus (died approximately 530), then by his sons. According to some later traditions Peisistratus commissioned the first written texts of the Homeric poems for the use of judges in contests of poetry at festivals. Peisistratus' economic expansion of Athens, especially in the wine, olive, and honey exports, produced a need for more pottery, the quality of which improved rapidly as migrant craftsmen exchanged ideas with existing local artists. The abundance of painted vases from this period gives us a visual insight into the mythical beliefs and imaginations of the Greeks before Romanization.

600–400   Secondary epic became increasingly encumbered as oral formulae merely appeared to be repetitive clichés in writing. New poetic forms emerged: **Lyric** and **Elegiac** poetry gave a poet a more verbally concentrated and less repetitious form in which to write and gradually increased the number of available metrical schemes. **Choral lyric** created a more grandiose effect than just having one singer perform a poem. This genre had already started to grow in Doric dialect-speaking areas before 600 and had not always depended on writing as a medium; poets had "coached" their choirs to learn the words of a poem by rote. Even more than in the case of a written poem, brevity was a positive advantage.

518–438   One of the later, and possibly the greatest, of the Lyric poets was **Pindar.** He was born near Thebes in Boeotia and composed a large number of victory-odes for winners in the four main games held regularly as Panhellenic (inter-state) events by the Greeks: the Olympic, Pythian, Nemean, and Isthmian games. There is a tradition that critics and fellow poets noticed an absence of mythological references from Pindar's early poems. When this was brought to his attention he compensated very drastically for this omission. An important part of the "flattery-content" of a victory-ode was the glorification of the winner's ancestors, who were very often considered to be demi-gods and heroes of antiquity.

Lyric poetry had already become popular in Athens before 500 (probably promoted at the festivals sponsored by the Pisistratids) but at about that time a major new development took place. Tradition ascribes this development to the poet Thespis. A soloist was required to participate with the choir and to take on the personality of the protagonist in the poem. This naturally became the origin of **drama**.

The number of characters required to be played by soloists grew later (see below) as the genre became more popular and sophisticated. Drama also includes, both visually and verbally, a strong ritual element in its 5th-century form.

c. 500–450   The philosopher **Xenophanes of Colophon** criticized the existing tendency within Greek religious belief toward anthropomorphic polytheism (see *ancient critics*).

An approximate contemporary of Xenophanes was **Democritus**, founder of the **Atomist** school of philosophy.

494–478   Ionian revolt against Persia and the two Persian invasions of mainland Greece **(Persian Wars)**. The Battle of Marathon took place in the first war, the battles of Plataea and Salamis in the second.

478   Formation of the Delian Confederacy, an alliance of maritime Greek states to keep Persian power out of the Aegean and compensate states for damage done during the Persian invasions.

Athens, as being probably the heaviest casualty, received large sums of money during the next 50 years, making possible a massive program of civic and religious buildings (especially the Parthenon and Erechtheum) and helping promote the growth of drama in the new theatres. Drama rapidly assumed two distinct forms: **tragedy** and **comedy** (see separate notes).

Aristotle (see below) records that the purpose of tragedy according to the classical Greek criteria was to observe, within practicable and comprehensible limitations, a true reverence for the majesty of the gods and the power of fate. Aeschylus and Sophocles are still regarded in particular as the prime representatives of all that is best in Greek tragedy.

Aeschylus himself became something of a legendary figure, a popular biography recording that he was killed in old age when an eagle dropped a tortoise on his head.

All the Athenian dramatists reinterpreted traditional narratives or motifs to comment on topical situations (for example, Aeschylus' treatment of the court of Areopagus in the *Eumenides*).

Similarly Euripides introduced the politics of democracy into the anachronistic context of the Achaean army under Agamemnon in his *Iphigenia in Aulis*.

440–404   The plots of old comedy were fair game for lampooning myths in contemporary topical terms, as can be seen in the *Birds*, *Clouds*, *Thesmophoriazusae* and *Frogs* of Aristophanes.

431–404   The **Peloponnesian War**, between Athens and Sparta, each with its allies and covering an increasingly wide area of action, spread to Sicily in 415 and weakened the power of both sides. The Mutilation of the Hermae occurred on the eve of the scheduled departure of the Sicilian Expedition; statues and small effigies of the god Hermes were defaced in parts of the city of Athens, an action which was perceived as inviting ill-fortune. At the end of the war, the Athenian democracy was subverted, an oligarchy was imposed, and the increasing limitations of political censorship narrowed the scope of literary composition, especially for the stage.

430–380   Growth of the Sophistic movement in Athens, started by Gorgias of Leontini. Gorgias was born about 490 and came to Athens in person in 427. The teachings of the Sophists centered around the art and science of logical argument.

Many sophists were also, like Gorgias, rhetoricians but soon a sharp division arose between them, exemplified in the speeches *Against the Sophists* and *Helen* by Isocrates (436–338) Isocrates firmly believed that philosophy could go too far in its speculation away from real life.

Another contemporary of Isocrates was Alcidamas, from Elaea in Asia Minor. He also wrote a speech *Against the Sophists* and has had attributed to him (though it is probably a later forgery) a prosecution-speech, *Odysseus against Palamedes* in supposed reply to the defense-speech by Gorgias.

Socrates (d. 399), left no known written works; the majority of his teachings have come to us via Plato's writings, the rest through the memorabilia by another of his disciples, Xenophon and through later biographies.

445–410   **Herodotus**, writing a complete history of the Persian Wars with a lengthy account of the origins of the conflict and growth of the protagonist nations, left a valuable collection of cross-cultural information. He is the earliest prose author whose works still survive and has earned the title, "Father of History." His occasional gullibility has also earned him the nickname, "Father of Lies."

The writings of earlier prose historians seem to have consisted mainly of lists of countries, cities, tribes, and genealogical lines with anecdotal stories appearing as "filling." These *Logographoi* (= storytellers) transmitted a great deal of information on local legends, beliefs, and practices in specific areas, but their lack of cohesiveness and uneven level of human interest appeal resulted in the failure of their works to be copied out in a complete form. Some specific details from their works were quoted either directly or in summary form by later authors or commentators (*scholiasts*: see below under "Aristarchus") on works which do survive. It is especially important that Herodotus saw the Persian Wars in the context of an "East-versus-West" conflict, a concept which continues in use as a political cliché to the present time.

428–347   **Plato**, using the figure of Socrates (see above) as "Chairman" of his dialogues, attempted to propagate human examination of one's own attitudes to life and questioning of public institutions and human values. Plato clearly believed in the immortality of the soul and in the concept that there are different levels of existence: the spiritual, the purely visual (including illusory manifestations), and the physical, or lowest, level.

Plato questioned traditional myths on several different levels in addition to the allegorical values of myths and the dubious adventures of the gods which made them poor role-models. He believed that myths preserved some concepts of world-history. He may have visited Egypt; at least he took an interest in stories brought from that country and in comparing them with the myths of Athens. He believed that the Nile valley retained the oldest continuous world civilization and that the Greeks, whom he considered to have an even older heritage, had (along with most other nations) been periodically interrupted in their development by floods and other natural disasters.

An approximate contemporary of Plato was **Palaephatus** (*see* Chapter 2, above, part 2c). Another collector and editor of mythic information was Asclepiades of Tragilos, whose *Tragodoumena* were mythical narratives based on the plots and contextual references of Attic tragedy.

370–345   The powers of Athens, Sparta, and the rest of the southern and central Greek states were progressively weakened by the incursions of King Philip of Macedon.

384–322   Aristotle, Plato's pupil, continued the practice of criticizing mythical stories and works of literature. His approach, however, was more from the viewpoint of analysis and literary criticism than from that of political ideals. His great work the *Poetics* includes much valuable information on literary genres and treatment of subject matter. Aristotle's chief importance for modern readers is that he was amongst the first thinkers to demand evidence and proof of theories as to how things worked.

Aristotle's pupil, Alexander the Great, died in 323 as a young but highly successful commander. He had conquered the furthest-reaching empire the world had seen at that time. He had inherited control of a large part of the already Greek-speaking world from his father, King Philip of Macedon. He had multiplied the size of his possessions by defeating the Persians, who had for the previous two centuries been in control of most of the Middle East.

On the breakdown of Alexander's newly-conquered empire after his early death, his successors (his former generals who divided up the territories amongst themselves) vied with one another in many ways besides open warfare. Within the next century the Ptolemaic dynasty in Egypt and the Attalids in Pergamon began to build libraries and endow positions for lecturers and research-scholars. The existence of the libraries and consequently an increasing body of potential students which in turn brought private lecturers looking for employment, created a new thirst for information.

Greek became the common international language for the countries around the Eastern Mediterranean for the next 700 years. The period which started with Alexander's victories and death, fading gradually under Roman annexation 300 years later, is now known as the **Hellenistic Era.**

c. 300   Euhemerus of Messene, active in the court of King Cassander in Northern Greece (317-297) wrote a *Sacred History*, relating the discovery on an island in the Indian Ocean of inscriptions which, pieced together, contained complete biographies of Zeus and other men whom posterity had called gods. This work of ingenious fiction gives us the origin of the term, ***Euhemerism***, the claim that the Olympian gods had been mortals on whom increasingly exaggerated stories had been based. Because of their noble birth and high degree of intelligence and strength, these men had become military and political leaders in their day like Alexander. Common memory had confused these characters with allegorical personifications of natural forces.

312–262   Zeno founded the **Stoic** school of philosophy in Athens, initially meeting in the Stoa of the marketplace. The Stoics stressed the power of fate even over the gods (an idea already exploited by some tragic poets). Zeno and his successor Chrysippus developed a theory that the universe was controlled by *Logos* (literally = "word"), a kind of universal mind-force. The monotheistic implications of this theory are very much apparent to modern Judaeo-Christianity and Islam, but it may be too tempting to regard the Stoics as early monotheists. Their debt to the earlier thinking of Xenophanes (see above) is clear.

The Stoics tended to de-emphasize the historicity of myths and to place greater stress on the significance of **allegorical** interpretation.

306–270   The teaching career of Epicurus in Athens. He was born on the island of Samos, c. 341. His school was to become the greatest rival of the Stoa in Athens. Epicurus based his theories on the "Atomist" teachings of Democritus (see above). The atomist doctrines seemed to have no place for the immortality of the soul; it did not automatically follow that, as many people thought, Epicureans could indulge themselves without limit, free from the fear of judgment after death.

While not acknowledging a "Hell" concept, the more serious Epicureans modified their behavior out of consideration for their fellow human beings, aiming at an ideal state of *Ataraxia* (= freedom from trouble).

285–247   Reign of Ptolemy II Philadelphos in Egypt. He developed the library at Alexandria, giving generous funding to the formation of the world's largest collection of books at the time. He also funded research connected with use and care of material in the collection plus prestigious posts for librarians who would be expected to acquire new works and maintain catalogues.

The first librarian, Zenodotus, is now chiefly remembered for his commentaries on the works of Homer. His comments only now survive in a few scattered quotations in later commentaries. Originally edited as "companion-volumes" to the text of the poems, Zenodotus' observations were later incorporated into marginal glosses written on the same page as the text, a practice popular in the Byzantine period.

276-272   Chremonidean War, in which Athens and Sparta, with Ptolemy II's help, tried to regain independence of Macedonia. During the war Philochorus of Athens, leading spokesman of the independence party, was murdered. Philochorus had written a massive corpus of material on the national histories of Attica, his chief work being an *Atthis*. He also composed and edited a series of antiquarian and mythological criticisms of Attic tragedies, plus a "Letter to Asclepiades," publicly attacking the *Tragodoumena* (see above).

300–260   Theocritus, the first pastoral poet, was born in Sicily but spent much time in Alexandria. Some of his poems touch upon mythical subjects, especially in the context of popular local motifs such as stories of a Cyclops wooing a nymph. Many of the pastoral idylls show the prominence of popular superstition in everyday life.

Zenodotus' successor as librarian at Alexandria was **Apollonius of Rhodes**, who made the most lasting Hellenistic contribution to Epic Poetry. His ***Argonautica***, the story of Jason's quest for the Golden Fleece, survives in its original four books. Apollonius incorporated much material from local legends which may already have been collected in a written form. In the last book of the poem the Argonauts return to Greece by a perilous and overly long detour up the river Danube; they carry the Argo across the Alps! It is very likely that this episode was composed or revised shortly after Hannibal invaded Italy by a transalpine route, 219 B.C.

While Zenodotus and Apollonius were in overall charge of the library, the specialist keeper of the comedy section was Lycophron of Chalcis. Little survives of his comic writing, but we have a complete text of his unique work, the *Alexandra*. Presented in the form of a messenger's speech in the tradition of Attic tragedy, this poem consists mainly of the prophetic words of the raving Trojan priestess Cassandra. The 1400 lines of Iambic verse are an absolute study in obscurity. The art of oblique references was here being developed as an art in itself. Hardly a line in the whole poem can be understood without the aid of a commentary.

300–240   The Alexandrian poet Callimachus wrote two major surviving sets of poems, the Hymns and the Aetia, which were only a small sample of his output. The hymns are a sort of Hellenistic equivalent of the Homeric Hymns, full of the allusions typical of Alexandrian writers. The *Aetia* were at the time a relatively new genre of poetry, mainly versified instances of poems illustrating origins of Greek myths, customs, ritual, places, and families.

246   Accession of Ptolemy III Euergetes in Alexandria; during his reign Eratosthenes became the third librarian. Eratosthenes is now remembered as a geographer and chronographer. As the latter he compiled a World History, listing information on monarchs, dynasties, and events in chronological sequence dating back beyond the First Olympiad at least to the Trojan War. His work formed the basis of the Christian World-Chronicle compiled 600 years later by Eusebius of Caesarea. In these chronicles, as much detail as could be taken literally or euhemerized was treated as historical data in fixing an absolute chronology around the relative chronologies of each nation.

Late 200's   Homeric criticism was continued by the fifth librarian at Alexandria, Aristarchus. His text of the *Iliad* and *Odyssey* was meant to be the absolute "critical edition." Each volume of the text was carefully written out line-by-line, with signs in the margin to indicate if a specific line required clarification, or whether the text was in any way doubtful at that point.

A commentary-volume, intended to be used alongside the text, would have to be used to convey Aristarchus' remarks. No such volumes now survive except in small fragments, but many of Aristarchus' comments have been preserved in marginal glosses written in annotated texts of the Byzantine period. The chief value of the **Scholia** (marginal glosses) is that they preserve a lot of literary and mythological information, especially on the identity of authors believed to have been responsible for introducing a particular motif into the accepted narrative of a given legend. They also quote extensively from otherwise lost literature. Examples of scholia are used below in the appendices, especially app. E.

It was also at approximately this stage at Alexandria that the *Iliad* and *Odyssey* were divided into 24 books each (there are 24 letters in the Greek alphabet). Previously each episode of the poems had been known by its own "subtitle," a fact which has occasionally created an impression that each episode had been a poem in its own right.

284-204
Livius Andronicus, born in Tarentum, south Italy (then the Greek-speaking state of Taras), was taken to Rome as a slave in c. 272. He prefixed Lucius Livius to his existing Greek name *Andronikos*, since he had been bought by a Roman citizen Lucius Livius. Not only did he teach Greek language and literature to his owner's (and possibly other) children, but he also translated the *Odyssey* into Latin, a language not yet quite ready to have hexameter verse imposed upon it. Livius' *Odyssey* seems to have used the old Saturnian Metre, and was regarded as a crude archaism by the end of the Republic. Livius' great contribution is that by selecting this poem and making it available to Roman citizens he caught their interest and directed it toward an appreciation of the Greek imagination, with its literary and mythical traditions. The Romans had no formal collection of their own literature and myth at the time. Livius Andronicus also produced, wrote, and acted in the first Latin comedy and Latin tragedy ever written on a large scale. Like the *Odyssey*, his plays were translated from Greek models.

270- 201
Cnaeus Naevius is recorded as the first true Latin poet who was also a Roman citizen. He too wrote tragedies and comedies, some for performance "in Greek dress" (*Fabulae palliatae*), others in Roman dress (*Fabulae Togatae*). His monumental epic poem, "On the Punic War,"

set a standard in taste and content that was to influence Roman poets for many generations to come; Roman epic poetry tended, with a few notable exceptions, to concentrate on Rome's own military and political glory rather than mythological themes. Naevius traced Rome's ancestry back to Troy in this poem. The Romans were apparently conscious already of a migration from Asia Minor somewhere in their own ancestry and acknowledged their descent from Anchises, the alleged lover of Venus (Aphrodite) and father of the Trojan hero Aeneas. This migration-story was especially strong in respect of the cult of the Penates, early Italian household gods supposedly brought from Troy by Aeneas.

500 to 300 B.C. The **Etruscans,** whose power Rome had pushed back, also claimed descent from migrants from Asia Minor. Surviving fragments of their language show it to have been non-Indo-European, but there is insufficient material now available for closer analysis. The Etruscan household gods were the Lares. By the classical period, cults of *Lares* and *Penates* had become almost indistinguishably fused within the general framework of Roman family-religion.

218–204 The Second Punic War (Rome vs. Carthage; Hannibal's invasion of Italy) ended in victory for the Romans, who then assumed control of all Southern Italy, Sicily, and the islands of the Western Mediterranean plus most of the Iberian peninsula. Roman power by this time was also spreading eastward across northern Greece and the Aegean.

205–204 The cult of the Great Mother of Mount Ida (Asia Minor, near Pergamon and the ancient site of Troy) was imported into Rome, apparently as a result of an oracular warning from the Sibylline Books (believed to date back to the early Roman king Ancus Martius and connected with the Oracle at Cumae) about the Punic War. Much credit for Scipio Nasica's final defeat of Hannibal at Zama was given to the importation of this cult, symbolized by the transfer of a large lump of meteoric rock, supposedly in the shape of the goddess, to Rome. Perhaps this same rock is to be identified with the "Palladium that fell from heaven," usually associated with the old Trojan version of the Athena-cult by Greek epic poets and writers of mythological handbooks dealing with the end of the Trojan War.

The matriarchical goddess, usually called *Cybele* or *Ma* by the Phrygians in Asia Minor, had as her consort *Attis,* who died in spring every year and was buried on March 24th. He was believed to rise again on the 25th. Legal restrictions had to be placed on Cybele-worship in Rome when it was realized that frenzied devotees practiced self-mutilation.

200/190
Hegesianax, from Alexandria in the Troad, seems to have been responsible for editing or forging a "Troica" (matters dealing with Troy), purportedly a narrative of prehistoric antiquity by Cephalon of Gergis, who probably never existed. Hegesianax is known to have represented the Syrian tyrant Antiochus III on a diplomatic mission to Rome in 193, when the Romans were starting to occupy the northern Aegean area. He may have been instrumental in reinforcing the Romans' conviction that they were descendants of the ancient inhabitants of the Troad.

197–159
Power of the kingdom of Pergamon, which had grown during the Hellenistic period in the North-Eastern Aegean area, reached a peak under Eumenes II, who defeated the Galatians in Asia Minor. Eumenes began an Altar of Zeus (a huge building with 3 wings) and was patron of the Second Pergamene school of sculpture. He established a library to rival that of Alexandria. The two libraries began to compete, each claiming to have a copy of every book ever written. Within a short time this rivalry reached the level of sheer bathos as supposedly ancient books were "discovered"—that is, forged.

149–146
Third Punic War (final Roman conquest of Carthage). Fall of Corinth, Roman annexation of Greece, and creation of the province of Achaea.

90–60
The Roman poet Titus Lucretius Carus translated Epicurus' works into Latin hexameter verse, "On the Nature of the Universe." This made Epicureanism available to a wider readership throughout the Roman provinces. Lucretius' younger contemporary Catullus wrote short, often romantically-inspired poems in a kind of "Latin/Alexandrian" genre. One of his main poetic models was Callimachus.

106–43
Life of Marcus Tullius Cicero, lawyer, statesman, philosopher, and poet. As a politician Cicero viewed with distaste Julius Caesar's rise to absolute power (see below). In his philosophical writings Cicero was chiefly influenced by the Stoics; he recognized it to be his patriotic duty to observe the feasts and sacrifices offered to the gods in the established state-cults, but privately felt that the whole realm of

creation was subject to a single divine intellect. He regarded the Epicureans as impious in their overall rationalization of the gods.

102–44 Life of Caius Julius Caesar, politician, general, and historian. After his conquest of Gaul, 58–52, and victory over Pompey in the Civil War (49–47), Caesar was regarded by many inhabitants of Roman-occupied territories as a god in human form. In strictly Roman terms this simply meant that his **Numen** (= protective spirit/genius) was greater than that of any other living human being, not that the man himself was a "god" as such.

However, from the 60s B.C. onward, the whole eastern Mediterranean world had come under Roman domination. In many of these countries (especially Egypt and Bithynia) it was already the established custom to regard a king or conquering general as a god in human form (see above).

Doubtless Caesar's opponents had been determined to prove his total mortality when they assassinated him. Unfortunately for them, not only did Caesar prove to have had greater popularity than the sum total of theirs, but also the passing of a comet close to the earth's surface not long after Caesar's death was construed by his supporters as a divinely-sent vehicle conveying the *Numen Caesaris* to join the gods.

59–30 Career of Diodorus of Sicily. He wrote a massive *Historical Library*, an attempt to encompass the history of the world as he knew it, in 40 books. The surviving books are an important source on much material not covered elsewhere. We can trace the remains of many of the otherwise lost books of Diodorus in the works of the 4th-century A.D. chronicler, Eusebius.

31 Battle of Actium. Octavian (Julius Caesar's great-nephew and adopted heir) defeated the forces of Marcus Antonius and Cleopatra (the latter was the last Ptolemaic ruler of Egypt). As a political move this victory was seen to establish the claims of the *Gens Iulia* (Caesar's family) to divinely-appointed world leadership. Egypt became no longer a nominally independent puppet-kingdom but a Roman province.

72–19 B.C.   Life of the Roman poet Virgil (also spelt Vergil; his full name was Publius Virgilius Maro). In his early days Virgil found distaste for the traditional Roman form of Epic Poetry, which was essentially the versification of military and political history. He found his own self-expression as a pastoral poet, becoming in his *Bucolic **Eclogues*** a kind of Roman answer to Theocritus. He then tried his hand at a more didactic form of pastoral poetry, addressing the four books of his ***Georgics*** not only to his patron Maecenas but also to the popularization of farming at a time when political and economic problems were already overshadowing Rome's new imperial government. The ultimate model for the Georgics is clearly Hesiod's "Works and Days," but each book of the Georgics is categorically aimed at a different aspect of farming. Like Hesiod, Virgil gave mythical precedent for his precepts, especially in his fourth book.

28   **First Settlement of Augustus**; Octavian made his first move toward a redefinition of his constitutional position, calling himself the "First Citizen" while claiming to have restored the Republic (only partially in reality) and assumed the new name **Augustus** (= revered, chosen by the gods).

   Virgil was commissioned at about this time by Augustus to compose an epic poem glorifying Rome's illustrious heritage. Virgil was at first unwilling to undertake epic writing, but decided to deviate from the most commonly established Roman custom and write a mythological epic which would still glorify Rome. Accordingly he embarked upon composing the **Aeneid**, a twelve-book epic poem on the hero Aeneas, his travels from Troy after a bitter fight with the Greeks, his arrival in Italy and the problems he encountered in establishing himself there. Even on his deathbed Virgil was dissatisfied with the work, but it became the standard Roman mythological poem comparable with both the *Iliad* and with the *Odyssey*.

43 B.C.–A.D. 17   Life of Publius Ovidius Naso (**Ovid**). He shared Virgil's distaste for dry historical epic and produced a vast output of poetry, much of it based on mythical themes. His *Heroides* (some of which are considered spurious) are a collection of imaginary correspondence in verse between pairs of mythical characters, often lovers. His greatest contribution to epic poetry is his ***Metamorphoses*** in 15 books, developing a tradition previously exemplified in Callimachus' *Aetia* (a set of etiological myths in poetic form). Each narrative (there are several in each book) is part of a loosely chronological sequence and shares a common theme in that a mythical character is supernaturally changed into another form, either as a punishment or as a reward.

A.D. 14   Death of Augustus. He had given the Romans their longest continuous period of peace for over a century. On his death he was officially proclaimed a god (though he had been unofficially worshipped as such in some of the Eastern provinces since 18 B.C.) and sacrifices were accordingly designated to his *Numen*.

CHAPTER 27

Germanic Myths: Historical Background from Tacitus

📖 *The following extracts are taken from the **Germania** of the Roman historian Cornelius Tacitus. Most of Tacitus' works were composed between about 80 and 120 A.D. In A.D. 77 Tacitus married Julia, the daughter of the famous Roman general Julius Agricola, who had commanded legions in Germany and later became Roman governor of Britain.*

The following extracts date from approximately a thousand years before our earliest written texts of primary source-materials for Germanic myths. Considering that such a long time had elapsed, it is really quite surprising how little the concepts of Germanic religion had changed between the beliefs recorded by Tacitus and those which lie in the background of the oldest poems in the Poetic Edda (probably collected in their present form between 850 and 1150 A.D.).

2. The people of Germany seem to me to be aboriginal, not interbred with foreigners who settled their land from outside or visited it temporarily. This is because ancient people used to effect their major movements by water, not by land. The huge and really quite hostile North Sea is rarely navigated by ships from our world. In addition to the dangers of a rough and dangerous sea, who would willingly leave Asia, Africa, or Italy for a rough land with a harsh climate, miserable to every visitor and cultivator except for those born and bred in it?

In their ancient songs, which are their only kind of historical records, they celebrate the earthborn god Tuisto and his son Mannus[1] as their ancestors. They say that Mannus had three sons[2] from whose names the people along the coast are called Ingaevones;

---

[1] *Mannus* simply is a Romanized form of the Germanic noun *man* (Modern German *Man, Mensch*, etc.).

[2] Ingaff, Hermann and Istaff. Ingaff's descendants, whose names Tacitus Latinizes into "Ingaevones," may be the Ynglinga (see the *Ynglinga Saga*, part I of Snorri Sturluson's *Heimskringla*, the fullest surviving version of the allegedly historical sagas of the Norse kings). One possible German interpretation of the names is that the Ingaevones are "*die Inwohner*," the Hermiones "*die Herumwohner*," and the Istaevones "*die Westwohner.*"

those in the central region are the Herminones, and the rest the Istaevones. Some people, however, taking liberties with history, claim that the god had more descendants who gave their names to more tribes, such as the Marsi, Gambrivii, Suevi, and Vandali. They say that these are the original names of the nations and that "Germany" is a modern term.

They also have their own regional version of Hercules, whose praises they sing as they advance into battle.

3. There is a strange kind of poetry form they use, calling its practice "bard" craft.[3] It stimulates their courage, while the sound itself[4] acts as an omen of the combat to come. As the cry rises up from the battle-line, terror is inspired or felt. It does not sound articulate as [the words of] a song, but is more like a wild chorus of valour. A harsh, piercing note and a broken roar are the favourite sounds, which they amplify in volume and sonority by applying their mouths to their shields.

Some people have supposed that Ulysses,[5] in the course of his long wanderings that are the subject of many stories, was driven into this ocean and landed in Germany, and that he was the founder of Asciburgium[6] (a town located on the Rhine) which is even inhabited today; they say Ulysses called it "Askipurgion." They claim that an altar was discovered here some time ago, with a dedicatory inscription to Ulysses, mentioning that he was the son of Laertes. Apparently there are still monuments and tombs inscribed with Greek lettering, around the borders of Germany and Rhaetia. I shall attempt neither to confirm nor to deny these claims; each person may believe about them what he wants.

---

[3]This is my translation of Tacitus' Latin word *barditus*. The word "bard" is actually Celtic. The Norse equivalent is *skaldr*. Tacitus is (accidentally: see next note) referring to the right concept, which in Norse was called *skáldskapr*.

[4]Tacitus is now using the term *barditus* to mean some kind of war-cry generated by warriors droning into their shields, using them as amplifiers. He may have been confusing different Germanic and other Northern European terms and pre-battle practices.

[5]There was an enormous proliferation of foundation-myths based on the travels of Odysseus/Ulysses throughout antiquity. See, for example, the references to the hero in the spurious last 30 lines of Hesiod's *Theogony* and in the appendix chapter on the *Telegonia*. It is quite possible that Tacitus may have been told about or even shown some kind of stone slab bearing a few legible Greek or Latin letters bearing a name beginning with the letters "OD-." The same letters, of course, might have originally been an attempt to write Odin's name in a classical-type alphabet. There is no longer any evidence of intentionally permanent runic-type writing prior to the eighth century AD, so this is entirely speculative.

[6]This town is probably Asburg in Meurs. The original Germanic etymology of Asburg is more likely to mean either, "Town of the Aesir" (= Norse *Asgarð*), or "Town of the Ash [Tree]." Tacitus took his information here from Greek or Latin-speaking historians, who were always trying to equate foreign settlements with the adventures of Classical heroes and gods. Later Snorri Sturluson described the first humans thus (*Gylfaginning* 8): "*The man was called Ask, the woman Embla, and from them was born the human race to whom the dwelling-place within Miðgarð was given. After that they built for themselves a city in the middle of the world, calling it Asgarð. We call it Troy.*"

9. In their religion, they pay the highest respects to Mercury.[7] On certain days they even see fit to make human sacrifices to him. They slaughter the more common types of sacrificial animal for Hercules and Mars.[8] Some of the Suevi also perform sacred rituals to Isis.[9] I have been unable to find out how this foreign religion became popular with them, except by noticing that they symbolize her with a sailing-ship.

They consider it unworthy of the dignity of sky-gods to be confined within walls or to be represented in human likeness. Woods and groves are their temples.

10. No people are more addicted to prophecy by omens and lottery. The latter is performed in the following simple way: they cut a twig from a fruit tree and divide it into small pieces which, distinguished by certain marks, are thrown haphazardly on a white cloth.[10] Then the local priest (in the case of a public ceremony) or head of the household (if private) calls upon the gods with his eyes raised to heaven. He takes out each piece three times and, as they come up, interprets their meanings according to the marks on them. If the result is an unfavourable omen, there is no further consultation on the particular subject on that day. If the omen is positive, they still look for confirmatory signs.

Like other nations the Germans are acquainted with the practice of prophesying from the sounds and flight of birds. What is more unusual is that they also derive

---

[7]According to the medieval chronicler Paulus Diaconus (*History of the Lombards*, I.9) "Mercury" is *Oðin*, or Woden, chief of the Germanic gods. This makes good mythological sense, *Oðin* being both the Psychopomp and the controller of runes (thus ensuring the working of sympathetic magic) in ancient Germanic culture.

[8]"Hercules" is presumably Thor, while "Mars" must be Tiw (Tyr). Tacitus strongly suggests that these gods are next after "Mercury" in order of priority. Thus, in the English week, Woden's Day has Tiw's Day and Thor's Day on either side of it. We normally regard the concept of a seven-day week as being essentially peculiar to the monotheistic tradition (and thus introduced to the Northern countries by Christian missionaries a century or more after Tacitus' time), but the system can equally be a natural consequence of depending on a lunar calendar ($28 = 4 \times 7$) and dividing the month into four stages. The ancient Germanic dependence on the lunar calendar is confirmed in paragraph 11, below. The current English names for the days of the week were preserved during the Middle Ages from their Germanic predecessors and commonly excused on the basis of being named from the "planets," which included the sun and moon before Galileo's time.

[9]Isis was the ancient Egyptian fertility goddess. It is uncertain whether Tacitus is really referring to an imported cult or identifying the early Suevic cult of Freyja with the closest equivalent he knew (see further on Freyja's symbols below). Tacitus himself, as we see in the following sentence, thought it was the former because to him the use of a ship emblem signified the importation of a foreign god, with the same intent that the Romans had initially adopted the rites of the Phrygian mother-goddess Cybele between 210 and 196 B.C.

[10]This account of divination from rune-sticks is more recognizably Germanic than the system used by the Scythians described by Herodotus (above, chapter 25).

certain omens from horses. Some of these animals, milky white[11] and untouched by farm-work, are pastured at public expense in the sacred woods and groves. These are harnessed to a consecrated chariot and accompanied by a priest, king or chieftain who listens closely to their neighing and snorting. They (not just the common people, but also the nobles and priests) consider this the most reliable form of prophecy.

11. In matters of minor import the chiefs consult each other. Major issues are decided by the whole community. Even so, the questions to be set before the people are first discussed in advance by the chiefs. Unless there is a special emergency they assemble on predetermined days, such as the new moon or full moon, which they consider the best times to undertake any new enterprise.[12] Unlike us, they do not measure time in numbers of days, but of nights.[13] This is how they organize their business and set their appointments: in their reckoning night always comes before day.

40. The Langobardi[14] derive their respect from the smallness of their numbers. Even though they are surrounded by many more powerful tribes, they maintain territorial integrity not from making concessions but by their martial enterprise. The neighbouring Reudigni, Aviones, Angli, ... and Nuithones are defended by rivers and forests. There is nothing remarkable about these tribes or their territories except that they unite in the worship of Hertha,[15] or Mother Earth. They believe that she interferes in human fortunes and visits her different nations. In an island of the ocean stands a sacred and unviolated grove, in which there is a sacred cart[16] covered with a veil. Only the priest

---

[11]The motif of the White Horse goes back a long way in British folklore: some images, more than 100 ft. long, are still visible, cut into the topsoil on the chalk-downs of Southern England. There is still much debate as to whether the images were first carved by Celts or by later Germanic invaders. As a name or title, 'The White Horse' still survives in England for some local public houses.

[12]This statement may be construed as a piece of evidence that some early Germanic tribes had used a lunar calendar. The moon's phases have always been an important measure of time. See note 8, above.

[13]This usage is still preserved in the English word "fortnight" meaning a period of two weeks: "fourteen nights."

[14]"Long-Beards." This tribe later invaded Northern Italy and settled in the territory still called Lombardy.

[15]"Earth" as a name in Norse is **Jordi**. A close modern English pronunciation would sound like "Yerthi". Some manuscripts read *Nerthus*, which looks like a male name and is difficult to reconcile with "Mother Earth." Saxo Grammaticus (c. 1200 A.D.) makes several disparaging comments about the effeminacy of the priests of Njǫrðr, a fertility god of the Vanir group. Njǫrð's name would certainly have been transcribed into Latin as "Nerthus." As a soil-based fertility god N's name joins the Pantheon of the Week as Saturn, a name much easier for non-Germanic people to pronounce.

[16]The partially fossilized remains of several carts have been found in former swamps in Denmark and Britain. From the excellent state of their preservation it is very likely that they were used for religious purposes.

is allowed to touch it. He alone knows when the goddess enters her sacred retreat and with deep respect he tends the vehicle, which is drawn by yoked cows.

At this season all is joy; every place the goddess visits is a scene of festivity. No wars are undertaken, weapons are untouched, and armour is all put away. This is the only time they celebrate peace both at home and away. Eventually the same priest returns the goddess, sated with the attentions of humans, to her sacred home. The chariot with its curtain and, if we may believe it, the goddess herself are all washed in a secret lake. This washing duty is performed by slaves who are afterwards drowned. This is the origin of a mysterious horror: holy ignorance of what actually happens. The sacred ritual is only seen by those who are on the point of death. This part of the Suevian nation extends to the most remote corners of Germany.

43. An extended mountain ridge separates the Suevian territory from that of various remoter tribes. Of these, the Lygians occupy the most extensive territories. The most powerful groups of Lygians are the Arii, the Helvecones, the Manimi, the Elysii, and the Naharvali.[17] In the last-named territory is a grove, dedicated to a very ancient religion. The priest who presides over this cult is dressed rather like a woman, but the gods worshipped there are said, as Romans interpret them, to be Castor and Pollux. The local name is Alcis.[18] No images or other trappings of foreign religion appear in their worship, but these gods are worshipped as young men who are brothers.

44. Next are the territories of the Suiones,[19] situated right on the edge of Ocean. In addition to their large numbers and physical strength, they also possess a navy.

45. Beyond the Suiones is another sea, sluggish and almost stagnant. People believe it is the Ocean which surrounds the world. This is because sometimes the last light of the setting sun is so bright that the stars are obscured. Some people even claim they can

---

[17]The lands Tacitus is now describing are farther to the East than before, around the prsesent borders between Poland and East Germany.

[18]The word which Tacitus transcribes as "Alcis" is probably cognate with Germanic "Alf" or "Alp," English "Elf," Norse "Alfr." Since Tacitus identifies them with the Gemini (*Dioscuri* in Greek), the religious cult is probably based on local perceptions of marsh-gas. Ancient Greeks and Romans commonly believed that the Dioscuri were patron gods of sailors and sent the luminescent phenomenon which we still call "St. Elmo's Fire."

[19]I have omitted some text here: Tacitus has now reached the Northern tribes in his circular tour of the Germanic nations. On the Suiones, their ancient wealth and religion, see the medieval historian Adam of Bremen (*History of the Church*, ch. 233): *"This nation possesses a temple of great fame, called Ubsol. In this temple, which is decorated throughout with gold, the people worship the statues of three gods. The most powerful, Thor, sits on a couch in the middle. Woden sits on one side and Fricca on the other."* Compare notes 7 and 8 above.

hear the Sun-god rising from the ocean and can see the shapes of his horses[20] with rays gleaming from their heads. This, they say, is as far as the laws of nature can reach.

On the East side of the Suevic Sea live the tribes of the Aestii, who dress in the same way as the Suevi, but whose language is more like British.[21] They worship the mother of the gods.[22] As a symbol of their superstition they wear on their persons the emblems of wild boars. They rely on these images[23] as if they were armour and every other form of defence. The devotee [thinks he] is safe even in the midst of his enemies. Their weapons are chiefly clubs, for they do not use iron very much. They grow wheat and other products of the soil and are more industrious than other Germanic tribes. They even explore the sea and are the only people who make a living from gathering amber, which they call "glese"[24] and collect it along the shore. With the usual indifference of barbarians, they have not troubled to ask or otherwise find out how it is produced in nature.[25]

---

[20] I translate *formas equorum*. Some manuscripts read "*formas deorum*" = "shapes of the gods." Perhaps this is a reference to the Aurora Borealis, or Northern Lights. Horses of the Sun are a frequent motif, often associated with myths which were themselves connected in other ways with Northern Europe, e.g. the Myth of Phaethon in Ovid, *Metamorphoses* II.1-366, especially the references to the amber imported into Rome from the North.

[21] Tacitus is referring to a form of Celtic which survived for a long time in remoter parts of Northern Europe. He does not mean "English," since he has already listed the Angli (who did not begin invading Britain in large numbers until after A.D. 400, when the Western Roman Empire had begun its collapse and Roman legions had already been withdrawn from Britain) in their old German homeland. When Tacitus speaks of a 'British' language he probably means one closer to the forms of Celtic which survive as Irish and Gaelic.

[22] The wild boar was Freyja's ancient symbol throughout Northern Germanic countries. When Robert Eaglesfield persuaded Queen Philippa to establish The Queen's College in Oxford, 1341, the student beneficiaries were from Eaglesfield's own home county in Cumberland. Many of these students were native speakers of West Norse or of Celtic, and brought their own customs to college with them. The Queen's College still celebrates the Boar's Head Gaudy every Christmas, explaining the custom by reference to a student called Thomas Copcott who killed a boar with a volume of Aristotle while walking outside town and brought the body back to College for the Christmas dinner.

[23] It is unclear whether Tacitus is referring to actual shields made from boars' hide, or to a belief in the magical protection of boar-shaped badges.

[24] The original Celtic word probably meant "bright stuff." It is cognate with Welsh "glas" (= green, the colour of most glass produced in the Roman period) modern English "glass."

[25] Compare this with the probable astuteness of Celts in earlier times, who seem to have sold amber to Greeks and other Mediterranean customers telling them that the pieces were the frozen tears of tree-goddesses. Baltic amber was well known to Herdotus (III.115). Hesiod introduces the amber-goddess Elektra as "Daughter of Oceanus," i.e., originating at the edge of the world. Apollonius of Rhodes (*Argonautica* IV.605-612) in the third century B.C. gave the Phaethon story as an etiological myth for amber as tears of tree-goddesses.

Norse Myths and their Sources

PART A: WHAT THE SOURCES ARE

1. The Poetic Edda

A very loose collection of assorted poems assembled from many manuscripts. No two or more independent manuscripts contain exactly the same set of poems. The poems were mostly composed and transmitted orally at first, in some cases possibly before 800 AD, the early Viking period. They were not committed to writing until at least the eleventh century, using the Latin-type alphabet introduced to the North by Christian missionaries. The runic system of writing (the *futhark*, not strictly an "alphabet" at all) was clumsy and was seldom used for writing poems unless they were extremely short. Some signs were added to the Latin characters from the runic system, such as *eth* (ð, pronounced as in English "other") and *thorn* (þ, pronounced as in English "through"), a useful patch when the more modern-looking "th" is not always intuitive to pronounce. These letters are still in use in the Icelandic written language, the closest living descendant of Old Norse. After the introduction of printing such signs fell out of use in printed English but survived for several years on handwritten signs, where they were often misunderstood.

As in the early Greek case with epics in Homer's time, poetry was intended to be memorized and performed "live": most people did not automatically associate it with writing.

Not all of the Eddic poems are narrative, that is, telling a story in order. There are **mantic** (prophetic) poems as well as many riddles. One occasionally also finds **skaldic** (political-style) poems mixed with Eddic material in some mss.

Examples of Eddic poems

Vøluspá: Sayings of the Prophetess (Mantic: found in two manuscripts, the *Codex Regius* and *Hauksbók*)

Balðsdrauma: Baldr's Dreams (a supplement to Vøluspá: see above)

Hávamál: Sayings of the High One (mantic)

Rigsþula (The Song of Rig): narrative of Heimdall's journey to Miðgarð (*þula*, pronounced **thoo**-la, means a list. The poem also takes the form of a song with a repeated chorus)

Lokasenna: Loki's Curse-Dialogue (a song in a kind of Skaldic meter)

Dvergatál: Catalogue of Dwarves (this list appears as stanzas 9–16 in the manuscripts of Vøluspá, where it is clearly an interpolation).

Link to text and translations of Vøluspá: http://www.voluspa.org/voluspa.htm

2. The Prose Edda, by Snorri Sturluson (1179–1241)

Without this textbook of Norse myth and poetry we would be quite unable to understand most of the poems in the *Poetic Edda*.

Organization of the *Prose Edda*:

Some manuscripts begin with a General Prologue, in which Snorri cites his Catechism to demonstrate that he is a Catholic Christian and does not believe in the "pagan" gods as such. He explains that he is preserving the myths for their cultural value to his people in Iceland and in neighboring countries (Norway, Sweden, Denmark, Iceland, and England). Snorri divides the Prose Edda into three sections, each being a kind of textbook on the cultural heritage of the Norse people.

A) *Gylfaginning* (The Tricking of Gylfi)
   The story begins with Gylfi, a long-dead king of Sweden, having a dream in which he entered a house in a remote place and was entertained by three men: The High One, Equally High One, and Third. He never saw their faces, but heard their tales and was able to ask questions. The stories thus framed within the dream-sequence outline the principal Norse myths, from the Creation story, via several important stories of the gods, to Ragnarøk (End of the World).
   Note: The opening sections of *Gylfaginning* are translated below in this chapter.

B) *Skáldskaparmal* (Guide to Skald-craft)
   This is a text on the content of traditional poetry. The second half is an attempt to explain one of the trickiest aspects of Skald-craft, the understanding of **kennings** (substitution-phrases, loosely corresponding to the use of epithets in Greek by Homer and Hesiod). Most of the book is organized as a kind of dictionary of kennings.

C) *Háttatal* (List of Metrical Schemes)
   This is a technical guide to the construction of Skaldic poems.

Link to text and translation of Prose Edda:
https://archive.org/details/proseedda00snor/page/n19

* * * * * * * *

3. History of the Danish Kings, by Saxo Grammaticus

We do not know exactly who Saxo was. There were several men called Saxo connected with the Danish court between about 1180 and 1220, the probable time the *History* was composed. "*Grammaticus*" shows that he was well educated (he wrote in Latin) and had a polished style in which he imitated the florid phrases and long, complex sentences of earlier writers from Italy and France. The *History* was probably intended to be a Danish counterpart of Geoffrey of Monmouth's *History of the Kings of Britain*, written between 1135 and 1155. Geoffrey had been one of the first historians to develop King Arthur as a historical figure and included among his pre-Roman kings some names that probably reflect euhemerized Celtic gods. Saxo, when referring to Norse gods, tended very often to euhemerize them. On other occasions, as in the case of *Ugardilocus* (Utgarð-Loki) in Book VIII, he treats the survival of the gods as an unclean piece of devil's work. A substantial part of Book VIII is translated in the *Intro to Mythology* textbook, Chapter 29.

PART B: THE TRICKING OF GYLFI (GYLFAGINNING)

Part 1 of the *Prose Edda*, **by Snorri Sturluson** (Translation & notes by J. G. F).

📖 *Snorri Sturluson (1179–1241) was born and spent most of his life in Iceland. He was a land-owner, lawyer, and politician. He felt very strongly that some aspects of Norse culture, especially its mythical, linguistic, and poetic traditions, should be preserved. He fully understood that such an attitude might be misrepresented in the growing uniformity of Catholic Christianity, which the* Althing *(Icelandic parliament) had formally adopted in the year 1000 AD. He composed a general prologue for the* Prose Edda *in which he demonstrated his Christian beliefs explicitly but argued the merits of cultural preservation. He re-drafted this prologue at least twice in different revisions of the work. His use of the character Gylfi (an actual king of Sweden who had died centuries before Snorri's time) shows a lawyer's skill in avoiding charges of writing inappropriate material. The following extracts are based on the reading of* Konungsbók *(Codex Regius / the Royal Manuscript). For a complete translation of Gylfaginning, published a century ago by A. Brodeur, link to:* http://www.sacred-texts.com/neu/pre/pre04.htm

1. King Gylfi ruled the land that is now called Sweden. It is said of him that he gave to a wandering woman, as a reward for entertaining him, a piece of arable land in his kingdom, as much as four oxen could plough in a day and a night. But this woman was one of the Æsir[1] and her name was Gefjun. She took four oxen from up North in Jótunheim[2] (they were her sons by a giant) and set them to the plough. The plough went in so hard and deep that the land was cut and the oxen dragged it out Westwards into the sea and it stopped at a certain bay. Gefjun let the land settle there, gave it a name, and called it Selund (Zealand). But the place from which the land had been torn up became a lake. It is now called Lögrinn (The Lake) in Sweden. There are as many bays in The Lake as there are headlands in Zealand. This is what the poet Bragi the Old says:

   > *Gefjun gladly drew from Gylfi the deep-ringed land,*
   > *So that steam arose from the swift haulers,*
   > *Increasing Denmark.*
   > *The oxen bore eight stars on their four foreheads*
   > *As they hauled their spoil, the wide island of meadows.*

---

[1] The Æsir were the family of Norse gods of whom Oðin was the head. Gefjun (or Gefion in English spelling) was a goddess of nature occupying a status roughly corresponding to Artemis in the Olympian system or Diana in the Roman system.

[2] Giant-Home." There is an actual district called Jótunheim in the mountainous North-West part of Norway

2. King Gylfi was a clever man, skilled in magic. He was astonished at the cunning of the Æsir-folk, that they could make things obey their will. He wondered whether they were accomplishing this by their own power, or whether this effect was caused by the gods they worshipped. He traveled to Asgarð[3] in secret, disguising himself as an old man. But the Æsir were too clever, having the gift of prophecy: they saw him coming before he arrived and made ready their tricky optical illusions.

When he came into the city, there he saw a high hall, so big that he could hardly see over it. Golden shields were laid over it like roof-shingles. Thjóðolf of Hvinir[4] says this about Valhalla's shield-roof:

> *On their backs they let them shine,*
> *As the stones stormed on them,*
> *Svafni's[5] house-tiles.*
> *Those men were thoughtful.*

In the doorway of the hall Gylfi saw a man juggling with daggers, keeping seven in the air at once. This man was the first to ask his name. He said his name was Gangleri,[6] that he had travelled a long distance and that he wished to stay overnight. He asked who owned the hall. The man answered that the owner was their king. "I will accompany you to see him," he said, "So you may ask him yourself."

He then moved on into the hall. Gylfi followed and the hall door closed right on his heels. He saw many rooms and many people: some were playing games, some were drinking, others were fighting with weapons. As he looked around him, what he saw was beyond belief.

> *"At every door,*
> *As you go through it,*
> *You must check carefully.*
> *You do not know*
> *What enemies sit*
> *Lurking ahead of you."*[7]

---

[3]Asgarð = "Yard (or enclosure, home) of the Æsir"

[4]The "shield-roof" was a popular kenning for Valhalla. Þjóðolf was a skaldic poet. An easier spelling of his name might be "Theodulf."

[5]*Svafni* (sleep-bringer) is a kenning for Oðin.

[6]Gangleri (weary traveller) is another of Oðin's kennings. Since Gylfi is in disguise according to Snorri's alleged dream-sequence, he is trying to use Oðin's own trickster style.

[7]These lines are quoted from the opening verse of *Hávamál*, the "Sayings of the High One." It is one of the main poems in the *Poetic Edda* collection. A complete translation may be found at: http://www.pitt.edu/~dash/havamal.html

He saw three high seats, one above the other, a man sitting at each. He asked the names of these chiefs. His guide answered that the one sitting in the lowest throne was a king and was called High One; the next up was called Equally High,[8] while the top one was called Third. High One asked the visitor if he had any more business, saying he was welcome to food and drink as were all in High One's hall. Gylfi replied that he wished to find out if there were any scholarly people present. High One answered that he would not leave a healthy man unless he became smarter:

> *"Stand forward*
> *While you ask;*
> *He who answers shall sit."*

3. So began Gangleri's questions: "Who is highest or oldest of all the gods?"

High One replied: "He is called Allfather in our language, but in Asgarð as of old he has twelve names. One is Allfather, the second Herran[9] or Herjan. His third name is Nikarr[10] or Hnikarr, his fourth is Nikuz or Hnikuðr,[11] fifth Fjölnir,[12] sixth Oski,[13] seventh Omi,[14] eighth Bifliði or Biflindi,[15] ninth Sviðarr, tenth Sviðrir,[16] eleventh Viðrir,[17] twelfth Jálg or Jálkr."

Then Gangleri asked, "Where is this god? What power does he have? What mighty deeds has he performed?"

High One said: "He lives through all ages and rules over all his kingdom: everything, great and small."

Then said Equally High: "He crafted heaven and earth and sky and all that is in them."

Then Third said: "What matters most is that he made mankind and gave him a soul that shall endure for eternity, even if the body should decay to mould or burn to ashes. So shall all righteous men live with him in the place called Gimlé[18] or

---

[8]*Jafnhár*, literally "Evenly-high"

[9]Lord, or Warlord

[10]Thruster (of a sword or spear)

[11]Another word for "Thruster"

[12]Knowledgeable

[13]Granter of wishes

[14]The one with the booming voice

[15]Spear-shaker

[16]Burner, scorcher

[17]Weather controller

[18]Gem-like, shining

Vingolf,[19] but wicked men will go to Hel and from there to Niflhel,[20] that is down in the ninth world."

Then Gangleri said, "What was he doing before heaven and earth were made?"

High One answered: "That's when he was with the frost-monsters."[21]

4. Gangleri said: "How did things begin? What was there before?"

High One answered: "As it says in *Völuspá*,

> *"It was long ago of old,*
> *That nothing existed.*
> *There was neither sand nor sea,*
> *Nor cold waves.*
> *There was no earth yet,*
> *Nor heaven up there.*
> *Space there was (tricky!)[22]*
> *But no grass.*

Then Equally High spoke: "Many long ages before the earth was created, Niflheim[23] was made. In the middle of it is a spring called Hvergelmir, and from that the rivers which flow out are called: Svöl, Gunnthra, Fjörm, Fimbul, Thul, Sliðr and Hrið, Sylgr and Ylgr, Við, Leiptr and Gjöll that is next to Hel's door."

---

[19]Friendly haven

[20]Cloudy/foggy hell

[21]The words *með hrimþussum* are normally translated "among the frost-giants." The normal Norse word for giant is Jótun (derived from *Jörði* = Earth, as in Greek *Gigas* is a contraction of *gēgenēs* = earth-born). Some scholars have argued that *Þursa* is from the same √IE stem as Greek *Theos* = God. The frost-monsters (definitely someone else's gods, never one's own) belong clearly to the trickster archetype and probably began in Northern myth as personifications of glaciers: They seem to be alive and have massive powers, but cannot be alive in the human sense of the term. There are many myths in which gods of the Æsir group have hostile encounters with this species.

[22]The poem here reads, "*Gap var ginnunga,*" which can also be translated, "There was Ginnungagap." I have tried to bring out the root meaning of the mythological word's components, split as they are here with great effect by the poet of *Völuspá*. The word *gap* in Norse means the same in English and both are cognate with the verb to *gape*, normally meaning to stand with one's mouth open, i.e. create a *gap*. The same semantic link works for *Chaos* and *cha'ein* in Greek: see above, ch.18 note 7.

[23]Cloud-home, i.e. The North Pole of the entire universe. *Nifl*, in Norse, is cognate with German *Nebel* (= cloud, mist) and with Greek *Nephele* (cloud): see chapter 13, note 2.

Then spoke Third: "First was the world that is in the southern half, called Muspell. It is bright and hot. It is so blazing and burning that those from outside who are not born there cannot go there. A being whose name is Surt stays in the land to guard its borders. He has a flaming sword, and at the world's ending he will come and cause the gods' downfall and burn every land with fire. As it says in *Vóluspá*:

> *Surt travels from the South*
> *With the stick consumer(=fire).*
> *Shining from his sword*
> *The sun of might.*
> *Great mountains clash together,*
> *And trolls will travel about.*
> *Men will walk the hell-road*
> *While heaven splits open.*

5. Gangleri said: "What shape were things in before generations came into existence and humanity increased?"

Then High One spoke: "Those Rivers that are called the Elivagar, when they had spread so far out from their source that the poison floating along on them hardened like the cinders that come from a furnace, turned into ice. When the ice stopped and flowed no more, the poisonous mist coming from it settled and turned to frost. One layer of this frost formed over another, right across Ginnungagap."

Then Equally High said: "Ginnungagap, on the side that faces North, filled up with thick and heavy ice and frost, while the inner parts [filled up with] rain and gusts. The southern part was lit up by the glowing coals that flew from Muspell-home."

Third said, "Just as everything cold and grim came forth from Niflheim, so everything close to Muspell was hot and bright. Ginnungagap was mild as air without wind. When the frost met the blowing warm air it thawed and dripped; when these melting drops quickened it took the likeness of a person and he was called Ymir. The frost-monsters call him Aurgelmir, and from him come all the generations of frost-monsters, as it says in the *Short Vóluspá*:

> *'All the shamanesses are from Viðólf'*
> *All the wizards from Vilmeið,*
> *But the sorcerers are from Svarthöfði.*
> *All the giants come from Ymir.'"*

And here is what the giant Vafthrúðni[24] says:

> *Where did Aurgelmir come from, with his giant-sons,*
> *First that wise giant?*
> *When from Elivagar*
> *Seeped venom-drops,*
> *They grew until there was a giant.*
> *That's where our generations*
> *Came from altogether.*
> *That's why we are all so wild.*

Gangleri then asked:"How did those generations come forth from him, and how did other men multiply? Do you believe that the one you are talking about is a god?"

Then High One answered:"We do not in any way consider him a god. He was evil and so were all his family. We call them frost-monsters. It is said that while he slept he sweated. There grew under his left armpit a male and a female,[25] and one foot begat a son on the other. From that source came descendants that are frost-monsters. The old original frost giant is the one we call Ymir."

6. Gangleri said, "Where did Ymir live, and what did he survive on?"

[High One said[26]]:"The next time the frost dripped, a cow took shape. She was called Auðumla and from her four udders ran milk. She fed Ymir."

Then Gangleri asked,"What did the cow feed on?"

High One answered:"She licked the ice-blocks, which were salty. On the first day, as she licked the stones, a man's hair appeared from the blocks in the evening. The next day it was a man's head, then on the third day it was the whole man. His name was Buri. He was fair-looking, big and strong. He begot a son who was called Bor. He (Bor) married a woman called Bestla, daughter of the giant Bolthorn, and they had three sons. One was Oðin, the next Vili, the third Vé. It's true as far as I'm concerned that Oðin and his brothers are

---

[24] *Vafþrúðnismal* 30.3 – 31: See **The Poetic Edda** translated by Carolyne Larrington (Oxford U.P. 1996) pp.39-49, or by Lee M. Hollander, (U. of Texas Press 1962, 1988) p. 47 for the full context.

[25] A male and a female frost-monster (*hrimthursa*). While this form of reproduction may seem like a bizarre twist on warnings about bad personal hygiene (we have already been told that the species are evil by nature), it probably reflects more directly on ways in which a glacier can seem to reproduce by splitting at its "limbs."

[26] This phrase is missing in the Royal Manuscript. It is found in other mss.

the rulers of heaven and earth. We think this his rightful title: he is the mightiest and most famous man we know, so you can take it that that is what he is called."

7. Then Gangleri asked, "How did things go between them, or which was the more powerful?"

High One answered: "Bor's sons killed Ymir the giant. When he fell, his wounds put out so much blood that with it all the race of frost-monsters was killed, except for one who escaped with his family. The giants call him Bergelmir. He got up on a boat with his wife and stayed safe there. From them come the families of frost-monsters, as it says here:

> *Countless winters before the earth was shaped,*
> *That's when Bergelmir was born.*
> *The first thing I remember*
> *Was when that wise giant*
> *Was laid on a trunk.*[27]

8. Then Gangleri said, "What did Bor's sons do then, if you believe that they are gods?"

High One said: "That's no little matter to tell. They took Ymir, moved him to the middle of Ginnungagap, and built the earth from him. From his blood was the sea and the lakes. The earth was made from his flesh and the mountains from his bones. They broke his teeth and jaw-bones – from those and the broken bones they made rocks and pebbles."

Then Equally High said: "From the blood that was squirting forth from his wounds they made the sea and used it to link the earth together, and they placed the sea in a ring round the earth. Most people would think it impossible to cross it."

Then spoke Third: "Then they took his skull and made the sky and set it up over the earth with four corners, and under each corner they set a dwarf. They are called East, West, North and South. Then they took hot coals and ashes that were flying wildly out of Muspell-home and set them in the middle of Ginnunga-heaven, both above and below, to light up heaven and earth. They gave places to all the lights, some fixed in heaven, some wandering about

---

[27]*Luðr* means a hollowed-out tree trunk, boat, or box. It can invite comparison with Noah's Ark, but the anonymous verse quoted here (actually verse 35 of *Vafthrúðnismal*) seems to refer to the witnessing of Bergelmir's funeral.

below the heaven, but prescribed their positions and designed their courses. So we have it from ancient knowledge that by their means days were counted and years were listed, as it says in *Vóluspá*[28]:

> *The sun did not know*
> *Where her home was.*
> *The moon did not know*
> *What mightiness he had.*
> *The stars did not know*
> *Where their stations were."*

Then spoke Gangleri:"This is great news that I have now heard.This is a miraculously arranged construction. How was the earth set up?"

High One answered:"It is a circle on the outside, and around that lies deep sea. Along the sea-coast they gave lands as a home to the generations of giants. Further inland they built a fortification around the world against the attacks of the giants.To fortify this wall the used the giant Ymir's eyebrows and called the fortification Midgard.They took his brains, threw them upwards and made the clouds in the sky from them, as it says here[29]:

> *From Ymir's flesh*
> *The earth was shaped,*
> *From his sweat[30] the sea,*
> *Mountains from his bones,*
> *Trees from his hair,*
> *And heaven from his skull.*
> *From his brows*
> *The delighted gods*
> *Made Midgard for men's sons,*
> *And from his brains*
> *Were all of those ill-tempered*
> *clouds shaped."*

9. Then spoke Gangleri:"I think it must have been a great accomplishment when earth and heaven were made and the sun and moon were set up to shape the days. So where did people come from, to make their home there?"

---

[28] *Vóluspá* verse 5.

[29] *Vafþrúðnismal* verse 21

[30] The primary meaning of *sveiti* is sweat, its direct English cognate. It has a secondary meaning, "blood." In view of the context most modern translators prefer the secondary meaning here.

High One answered: "When Bor's sons were going along the sea-shore, they found two tree-stumps. They took these trees and shaped people from them. The first gave them breath and life, the next gave them wits and movement, the third gave them expressions, speech, hearing and sight. They also gave them clothing and names. The male was Askr and the female Embla[31]: from them came all mankind that was given its home down in Miðgarð. Then they built a fortress for themselves in the centre of the world: it is called Asgarðr. We call it Troy.[32] There the gods and their families lived and their many acts and deeds were wrought both on earth and in heaven. There is a place there called Hliðskjálf,[33] where Oðin sat so that he could see over all the worlds, so he saw and knew what everyone was doing. His queen was Frigg the daughter of Fjörgvin: their descendants are those we call the Æsir who lived in ancient Asgarðr and the territories that belong to it. They are a divine race. This is why he is called All-father: he is father of gods and men and everything he accomplished with his power. Earth[34] was his daughter and his wife. From her he had his first-born son, that is Ásaþorr.[35] He was noted for power and strength, enough to defeat all living things."

---

[31]*Askr* = Ash (tree), *Embla* = elm.

[32]References to Troy in national histories were quite frequent throughout the Middle Ages. The success of Vergil's *Aeneid* at the beginning of the Roman Empire had set a cultural expectation of divine destiny linked to Rome's successful growth over the next 400 years. The end of that empire did not stop future leaders from wanting to claim Rome's legitimacy for themselves. For example, the British historian Geoffrey of Monmouth in the 1130s claimed that Britain's name was derived from Brutus, a refugee from Troy who had crossed Gaul and the Channel a generation after the sack of Troy and landed where the town of Totnes, in Devon, is now located.

[33]Literally door-shaker, Oðin's watch-tower.

[34]*Jörðin* is a female name for earth. She may be an alternate name for Frigg here, but we are reminded very much of Zeus' multiple wives in the Olympian system.

[35]Ása -Thor. *Ása* is the singular form of which the plural is *Æsir*.

The Story of Thorkill
(from Saxo Grammaticus)

📖 Saxo wrote this history in Latin between the years 1185 and 1200 A.D. The extract translated below is taken from a portion of the History that deals with the period between approximately 690 and 750 A.D.

Observe the references to "Thule": this name was semi-mythical in the early middle ages. It was first mentioned by the Greek geographer Pytheas of Massilia (about 300 B.C.; Marseilles, in the South of France, was in ancient times the Greek colony of Massilia). The works of Pytheas are now lost, but his account of Thule is mentioned several times by the 1st century B.C. geographer Strabo, who is very skeptical about this island in a frozen sea. Our next record of it is in the *Life of Julius Agricola,* written in approx. 97 A.D. by the Roman historian Cornelius Tacitus. In Chapter 10 of the *Agricola* Tacitus tells of a Roman surveying party who had circumnavigated the island of Great Britain (modern England, Wales, and Scotland) and had discovered the further group of islands which was named the Orcades (modern Orkneys). Tacitus says the party also surveyed Thule, but withdrew because of the approach of winter and because the waters were "too sluggish" for normal sailing. Most modern scholars think Tacitus' account relates to sightings of the Shetland Islands, while Pytheas may have actually meant Iceland, since he specified that it was "six days' sail" beyond Britain. We must not, however, ignore the possibility that either author or his sources may also have been misled by references to the West coast of Norway. Tacitus later (*Agricola* 28) mentions a group of Usipi, German auxiliary soldiers, who had been serving in the Roman army in northwestern Britain (probably near the Cumbrian or West Scottish coast). These Usipi rebelled against their Roman officer's discipline and hijacked three ships to return home to Germany via the North Sea. When recaptured by Suebi and Frisii (Germanic tribes on the North Sea coast), the men gave some details of their adventures raiding the Northern coasts of the British Isles. It is obvious that explorations of the North Sea and North Atlantic Ocean this time onwards became a subject of high adventure, especially among Germanic peoples. At about the same time as Tacitus, the Greek author Antonius Diogenes wrote a fantasy story called *The Wonders beyond Thule*, claiming in the introduction that the text was in fact much older and had already existed in the time of Alexander the Great.

Several commentators on Saxo's history think that "Thule" means Iceland (basically because many authors had passed on the remarks of Pytheas). Yet Iceland was not discovered by Norse people until about 860, when Gardarr Svavarsson (a Swede living in Denmark) was blown too far west in a storm. It is more likely that "Thule" here refers to an unspecified part of Scandinavia which was still uncharted as early as 700. Saxo was very likely using an earlier written source for this story. At the time he was writing, the Norse genre of *saga* literature in prose was just beginning to take shape and heroic ballads had already been circulated for centuries in verse (see previous section). Whether the source-story had been centered around the character of Thorkill himself, or whether it had been about the king (thus probably entitled, for example, *Gorms Saga Haraldssonar*) we cannot be certain.

I have replaced Saxo's Latinized spelling of the names (Gormon, Geruthus, Ugarthilocus, etc.) with simplified versions of the probable Norse forms of the names ("Gormr," *Geirroðr* becomes "Geirrod," *Utigarðr* becomes "Utgard," thus Utgard-Loki instead of the clumsy Latin *Utigardilocus*, etc.).

The bold numbers on the left hand side refer to the page numbering of the *Editio Princeps* of Saxo's history (Paris, 1514).

📖

85b After the death of Harald Bjornsson the next king was Gormr Haraldsson. He was distinguished amongst the ancient Danish military kings for his achievements. But he put the courage he had inherited to the test in ways other than warfare; he searched out the secrets of nature. His heart thirsted to investigate marvels, whether he had experienced them himself or had simply heard of them from others.

Being so desirous of seeing everything that was foreign and extraordinary, he decided to test a report he had heard from the men of Thule about the home of a certain Geirrod. The men made fantastic claims about the mighty piles of treasures in that country, but said the way was beset with danger and was virtually impassable by human mortals. For those who had tried it claimed that one must sail over the Ocean that surrounds the lands, to leave the sun and stars behind, to journey down below Ginnungagap,[1] and finally to enter a land where there was no light, but darkness ruled eternally.

---

[1] The Latin reads, *sub Chao,* = *"under Chaos."* I have substituted *"Ginnungagap"* as being the closest Norse equivalent.

But Gormr the warrior trampled down in his soul all fear of imminent danger. He did not so much want the treasure as the glory, for he hoped that his fame would increase if he were to venture on a completely unprecedented quest. Three hundred men announced that they shared the king's ambition. Gormr decided that Thorkill, who had brought the news, should be chosen to guide them on their journey, since he knew the land and was acquainted with the approaches to that country. Thorkill did not refuse the task, but warned that ships must be specially constructed to be strong enough to withstand the unusual fury of the sea; that they must be fitted with plenty of knotted ropes, with timbers closely nailed together, filled with plenty of provisions, and that the storage spaces onboard should be waterproofed with ox-hides. The men sailed off in only three sailing ships, with a hundred chosen men in each ship.

When they had reached Heligoland they lost their favourable winds and were driven around over dangerous seas in different directions. Finally, in extreme need of food, having even run out of bread, they kept off hunger with a small amount of stew. After several days they heard the rumbling of a storm in the distance, as if rocks were being flooded. From this they deduced that land must be close. A young man of great agility was sent up the mast to look out. He reported that a steep-sided island was in sight. The whole crew, overjoyed, looked eagerly for the land at which he was pointing, hoping for refuge on the aforesaid shore. At last they managed to reach it, and climbed up the steep cliffs which blocked their way to the higher ground.

There were plentiful herds of large cattle wandering about on the shore; Thorkill told the men to kill no more of these than they would absolutely need to stave off their hunger. If they disobeyed, he said, the gods who guarded the place would not let them leave.

86a But the sailors, more anxious to fill their bellies than to obey orders, ignored safety in favour of gluttony. The holds of the ships were now empty of food, so they filled them up with the carcasses of the cattle they had killed. These animals were very easy to catch because they crowded round to look at the men, not being used to them and having no fear.

That night, monsters rushed down to the shore, filled the forests with their noises, and surrounded the ships. One of them, much bigger than the rest, waded out into the water carrying a huge club. When he got close enough, he shouted out to the men that they would never sail away until they had paid for the crime they had committed in killing the cattle; the penalty to the gods was to be a price of one man for each of their ships. Thorkill gave in; to preserve the safety of the majority at the cost of a few he singled out three men by lot and gave them up.

After this they got a favourable wind and sailed to the further end of Permland. It is a region of eternal cold, covered in very deep snow. Even in summer the heat does not reach it. There are forests which cannot be crossed, no produce of grain, and wild animals which are rare in other places. Its many rivers pour themselves forth in a hissing, foaming flood because of rocks embedded below the surface. Here Thorkill beached his ships and told the men to pitch camp on the beach since, he said, it was only a short distance to Geirrod.

He told them not to speak to anyone who approached them, since any inappropriate words they might utter would give the monsters power to harm visitors. It was therefore better to keep quiet; he was the only one who had seen all the manners and customs of this country before, so only he could speak safely.

At about sunset, a man of unnatural size greeted the sailors by their names and came to join them. The men were all horrified, but Thorkill told them to smile at him pleasantly.

"This is Gudmund," he said, "The brother of Geirrod. He is the most reliable guardian of anyone who lands in this spot."

"Why don't your friends speak?" asked the giant.

"Sir," replied Thorkill, "My friends have no skill in your language. They are embarrassed to use a foreign speech."

Gudmund then invited them to be his guests and gave them transportation on his carriages. As they travelled on they saw a river which could be crossed by a golden bridge.[2]

They wanted to cross the river, but Gudmund discouraged them, saying that this was the river by which nature separated the world of men from the world of monsters; mortals were not to cross it.

Then they reached their guide's home. Here Thorkill took his men aside and warned them to act sensibly, since there would be a lot of temptation coming their way.

"Don't eat any of the strangers' food", he said, "but feed yourselves only on what you have brought with you. Sit together when you eat, and don't sit with the locals during the meal time. If you eat any of their food, you'll lose all recollection of who you are and spend the rest of your lives among these filthy creatures, being just as unclean as they are. Likewise, keep your hands off the servants, and don't touch any of their eating or drinking utensils."

---

[2]This bridge seems to be *Giallar-brú*, the Golden Bridge which traditionally joined Jótunheim to Miðgarð over the river Vimur, which separated the two worlds.

Gudmund's twelve sons and twelve daughters (who were outstandingly beautiful) stood round the table. When Gudmund noticed that the king was barely tasting what his servants brought, he complained that Gormr was rejecting his hospitality; he said he found this behaviour insulting.

But Thorkill interrupted with an excuse. He reminded Gudmund that men who ate food to which they were not accustomed often suffered serious consequences.

"The king certainly appreciates your hospitality," said Thorkill, "but he must take care of his health. He must only eat the food he is accustomed to, so that is why he has brought his own supply with him. Please don't be insulted by the king's refusal to eat foreign food: he simply doesn't want to suffer indigestion."

When Gudmund saw that his trick had been foiled by the politeness of his guests, he decided that, if he couldn't corrupt their hunger and thirst, then he would corrupt their self-control in other respects. He offered the king his daughter as a partner, and promised the rest that they could have whichever of the women they chose. Most of the men showed some interest at this offer, but Thorkill quietly reminded them of the warning he had already given. With the utmost diplomacy he played off the intrigued guests against the suspicious host. Four of the Danes, too full of lust for their own salvation, accepted Gudmund's offer. They must have caught some terrible infection which maddened them and addled their wits, confusing their memories. They are reported never to have been in their right minds again after this adventure.

86b Gudmund tried another trick: he told his guests what a delightful garden[3] he had, and invited the king to come and see it and to try some of the fruit which grew there. Thorkill quietly reminded the king of his previous warnings.

"Thank you kindly for the offer of a visit to your garden," he said, "but I must hurry on my journey."

Gudmund realized by now that Thorkill was smarter than he was at every trick. He therefore gave up trying to trick them and took them all across the river so that they could continue their journey.

The Danes went on their way. Not far off, they came to a gloomy, neglected town which looked more like a cloud with vapour oozing from it. Along the fortifications of the wall there were stakes protruding, with the severed heads of warriors fixed to the ends. Fierce-looking dogs guarded the doorways with watchful, hungry expressions.

---

[3] In ancient times private gardens were surrounded by the rooms of the rear portion of the house, like the Greek and Roman *Peristyle.*

Thorkill took a horn and smeared on it some fat. He threw this to them and left them to fight over it.

"That will keep them busy!" he said.

The gates were open, but only at a high level above the ground. The men entered with difficulty, only reaching the entrance with ladders. The interior of the town was gloomy and haunted by vague, misshapen phantoms. It was hard to say whether the screaming shades were more offensive to the eye or to the ear. Everything was filthy; the stink of the mud assailed their nostrils with an unbearable stench. Then they found the rocky home which, they had been told, was where Geirrod lived. They decided to pay him a visit, but they stopped in horror at the doorway. Thorkill, noticing their hesitation, encouraged them to go on.

"You are quite safe," he assured them, "as long as you show restraint. Don't touch any goods or furniture in the house, no matter how desirable it may look. Arm yourselves against greed as well as fear. If you try to take anything, your grasping hands will suddenly be caught fast; you won't be able to let go of whatever you touch. As you go in, advance in small groups, four by four."

Broder and Buki[4] were the first to go in. Thorkill and the king followed, then the rest of the men moved on in organized groups.

The whole interior of the house was ruinous and stank abominably. As for the kinds of things that could disgust a person, there was plenty of them: the door-posts had a thick layer of soot and grime; the wall was plastered with filth; the roof was made of spear-heads; the floor was awash with every kind of filth and crawling with snakes.

As the men moved on they recoiled with a mixture of horror and revulsion. Bloodless ghosts huddled on the iron seats. The regular kind of seats were partitioned off with trellises made of lead. Hideous doorkeepers stood on watch at the thresholds. Some of them, armed with clubs lashed together in a bunch, screeched horribly. Others played a gruesome game of catch with a goatskin.

Thorkill again warned the men of the dangers of greed.

The men continued through a gap in the cliff. They saw an old man with his body pierced through, sitting a short distance away on a high seat facing the gap in the cliff. There were also three women, covered with tumors and apparently without the support of their backbones, on adjacent seats. Thorkill's companions were very curi-

---

[4] This phrase could equally well have meant, "Buki and his brother," if Saxo had been translating from a Norse original.

ous. Thorkill, who already knew the story,[5] told them that a long time ago the god Thor, driven to anger by the insolence of the giants, had driven red hot irons through the body of Geirrod after a fight. The iron had gone right through Geirrod's body and had torn through the mountain, causing part of its side to break away. As for the women, they had been stricken by Thor's thunderbolts and this was why their backs were broken.

87a As the men left, seven round jars, bound up with golden bands, were opened for them. From these hung silver rings wrapped around them in tight knots. Near them the tusk of a strange animal was found, with gold work on its ends. Next to this lay a huge wild ox horn, painstakingly decorated with flashing jewels of a rare kind; this too was not without the work of a craftsman. Next to these was a bracelet of tremendous weight. One man, overcome with greed, laid his grasping hands on this bracelet, not knowing that the utmost danger lay hidden under the shining metal. Another man, unable to restrain his desire, stretched out his uncontrollable hands to the horn. A third man, following the boldness of the previous men, and not exercising control over his fingers, lifted the tusk to carry it over his shoulders.

Their plunder was as pleasant to look at as it likely would be to use. But the bracelet suddenly turned into a snake and attacked the man who was wearing it with its poisonous fangs. The horn turned into a dragon and tore out the life of its carrier. The tusk turned into a sword and plunged into the side of its bearer.

The rest of the men, fearing the same fate as their comrades, thought the innocent might perish like the guilty. Then the door of another side-room opened, revealing a narrower storage-space in which there were even richer treasures. Pieces of armour were exposed, too big for the human body. Among them were a royal robe, a well-decorated hat and a belt of amazing craftsmanship. Thorkill, seized with admiration for these objects, gave in to his greed and threw off his self-restraint. He grabbed the robe, and in doing so he set an example in plunder to the rest. As soon as they did this, the inner rooms began to shake from their lowest foundations like a tidal wave.

Suddenly there was a shout from the women: "The unspeakable robbers have outstayed their welcome!"

Then the figures, which they had previously thought were half-dead people or lifeless dummies, jumped up unexpectedly from their seats on hearing the women's voices, and attacked the visitors furiously. The other creatures made a harsh bellowing noise. Then Broder and Buki resorted to their old familiar skills and fell upon the attack-

---

[5]The story of Thor, Geirrod and Geirrod's daughters is narrated by Snorri in *Skáldskaparmal.*

ing vampires with their spears at the ready on all sides. With a shower of missiles from their bows and sling-shots they wore down the monsters' battle line. There was no more effective way to drive them back.

Only twenty men from the entire royal bodyguard were saved by the arrival of the skilled archers. The rest were butchered by the monsters. Gudmund rowed the survivors across the river and accommodated them at his home. Although he tried he could not persuade them to stay, and finally let them go after giving them gifts.

Buki became careless over his own self-restraint, inflamed with uncontrollable love for one of Gudmund's daughters. He sought marriage with her, to his own destruction, and suddenly his brain became dizzy; he lost his memory of the past. And so this hero, once the conqueror of so many monsters, and who had endured so many perilous adventures, was overcome with ardour for a single girl. He let his mind go under the yoke of desire.

As the king was about to leave, Buki was going to accompany him out of respect. As he was going to ford the river in his cart, he was sucked into the waves and drowned. The king moaned to see his friend's death, but resumed his voyage in a hurry. This was at first successful, but later he was tossed about by contrary winds.

Only a few of his men survived, so he began to feel so close to ultimate danger that he started making vows to the gods, thinking that they were his safest protection. At last, when the others tried different prayers to various gods, he himself approached Utgard-Loki with his vows and offerings. The result was the kind of weather and sky he had hoped for.

87b When he got home after experiencing all these travels and toils, Gormr decided that it was time for his tired spirit to take a rest away from business. So he married a queen from Sweden and took up meditation and relaxation instead of his old pursuits. He spent his life in the utmost peace and tranquillity, but when he had almost reached the end of his days he started to believe (convinced by the most likely forms of proof) that souls were immortal. He therefore kept pondering over what place he would go to when his limbs gave up their life, or what the reward would be earned by paying respect to the gods.

As he was thinking about this, certain men who had evil intentions towards Thorkill came to the king and told him that he must consult the will of the gods.

"You need to be absolutely certain," they said, "and so the matter is too deep and difficult for a human mind to give you an answer, so you must approach the oracles of the heavens. For this reason, you must make your peace with Utgard-Loki. Nobody is better qualified to do this for you than Thorkill."

There were also other people who laid charges against Thorkill as a traitor and an enemy to the king's life. When he saw that he was heading for the utmost danger, Thorkill demanded that the people who brought these charges should be his companions of his journey. Then the people who had maligned an innocent man saw that the danger they had prepared for him had rebounded upon themselves, so they tried to take back their allegations. In vain they tried to fill the king's ears; charging them with cowardice he forced them to sail under Thorkill's leadership. This is the penalty one has to pay for plotting evil against another. When they realized that they were bound to a danger and could not escape it, they obtained ox-hides to pad out their ship, then filled it with plenty of provisions.

Sailing off in this ship, they reached a place without sunlight, where the stars were unknown, daylight had no hold, and eternal night hid them in its shroud. When they had sailed for a long time in this unusual type of climate, they finally ran out of firewood, so there was nowhere to boil their food. They kept off starvation with raw food. But several of those who ate this raw food caught a deadly disease from failing to digest it properly. This unusual diet made sickness gradually creep over their stomachs, then the infection spread further and affected their vital organs. So it was dangerous in either case: they would starve if they did not eat, and suffer from food poisoning if they did.

Just as they were casting off all hope of survival, protection appeared to them from an unexpected quarter, just as a bowstring is most likely to break when the bow is stretched tightest.

Suddenly, as they were exhausted, they saw a fire gleaming not far away. Thorkill decided that this fire was a gift from the gods, so he should go and obtain some of it. So as to be sure of returning to his friends, he fixed a gemstone to the top of the mast of his ship. When he reached the shore he fixed his eyes upon a cave with a narrow mouth.

After ordering his companions to wait outside, he went in. He saw two men, monstrous and swarthy, with horn-like noses, feeding their fire on whatever fuel they chanced to get. The entrance to the place was ugly. The door-posts were rotten, the walls were dirty and mouldy, the roof was dirty and the floor was swarming with snakes which were even more offensive to the mind than to the eye.

Then one of the giants greeted him: "You have started a crazy adventure if you're so keen to visit a strange god: let's see if you can face him! You're now stepping outside your own comfortable, familiar world. I'll tell you the way to go and give you directions, if you will tell me three true judgments in the form of the same number of riddles."

Thorkill replied, "By Thor, I don't remember ever seeing a family with noses as ugly as your lot. Nor have I ever reached a place I'd be less willing to live. I think my best foot is the one I can get out of here soonest."

88a The giant was delighted with Thorkill's wit. "Those are true judgments, sure enough!" he said. "First, you must go to a land where grass is scarce and the darkness is thick. But first, you must get there at the end of a four-day non-stop rowing trip, to reach your goal. There you can see Utgard-Loki, who prefers to live in dark, dingy, filthy caves."

Thorkill was horrified at being told to travel on such a long and dangerous journey. But his hopes, though uncertain, prevailed over his immediate fears.

"May I have some firewood?" he asked.

"If you need fire," said the giant, "you must answer with three more judgments in the form of riddles."

Thorkill replied, "Advice must be followed even if a real loser gave it. Likewise, I've reached such a foolhardy stage that if I finally get back I'll owe my safety to nothing but my own legs. Again, if I had the chance to get out of this right now I'd make sure I never came back."

Then Thorkill took some firewood to his companions. After finding the wind in his favour, he landed on the fourth day at the harbour of which he had been told. With his companions he approached a land where darkness was never interrupted by occasional breaks of daylight. He could hardly see the view with his eyes' help, but faintly observed in front of him a cliff of enormous size. Eager to examine it, he stationed some of his companions to keep watch at a cave entrance. He told them to use their flints to make a fire to burn in the doorway and keep them safe from demons. Some other men went forward with torches and Thorkill crouched down to squeeze into the narrow archway of the cave. The inside was crawling with snakes and there were iron seats placed at regular intervals. The next thing that faced him was a rather quiet patch of water flowing gently over a sandbank. He crossed this and approached a cave with a floor which had a steeper slope.

From here the visitors came upon an opening onto a dark, dirty cave. Inside it they saw Utgard-Loki, loaded down with huge chains on his hands and feet. His individual hairs, which stank, were each as large and stiff as a cornel-wood spear. Thorkill took one of these, with the help of his companions, from Utgard-Loki's chin—and he allowed it! This was to be a more certain token later of the truth of his deeds.

Immediately such a foul stench spread to the bystanders that they could not breathe without pressing their cloaks to their noses. They only escaped with difficulty, being the targets of poison which the snakes spat at them from every direction.

Only five of Thorkill's companions made it back to the ship with their leader; the rest were overcome by the poison. The demons hovered over them savagely and threw poisonous spit-balls[6] at them as they passed below. But the sailors held up their ox-hide shields in front of them and made the spit-balls bounce back at the throwers. When one sailor put out his head from behind cover, the poison touched his head and took it off as if it had been cut off with a sword. Another, peeping out from behind the shelter with his eyes open, brought his head back in with empty eye-sockets. Another, while unwrapping his leather cover, exposed his hand. When he drew back his arm it was shriveled up with the same poison.

The men began to call upon their various gods to protect them, but in vain until Thorkill called upon the universal god in his prayers, and poured out to him libations as well as just prayers.

Then, when the condition of the sky and weather was back to its usual shape, he enjoyed safe sailing. Now they seemed to be in a different world, in the reality of human beings.

Finally he was blown towards Germany, which had by then been converted to Christianity. Amongst its people he learned the basics of religion. His men had been almost wiped out because of the hostile air they had been breathing. He finally got back to his own country with only two of his companions. But the foul poison had disfigured his face and body so badly that not even his friends recognized him.

Finally, he wiped off the filth and made himself recognizable to those who saw him. This filled the king with the utmost anxiety to find out about the success of his quest.

But Thorkill's rivals still did not quieten down from slandering him. Some of them claimed that the king would die if he received the news. A prophecy that the king would die under suchlike circumstances made the king's disposition worse.

Therefore, at the king's command, men were hired to murder Thorkill during the night. But somehow he found out about the plot; he left his bed during the night without telling anyone and left a heavy log in his place. So the plan was foiled and the hired murderers only cut up the log.

The next day he approached the king as he was having a meal.

88b "I forgive you," he said, "for your cruelty. I suppose it must be a mistake, that you gave instructions to punish me instead of thanking me for the trouble I have gone to in bringing you good news of my mission. But I do not seek to be avenged. I am satisfied if you feel ashamed at the wrong you have done me. It seems to me that you must be worse than all the demons in your anger, if I have escaped all the tricks of those monsters but fail to be safe from yours."

---

[6]This is the closest rendering I can attempt in English. I suspect that Saxo may be thinking of "Greek Fire," the medieval incendiary/artillery device which was the closest equivalent of modern napalm.

The king, wanting to hear everything from Thorkill in person, and deciding that it was a tough thing to stand in the way of fate, told Thorkill to describe the whole adventure in order. He had listened to all the other adventures attentively, but when he finally heard a reference to his own god, he could not stand to hear an unfavourable judgment. He could not bear listening to the charges of filthiness which were brought against Utgard-Loki. He was so outraged to hear the god defamed that he gave up his life in the middle of Thorkill's story.

Furthermore, the stink of the hair, which Thorkill had plucked out of the giant as evidence of his adventure and personal heroism, wafted out over the bystanders in such a foul way that several people died from breathing it.

Last poem of the Troy Cycle

Ancient Sequels to Homer's *Odyssey*

Homer's *Iliad* and *Odyssey* were not the only epic poems that existed in the early Greek period that were based on the Troy cycle, that famous chain of events that traditionally started with the abduction of Helene to Troy (and what, in turn, had led up to that abduction), through the war itself and continuing to the fates of the surviving heroes who returned to Greece. We still have summaries of the contents of some poems on the subject that seem to have been composed around Homer's time or shortly afterward. None of these others survive as complete poems any longer: from the lack of evidence in papyrus fragments that scholars in past 150 years have been identifying and/or transcribing, it seems that copyists and their clients had already lost interest in the "cyclic" poems by the time Rome became the capital of an empire. By that time handbooks were starting to appear that contained the same information in a shorter and simpler form[5], similar in purpose to the "Cliff's Notes" booklets that were once popular amongst students preparing for tests or school essays. On the other hand, written copies of the "Cyclic" epics were in circulation and were quoted by historians such as Herodotus and philosophers like Aristotle between about 440 and 320 BC. The Troy-cycle, to use the simplest term, was just one chain among several of ancient epics.

---

[1] A good example is the *Library of Mythology* attributed to an otherwise unknown Apollodorus, compiled at some point between about 100 BC and 200 AD. It is quoted extensively in Chapters 16 and 23 above.

The "complete" Epic Cycle, as it was known in a very vague and indirect way to Greek scholars during the late Roman Empire and early Middle Ages, took this form:

1. The *Marriage of Earth and Heaven* (evidently a Creation Epic: perhaps lines 116–210 of Hesiod's *Theogony*[2] represent a shorter counterpart of this poem)

2. The *Titanomachia*[3] (Battle of the Titans, again perhaps overlapping with some of the second half of the *Theogony*)

3. The *Oidipodeia* (Epic of Oedipus, first part of the decline and fall of Thebes[4])

4. The *Thebaid* (centering upon Oedipus' sons and the siege of Thebes[5])

---

[2]Whether the *Marriage of Earth and Heaven* was intended and received as a self-contained poem before its title entered lists in the Christian era is uncertain. A. Bernabé (*Poetae Epici Graeci* I, Leipzig, Teubner 1987, p. 10) gives under the title *Theogonia* three citations from Byzantine sources, all of which mention "*The mythical Marriage of Heaven and Earth.*" There are no actual fragments of such a poem surviving; in fact it is entirely possible that the first two titles cited above were parts of a larger theogonic poem, whether it was the one attributed to Orpheus or another. For a discussion of "Theogonies and Theomachies" by Eumelus of Corinth and others, see G. L. Huxley, *Greek Epic Poetry*, Chapter 1. Athenaeus (VII.277d) quotes from *The Second Book of the Titanomachia*, admitting uncertainty as to whether its author was "*Eumelus, Arctinus, or whoever.*" There certainly seems to have been a theogonic poem included in the "greater" Epic cycle during the Hellenistic period (see below): M. L. West, in *The Orphic Poems* (Oxford 1983, 123–139) discusses the possible survival of some fossils of it in Apollodorus' *Bibliotheke* and (264) extrapolates its stemma. Malcolm Davies (*Epic Cycle* 13) prefers to believe that Apollodorus had simply re-edited a lot of material from the Hesiodic Theogony. In either case the relationship is unlikely to be direct, since epic material on the creation myth was also re-worked by early prose historians such as Acusilaus, Pherecydes, and Hellanicus, whose works were known to "Apollodorus" in a fuller form than we know them today. Bernabé (o.c.8–10) includes a *testimonium* from Eusebius, *Preparation for the Gospel* I.10.40, probably derived from Herennius Philo of Byblos at the end of the first century AD, referring collectively to Hesiod and the "Cyclic poets" as authors of "Theogonies and *Gigantomachiai* (Giant-Fights)."

[3]Fragments: Allen pp.110–11; Evelyn-White 480–3; Davies *EGF* pp.16–19; Bernabé in previous note. On the interchangeability of the titles *Titanomachia* and *Gigantomachia* (Titan War and Giant War), which were probably regarded rather as generic labels and the frequent overlapping of both with theogonic material, see Davies *Epic Cycle* 13–18.

[4]This poem was composed by Cinaethon of Lacedaemon, according to the *Tabula Borgia*, IG XIV 1292: Huxley *op. cit.* p.86; Bernabé p. 17. Cinaethon was also a candidate for a *[Little?] Iliad* and a *Telegonia.*

[5]Athenaeus (XI.465e = fg.2 in both Bernabé and Davies, where the latter cites Book "14") refers to a "Cyclic" *Thebais*, distinguishing it from the one by Antimachus (of Colophon: there was also an earlier Antimachus of Teos, who may have composed a *Nostoi*, according to Huxley, *op. cit.* 162). Pausanias (IX.9.5 = Bern. *Thebais* T2, Davies *Epicorum Graecorum Fragmenta* T1) refers to its being ascribed to Homer. See also *The Contest of Homer and Hesiod*, 15.42,29 Wilamowitz. If one equates the name of Homer with Ionian epic generally (as was sometimes the case in antiquity), then the belief that Homer had written a *Thebais* may reflect an early Ionian interest in the story, as Huxley suggests (*op. cit.* 43–4).

5. The *Epigonoi* (Sons of the Seven who fought against Thebes[6])

6. The *Cypria* (beginning of the Trojan War)

7. Homer's *Iliad*

8. Arctinus' *Aethiopis*

9. Lesches' *Little Iliad*

10. Arctinus' *Iliou Persis* (Sack of Troy)

11. Hagias' *Nostoi* (Returns of the Greek Leaders)

12. Homer's *Odyssey*

13. Eugammon's *Telegonia*

By this definition the sequence of epics devoted to the Trojan War consisted of numbers 6–13. We are simply concerned with the last, even though there is not a single line of quoted poetry that we ascribe to it with any certainty. We only have the summary that begins the next section of this appendix, plus some other miscellaneous accounts, references, and other by-products of a widespread desire to keep Homer's still-popular epic going into at least one sequel.

Eugammon of Cyrene appears to have lived during the mid-500s BC, making him at least a century later than the poet of the *Odyssey*. The material he used, however, was probably in many cases much older and may date back to the same raw material of heroic ballads that had pre-dated Homer but had not previously been recorded in writing. It is not our concern to worry about what Eugammon had said beyond the summary we have. The summary itself may only date back to the late Roman Empire (there was more than one writer named Proclus), but the amount of other material presented here shows that Odysseus' adventures continued to demand an audience.

---

[6]Again attributed to Homer, according to the *Contest* (note above). There may have been a poem of this name by Antimachus of Teos: see list of scholars in Bernabé p. 29.

The *Telegonia*,
by Eugammon of Cyrene

A) SUMMARY OF THE *TELEGONIA*, ATTRIBUTED TO PROCLUS

📖 from *Codex Venetus A* of the *Iliad*.

After this[1] is Homer's *Odyssey*. Then are the two books of the *Telegonia* by Eugammon of Cyrene; their contents are as follows:

The suitors are buried by their next of kin.[2] Odysseus, after sacrificing to the Nymphs, sails off for Elis in order to survey pasturage[3] for cattle. He is entertained by Polyxenus[4] and receives as a gift a mixing-bowl on which are depicted the

---

[1] The summary of the *Nostoi*. See appendix A, above.

[2] This has already happened at the end of our *Odyssey*. Many scholars believe that the last book and a half of the present *Odyssey* form a "continuation" and that the original poem had ended at the present line XXIII.296, which the ancient critics Aristarchus and Aristophanes called "The Limit."

[3] In Herodotus the Greek word just means "cattle" and is here translated accordingly by Evelyn-White. The late Hellenistic author Heliodorus (I.5) uses it in a more geographical sense, specifically of a cattle-raising area in lower Egypt. In the present context, Odysseus' interest in Elis seems to be territorial. Davies (*Epic Cycle* 89) takes Odysseus' interest as being in "*the famous cattle-sheds of Augeas king of Elis*" and reminds us of Herakles' labour there (see below, n.6).

[4] A Polyxenus, king of Elea, is mentioned by Apollodorus (*Bibl. II.4.6*) as custodian of some cattle entrusted to him after a raid by a group of Taphians. The cattle are then ransomed by Amphitryon, who has not yet married Alcmena; these events take place before Herakles' conception. Presumably the present Polyxenus is a descendant of the one in Apollodorus. Since *Polyxenos* means "much-entertaining", or "many-hosting" he seems to be a convenient and generic background figure, exploited in the *Telegonia* much as Nestor is in the *Odyssey* to provide the context for a digression. Eugammon seems to have set this digression visually, describing pictures on a cup (compare also the shield pictures inserted into the *Iliad* and the *Catalogue of Women*). Another Polyxenus, son of Agasthenes, is mentioned as a suitor of Helen (Apollod. *Bibl*.III.10.8).

stories[5] of Trophonius, Agamedes and Augeas.[6] Then, after sailing back to Ithaca, he performs the rituals[7] specified by Teiresias.

---

[5]G. L. Huxley (*Greek Epic Poetry* 171) concludes that the digression prompted by the decorated cup was "*the story of Augeias' treasury and how Trophonius built it.*" It is certainly true that the brothers Trophonius and Agamedes were celebrated in Boeotia as culture-heroes of building, construction and excavation from quite early times to the Roman period (Pausanias IX.37.3) but it is also clear that the cult of Trophonius, at least, was associated at Levadeia, near Orchomenos (*ibid.* 39) with an ancient form of initiatory katabasis. Trophonius' cult, with its famous ritual of personal initiation by descending into an underground chamber, was already famous throughout Greece by Eugammon's time: Trophonius was, according to Pausanias (X.5.5) the traditional builder of the fourth Oracle building at Delphi (though archaeological evidence suggests that this Doric structure was only built around 600 B.C.) which, according to Pausanias, was burned down in the 58[6] Olympiad (548 B.C.). Aristophanes (*Clouds* 505-8) speaks of the initate's fear at entering the oracle (which we known from several sources was accomplished by sliding down a chute from one subterranean chamber into a lower one) as being proverbial. A votive relief (Athens, National Archaeological Museum 3942) of the third century B.C., found in Levadeia, shows alongside Trophonios an impressive array of chthonic and initiatory deities, namely Cybele, Persephone with a key, Dionysus, Hecate bearing a torch, three Curetes and the Dioscuri. Trophonius' name, possibly derived from √*troph-*, = nutrition, has chthonic associations (in Pausanias IX.39.5 he is nursed by Demeter), but Sir James Frazer (notes *ad loc.* to Pausanias, vol. V p.200, London, Macmillan 1898) cites in several examples a dedication, a priest and an oracle, of *Zeus Trophonios* and concludes that Trophonius was the old local god of Lebadea sometimes (and probably at a late date) confused with Zeus. As to the hero and his association with building, Huxley cites two vase-scenes showing "*Trophonios erecting a tholos or treasury,*" and points out that since Augeas was a predecessor (but presumably not a direct ancestor: see next note) of Polyxenus, the illustrations on the bowl reflected how Augeas had acquired his wealth. The descriptive digression also, however, serves an important structural function: the scene suggests the completion of what Odysseus had already learned in his own *katabasis* (*Odyssey* XI). Pausanias (I.17.5) discusses the latter in a way that suggests a strong association with Ephyra in Thesprotia, in North-West mainland Greece. The comparability of the two oracles (at Ephyra and at Lebadea) is discussed by Walter Burkert in *Greek Religion* (English translation by J. Raffan, Harvard U.P. 1985) 114-115. Eugammon seem to have visualised the fulfilment of Teiresias' prophecy as being accomplished in the central Peloponnese, probably in Arcadia (very much in accordance with the general local associations mentioned by Pausanias (VIII.10 - 12, discussed further below) and prior to his return to Ithaca which again preceded the Thesprotian episode. Whether Eugammon had also visualised the interview with Teiresias (*Od. XI*) as having taken place in any part of the known world is impossible to tell, but later associations between the episode and the location must have been strong.

[6]Augeas is presumably the king of Elis whose stables are cleaned by Herakles: Apollod. *Bibl.* II.5.5. Apollodorus also (II.7.2) says that Herakles afterwards marched against Elis, killing Augeas and his sons. See also Theocritus XXV.7; Diodorus Siculus IV.13.3; Hyginus *Fab.* 30; Pausanias V.1.9ff. & VI.20.16.

After this he reaches the territory of the Thesprotians and marries Callidice the queen of Thesprotia.[8] Then a war breaks out between the Thesprotians (under Odysseus' leadership) and the Bryges. Then Ares puts to flight the followers of Odysseus, and a fight breaks out between Ares and Athena. Apollo breaks up the fighting pair.

After the death of queen Callidice her successor is Polypoetes[9] the son of Odysseus, while Odysseus himself travels to Ithaca.

Meanwhile Telegonus, sailing off in search of his father, lands on Ithaca and pillages the island. Odysseus, rushing out to help defend the land, is killed by his son in ignorance. Telegonus, discovering his mistake, takes his father's body, along with Telemachus and Penelope, to his mother. She makes them immortal, and Telegonus lives on with Penelope, while Telemachus lives with Circe.

---

[7]These "rituals" (literally "sacrifices") are prophesied by Teiresias in *Odyssey* XI, 119-134: see below, frag. 3. The specific sacrifices are first to Poseidon then, on Odysseus' return to Ithaca, to the other gods *"in due order."* Since the summary places the rituals directly after the visit to Elis, we must suppose that Odysseus was portrayed in the poem as having sailed to the Thesprotian mainland as the final part of the fulfilment of this sacrificial duty. Something is probably omitted in the summary, since Odysseus was more commonly believed to have been in the central Peloponnese when he encountered the man who thought the oar was a winnowing-fan. In Mantinea (Arcadia) there was a cult of Poseidon the Horse-god (Paus. VIII.10.4) associated with an ancient belief that the waves of the sea reached the sanctuary in spite of its great distance inland. Huxley (*ibid.* 170-171) also mentions coins of Mantinea featuring Odysseus with an oar on his shoulder and cites Herodotus IV.161-2 on Mantinean links with Cyrene: Demonax the Mantinean lawgiver went to Cyrene to settle disputes in the time of Arcesilaus III. We thus have strong support for the depth of interest that the Arcadian episode would have held for Eugammon's audience in Cyrene. Pausanias also mentions (VIII.10.2) that the Mantinean sanctuary was built by Trophonius, thus confirming the strength of the link between this ancient culture-hero and Odysseus in the region around Arcadia.

[8]The story of Odysseus and Callidice seems to have been narrated both in the *Telegonia* and in another early poem, the *Thesprotis*, or Epic of Thesprotia: see **supplementary summary 1** (pseudo-Apollodorus) below. Proclus here is somewhat fuller in detail.

[9]Odysseus' son Polypoetes (Much-Doer, perhaps Over-Achiever, or in a derogatory sense, Busybody) is only attested elsewhere in the pseudo- Apollodorus *Epitome* (VII.35, given below). The *Epitome* may itself be a product of the Byzantine scholar John Tzetzes, who would certainly have been familiar with the present Proclan summary (see introduction). The story of Polypoetes may go back to myths of early Thesprotian kings, or it may have crept into the Odysseus-saga as a phonic doublet for Ptoliporthes (see below).

B) SUPPLEMENTARY SUMMARIES

1. Pseudo-Apollodorus, Epitome VII.34–38

34. On completing his sacrifices to Hades, Persephone and Teiresias, [Odysseus] travelled on foot through Epirus and reached the territory of the Thesprotians. After sacrificing according to Teiresias' prophecies he completed his propitiation of Poseidon. But Callidice, who was then queen of Thesprotia, prompted him to stay by offering him the kingdom.

35. After mating with him she bore him a son Polypoetes. Odysseus married Callidice, ruled the Thesprotians and conquered in battle those of the neighbouring tribes who marched against him. On Callidice's death he handed the kingdom over to his son and travelled to Ithaca; there he found Poliporthes,[10] whom Penelope had borne to him.

36. When Telegonus learned from Circe that he was Odysseus' son, he sailed away on a quest to find the man. On reaching the island of Ithaca he drove off some of the cattle, and when Odysseus ran up to protect them, Telegonus wounded him with a spear that he had in his hands, tipped with a [sting-ray[11]] barb, and Odysseus died.

---

[10]Ptoliporthes (as in Aeschylus, *Agamemnon* 476) is another form of "City-Sacker." A character of this name was Odysseus' son by Penelope in the early epic *Thesprotis*. Apollodorus' ultimate sources were usually poetic. I suspect that at least one early poet had invented or exploited the contrasting name-sounds, P(t)oliporthes and Polypoetes, just as Eugammon had exploited (if not invented) Telegonus in contrast with Telemachus. The sixth-century B.C. Hesiodic continuator responsible for *Theogony* 1017-8 had likewise concocted another pair, Nausithous and Nausinous, two names which proved to be quite unremarkable. Nausithous (*Od*.VIII.564) was also the name of Alcinous' father. By the time the Hesiod-continuator inserted the name into the present context, it had probably passed through several stages of development: **a)** it was, in the "Homeric" tradition, necessarily associated with kings of Phaeacia; **b)** it was a natural choice of name for a son of Nausicaa; **c)** a poet who ignored the possibility of a union between Odysseus or Telemachus and Nausicaa transposed the name to another son of Odysseus.

[11]This word is not in the Sabbaitic manuscript (the only one which extends to cover this part of the *Epitome*), but was supplied by Bücheler, on the understanding that the detail was a well-known motif (see below on Dictys VI). Bücheler had noticed the reference to the sting-ray barb, in the context of the Telegonus story, in Oppian's *Halieutica*, II. 497-505.

37. But when Telemachus recognized him and lamented grievously, he took the body [and[12]] Penelope to Circe, and there he married Penelope. Circe sent them both away to the Isles of the Blessed.

2. Hyginus, *Fabula* 127

Telegonus, son of Ulysses and Circe, is sent by his mother to seek out his father. He is brought to Ithaca by a storm and there, driven by hunger, begins to plunder the fields. Ulysses and Telemachus, unaware of who he is, make an armed attack on him.

2. Ulysses is killed by his son Telegonus: an oracle had warned him to beware death from his son. After finding out who [the dead man] is, they[13] return at Minerva's command to his homeland, the island of Aeaea, along with Telemachus and Penelope. They also convey Ulysses' dead body to Circe and there hand it over for burial.

3. At the advice of the same Minerva Telegonus marries Penelope, while Telemachus marries Circe. Circe and Telemachus have a son, Latinus,[14] who gave the Latin language its name from his own. Penelope and Telegonus had a son Italus,[15] who called Italy after himself.

---

[12]The bracketed conjunction was inserted by Wagner, prompted by comparison with Proclus' *Telegonia* summary. The general sense agrees with Hyginus' narrative.

[13]Presumably Telegonus and his surviving companions.

[14]Latinus is Odysseus' and Circe's son according to the late Hesiod-continuator (*Theog.* 1013: see M.L. West's comment on the line, 1966 p.434). Hyginus is probably repeating a popular folk-etymology for the Latin language. Telemachus' son is usually (frag. 2b, below) Persepolis, meaning "City-destroyer." In Greek it is synonymous with *Ptoliporthos*, a term which appears as Odysseus' epithet twice in the *Iliad* and six times in the *Odyssey*: see C. Robert, *die Griechische Heldensage* 1405, n.3. The same epithet is used several times for Achilles in the *Iliad* and is a common epithet of Ares.

[15]Italus is obviously a generic eponym. Attic dramas based on material from the *Telegonia* had probably sustained the popularity of speculation about Odysseus, Penelope, and the next generation, especially in the context of Western exploration and foundation myths.

3. Dictys Cretensis,

a) Latin version: *Diary of the Trojan War*, VI.14-15[16]

14. At the same time[17] Ulysses, frightened by frequent inauspicious omens and dreams, hired all the most experienced interpreters of dreams from all the districts under his dominion. He reported to these men, amongst other things that he had seen, the most frequent one: a certain apparition half way between human and divine, of a form that certainly inspired praise, would suddenly appear from the same place. When he reached out his hands to embrace it, seized as he was with the utmost desire for it, he received an answer in a human voice, telling him that a relationship of this sort was scandalous, since they were (it said) of the same blood and ancestry. For each one of them would perish by the other's doing.

So, as he turned this over in his mind and became increasingly anxious to learn the cause of this phenomenon, a certain sign appeared to come up from the sea and to move between them. This entity cast itself towards him[18] at the first [apparition's] command, and thus separated them.

All of those present declared unanimously that this vision boded death. Furthermore they warned him to beware treachery on his son's part. Coming thus

---

[16]For more on Dictys, see Appendix A, above·Dictys' *Diary*, in its original Greek, was forged in nine books. The Latin translator, Lucius Septimius, says in his introductory letter that he had translated the first five books in full but summarized the last four, all of which dealt with the returns of the Greeks, into a single book. The portion translated here is from the last two chapters of the entire work, and probably represents a large portion of the original ninth book.

[17]The previous chapter describes Orestes' plot to kill Neoptolemus. The phrasing of the Latin in ch.13 is curiously ambivalent, hinting that Orestes was only *believed* to have killed Neoptolemus, whose death is never stated directly. This may be caused by the extreme brevity of Book VI (see previous note) or we may be dealing with an abbreviated rationalization for the hero-cult of Neoptolemus at Delphi. Other extant Greek versions of Dictys are too confused and contaminated at this point to be of any help.

[18]The previously held idea that the first image is Telegonus, while sanctioned by the *prima facie* interpretation of the fullest surviving Greek version (see **3b**, below), should be questioned. The first image makes more sense in a wider context as his mother, while the second image is Telegonus himself. Circe was the one with whom Odysseus had already conjoined, and she commanded her son to find his father. Circe was traditionally the daughter of Helios, so she is the "divine form" who "inspired praise." Dictys is doing two things here: he is rationalizing Circe's divinity, and at the same time was adhering to the elaborate nexus of dreams and oracles which traditionally must have surrounded Odysseus' death, exemplified not only in Teiresias' prophecy (*Od.* XI) but also in the extant fragments of Sophocles' *Odysseus Akanthoplex* (S. Radt, *Tr.Gr.Fr.* IV pp.374-8, esp. fgs. 455-461; Lloyd-Jones *Sophocles* III pp.238-241).

under his father's suspicion Telemachus was sent off to the property[19] in Cephalenia and with him were sent the most trustworthy guards available. Meanwhile Ulysses, in withdrawing to another place that was secluded and distant, tried to avoid the violent outcome of his dreams.

15. At this same time Telegonus, whom Circe had borne as Ulysses' son and had raised on the island of Aeaea,[20] reached maturity. He set out on a search for his father and reached Ithaca carrying in his hands a certain spear, armed at the tip with the bone of a marine turtle-dove,[21] a kind of token of the island[22] in which he was born. On being informed of Ulysses' whereabouts, he went to him. There he was denied access to his father by the wardens posted over the territory.

When he persisted rather keenly and was pushed back from all sides, he began to shout that it was a shameful crime for him to be denied access to his father's embrace.[23] So, in the belief that Telemachus had arrived to offer violence to the king, they resisted more keenly, since none of them knew that Odysseus had another son. When the young man saw that he was being pushed back more persistently and with force, in a fit of anger he killed many of the guards, wounding or seriously disabling some of the others.

After Ulysses discovered what was happening, and believing that the young man was sent by Telemachus, he cast at Telegonus the lance which he usually kept with him for his personal safety. But the young man, blocking this mode of attack with some kind of dodge, threw his own remarkable spear at his father, intending to do serious damage by wounding him.

But Ulysses, as he fell from the blow, began to offer thanks to his fortune and to acknowledge that this was the best thing that could have happened to him, to be killed at the hands of an outsider and thus to have freed Telemachus, who was most dear to him, from the charge of parricide. Then, holding on to what breath he had left, he asked

---

[19]Literally, "to the fields that were in Cephallenia." The clear implication is that Odysseus owned land there.

[20]Aeaea was traditionally Circe's home: *Od.* X. 135ff.

[21]*os marinae turturis*: this does not agree with the Byzantine versions, where the point is the barb of a sting-ray as in Oppian (see next section).

[22]Compare with the Greek version in *Ekloge*, below.

[23]The Dictys -forger frequently used the plots of tragedies for his material (see introduction). We have already noted one play at least, Sophocles' *Odysseus Akanthoplex*, or *Niptra*. The current context seems especially condensed from a stage setting: the guards are attempting to restrain Telegonus, who is arguing vehemently for access to his father. The guards may or may not have been on stage; either they or a group of herdsmen would have formed the chorus in the orchestra. The ensuing violent scene of fighting would not, of course, have taken place on stage in classical Attic tragedy.

the young man who he was, where he was born, and how he dared to kill Ulysses the son of Laertes who was renowned at home and in war.

Then Telegonus, on realising that this was his father, started tearing the hair from his head and uttering the most wretched lament in agony at the death he had brought upon his own father. So he revealed to Ulysses, in response to the latter's wish, his own name and that of his mother. He told him on which island he had been born and finally revealed the device of the spear. Thus Ulysses remembered the impact of his threatening dreams and that the end of his life had been prophesied by the dream-interpreters. Wounded by the man he had least believed would do it, he died three days later, already rather old in advancing years but nevertheless not weakened in his physical strength.

b) Anonymous *Ekloge Historiôn*

(ed. J.A. Cramer,[24] in *Anecdota Graeca Parisiensia* II.214-5)

📖 *The following extract[25] (corresponding in content to the beginning of the above passage from the Latin Dictys) begins immediately after Telemachus' marriage to Alcinous' daughter Nausicaa and the defeat of the Suitors' kinsmen (the passage which corresponds to VI.6 in the Latin version).*

As time went on, Odysseus began to see dreams signifying his own end, and on waking summoned all those who had interpretative skills to explain his dreams. One such interpreter was Cleitophon of Ithaca, another Polyphemus from Argos. He described his dream to them and said, "I dreamed that I was lying down on my own bed, and there was also [present] a beautiful and terrifying god-like animal. It was not able to retain a completely human shape, but yet I looked at it with pleasure, and tried, uncomprehending, to take hold of it. As to the union from which it had been bred, that was not

---

[24]J. A. Cramer, Provost of New Inn Hall, Oxford, discovered this chronicle in Codex Parisinus Graecus 854. This manuscript, dated A.D. 889 (see Cramer's introduction, p.165), is for the most part a unique compilation, depending on Malalas only for the episode on the Trojan War. The same episode is covered less fully in the better-known Barocci ms. of Malalas and in the Slavonic version which follows Barocci very closely.

[25]The only other available English translation of this extract is, to the best of my knowledge, given by E. M. Jeffreys, M. Jeffreys and R. Scott, in *The Chronicle of John Malalas* (Melbourne, Australian Association for Byzantine Studies, 1986), pp. 64-66 footnote.

clear to me, either by personal acquaintance[26] or by knowledge. On taking in[27] this vision I dearly wanted to embrace it in my arms. But it, whinnying[28] with human speech, said that it was god-sent[29] and was a bond of kinship between both of us, and that it was ordained that I should be killed by it. When I became anxious on account of it, an unexpected sting came upon me at the being's command, manifested in a way that could not be seen.[30]

---

[26]Odysseus seems to be saying that he had neither personally seen nor even heard sailors' tales of such a creature. If this text is any closer to the original wording of the Dictys-text than other extant versions (compare the Latin, above), one is inclined to suspect that the Dictys-forger was indulging his penchant for rationalized versions of standard mythic concepts, in this case attempting to convey a dream-image interpretation of the old Proteus theme. Proteus was the shape-changer prophet, a kind of shamanic "Old Man of the Sea," described in *Od.* IV.455ff. The verb used later (see next two footnotes) suggests the whinnying of a horse. I am strongly inclined to suspect that "Dictys" had been using and partially rationalizing a poetic source in which the creature was described as resembling a hippocamp, or sea-horse.

[27]The Greek verb here implies knowing or recognition. Jeffreys & Scott translate, *"when I saw it,"* which surely has a weaker meaning.

[28]Jeffreys & Scott translate, *"But it, (protesting) in a human voice.."* The verb bracketed by them is legible in the Ekloge manuscript, observed by Cramer to have been a mis-spelling. The verb normally signifies an animal noise such as whinnying or grunting. The compiler of *Ekloge* must have used a recension of Malalas which retained not only more details than other extant versions of the chronicle, but was fuller here than the Latin version of Dictys. The original Dictys-forger may have been attempting to convey, incorporated into his Dictys-narrative, a rationalization of Circe's famous trick of turning men into animals (*Od.* X.233-454). Previous commentators on this sentence do not seem to have drawn much attention to Dictys' efforts to portray a visionary beast which is not essentially human.

[29]Ordained by fate. The beast in the vision only seems to represent Telegonus in a very indirect way. It also seems to represent Circe's power of transformation (see previous note).

[30]The oxymoron is deliberately cryptic. It has already been noted that Dictys used tragic material (see introduction) and we have evidence of several plots which made use of Odysseus' forebodings of death: in addition to Sophocles' *Niptra* or *Odysseus Akanthoplex*, there was also the *Euryalus*, summarized by Parthenius in *Narr.* III: *"Even after his wandering, when he had killed the suitors, he went to Epirus by reason of certain oracles. There he seduced Evippe the daughter of Tyrimmas."* The latter, in this story, turns out to be the wronged host (a variant on the familiar "Paris in Sparta" motif) and the child is Euryalus, later killed by Odysseus as a result of a jealous plot on Penelope's part. The oracle may already have been an old feature of this myth, dating back to the early epic *Thesprotis*. Of our surviving fragments of the *Odysseus Akanthoplex*, several mention Dodona, the famous oracle in Northern Greece.

But I, in a great panic, became powerless and died shortly afterwards. This is what I saw. As for you, don't be afraid of making judgements, for I understand that the vision was inauspicious."

The interpreters went off by themselves and studied its meaning. They told him that Telemachus should be put out of his way. When he was out of earshot they said that Odysseus would die on being struck by his own son. He promptly rushed after Telemachus, wishing to kill him. But when he saw his son weeping and begging him he came to his fatherly senses and decided to send his son away. He ordered him to be under guard and banished him to the remotest parts of Cephallenia, removing him from the threat of death.

Again, not many days later, Odysseus had the same dream and, having already learned its meaning, he spent the rest of his life in a happier state of mind. But he had another son whom he did not know, the one called Telegonus, born to him by Circe. She realised that her son was the complete likeness of his father as soon as he came to maturity, so she gave him the spear that she had received from Odysseus, the one with the point tipped with the barb of a sting-ray, so that this would be a token and a sure means of recognizing his paternity.

Telegonus therefore, taking the spear, reached Ithaca by night on his quest for his father. On learning that Odysseus was out in the fields[31] he presented himself there, having a violent confrontation with the guards so as to see his father. They, not recognising him, tried harder to resist. When Telegonus called on the gods as witnesses that Odysseus was his father and that they were hindering him from seeing him, they resisted even more, supposing that it was Telemachus and that he had come by night to kill his father. For no-one knew that Odysseus had another son.

When an uproar broke out they announced to Odysseus, "Telemachus, dressed in a foreign costume, has come and attacked us by night!"

He, on learning this and seething with anger, came out with his spear and promptly cast the spear at Telegonus. It missed him but stuck in an apple tree[32] next to him.

---

[31]This simply means that Odysseus was away from his house, supervising work in the countryside. Such an occupation would take him away from home for several days in a row, perhaps camping in remote areas in the meantime.

[32]Oppian (*Hal.* II.490-6, immediately preceding the Telegonus anecdote) says that if one takes a healthy tree with a good crop of leaves and fruit, and pierces it down in the roots with a sting-ray barb, it will wither and die. Dictys' original poetic (tragic?) source may have included an etiological anecdote for a local landmark at this point.

Telegonus, not seeing that it was his father who had thrown the spear, threw his own spear in turn and scored the unluckiest of lucky[33] shots. He wounded Odysseus in the side.[34] As Odysseus was becoming aware of this man's daring, he learned from Telegonus that he was his son by Circe. He believed that he himself was Telegonus' father when the latter showed him the marine spear-point that he had given to Circe. He threw himself on the ground, uttering many groans.

When Odysseus realised that it was not Telemachus he blamed the dream-interpreters. They, in turn, asked Telegonus where he had come from and of which parents he was born, since he had killed such a man whom no-one in Ilium had wounded and who had accomplished so many wonderful things in his life. Odysseus was then carried, half dead, to Ithaca and ended his life shortly afterwards. He left his political power to Telemachus and to Ptoliporthus his[35] son. Telemachus divided the command, ruling all of Ithaca himself, but he gave the more distant territories to Telegonus. He made Ptoliporthus commander over the middle territories.

He[36] wanted to kill the dream-interpreters, but when Telegonus disagreed with this judgement he ordered them to stay in Sparta.[37] Some of them, after they had arrived there, explained the whole story to Dictys. So much for Odysseus.

4. Lucian, *True Story* II.22-35

(The following extracts have been included primarily as an example of the kinds of Homeric parody and pastiche which were current in the second century A.D. *Lucian claims, in the story, to have visited the Isle of the Blessed, ruled by the Cretan king and legendary judge Rhadamanthus. The story is taken up here on the day of*

---

[33]In Greek this is a play on three words sharing a common root. Again it has all the hallmarks of an origin in dramatic, elegiac or mantic poetry.

[34]Lycophron (*Alex.*795) also specifies that Odysseus was struck in the ribs (plural form of the same noun) by Telegonus' spear. Such incidental details probably antedate the Hellenistic period at least.

[35]Telemachus had married Nausicaa (Alcinous' daughter) and had a son, Ptoliporthus, in Dictys VI.6.

[36]Presumably Odysseus who, according to the Latin version given above, took three days to die.

[37]Why Sparta should suddenly become relevant here is unexplained. One of the seers was from Argos, but otherwise there have been no references to the Peloponnese. The allusion probably refers to the ancient association between Odysseus' fulfilment of prophetic warnings (such as that from Tiresias) and the central Peloponnese, especially Arcadia. See Pausanias VIII.12.6, quoted below.

the Games of the Dead, perhaps a satirical inversion of the ancient custom of funeral-games.)

22. The referees were Achilles (his fifth time in office) and Theseus (seventh time). The whole event would be a long story, but I shall outline the main things that happened. The winner of the wrestling match was Caranus the descendant of Herakles, defeating Odysseus for the crown. In boxing there was a draw between Areios the Egyptian (who was buried at Corinth) and Epeius. They offer no prizes in the Pankration. I don't remember who won the foot-race. As for the poetry contest, Homer was vastly superior, but Hesiod won.[38]

(After the games, some dead villains escape from the place of torment, but are rounded up by Theseus, Achilles, Ajax and Socrates.)

24. Homer even wrote an account of this battle and gave me the book as I was leaving, to take to people in our world, but later I lost it along with everything else. The beginning of the poem was like this:
"Now sing for me, Muse, of the Battle of Dead Heroes."

28. On the day following [my preparations for departure] I went to Homer, the poet, and asked him to compose for me a two-line epigram. As soon as he had done it I set up a pillar of beryl-stone near the harbour and carved the verse on it. The epigram was as follows:
"Lucian, dear to the blessed gods, saw
Everything here and returned home to his dear native land."

I stayed that day and set sail on the next, escorted by the heroes. At this point Odysseus approached me without Penelope's knowledge and gave me a letter to take to Calypso on her island of Ogygia. Rhadamanthus sent me Nauplius[39] as my pilot so that, if we were to stop by any of the islands,[40] no-one would arrest us on a charge of landing there for other business.

- - - - - - - - - - - -

---

[38]This reference to the verdict is a comment on an old biographical tradition going back at least to the work of the early orator Alcidamas, that Hesiod had defeated Homer in a poetry contest on the island of Euboea. See Appendix A.

[39]Nauplius, Palamedes' father, was especially noted as a marine pilot. See Alcidamas, *Odysseus against Palamedes.*

[40]One of these islands proves to be the place of punishment for dead wrongdoers (31-2), amongst whom are the Great Liars. They include Ctesias of Cnidos (author of the *Persika*, a history of the Persian Empire now lost but surviving in quoted fragments.) and Herodotus. Another island is the Land of Dreams.

35. On the third day out [from the Land of Dreams] we put in at the island of Ogygia and landed. But first I opened the latter and read its contents. It said:

"Odysseus sends greetings to Calypso.
You must know that, as soon as I had sailed away from your home with the raft I
had built there, I suffered a shipwreck but with difficulty, and thanks to Leucothea,
I managed to reach the land of the Phaeacians in safety. They escorted me home and
there I came upon many suitors of my wife, living in luxury at our expense. I killed
them all, but later I myself was killed by Telegonus, my son by Circe.

Now here I am on the Isle of the Blessed, entirely regretting the life with you that
I gave up and the immortality that you offered me. So, if I get an opportunity, I shall
run away and join you."

In addition to this the letter contained instructions about us, that we should be entertained.

36. When I went inland a short distance from the seashore I found the cave, exactly as Homer described it, and found Calypso herself spinning wool.

QUESTIONABLE FRAGMENTS[41] POSSIBLY ASSOCIATED WITH THE *TELEGONIA*

1. Athenaeus X.3 (412D)

When Odysseus was an old man,[42]
"He ate endless meat voraciously; [he drank] sweet wine too."

---

2. a) Odyssey XVI.117-121

But sensible Telemachus answered him[43] in turn:

---

[41]Not a single extant fragment of verse can safely be attributed to Eugammon. Even when the *Telegonia* is cited, as in fragment 2b, below, its contents are garbled as a result of poor copying.

[42]This phrase is the strongest suggestion that the line which follows is not meant to be from the *Odyssey,* but describes a later time in Odysseus' life. It certainly is not found in any of the "Homeric" poems. T.W. Allen (*Classical Review* 27, 1913, 191) was the first to suggest that the line should be ascribed to the *Telegonia* or possibly to a *Thesprotis.* The same line is also quoted, again without source-citation, by Eustathius in a comment on *Odyssey* XVIII.53-4, where the subject is excessive eating.

[43]Odysseus is still disguised as a beggar and has just been questioning Telemachus as to the state of affairs in the family home, as well as passing remarks concerning attitudes (including his own) in the household towards the suitors.

"Well, then, stranger, I shall tell you the plain truth.
The whole people are not hostile to me, nor bear me a grudge,
Nor do I blame any relatives, the sort that a man   115
Usually relies upon in a fight, even if a great feud were to arise.
For in this case Cronus' son has made our family single-lined:
Arceisius begat Laertes, an only son,
Who in turn as father begat Odysseus alone.

*   And Odysseus begat only me, left me in our halls and had no joy of me.   120

So now, indeed, there are countless enemies in the house."

b) Eustathius, **Commentary on *Odyssey*** XVI. 120 (p. 1796)

(Allen I, Bethe 2, Evelyn-White 2, Bernabé 3,)
* You should know that genealogists trace Arceisius' parentage to Zeus and Euryodia.
Arceisius in turn begat Laertes upon Chalcomedusa. Laertes and Anticleia had
Odysseus. He in turn had Telemachus by Penelope. Telemachus married Polycasta the
daughter of Nestor and they had Persepolis, as Hesiod tells:

"*Well-girdled Polycaste, youngest daughter of Neleus' son Nestor* ,[44] *Bore to
Telemachus Persepolis after joining him through golden Aphrodite.*"

Aristotle, in his *Ithacan Constitution*, and Hellanicus,[45] say that Telemachus married Nausicáa the daughter of Alcinous and they became Persepolis' parents.

Some authors fill in[46] the story in these terms: Circe bore to Odysseus, according to Hesiod,[47] Agrius and Latinus; Calypso bore him Nausithous and Nausinous.
But the Cyrenean poet of the *Telegonia* says it was Calypso[48] who bore Telegonus,

---

[44]This "Hesiodic" reference (presumably from the *Catalogue of Women*: listed as fg. 221 by
Merkelbach & West) is very similar in wording to *Od.* III.464-5, except for the reference to
Telemachus.

[45]Aristotle *Ithacan Const.* Frag. 506 Rose. Hellanicus FrGrHist 4F156.

[46]Liddell-Scott-Jones give "pass one's time in" as a translation for this verb.

[47]*Theogony* 1011-1018.

[48]This cannot be right: it not only disagrees with "Hesiod" (which Eustathius means it to do here),
but also with Proclus. There must have been some confusion already existing in Eustathius' source,
compounded in the transmission of his comment. Bergk's reading would substitute, "*it was Calypso
who bore Teledamus <and Circe Telegonus>.*"

or Teledamus, to Odysseus, but that Penelope bore him Telemachus and Arcesilaus.[49]

---

3) a) **Odyssey** XI. 119-137

(The ghost of Teiresias is prophesying to Odysseus in the underworld)

"But when you have killed the suitors in your own residence,
Either by trick or openly with a sharp sword,   120
Then you must surely go, taking a well-balanced oar,
Till you arrive in a land where people do not know the sea,
And do not eat food that has been mixed with salt,
And where they do not know about ships with painted cheeks,
Nor anything about well-balanced oars which act as wings for ships.   125
A sign shall I tell you, and unmistakable it is: do not miss it!
Whenever another traveller should meet you
And say that you are holding a winnowing-fan on your illustrious shoulder,
Then set your well-balanced oar right in the earth.
Make sacrifices to lord Poseidon: 130
A ram, a bull and a boar that is the mate of sows.
Then return home and offer up sacred hecatombs
To the immortal gods who occupy broad heaven,

*   To all of them in order. As for yourself, death

*   Will come to you out of the sea. Such a very gentle end will take you 135
When you are worn out with comfortable old age. Around you
Will be prosperous people. This I tell you assuredly."

b) **Q**-Scholion to line 134, above
"Out of the sea" means "away from" the sea, for the poet did not know[50] the story of Telegonus and the sting-ray barb.

---

[49]Evelyn White reads "Acusilaus" for this name, unsupported by any other current editor or by any manuscript to the best of my knowledge. Huxley (*Greek Epic Poetry* 172) suggests that Arcesilaus' name appears by way of a royal tribute, since Eugammon was probably living in the time of Arcesilaus II, king of Cyrene. For more on Arcesilaus I and II, see Herodotus IV.159-160.

[50]We note again the tendency of ancient commentators to presume awareness of what Homer "knew" and "did not know."

c) **H & Q** Scholia to the same lines   (Bernabé 4)

The word[51] *exalos* works like *ekbios* [=lifeless, so by analogy "sealess"], meaning "on land," as opposed to being at sea. Some commentators, by way of comparison, render *ex halos* as "originating in the sea," as in the expression, "*a god may send some kind of big monster from the sea.*"[52] They say that Hephaestus,[53] at Circe's intercession, fashioned for Telegonus a spear made from a sting-ray of the sea, the creature which Phorcys had captured at the time when it was eating fish in Lake Phorcis. The head of the spear was made of adamant, and its lower point was golden. This was the spear that killed Odysseus.

d) **"Vulgate"** Scholia to the same lines
   Later poets[54] invented the story of Telegonus, son of Circe and Odysseus. Apparently this character came to Ithaca on a search for his father and in ignorance used his sting-ray spear point against his father.

4. Pausanias VIII (**Arcadia**) 12.5-6

On the right hand side of the road[55] there is a high barrow: people say it is Penelope's grave, but this disagrees with the poem called *Thesprotis*. (**6**) In this poem is the story that, when Odysseus returned from Troy, Penelope bore him a son called Ptoliporthes. But the Mantinean story says that Penelope was accused by Odysseus of bringing lovers to the house, and when she was sent away by him she went directly to Lacedaemon, but that she later moved from Sparta to Mantinea; this is where she lived out her days.

---

[51]*Ex* and *halos* are now being conflated into a single word by one of the older commentators.

[52]A reference to *Od.* V. 421

[53]We may speculate that, if the reference to Hephaestus in this context has any source in an epic poem, it was akin to Thetis' request to Hephaestus for new armour for Achilles (*Iliad* XVIII). Arming scenes are certainly an old and widespread part of the epic tradition. Introducing the manufacture by divine agency of a weapon with the request of a goddess (who also happens to be the central character's mother) may even have been a stock idea before it was exploited in the *Iliad*.

[54]The word used by the Scholiast here is *Neoteroi*. In the next sentence after the cited extract, the scholiast gives a cryptic quotation from the *Psychagogoi* of Aeschylus, in the form of a prophecy that Odysseus would die from a sickness brought upon his skin and hair by the droppings of a bird. Radt (*Tr.Gr. Fr.* III.275, p.373) suspects that the prophetic words in the script were uttered by Teiresias.

[55]from Mantinea to the Arcadian Orchomenus